CLASSROOM COMMUNICATION AND DIVERSITY

Enhancing Instructional Practice

Third Edition

Dana L. Powell and
Robert G. Powell

NEW YORK AND LONDON

This edition published 2016
by Routledge
711 Third Avenue, New York, NY 10017

and by Routledge
2 Park Square, Milton Park, Abingdon, Oxon, OX14 4RN

Routledge is an imprint of the Taylor & Francis Group, an informa business

First published 2004 by Lawrence Erlbaum Associates, Inc.

Library of Congress Cataloging in Publication Data
Powell, Dana L.
Classroom communication and diversity: enhancing instructional practice/
Dana L. Powell and Robert G. Powell.—Third edition.
pages cm.—(Routledge communication series)
Includes bibliographical references and index.
1. Multicultural education—United States. 2. Educational equalization—
United States. I. Powell, Robert G. II. Title.
LC1099.3.P694 2015
370.11′7—dc23
2015003039

ISBN: 978-1-138-89790-8 (hbk)
ISBN: 978-1-138-89791-5 (pbk)
ISBN: 978-1-315-70890-4 (ebk)

Typeset in Bembo
by Florence Production Ltd, Stoodleigh, Devon, UK

Printed and bound in Great Britain by CPI Group (UK) Ltd, Croydon CR0 4YY
on sustainably sourced paper.

CONTENTS

FIGURES

TABLES

PREFACE

Our aim in this, the third edition of *Classroom Communication and Diversity: Enhancing Instructional Practice*, is to provide a useful framework for teaching in today's diverse classrooms. We believe effective communication is at the heart of the teaching process. Lesson plans, state standards, textbooks, and technologies do not stand on their own but are activated through communication. We believe good teachers are effective communicators.

One of the challenges to effective communication is diversity. There are many approaches to studying and teaching about diversity. Some theorists equate this term with multicultural education (e.g., Banks, 1999). Banks and Banks (1989), for example, defined multicultural education as "a field of study and an emerging discipline whose major aim is to create equal educational opportunities from diverse racial, ethnic, social-class, and cultural groups" (p. xi). Wlodkowski and Ginsberg (1995) acknowledged the different interpretations of diversity and for the purposes of their research argued that it "conveys a need to respect similarities and differences among human beings and to go beyond 'sensitivity' to active and effective responsiveness" (pp. 8–9). Nieto (2002) described diversity as "[the] range of differences that encompass race, ethnicity, gender, social class, ability and language" (p. 183). We build on these definitions but also consider diversity to be a fluid and multidimensional concept. Culture, ethnicity, gender, class, and exceptionality emerge and converge in a number of communication spaces. Consider, for example, a crystal. It is multifaceted and complex. Depending on the way light reflects through it, certain features become prominent and others stay in the background. Similarly, people are multidimensional; different features of identity are enacted and negotiated in different contexts. In our experience, too many teachers view diversity as something students must overcome if they are to be academically successful. We would like educators to view diversity as a valuable resource that help them forge positive relationships that will in turn promote positive student learning outcomes.

There are four units in this text. Unit I focuses on the foundations of communication in the learning context. In Chapter 1 we explain the components of the communication process discussed throughout the text. This chapter contains a discussion of language and its role in learning. We also discuss nonverbal communication and listening. Chapter 2 explores the relationship between communication and learning outcomes. We discuss three major areas: student abilities (the competencies that students bring to the classroom), student motivation, and communication processes. Four major theories of motivation are reviewed: self-efficacy theory, attribution theory, self-worth theory, and achievement goal theory. We also discuss teacher efficacy, the belief teachers have about their ability to be effective in the classroom. We conclude Chapter 2 with a discussion of the communication processes used to manage instructional discourse and impact student attitudes about learning.

Unit II explores diversity. In Chapter 3 we introduce readers to the value dimensions of culture and the way those dimensions impact classroom behavior. Culture, language, and identity are examined in detail. We challenge the reader to consider attitudes about language, how it varies from situation to situation, and what it means for academic connection and learning. We examine the impact of culture on preferences for learning and conclude the chapter by discussing strategies for culturally responsive teaching. Chapter 4 examines studies on sex and gender. Researchers and teachers frequently use gender and sex interchangeably but they are different and lead to very different conclusions about female and male behavior. This chapter begins with a brief discussion of research on the differences and similarities of females and males. The second section examines the way in which schools shape and reinforce gender identities. The chapter also reviews research on male and female academic performance and discusses strategies for engaging males and females in learning. One of our goals is to challenge teachers not to tie academic and social expectations to attitudes about sex differences.

The final chapter in Unit II provides an overview of students who are at risk of school failure. We discuss a broad range of factors that place students at risk and review the pertinent legislation that is used to provide appropriate accommodations to meet students' needs. Students who are culturally and linguistically diverse and have disabilities present some unique challenges for educators. Specific teaching strategies for helping students succeed both academically and socially are included in this chapter.

In Unit III, we examine research on ways to build, sustain, and manage teacher–student relationships. Instructional goals are more easily accomplished when teachers have positive relationships with their students. We begin Chapter 6 with a discussion of the research documenting the impact of positive teacher–student relationships on academic engagement and achievement. The next section examines how teacher–student relationships change over time. We discuss the relational constructs predicting academic achievement and conclude the chapter by discussing specific strategies for building positive relationships with students and families. Chapter 7 focuses on ways to build a community of learners. We outline the defining features of community and explain how to build community in a classroom setting. Among the topics examined are teacher support, peer-mediated learning, cooperative learning, peer mediation, classroom meetings, and service learning.

Proactive behavioral support is the focus of Chapter 8. Educators' perceptions of the underlying causes of behavior will inform the way they attempt to manage it. Chapter 8 covers several theoretical perspectives on behavior including the etiology and educational application of each perspective. We also consider the way culture influences the perception of behavior. In this chapter we examine the negative effects of punishment and offer instead proactive strategies for managing behavior.

The goal of Unit IV is to provide insight on strategies for presenting instructional material. Planning is key to effective teaching. We provide information on common-core standards, differentiated instruction, and the design of effective lesson plans. Differentiated instruction is especially designed to help teachers design curriculum for diverse learners. Following this discussion, we offer communication strategies for presenting and managing academic content. Specifically, we discuss lecturing, small groups, cooperative learning, ways to enhance explanations, and the use of questions.

We conclude the text with an examination of the role of technology in the classroom. In addition to providing the reader with ways to use technology in the classroom, we have added a section on the attributes of meaningful learning using technology. We examine the use of social media and ways in which media can be used to accomplish instructional tasks. We identify changes in access and offer different strategies for implementing technologies into instructional practice.

We believe that learning is best served when students and teachers have an ongoing conversation about concepts and ideas. As in the first edition, we have provided "reflection" questions to promote discussion. At the end of each chapter we have also provided examples of learning activities to enhance understanding. Finally, Internet and other resources are included for further information.

New in This Edition

This edition of *Classroom Communication and Diversity: Enhancing Instructional Practice* is a substantial revision of the second edition. We believe these changes have improved the text considerably.

Chapter 1

- Discussion of the zone of proximal development has been expanded and a new discussion of "the instructional conversation" added. Both of these concepts emphasize the link between communication and learning.
- Data on the changing demographics are added and used to establish a context for the third edition.

Chapter 2

- Examples of different types of questions are included in Chapter 2. We introduce the reader to two categories of questions: reproductive and productive. Reproductive questions are designed for students to report their understanding of the information provided by the teacher. Productive questions are higher order and require students to use prior knowledge to create, evaluate, or analyze material.
- A section on teacher efficacy is included in Chapter 2. Research indicates that high-efficacy teachers are more innovative and make positive connections with students.

Chapter 3

- An extended discussion of African-American ethnic identity is included in Chapter 3. We contrast the oppositional perspective discussed in the second edition with other research demonstrating that African-American students with a strong cultural identity are highly motivated to be successful in school.
- We include a discussion of immigrant students and address the implications for classroom communication.

Chapter 4

- The discussion of the differences between males and females is revised. The difference and similarity hypotheses are examined in this edition. This research challenges the belief that females and males are predisposed to certain tasks and competencies because of biology.
- A discussion of "Alpha" girls has been added to this edition. New research indicates that many females born after 1980 are highly motivated academically and socially. We use this research to contrast the vulnerability perspective illustrated in the discussion of *Reviving Ophelia* from the second edition.
- Specific strategies for teaching males who struggle in school are added to this edition.

Chapter 5

- Substantial changes are made to Chapter 5. We have changed the title from *Students with Special Needs*, to *Students with Diverse Learning Needs.* The disability category, *Communication Disorders*, is changed to *Speech or Language Impairments.*

- To reflect the diversity of students in today's classrooms, we include a new section, *Students with Other Diverse Needs*. In this section, we describe prevalence, characteristics, and learner needs of *Gifted and Talented Students*, *Immigrant Students*, *English Learners*, and *Students at Risk of School Failure* due to such conditions as poverty and homelessness. Pertinent laws and regulations that mandate programs and services for students with diverse needs are described.
- We discuss the implications of "deficit thinking" when working with students with diverse needs. This type of thinking often leads teachers and administrators to place the blame for school failure on the child and family. Learners are guided to challenge the destructive assumptions that emerge from the deficit paradigm and encouraged to consider students' life experiences and families as strengths to be celebrated and integrated within school culture.
- The section *Response to Intervention and Universal Design* has moved to Chapter 9.
- The section *Working Effectively with Parents and Families* has been changed to *Partnering with Families* and moved to Chapter 6: *Building Relationships and Communities of Learners.*

Chapter 6

- We review new literature documenting the impact of teacher–student relationship quality (TSRQ) on student academic performance.
- Specific strategies for building positive relationships are added to Chapter 6.
- A section on working effectively with parents is added to Chapter 6. Research on caring teachers, previously in the section *Teacher Support* in Chapter 7, now appears in Chapter 6.

Chapter 7

- A new section, *Building Caring Classroom Communities*, replaces the discussion of *Social and Emotional Learning* from the second edition.
- The section titled *Service Learning* now becomes *Connecting Students to the Community*. Research findings related to the benefits of service learning to student engagement and effective instruction are addressed. A model for the development of meaningful school involvement as a process for engaging students as partners in the classroom and community is presented.

Chapter 8

- The title of Chapter 8 is changed from *Behavior Management* to *Positive Behavior Supports*. A new introduction to Chapter 8 includes research related to public and teacher concerns about classroom management. We discuss the cultural disconnect between teacher and student that often exacerbates the potential for problem behaviors to occur.

- Added to the section *Cultural Influences* is a discussion of the research on ways that race and ethnicity influence disciplinary actions taken by teachers and administrators.
- In a new section, *Positive Behavioral Supports*, we discuss evidence-based interventions teachers can use with students who do not respond to typical classroom rules and procedures and whose persistent behavior interferes with their own learning and the learning of others.

Chapter 9

- We begin the chapter with a section on curriculum design including a description of common-core standards in language arts and literacy and mathematics. We follow with a discussion of Response to Intervention (RTI) and Universal Design for Instruction (UDI). RTI and UDI were discussed in Chapter 5 in the second edition of the text.
- A new version of Bloom's taxonomy and guidelines for providing effective feedback has been added to this third edition.

Chapter 10

- In Chapter 10 we include a discussion on social media and its impact on instructional communication. We also discuss the increase of educational Internet sites that can be used to support instructional goals and objectives.
- A new section on effective teaching with technology was added to this edition. The National Education Technology Standards (NETS) for teachers are introduced. These standards specify what teachers should know in order to teach in a technologically rich environment.
- We update information on the digital divide.

In this edition, specific learning objectives are included in each chapter. Additionally, updated Internet sites and new learning activities are provided in each chapter.

ACKNOWLEDGMENTS

There are several people we would like to acknowledge. First, we would like to thank Linda Bathgate, and Ross Wagenhofer from Routledge for their support and help in the preparation of this edition. We express our gratitude to Jennifer Hinchliffe, copy-editor, for her upbeat attitude and careful attention to detail throughout the process. Second, Angela Munoz uses the text in the instructional communication classes she teaches and has provided valuable suggestions on ways to make the content relevant and meaningful for classroom teachers. We would like to thank the students who, through their responses to the text, inspired us to write a third edition. Finally, we are grateful to our family and friends, who encouraged us to complete this revision.

ACKNOWLEDGEMENTS

Unit I

FOUNDATIONS OF CLASSROOM COMMUNICATION AND DIVERSITY

This unit lays the groundwork for effective instructional communication in diverse classrooms. Chapter 1 focuses on the communication process and its role in learning. First, we review three models of communication. These models are helpful in showing the development of our understanding of the factors influencing the communication process. Barnlund's (1970) model represents our view of classroom communication and the ways meanings are negotiated between students and teachers. Second, we discuss language and its role in learning. We contend that language and knowledge are inextricably intertwined and further, that today's classrooms are becoming increasingly diverse, creating significant challenges for teachers. Third, we discuss nonverbal communication. Nonverbal messages have a profound influence on the ways meanings are managed and constructed. We conclude Chapter 1 with a discussion of listening. Specifically, we discuss different types of listening and barriers to effective listening.

The major factors influencing instructional outcomes are discussed in Chapter 2. We outline three major predictors of academic performance: individual ability, motivation, and communication. First, we review the literature on multiple intelligences and emotional intelligence. The intellectual and emotional skills students bring to the classroom play a powerful role in academic performance. Second, we overview four major theories of motivation. Motivation is at the heart of learning and we believe teachers need to develop strategies for engaging students in their own learning. Finally, we discuss the communication processes that are used in instructional practice. In this final section we describe typical classroom patterns and then explain the communication processes that predict academic achievement.

1

COMMUNICATION IN THE CLASSROOM

Learning Outcomes

1. Differentiate message-centered from meaning-centered perspectives of communication.
2. Describe the "zone of proximal development."
3. Explain the impact of language diversity on classroom communication.
4. Identify the functions of nonverbal communication.
5. Contrast the different types of listening.
6. Identify barriers to listening.

Classroom Scenario

John, a first-year second-grade teacher, is about to begin his reading group. Desmond, a Native-American, sits at the table with his arms crossed, looking down. When it is his turn to read, Desmond remains silent. The teacher calls him by name: "Desmond, why aren't you reading? Are you tired? Did you stay up late last night?" The more the teacher implores, the more Desmond resists. The teacher threatens Desmond and says, "If you don't read, you will lose recess time." Finally, Desmond gets up from the table and leaves the classroom. The teacher follows, directing Desmond to the vice principal.

This scenario reveals the complex relationship between communication and culture. Desmond is a Native-American child who has been taught that silence is appropriate, and revealing private feelings and emotions is inappropriate. The teacher, a white male, expects the student to engage in a learning task when called on. These different orientations are underneath the surface, but they can result in conflict, misunderstanding, and alienation. These types of events occur every day in America's schools as teachers and students navigate their interpersonal relationships, instructional goals, and objectives. The aim of this book is to inform teachers and potential teachers about the central role of communication in today's classroom. We are particularly interested in helping teachers understand the ways in which diversity influences classroom communication and orientations to learning.

Communication

Human communication is ubiquitous. It exists everywhere and has a profound impact on what unfolds in a communication setting. All that happens in the classroom is created and sustained through communication processes. Lesson plans, teaching methods, discipline strategies, explanations, and critiques of student work occur through the communication exchanges between teachers and learners. Communication is dynamic and complex, but it can be learned and understood if we carefully examine it in "chunks" and apply what we learn to real-world circumstances.

To begin our examination of classroom communication, we will first describe how our understanding of communication has evolved. The way in which we approach and manage communication is related to our definition of it. The early theorists focused on the message. Communication was considered a one-way phenomenon. Different occasions called for different types or forms of speech. Campaign speeches required one kind of communication, funeral orations another. Thus, the early theorists contributed to our understanding of communication by suggesting that messages were connected to the setting. An effective communicator needed to master these different forms of discourse. A message-centered approach to human communication continued for many years. Shannon and Weaver (1949) refined the message-centered approach by describing the processes that influenced the clarity of messages (see Figure 1.1).

Communication was considered a linear process, with the initiation of a message at one point (information source) and the termination of it at another (destination). The key to effective communication was the clarity of communication exchanges. Clarity was achieved when the message sent was the message received. Noise, both external and internal, distorted a message and interfered with clarity.

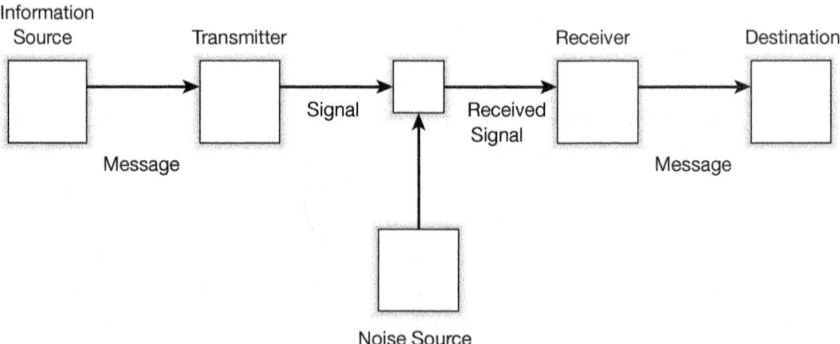

Figure 1.1 Message-Centered Model of Communication: The Shannon and Weaver Model

Consider, for example, a lecture. The instructor (information source) presents the information in front of a class (transmits through speech and perhaps PowerPoint slides). As the instructor presents the information a lawnmower is roaring outside the classroom (external noise). Some of the students are focusing on the lawnmower noise and others on a tiny white piece of tissue that is stuck on the chin of the teacher (internal noise). The students receive the information in light of the processes that influence its reception.

David Berlo (1960) dramatically influenced our thinking about human communication. His book, *The Process of Human Communication*, built upon previous thinking but also introduced a number of new ideas. He continued to maintain a focus on the message but he addressed the factors influencing the production and reception of messages (see Figure 1.2).

Berlo's (1960) model is important for a number of reasons. It introduced the complexity of the human communicator. Notice that any message is influenced by a number of individual difference variables. Let's focus on teachers for a moment. They come to the classroom with a variety of communication skills. Some are good listeners, some are organized, and some are funny. They also have different attitudes. Some like athletics, some like math. Teachers have different levels of knowledge. Some seem to know a great deal about the subjects they teach, others seem to struggle. Teachers come from different social systems and cultures. Cultures and social systems influence perceptions, language use, and rules for appropriate behavior. Taken together, these factors shape the way in which a message is structured, what is emphasized, and how it is coded.

Messages are sent through a variety of channels. The senses—seeing, hearing, touching, smelling, and tasting—can be part of a communication exchange. The reception of a message is also influenced by the receiver's communication skills, attitudes, knowledge, social system, and culture. The farther apart the sender

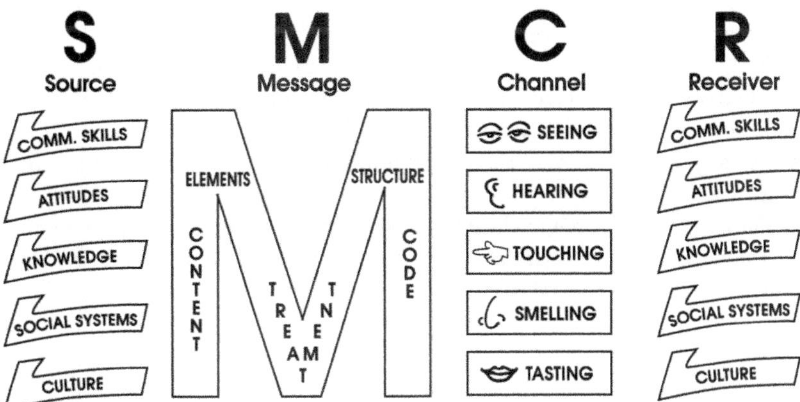

Figure 1.2 The SMCR Model of Communication

and receiver are on these variables, the more problematic the communication becomes.

Berlo went on to introduce other principles of communication that previously had not been discussed. One principle is that communication is a process. Berlo drew from Heraclitus, an ancient scholar, who posited that people could never step in the same river twice. Over time, the people and the river are different. Berlo explained the importance of process when he stated:

> If we accept the concept of process, we view events and relationships as dynamic, on-going, ever changing, continuous. When we label something as a process we also mean that it does not have a beginning, an end, a fixed sequence of events. It is not static, at rest. It is moving. The ingredients within a process interact; each affects all of the others. (Berlo, 1960, p. 24)

Consider an apology. When you have done something to hurt someone, saying "I'm sorry" does not erase the action that caused the hurt. In communication we are constantly building and responding to actions that have occurred. We build and rebuild but we never start from scratch. Every communication has a consequence and each exchange builds upon previous ones. Even though we might like to start each day anew, the reality is that we build upon the residue of previous events.

Another principle Berlo introduced is interdependence. He contended that any source (speaker) is dependent on a receiver to carry the communication forward. Consider the way interdependence plays out between students and teachers. A student needs a teacher to do "teacher things," such as constructing lesson plans, assigning homework, correcting student projects, and imparting information. Teachers in turn need students to do "student things," such as asking questions, completing homework, and listening attentively to the teacher. This interdependence helps shape an educational context with expectations about appropriate behavior.

Berlo made significant contributions to our understanding of communication behavior; his model continued to emphasize the message. In 1970, Dean Barnlund produced a transactional model of communication (see Figure 1.3), which focused on the way that communicators act upon the meanings they construct.

Barnlund's model reintroduced the importance of the setting or context of communication. In the Barnlund model, communicators respond to a number of internal and external cues. A communicator is simultaneously a sender and receiver. In a communication event, senders and receivers may focus on public cues such as the type of setting. A cramped classroom is different from a roomy comfortable one. A church provides different guidelines from a mosque. Senders and receivers also act on private cues. Teachers may say to themselves as they give a lecture, "These students have no idea what I am talking about." Senders

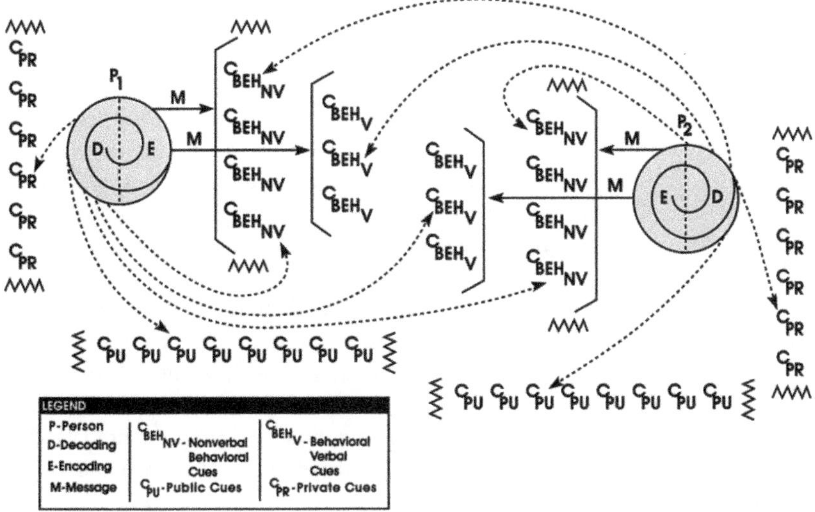

Figure 1.3 Barnlund's Meaning-Centered Model of Communication

and receivers also respond to nonverbal behavioral cues. One teacher used to spit so much when he lectured that the students stopped sitting in the front row. Students may focus on the way a male teacher tugs at his mustache while answering questions or the way he uses his hands to emphasize important points. Finally, there are verbal cues. The words and language styles that senders and receivers use impact communication. One philosophy teacher used to spice his lectures with Latin phrases and then say, "which needs no translation." Needless to say, several of the students were very confused.

Barnlund's transactional model stresses the fact that communication is complex and individuals ultimately act on the meanings they construct. Some receivers may get their meanings from private cues and others may focus on the verbal message. All the elements of the context interact to help shape understanding. The nonverbal style of the teacher (gestures, mannerisms), the verbal style (sentence structure, vocabulary), the physical environment (a warm and inviting room, or a cold and unappealing setting) all influence the meanings constructed by students.

The Barnlund model also notes that meanings are negotiated between communication participants. Teachers and students work through course content and teacher–student relationships through the process of communication. Frymier and Houser (2000) examined the communication skills associated with this process. The authors extended Burleson and Sampter's (1990) research on the skills necessary for friendship to the classroom setting. Eight communication skills were assessed: conversational skills (the ability to initiate, maintain, and terminate conversations), referential skill (the ability to convey information), ego-supportive skill (the ability to make others feel good about themselves), comforting skill (the ability to make others feel better when depressed), conflict management (the ability to reach mutually satisfying solutions to conflicts), persuasive skill (the ability to get people to modify their thoughts or behaviors), narrative skill (the ability to entertain through jokes and stories), and regulation (the ability to help someone who has violated a norm to fix the mistake effectively). Although each of the skills was considered important, referential skill, ego support, and conflict management were particularly significant. In addition, the authors found that communication skills positively correlated with student learning and motivation.

A meaning-centered view helps us understand the differences in the way teachers respond to classroom activities. Expert teachers, those with a great deal of experience in the classroom, see classroom events differently from novice teachers (Bransford, Brown, & Cocking, 2000). In addition to being more knowledgeable, experts are better able to contextualize learning material. That is, because they are well-versed on the information, they can adapt it to the world-views of different students.

So where are we today? Contemporary theorists do not believe that communication rests in the production and presentation of a single message. Rather, any communication event involves a context in which a number of factors play roles in the way the communication unfolds. Among the issues that are important are the physical setting, the relationship between the participants, and the goals of participants. In summary, our concept of communication has evolved from a linear notion that focused exclusively on the message to a "transactional one" in which participants share in the construction and management of meanings.

Several factors are related to the way in which these meanings are managed. Each individual enters a communication exchange with a set of experiences, values, and beliefs. In addition, each person has a wide range of competencies that also influence the production and reception of messages. At the center of these processes is the individual's symbol system.

Verbal Symbols

Verbal messages, the symbols we use to communicate, play a dramatic role in the classroom. Symbol making and symbol using are fundamental to human communicative behavior. A symbol is something that stands for something else. Words, icons, and some gestures are symbols. Symbols are contextually flexible; the meanings for symbols vary from situation to situation. In Milwaukee, a drinking fountain is called a bubbler. The machine used to harvest wheat is called a combine in Nebraska and a harvester in the San Joaquin Valley. We drink a soda in California and pop in Cleveland.

Symbols are also arbitrary. We make up words to represent something. Think about the nicknames people have. How did they get them? What do they signify? Educators are notorious for creating new labels for students. Labels such as jock, shy, gifted, bilingual, ADD, prep, skater, and nerd have specific meanings and imply expectations about academic performance and classroom communication. Although labels might be efficient, they can also be problematic. We can lock people into an expectation based on the words we use to describe them. Words and situations change, but if individuals do not have an understanding of the context in which the symbol is being used, misunderstanding and sometimes embarrassment can result.

Reflection

- What are some of the labels used to describe students?
- What do these labels imply or suggest about these students?

Finally, symbols are abstract. Some words are quite concrete and are easily understood. Words such as basketball, notebook, and desk have a limited range of interpretations, but words such as love, democracy, and racism are more difficult to understand.

We cannot underestimate the role language plays in the instructional setting. Our model of communication presupposes that individuals act upon the meanings they construct. These constructions are inextricably tied to the symbol system individuals possess. Teachers are constrained by the symbols they use to impart information and students are constrained by the symbols they use to understand the teacher. A young Latina tried to explain a *quinceañera* to her Anglo teacher. The young woman struggled to find ways to explain this cultural tradition in a way her teacher would understand. She grew frustrated and closed off the exchange by saying, "Oh, never mind." How many times have teachers grown so frustrated over trying to explain a concept that they have given up and moved on to a new or different idea?

Human symbolic behavior influences not only the content of messages but also the way we organize and structure interaction. For example, students must understand the difference between a question and a directive. A teacher may say to students who are talking during a lesson, "Are you finished with your work?" The teacher is really saying, "Get to work and stop talking," but for that utterance to be effective, the student must also understand that this utterance is a directive. The student who says "Yes" and continues to talk, seeing the comment as a question, may be chastised for being disrespectful.

Language and Learning

Theorists also argue that there is a relationship between language and knowledge. Dance (1982) contended that human capacity to use speech, to talk and listen, leads to the development of human conceptualization, which is necessary for the development of intellect, understanding, and knowledge. Language does more than package or represent something; it embodies an individual's understanding of the world (Langer, 1942; Stewart, 1986). Knowledge, then, is socially constructed rather than individually received. Sprague (1992) argued that individuals interested in instructional communication have focused too much on the role of teacher talk in the classroom. She contended that student talk facilitates learning of all subjects and should therefore be understood by teachers and researchers as well.

Vygotsky (1962/1981), a prominent Russian scholar, contended that mental processes and communication are inextricably intertwined. That is, the ability to learn and think is connected to communication processes. One of Vygotsky's major contributions was the zone of proximal development (Vygotsky, 1978). The zone of proximal development is the distance between independent problem-solving ability and the potential development that can be accomplished through adult guidance or in collaboration with more skilled peers. According to Vygotsky, by collaborating with a mentor or peer, students can develop competencies they would not obtain working independently. Glassman (2001) identified three conditions that must be met to accomplish the zone of proximal development. First there is an emphasis on joint action between a mentor and student. Second there is recognition by the mentor that subgoals must be met before the major goal is achieved (this is referred to as scaffolding; Grant & Sleeter, 2011). Finally, there is an emphasis on the social relationship between the mentor and student in accomplishing the goals. Communication, therefore, is the mechanism through which these developmental processes occur.

The Instructional Conversation

According to Tharp and Gallimore (1988) the zone of proximal development is supported through a process they label the "instructional conversation." It is through instructional conversations that teachers, parents and peers enable learners by engaging them in joint activities and assisting them in accomplishing parts of the activity they cannot master by themselves. As we noted earlier, students use language structures to make sense of instructional material. Consider for example, how young people learn how to ride a bicycle. Few people climb on the bike and competently ride it even though they may have seen many people riding. Rather, a peer, a sibling, or a parent assists the child in learning to ride. Some may use training wheels (scaffolds) that provide an aid in balance. Others have someone hold the seat as they push the pedals and wobble down the street. During this process, the novice and expert are in constant conversation. The mentor provides assistance and coaching on how to steer, move the pedals, and use the brake. So it is with learning math, language arts, or social science.

Forman and Cazden (1998) argued that communication with more competent peers, teachers, and tutors requires individuals to reconcile different perspectives on an issue or problem and, as a consequence, experience cognitive growth. Negotiation is one of the communication activities that influences cognition (Azmitia, 1998; Miller, 1987). As individuals move from childhood to adulthood, they must learn to manage situations involving alternative viewpoints. Negotiation requires individuals to engage in arguments that reveal strengths and weaknesses of a perspective. Think about the way in which students deliberate on classroom projects. The tension fueled by these exchanges must be resolved. Learning a new perspective or developing a new insight is one way the tension is resolved (Piaget, 1965). Knowledge, then, is not passively received, but emerges through interaction with peers and teachers.

The relationship between learning and language is at the core of constructivist approaches to education. Constructivism is predicated on the belief that learners construct their own meaning from interaction with texts, problems, materials, students, teachers, and other features of the learning environment (Arends, Winitzky, & Tannenbaum, 2001). Students are not empty vessels to be filled with some type of intellectual fluid. Each student comes to the educational environment steeped in experiences, competencies, and beliefs. Communication processes play a significant role in the way instructional processes are managed.

Language Diversity

American classrooms are linguistically diverse spaces (Nieto, 2002). One of the more challenging tasks students face is learning the language of the classroom. Reagan (2002) observed that participation in classroom discourse practices requires students to learn a linguistic system different from the one they are used to. This language tends to utilize formal grammar and syntax. Yet there has been phenomenal growth in the number of English language learners (ELLs) in the last decade. English language learners are those who have acquired their primary listening and speaking skills in a language other than English. In addition to learning English, these learners must merge their cultures, backgrounds, and experiences with those of their new environment in order to achieve academic success. The number of English language learners in public schools increased from 3.5 million to 5.3 million, or 51 percent, from the 1997–1998 school year to the 2008–2009 school year (National Clearinghouse for English Language Acquisition, 2007). English language learners represent over a quarter of the school population in California and Texas. By 2015, the number of ELLs enrolled in public schools is expected to reach 10 million and by 2025 one in every four students is expected to be an English language learner (National Clearinghouse for English Language Acquisition, 2007).

It is estimated that in today's classrooms, approximately 19 percent of students (ages 5–17) speak a language other than English (National Center for

Education Statistics, 2006). Many school districts have 50 or more languages represented. Students identified as ELL speak a variety of languages. Spanish-speaking students represent the majority of ELL students (72 percent) followed by Vietnamese (2 percent), Hmong (1.6 percent), Cantonese (1 percent), and Korean (1 percent) (Zehler et al., 2003). Indeed, language diversity presents several challenges and some teachers and administrators have negative attitudes about students whose first language is not English, and believe that these students enter the class with language deficits that must be fixed if they are going to be successful. Numerous theorists challenge this belief and contend that it creates a power differential that privileges not only a style of discourse, but also the person who speaks it (e.g., Bernstein, 1990; Bourdieu & Passeron, 1990; Cazden, 1988; Reagan, 2002). Nieto (2002) argued:

> It is evident that issues of status and power must be taken into account in reconceptualizing language diversity. This means developing an awareness that privilege, ethnocentrism, and racism are at the core of policies and practices that limit the use of languages other than officially recognized high status languages allowed in schools and in the society in general. When particular languages are prohibited or denigrated, the voices of those who speak them are silenced and rejected as well. (pp. 81–82)

It is not surprising, then, that bilingual students also face challenges. Bilingual education is one of the more controversial topics in education today. Gollnick and Chinn (1994) observed that rather than valuing children who speak more than one language, we expect them to give up their home language as soon as possible. There is a prevailing belief that bilingual children are educationally disadvantaged. The data supporting these educational attitudes are not clear. Yeung, Marsh, and Suliman (2000) conducted an extensive investigation of the effects of home language on academic performance. The results indicated that proficiency in a language other than English as a home language had a positive effect on objective tests of English proficiency. Vang (2005) reported that Hmong youth who could read their native language were more proficient in learning English than Hmong youth who could not read in their native language.

The child who is competent in a home language and regularly uses a language other than English may over time reap some important educational advantages. The child who does not have proficiency in a home language, however, is in a precarious position. Some students speak linguistic blends such as "Spanglish," which is a casual form of discourse. Yeung et al. (2000) acknowledged that if the learner's first language was not established, there would not be positive effects of home language on second-language acquisition. Many students who sit in linguistic limbo may be the students at most risk.

Reflection

- Discuss Nieto's claim about language and power differentials.
- How will the increase in the number of ELL students impact classroom communication patterns?

Nonverbal Communication

In addition to verbal language, nonverbal cues affect meaning (see the Barnlund model in Figure 1.3). Literally hundreds of studies have been conducted on this area of communication (e.g., Burgoon, 1985; Knapp, Cody, & Reardon, 1987; Knapp, Wiemann, & Daly, 1978; Smith, 1984).

Lustig and Koester (1999) suggested that nonverbal communication serves to accent, complement, contradict, regulate, and substitute for verbal messages. We can use a nonverbal message to emphasize a point, to say Donny got it right! Nonverbal messages can be contradictory. Think about the teacher who looks at his watch while saying, "Come in and see me; I always have time for my students." Nonverbal communication can be used to substitute for verbal messages. For example, a teacher might put an index finger over the mouth to ask for silence.

These general functions of nonverbal communication become problematic when we introduce culture. Students from different cultural backgrounds have different interpretations for nonverbal communication. White students often "grin and nod" when they agree with a teacher, and Asian students may "grin and nod" even if they don't understand the teacher.

Knapp and Hall (1992) provided a useful typology for examining nonverbal communication in the classroom. Their classification consists of: (1) environmental factors, (2) physical appearance, (3) proxemics, (4) kinesics, and (5) paralanguage.

Environmental Factors

The physical setting is an environmental factor that influences communication in a number of ways. We cannot identify a direct relationship between a physical setting and learning, but we can conclude that the physical setting establishes a set of expectations and constraints that influence attitudes and communication. We may have a very aesthetically pleasing classroom with tasteful artwork, well-organized workstations, and moveable desks designed to facilitate learning tasks and communication, but we cannot be sure that learning will occur in that setting. Similarly, we cannot conclude that learning will not occur in classrooms with tiles falling from the ceiling, faded paint on the walls, and outdated equipment. Ultimately, educational outcomes are most directly related to the activities occurring in the context of instruction.

Physical Appearance

Knapp and Hall (1992) noted that the physical characteristics of students and teachers influence communication in a number of ways. We live in a culture obsessed with physical looks so it is not surprising that attraction plays a substantial role in the classroom. Research indicates that attraction correlates with grades and that teachers interact more with students considered attractive (Gibson, 1982; Richmond, McCroskey, & Payne, 1987). Attractiveness is also related to popularity (Boyatzis, Baloff, & Durieux, 1998).

One feature of physical appearance discussed by Knapp is artifacts. Artifacts are clothing and other materials worn or displayed by individuals. These symbols are significant because they play a central role in identity management. Skaters, preps, and jocks dress in ways to signify who they are. Students may have tattoos, wear jewelry, or fix their hair in ways that reflect their identity. More and more students are getting tattoos and piercings to express their individuality. In some school systems, students are not allowed to wear clothing that can be construed as gang related.

A growing body of research has examined the effects of attire on judgments of teachers. Morris, Gorham, Cohen, and Huffman (1996) examined the effects of the attire of teaching assistants on their credibility. Three conditions of attire—formal professional, casual professional, and casual—were tested. The study found that perceptions of competence were directly affected by dress. The more casual the dress, the less competent the teaching assistant was perceived to be. The results also indicated that a casual dress style was related to sociability.

Roach (1997) examined the effects of graduate teaching assistant attire on student learning, misbehaviors, and rating of instruction. The research found correlations between teaching assistant attire and student learning (affective and cognitive). Learning increased with professional attire. Interestingly, teaching assistants who dressed more professionally also encountered less student misbehavior. Professional dress helped the instructor establish and maintain appropriate distance and boundaries. In addition, teachers who dressed professionally received higher teacher evaluations. Students seem to expect professionalism from an instructor, and dress style helps the teacher fulfill this expectation.

The research reported above is consistent with a wide range of studies that have examined the effects of attire (Davis, et al., 1992; Gorham, Cohen, & Morris, 1997; Hensley, 1981; Kleinke, 1977; Lang, 1986; Lukavsky, Butler, & Harden, 1995; Molloy, 1975; Newhouse, 1984; Schneider, 1974). Individuals in professional contexts, such as teaching, positively influence their credibility by dressing in a professional fashion. Simmons (1996), a longtime supervisory teacher, summed up the issue of dress in the following way: "Without a question, dress sends a strong message about who teachers are as individuals and as professionals. The message is clear—those who want respect for themselves and their profession must dress accordingly" (p. 293).

Proxemics

Proxemics is concerned with the management of space. Research has been rather consistent in this area. The proximity of the teacher influences the participation of the student (Smith, 1984). In traditional classrooms, there is a zone of classroom participation (see Figure 1.4).

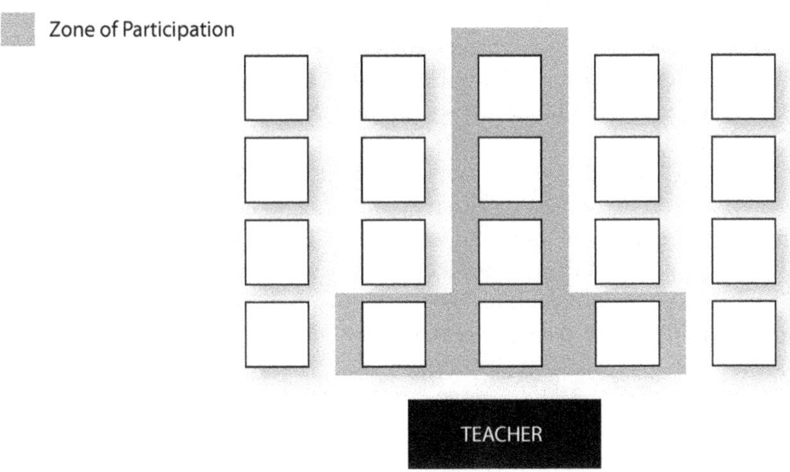

Figure 1.4 Zone of Participation

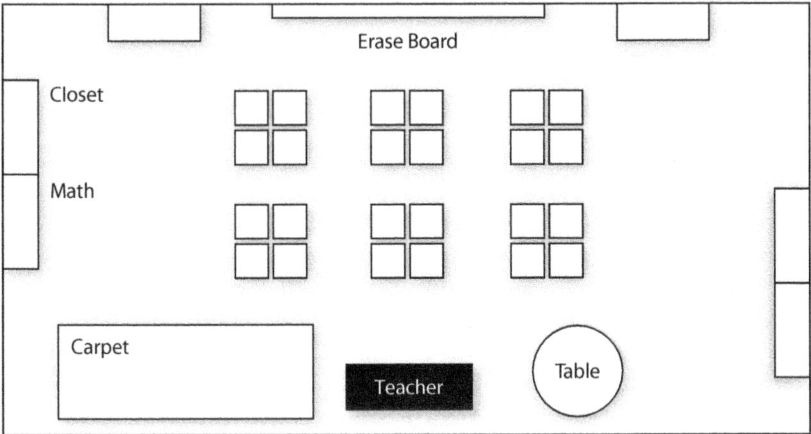

Figure 1.5 Classroom Arrangement

The shaded area shows where most of the interaction occurs. Students sitting on the sides and in back do not receive as much attention and do not engage in as much interaction.

Teachers must remember that no single seating arrangement is ideal for all classes, learning situations, or individuals (Williams, Alley, & Hensen, 1999). The classroom shown in Figure 1.5 reflects the instruction goals of one fourth-grade class.

In this class, the instructor has created several different "classrooms," each designed to accomplish a different goal. At the center are cooperative teams. Four students are placed in the center, where group activity and direct instruction occurs.

The carpet is a place where students can go for free reading, work on puzzles, or do other tasks. There is a table where reading groups can work without distracting other groups. In this classroom, students can work on several instructional activities simultaneously. Notice that the teacher's desk is not at the center of the room.

Given the choice, students will seek out areas in the classroom that accommodate their orientation to communication. Those who do not like to participate generally seek out areas where there is a lower probability of being called on by the teacher. Teachers, therefore, must think about ways to organize their classrooms to accomplish their goals. Teachers might experiment with different arrangements throughout the school year.

Reflection

- What are the advantages and disadvantages of placing the student desks in the center of the room?
- What is the purpose of placing the computer station in the front of the room?
- How would you arrange this classroom?

Kinesics

Kinesics, according to Knapp and Hall (1992), refers to gestures, posture, touching behavior, facial expressions, and eye behavior. Ekman and Friesen (1969) studied body movement and contended that there are five primary categories of movement: emblems, illustrators, affect displays, regulators, and adaptors. Emblems have a direct verbal translation. Americans wave to say hello whereas Eastern Indians clasp their hands together in front of the face. Illustrators are used to highlight or explain a verbal message. We can pretend that we are holding a fork and move it to our mouth to show, or illustrate, something about eating. Affect displays are those gestures that reveal emotion. These are primarily seen in the face. A smile is one way we show we are happy. Regulators are used to manage the give and take of conversation. People raise their voice when they do not want to give up the floor; they shift their posture when they wish to give the floor to someone else. Postural shifts occur as individuals participate in conversations. Finally, individuals use adaptors to manage stress or arousal. Some students tap their feet when they are anxious. Other people play with pens, tug at their hair, or snap gum to manage tension.

The way in which teachers carry themselves has a great impact on the attitudes of students. A great deal of research has been conducted on teacher immediacy, a concept developed by Mehrabian (1970a, 1981). According to Mehrabian, immediacy behaviors signal approach. The behaviors considered immediate are smiling, eye contact, forward body lean, proximity, and a relaxed posture. A number of studies have shown that immediate teachers are perceived positively regardless of student cultural identity (Collier & Powell, 1990; Powell & Harville, 1990; Sanders & Wiseman, 1990). Teachers using immediacy behavior indicate that they are open and they like their students.

One of the most controversial nonverbal behaviors is touch. Although touch is considered an essential component of human development, it can be problematic in the classroom. Touch can be used to comfort, discipline, and focus attention. When appropriate, it can send powerful messages of affirmation and care. When used inappropriately, the results can be devastating. Behaviors that appear nurturing in one situation can be litigious in another. Hugging a third-grader who falls from the swing may be appropriate whereas hugging a student in an empty classroom for being a "good student" may have a very different implication. Mongeau and Blalock (1994) found that, of all the teacher immediacy behaviors they studied, touch was the only one perceived to be inappropriate.

Paralanguage

The final area discussed by Knapp and Hall (1992) is concerned with the nonlinguistic features of speech, such as voice volume, tempo, pitch, and intensity as well as intruding sounds. Accent is certainly a paralinguistic feature that influences communication in the classroom. Research reveals that accent influences speaker credibility. Powell and Avila (1986) compared Anglo, Latino, Asian, and African-American students on the Communication Competency Assessment Instrument (CCAI) and found that students from Latin and Asian cultural backgrounds were considered less competent than individuals from other groups. One of the variables accounting for this difference was pronunciation, which is influenced by accent.

Gill (1994) investigated the effects of accent on comprehension. The results indicated that listeners had more favorable responses to teachers with standard North American accents than to those with British or Malaysian accents. Further, the students were able to comprehend more information from North American teachers than from foreign teachers.

Student attitudes may influence how they perceive a teacher who has an accent. Students who do not do well in a course may use the teacher's accent as a reason for their poor performance. The accent of the teacher may be less significant to the students who do well in the course. Students accepting of culture may be more tolerant of a non-mainstream accent whereas students less accepting may be much more critical of a nonmainstream accent. Similarly, teachers may develop expectations about students based on stylized features. Students with a non-dominant style of speech may not be perceived as bright, motivated, or as interesting as a student with a dominant style of speech. Some teachers feel that it is the obligation of education to create a homogenized community that uses the same code. Students with accents, regardless of their intellect, may be inappropriately pushed to the margins. Teachers need to be very aware of the attributions they make about students who have accents.

Listening

The final aspect of the communication process that we wish to discuss is listening. Meanings are intimately tied to listening ability. Students who are distracted do not focus on main ideas and have difficulty following instructional messages. Wolvin and Coakley (1993) provided a useful typology of listening consisting of five major functions.

According to Wolvin and Coakley (1993), *discriminative* listening is distinguishing among auditory and visual stimuli. This type of listening undergirds all other forms of listening. In the classroom, teachers and students must sort through a wide range of auditory stimuli. Students talking, shuffling papers, snapping gum, the squeak of chalk are among the sounds that are processed in the classroom context.

Discriminative ability is fundamental to musicians, auto mechanics, parents, and teachers. Each must determine the significance of certain sounds and how to respond to them. The musician learns how to coordinate certain tones and blend them into melodies. The mechanic listens to the "ping" in an engine to determine why it isn't running smoothly. Parents learn to differentiate cries for attention from cries of fatigue. Students and teachers must sort out a multitude of stimuli as they negotiate the meanings of instructional material.

Listening for *comprehension* builds on discrimination of stimuli to an understanding of the message. Many of the educational processes engage this listening function. Students listen to lectures, student reports, classroom discussions, announcements, and the admonitions of teachers. Successful comprehension requires that listeners avoid an evaluative attitude about the topic being discussed or the speaker. A student who does not like history may have difficulty attending to a lecture on the Revolutionary War. Listening is made particularly difficult when the listener does not like the speaker. It is easier to attend to messages from people we like and tune out messages from people we dislike.

Listening is facilitated when the listener can identify the speaker's main ideas. As we have observed, in any instructional context a multitude of messages is shared. Listeners must learn to discard extraneous information and focus on that which is most relevant to the instructional task. Comprehension is difficult in diverse classrooms where there may be vast differences in vocabulary. Students may hear many words but not know what they mean. Finally, comprehension requires listeners to store information in short-term memory, rehearse it, and move it into long-term memory so that it can be retrieved later.

Therapeutic listening, according to Wolvin and Coakley (1993), requires that the listener help the speaker solve problems. To fulfill this function, the listener serves as a "sounding board" so that the speaker can identify ways to define and solve a problem. Teachers often play this role when they listen to the difficulties students have at home or the struggles they have with friends at school. In these contexts, the teacher attempts to empathize with the speaker and show understanding. However, when students are experiencing more serious emotional difficulties, they should be advised to consult with professionals who are trained in counseling.

Critical listening requires the listener to render a judgment about the information received. This skill is invoked in several ways. When a speaker's purpose is to persuade, a listener must make a judgment about the validity and strength of evidence. Effectiveness in this situation requires listeners to understand the way in which persuasive arguments are structured and supported. Teachers put on their "critical" listening hats when they listen to student accounts for late work or a problematic pattern of behavior. They also model good listening when they help students process good arguments from more problematic ones. Students must learn that criticizing an argument does not mean criticizing the person.

The final function Wolvin and Coakley (1993) discussed is *appreciative* listening. Listening to music, the sounds of a mountain stream, or a favorite television program are examples of appreciative listening. This type of listening is subject to individual tastes and standards. Conduct a survey of your class and identify the different music forms the students like.

There are numerous circumstances that make effective listening difficult. One is that listening is always part of an interpersonal relationship. I have frequently heard teachers ask students, "Are you listening?" What they are really saying is that the students are not doing what the teachers want them to do. It is easier for participants to listen to individuals they respect and like, and tune out and counter-argue with individuals they do not like. In addition to these relational features, there are other blocks to effective listening worth mentioning:

- *Preoccupation*: Listeners feign attention while they think about other things. Students may grin and nod, exhibiting attentive behaviors, while thinking about what they want for lunch.

- *Noise*: As we noted earlier in this chapter, internal and external noise can distort instructional messages and interfere with the creation of meaning.
- *Information overload*: Listeners process information better in manageable chunks. When students receive too much information too quickly, they may tune the teacher out.
- *Boredom*: Listeners easily tune out a speaker who speaks in a monotone, is slow paced, and uses no vocal variety.
- *Selection*: Listeners will tune into information they perceive is relevant and tune out information they believe is irrelevant. These choices are based on personal tastes and attitudes.
- *Counter-argument*: Listeners listen to those features they can refute. As a consequence, they may miss other important features of communication.
- *Language competency*: Listening is difficult when listeners do not understand the language being spoken. This is especially true when speakers are continually translating the messages they hear.

Listening is often treated as an independent category of the communication process. We believe that listening is part of a host of behaviors that are used to make sense out of instructional material. Cooper and Simmonds (1999) contended that effective listeners are actively involved in the communication process. One effective strategy is to paraphrase another person's message. The goal of paraphrasing is to capture the content and feelings of the other's response. A student who feels that an assignment is too difficult may blurt out, "I don't get it; this isn't clear." A teacher might paraphrase this statement by saying, "You seem anxious about this assignment."

Another strategy Cooper and Simmonds discussed is *perception checking*. The purpose of this technique is to assess another's thoughts, feelings, or perceptions. According to Cooper and Simmonds, perception checking involves three ideas: (1) a reference to the sensory data leading to a conclusion; (2) the conclusion that has been drawn; and (3) a question asking the other if your conclusion is accurate. For example, a teacher may have a student athlete who has been late with homework and is inattentive in class. The teacher may be concerned that the student is spending too much time on the athletic field and not enough time studying. In probing this situation, a teacher may ask this student if she understood the assignment that was due. The student may look down and say, "I understood it but I had so much to do that I couldn't get it done." This perception can be assessed in the following way: "Julie, I know that the playoffs are coming up this week and you do not seem focused on your studies. Are you spending so much time practicing that you are not attending to your schoolwork?"

There are other ways to facilitate effective listening, however. We want to emphasize that listening is part of an on-going interpersonal relationship that is established and maintained. Effective listening involves more than implementing a few techniques. Good listeners and good communicators are sensitive to a host of behaviors that are involved in the communication process. As your knowledge of this process increases, so will your communication ability.

Summary

Over the years, researchers have come to appreciate the complexity of human communication. Early theoretical approaches were linear and simplistic. Contemporary orientations are complex and circular. Communication processes are negotiated among participants as they act upon the meanings they construct and share. Verbal and nonverbal behaviors are the mechanisms through which instructional sense making is achieved. Contemporary theorists also emphasize the powerful relationship between learning and communication. How we come to understand instructional material is a function of communication. After reading this chapter, our hope is that you recognize that understanding communication is an exciting and difficult challenge.

Learning Activities

- The Ideal Teacher
  Pair up with another student and go for a learning walk. On this walk discuss the defining characteristics of the ideal teacher. When you return to class, list the characteristics on a wallboard or flip chart. Note the similarities and differences among the descriptions.
- Nonverbal assessment
  Analyze the way nonverbal communication influences the meanings you construct. Specifically, contrast communication differences in two or three different physical settings. How were people dressed and how did their dress influence the impressions you formed? What types of gestures did you observe? How did space impact communication? Finally, what different accents, languages, or styles of speech did you hear and how did you react to them?
- Build a communication model using the concepts discussed in the chapter.

Resources

- Communication activities
  www.essortment.com/all/communicationte_rqmd.htm
- The essentials of language teaching
  www.nclrc.org/essentials/listening/liindex.htm

2

FACTORS INFLUENCING LEARNING AND COMMUNICATION

Learning Outcomes

1. Explain a constructivist view of education.
2. Identify your strongest intelligence.
3. Differentiate four perspectives on motivation.
4. Describe the primary dimensions of teacher efficacy.
5. How does teacher immediacy impact learning?
6. Explain the difference between productive and reproductive questions.

Classroom Scenario

Enrique and Danielle are in the teachers' lounge savoring the last drops of their coffee before scurrying off to their first period class. Rosa Parks Middle School, where Enrique and Danielle teach, is located in a low-income ethnically diverse community. For many students, English is not their first language and the verbal skills of many other students are below grade level. The test scores at Rosa Parks have been low and the principal has made it very clear that she expects substantial improvement. Teachers such as Enrique and Danielle face a daunting task—they must meet state standards, raise test scores, and excite the students about learning. It is in this context that teachers can easily forget their fundamental charge—to help students learn.

Learning is a complex process entailing a number of interrelated factors. Enrique and Danielle will be more effective in the classroom when they have a deep understanding of these factors, then they can develop teaching strategies to meet their instructional goals and address the needs of students. In this chapter we will define the learning context and examine three areas that are related to the teaching– learning process: student abilities, student and teacher motivation, and classroom communication.

Reflection

- What role does communication play in the learning process?
- How can a teacher motivate a student to learn?

The Learning Context

Our definition of communication states that people act upon the meanings they construct. Our view of learning follows from our definition of communication. It is not fruitful to believe that students are empty vessels to be filled with intellectual fluid. Rather, students are active agents in the creation and management of educational material. Constructivism, a perspective that has been studied in communication and education, resonates with our view. Kelly's (1955) Personal Construct Theory, Piaget's (1955) Developmental Theory, and Mead's (1934) Theory of Symbolic Interactionism provide the conceptual basis for this perspective. Brooks and Brooks (1993) summarized constructivist processes when they stated:

> Each of us makes sense of our world by synthesizing new experiences into what we have previously come to understand. Often we encounter an object, an idea, a relationship, or a phenomenon that doesn't quite make sense to us. When confronted with such initially discrepant data or perceptions, we either interpret what we see to conform to our present set of rules for explaining or ordering the world, or we generate a new set of rules that better accounts for what we perceive is occurring. Either way our perceptions and rules are constantly engaged in a grand dance that shapes our understandings.
>
> (p. 4)

Thus, learning occurs through the continuous building, integration, organization, and rebuilding of material. At the core of this perspective is the recognition that language, culture, home, and community play important roles in the knowledge structures students possess. Consider, for example, the way that a class discussion on music would be impacted by culture. One family may listen to *rancheras*, *corridos*, *cumbias*, and *marriachi* music. Another may listen to country western, bluegrass, and gospel. The discussion of music will be intimately tied to the students' experiences.

Culture also influences the constructs that students have for managing social situations. An Iranian student new to America went shopping for clothes at a department store. After selecting the shirt he wished to purchase, he haggled with the clerk over the price. The Iranian student equated buying a shirt in a department store with buying a shirt in the open marketplace in Tehran where negotiating the price is the common practice.

Constructivist approaches recognize that students come to the instructional context with different levels of competencies, interests, and experiences. Unfortunately, much of our educational curriculum is based on a "one size fits all" metaphor. As students move through the system, little effort is spent on tailoring instructional cloth to better fit each student. Unfortunately learning does not follow this pattern. Students come to class in many different shapes and sizes.

Indeed, students draw upon a range of interpersonal and educational constructs to learn instructional material and manage classroom relationships. Garcia (1999) stated that meaningful instruction accounts for the sociocultural, linguistic, and experiential background of students. While an instructor may have jurisdiction over curriculum, ultimately the student has jurisdiction over what it means (Wenger, 1998). In other words, students use their experiences and abilities to make sense out of the instructional material.

Because learning entails the negotiation of instructional material, it is difficult to isolate the specific ways that teaching influences learning. Some theorists go as far as to contend that teaching plays a rather minor role in learning (e.g., Coleman et al., 1966; Heath & Nielson, 1974; Mosteller & Moynihan, 1972). The findings of this early research indicated that family socioeconomic status, ethnicity, and family background are more important predictors of achievement than teaching. Think about arguments teachers like Enrique and Danielle make when they try to explain the low scores of their students on state achievement tests. These teachers recognize that there are significant factors outside of the school that influence learning. At the same time, we do not want to argue that teachers do little to influence the learning process. Friedrich (1982) argued that three sets of interrelated variables account for classroom learning: student ability, student motivation, and the quality of classroom communication are the primary factors influencing achievement. These three areas provide a useful starting point for our discussion of the relationship between teaching and learning. In fact we strongly believe that teachers can make profound differences in the lives of students, even those who live in difficult circumstances.

Student Ability

We argued earlier that students enter the classroom with a wide range of abilities and competencies. Friedrich (1982) contended that these abilities account for a substantial amount of variance on a range of cognitive outcome assessments (i.e., achievement tests, aptitude tests, general intelligence measures, unit measures). The scores that students receive on standardized assessments, such as multiple choice tests, may have more to do with the intellectual predilections of the student than with the classroom instruction.

Recent developments in cognitive psychology give insight into the intellectual capacities that students possess and bring to the instructional scene. Gardner (1983, 1993, 1999) proposed a provocative framework that has dramatically influenced educational practices. In his original work, *Frames of Mind*, Gardner outlined seven intelligences, and in *The Disciplined Mind* he added an eighth intelligence. Following is a brief discussion of these intelligences:

- *Linguistic Intelligence* entails the ability to use words effectively in both oral and written modes for a variety of purposes such as debate, poetry, prose writing, storytelling, and persuasion. Individuals with highly developed linguistic intelligence enjoy verbal jousting, puns, and other forms of word play. These individuals achieve best when they can speak, listen, read, or write.
- *Logical-Mathematical Intelligence* involves the capacity to reason, to think atomistically, and linearly. People who employ logical-mathematical intelligence are effective at finding patterns, establishing causal relationships, and working through formulas. Among the processes that emerge with this intelligence are categorization, classification, hypothesis testing and generalization.
- *Spatial Intelligence* addresses the ability to perceive, create, and recreate visual images and pictures. Individuals who are strong in spatial intelligence, perceive small details, and are sensitive to color, tone, composition, shape, and form. This intelligence entails the capacity to visualize and represent ideas graphically or spatially.
- *Bodily-Kinesthetic Intelligence* involves the ability to use one's body to express ideas and feelings. Among the defining features of this intelligence is heightened tactile competence, coordination, balance, dexterity, and flexibility.
- *Musical Intelligence* is the ability to understand, create, interpret and discriminate among musical forms. Musically intelligent people have the ability to sing in key, keep tempo, and are sensitive to rhythm, pitch, and melody.
- *Interpersonal Intelligence* requires individuals to be socially and personally perceptive. These individuals are able to perceive the moods and feelings of others and adapt messages to the demands of social situations. Interpersonally intelligent people enjoy social settings and work well with other people.
- *Intrapersonal Intelligence* entails the ability to be in touch with one's emotional state and predispositions. Individuals who are aware of their inner moods, intentions, motivations, temperaments, and desires and have the capacity for self-discipline are intrapersonally intelligent. This intelligence helps individuals create a "realistic" view of their strengths and weaknesses.
- *Naturalist Intelligence* is the capacity to be attuned to the natural world of plants and animals. Individuals who possess this intelligence enjoy the

outdoors, are aware of patterns in nature and have a deep appreciation for the environment.

It should not be surprising that students will be drawn to academic tasks where they feel most competent. Students with logical-mathematical intelligence will enjoy and perform well in math and science and students with linguistic competence will enjoy and perform well in language arts.

Gardner cautioned against viewing these intelligences as fixed and discrete. Individuals possess each of the intelligences to a degree but one or two may be particularly dominant.

Reflection

- What are your strongest intelligences?
- How are these intelligences manifested?
- How can teachers build on student intelligences?

A number of recent educational textbooks discuss ways to integrate multiple intelligences into educational practice (Armstrong, 2000; Carrozza, 1996; Silver, Strong, & Perini, 2000). Silver, Strong, and Perini (2000), for example, outlined strategies for realigning the curriculum to account for learning style and multiple intelligences (MI). The authors also provided guidelines for developing authentic assessments. Armstrong (2000) discussed ways to develop an MI portfolio. He identifies what should be included in such a portfolio and ways to evaluate it. The instructional approaches using multiple intelligences are concerned with measuring student growth and development, not with indexing student deficit. Building and extending student strength is one way to create more engaged and enthused learners.

Emotional Intelligence

Goleman (1995) extended Gardner's work into the area of emotional ability. Individuals who are emotionally intelligent are tuned into their affective states. There is growing interest in the area of emotion and learning. Goleman identified five dimensions of emotional intelligence:

1. *Knowing one's emotions*: Recognizing a feeling as it happens. The ability to monitor feelings is crucial to psychological insight and self-understanding.
2. *Managing emotions*: Appropriately handling feelings. The ability to work through anxiety or gloom is central to success.

3. *Motivating oneself*: Marshaling emotions in service of a goal is essential to paying attention, for self-motivation and mastery.
4. *Recognizing emotions in others*: Empathy is a fundamental social skill. People who are empathic are attuned to subtle social signals indicating how people feel.
5. *Handling relationships*: Skill in managing relationships, popularity, leadership and interpersonal effectiveness.

Emotional intelligence plays an important role in the classroom. The way in which students manage their emotions influences their approach to academic tasks and their ability to work with other students. Healy (1998) argued that socio-emotional factors are important predictors of academic and lifetime success. She described a study that investigated preschoolers' ability to delay immediate gratification. The preschoolers were given one marshmallow and told that if they could wait 15–20 minutes, they would get two marshmallows. These students were evaluated 14 years later. The results indicated that the students who could delay gratification scored higher on the SAT, were better liked by teachers and peers, and were more emotionally stable.

The research on emotional intelligence is compelling. Encouraging students to work before play, to be diligent in the face of adversity, to be respectful and caring, helps foster an attitude of self-efficacy, which in turn positively impacts academic achievement.

Perspectives on Motivation

Student interests, attitudes, and self-views relate to how motivated and engaged they are in the learning material. Maehr and Meyer (1997) argued, "motivation is at the heart of teaching and learning" (p. 372). Adolescents spend tremendous amounts of time e-mailing friends, connecting on networks such as Facebook, and talking on the telephone. Redirecting these energies to academic tasks is more challenging. To better understand the role of motivation it is helpful to review the perspectives that have been used to explain how motivation works in educational settings. In the next section we will examine some of the contemporary perspectives on motivation in education.

Seifert (2004) argues that four major theories—self-efficacy, attribution theory, self-worth theory, and achievement goal theory—are prominent in education. Each of these perspectives offers important insight into the factors that influence students' academic investments.

Self-Efficacy Theory

The key theorist of self-efficacy theory is Albert Bandura (1981, 1986, 1991, 1997). He argued that individuals develop judgments about their personal effectiveness which he labeled self-efficacy. Individuals who believe that they can successfully complete a task will expend the necessary effort to accomplish it. When individuals have low expectations, they are less likely to expend the time and effort on the task.

Bandura (1997) discussed four factors that influence a person's judgments of self-efficacy. The first factor is enactive influences. These judgments result from the way in which a person performs certain tasks. According to Bandura (1997), enactive experiences are the most powerful because they provide the most authentic evidence of whether the individual can access what it takes to succeed. Success leads to a strong belief in one's personal efficacy. However, efficacy does not always follow on from success. Individuals who only succeed at easy tasks may come to lose patience and not persist when the tasks become more troublesome.

A second factor influencing self-efficacy is vicarious experience. Individuals continually compare their own competencies with others. Modeling, then, serves as another way to achieve personal efficacy. The most powerful effect is based on peer comparisons. An individual's self-efficacy is not affected by comparisons with substantially younger, older, or substantially more talented others.

Miller (2000) examined the effects of internal and external comparisons on self-regulated learning. Self-comparisons (internal) occur when students compare their ability in one area, such as English, with their ability in another area such as math. External comparison occurs when students compare their performance in an academic area with that of their peers. The results indicated that students gave more weight to external comparisons than self-evaluations. This tendency, although understandable, is also problematic. Individuals do not always have information to make accurate comparisons. Skill levels, the amount of time on task, and interest can vary from student to student and are frequently ignored when comparisons are made. Miller (2000) suggested that educators should help students develop more balanced constructs of their abilities.

The third way that individuals develop self-efficacy is through persuasion. Bandura (1997) argued that persuasion has its greatest impact on those who have some reason to believe that they can achieve their goals. Persuasive information focusing on the target's ability and effort seems to positively influence efficacy. Persuasive messages focusing only on effort, however, can be counterproductive to the development of efficacy. If an individual does not have the necessary skills, no amount of effort will impact self-efficacy. Simply telling a student to work harder will not be an effective strategy.

Two additional features play an important role in the effects of persuasion. One involves the credibility of the source and the second entails the discrepancy between what individuals are told and their view of themselves. Research in persuasion clearly indicates that source credibility is one of the most powerful features of persuasive communication (Bostrom, 1983). Information from a low-credibility source, even when it is accurate, may be distorted or discounted. The persuasive effects on self-efficacy are directly related to the credibility of the sender.

Self-efficacy is also related to the degree of disparity between the information received and the individual's view of self. Bandura (1977b) noted that information might differ minimally, moderately, or markedly from a person's view of self (p. 105). For example, one high school baseball player had a successful season in his senior year in high school and received an offer to play baseball at a major university. The youngster's coach encouraged him to consider taking this opportunity, but the young man did not believe that he had enough talent, regardless of the statistics and the arguments from his coach. Rather than going to the large school, he decided to attend a local community college where he believed that there was a better fit for his talent.

The final factor influencing self-efficacy involves physiological and affective states. Arousal states can vary from falling asleep in class to suffering panic attacks. Some tasks create great anxiety for students, which influences their ability to complete the task. For example, many students have tremendous fear of public speaking (communication apprehension) and the anxiety attached to this activity negatively affects performance. High apprehensive students break out in hives, their voice quivers, and their stomach aches in anticipation of a five-minute presentation. Other students enjoy public speaking and channel their energy and excitement into dramatic delivery.

Self-efficacy is impacted by the way individuals work through these affective states. Bandura (1997) stated that an understanding of emotional states is developed through a process of social labeling that is coordinated with lived events. Children may experience an internal state (anger) and behave in a way that is connected to the emotion. Parents, teachers, and peers help identify the emotional state (e.g., "You're mad because you didn't get your way," "Are you too embarrassed to read?"). The effects on self-efficacy relate to the way in which individuals learn to label and manage these emotional states. The manifestation of these emotions and the way they are processed, explained, negotiated, and managed has a great deal to do with the development of efficacy. Students with higher levels of emotional intelligence are better able to stay focused on a task and persist through difficult situations.

Attribution Theory

Attribution theory builds on many of the assumptions of self-efficacy theory and also provides important insight into the factors influencing motivation. The conceptual foundation of attribution theory comes from Heider (1958), Jones and Davis (1965), and Kelley (1967). These theorists proposed that individuals are "naïve scientists" who search for causal reasons that explain behavior. Heider (1958) contended that a task outcome might be attributed to four attributional variables: the degree of ability possessed by the actor, the amount of effort expended, the difficulty of the task, and chance factors in the environment.

Weiner (1984, 1985) contended that attributions invoke emotions which influence task engagement. For example, an outcome such as failing or passing a test may result in an emotional reaction. To assess this emotional response, the individual turns to three primary characteristics: locus of causality (the cause resides in the individual or the situation), stability (the cause is always present, or the cause varies), and controllability (the agent can affect the cause or the outcome is out of the agent's control). Research on attribution theory suggests that individuals who are successful tend to attribute success to internal causes (ability, effort) and individuals who are unsuccessful tend to attribute failure to external causes (unclear instructions, lack of time).

Seifert (2004) stated that students who attribute success and failure to internal, controllable causes have higher self-esteem, will engage in more difficult tasks, and will persist in the face of adversity. On the other hand, students who attribute success to external forces (luck, the task was easy) are less likely to experience positive emotions such as pride or confidence. And learned helplessness, the most problematic attribution, occurs when students feel that no amount of effort will make a difference because they do not have the ability to control or influence an outcome.

Heidi and Harackiewicz (2000) argued that interest also influences attributional processes. Interest was conceptualized as the "interactive relation" between individuals and certain aspects of their environment (Heidi & Harackiewicz, 2000). Some individuals are interested in social studies, some soccer, others fashion. Interest can be considered a state and a disposition of the individual and has cognitive and affective features. Research suggests that interest plays an important role in academic performance. It stands to reason that students will be more attentive to and expend more effort in subject areas that interest them.

Researchers differentiate between two types of interest. Individual interest is a stable internal disposition that develops over time in relation to a particular topic or subject area. A student, therefore, may develop an interest in history that lasts throughout his or her educational experience. Situational interest, on the other hand, is generated by certain features of the environment that draw attention and focus to a particular area. The interest fostered in this context, may or may not last. For example, a dramatic lecture or a novel experiential activity may activate student interest in a topic that was previously considered boring.

Heidi and Harackiewicz (2000) noted that individual and situational interests may be distinct but they are not bipolar. Individual interest can serve as a filter for situational interest and situational interest may feed individual interest. The authors contended:

> individual interest in a particular topic may help students persevere through boring presentations or text about that topic, and situational interest elicited by presentations or texts may maintain motivation and performance when individuals have no personal interest in particular topics.
>
> (p. 155)

We can see how interest is also related to intrinsic motivation. Intrinsic motivation is defined as the motivation to engage in activities for their own sake (p. 155). This definition incorporates both individual and situational interest. Some students may read the Harry Potter novels simply because they are positively disposed to reading. Interest in reading may also be promoted for situational reasons. Individuals may be assigned a Harry Potter novel for a class assignment and become so interested in it that they read the entire series.

Self-Worth Theory

Covington (2000) argued that academic goals embraced by students represent an attempt to create and maintain self-worth in a culture that values competency and success. He contended that grades play a dominant role in the way a student judges self-worth. He further argued that while grades are important, they are only one measure of success. Some students attempt to be the best they can be and do not compare their performance to others. These students are likely to take on difficult tasks and feel comfortable with academic challenges. Other students see ability as a function of status and thus compare their performances with others. These students are more likely to avoid failure rather than strive for success. Students who are driven to avoid failure employ several self-protective mechanisms, according to Covington (2000).

Self-worth protection involves withholding the effort when risking failure. When this strategy is invoked, the self-concept appears to be protected because the cause of failure remains ambiguous. Students who are reprimanded by friends, teachers or parents for not trying are receiving an external message that they are incompetent. They failed because they did not try.

A second strategy is self-handicapping. Here the student creates a real or imagined barrier, which provides a convenient excuse. According to Covington, procrastination and setting unrealistic goals are typical tactics that failure-avoiding students employ. The student who studies at the last minute and fails cannot be criticized for not having the ability. And the student who succeeds is perceived to be especially talented. Another tactic is to establish unrealistic goals. A student cannot be blamed for failing at a difficult task. Finally, a student may state a worthy goal such as claiming he or she will do better on the next exam without a reasonable analysis of how to achieve it.

According to Covington (2000), the third strategy is defensive pessimism. Students using this defensive strategy maintain low expectations of ever succeeding or trivialize the importance of the assignment. Defensive pessimism helps the student manage the anxiety that may occur when the student takes an assignment seriously but knows they do not have the ability to fulfill it.

Effort is a key feature of self-worth theory. Failure-avoidant students link effort with ability. Because successful students are bright, they don't have to work hard. People who work hard are not considered to be bright. Seifert (2004) stated that success that comes from ability results in pride. Success that comes from low effort implies ability and also results in pride. Failure that is a function of low effort results in guilt but failure that results from low ability results in humiliation. Covington (2000) contended that students would rather experience guilt than humiliation. Thus, rather than work hard and fail (leading to humiliation), they will not work hard and fail (guilt). Self-worth theory helps teachers understand the choices students make. According to Covington (2000), the central issue for students is to protect their sense of self-worth.

Achievement Goal Theory

Dweck (1986) contended that motivation is related to the way students conceptualize their learning goals. She specified two sets of goals. Learning goals refer to increasing an individual's competence, understanding, and insight. Intelligence and learning for these individuals is malleable. Success or failure does not have a substantial effect on the learner's identity or sense of self-worth. Performance goals, in contrast, are those in which individuals seek a favorable evaluation of their competence. Intelligence following from a performance goal orientation is considered fixed and static. According to Dweck (1986), these different cognitive sets take students in vastly different directions. The individual who is competency oriented is more likely to attribute success to persistence and effort. Failure is not viewed as a reflection on personal identity. The individual who is performance oriented and sees intelligence as fixed does not see that effort and ability lead to success and, therefore, may take on academic tasks that are less challenging. They ask for a great deal of guidance on assignments, may avoid certain classes or teachers and may be more inclined to cheat.

Each of the perspectives reviewed above offer important insights into the processes influencing motivation. Each perspective addresses the role of perceived competence. That is, a student is likely to invest in an academic task when they feel they can successfully accomplish it. When they do not feel that they can be successful, they use strategies to protect their personal identities. The other common thread is the important role that emotions play in motivation. How students feel about their abilities and the meaningfulness of the task they are performing are what Weiner (1984, 1985) labeled motivational catalysts. The affective orientation can serve to bolster or constrain effort and learning.

Seifert (2004) identified five major patterns that are reflected in the perspectives used to study motivation. The first pattern is concerned with mastery. Students who have learning goals or who are internally motivated, will have positive affect, will persist in tasks, are resilient and learn from their mistakes (e.g., Dweck, 1986; Weiner, 1984, 1985).

A second pattern is failure avoidance. These students have performance goals, are externally motivated, and are driven to protect their individual identities. According to Seifert (2004), these students believe that outcomes are beyond their control and as tasks grow in difficulty, they are likely to engage in failure-avoiding behaviors to reduce threat to self.

The third pattern is learned helplessness. These students will not expend the effort because they believe it will result in success. Such students make internal, stable and controllable attributions for failure but make external attributions for success. In other words, this student will say, "I failed because I am incompetent" or "I succeeded because I was lucky." Students with this orientation are particularly challenging for teachers.

The fourth pattern involves students who are bright but bored. These students do not see meaning or value in the task and spend only the necessary effort to fulfill minimal expectations. Seifert contended that the student with learning goals would seek out meaning in the task while the bored student expects the teacher to make the task meaningful.

The fifth is the hostile work avoidant pattern. Seifert stated that the hostile student does not engage in academic tasks as a way to punish the teacher. This strategy may be another way the student protects self-worth. They may resent the work required and therefore refuse to do it. Several years ago one of the authors had an athlete in class who refused to complete a required assignment. When asked why, he stated, "I don't have to do this crap, I'm on the basketball team." This response is typical of hostile students. What then can teachers do with this information on motivation? This is a difficult question but the literature reviewed above suggests that student motivation is enhanced when they develop mastery over the tasks they are required to perform. Gettinger and Stoiber (1999) provided recommendations that may enhance motivation. They suggested that teachers should assign tasks that are moderately challenging but within the students' ability. Second, teachers should link student success to the effort they put forth. When this occurs, students are more likely to take control of their academic engagement. Third, teachers should create opportunities for students to be successful. Consider the following example. George is struggling with algebra. He studies but continues to fail the examinations at the end of the week. He questions his ability and spends less time studying. For George, it is too painful to work hard only to fail. One day, while grading the tests, the teacher discovers that George transposes numbers when he is writing the algebra formulas. Rather than writing down the number 23 in a formula he writes the number 32. The teacher reviews all of George's previous quizzes and finds that this is a consistent pattern. The teacher has a conference with George and carefully explains this error. In the next quiz, the teacher continues to remind George to make sure that he has not transposed any numbers. After George turns in the quiz, the teacher checks his answers and tells him that his scores have improved significantly. After this intervention, George continues to show improvement in algebra and is spending more and more time in this subject.

In this example, the teacher used a strategy that would directly influence George's mastery over the content. He is frustrated with his math scores and wants to understand why he is having a problem. His interest is piqued when the teacher explains why his answers have been incorrect. She encourages George and states, "Hey bud, you can do this, but make sure you don't flip your numbers. I will watch to see if you make this mistake during the quiz."

George now understands his error and corrects it, and as a result his test scores improve. When he corrected the problem and improved his quiz scores, his feelings of competence increased because he felt more control over the outcome. This scenario is designed to illustrate the subtle ways that teachers can help students increase their competence, which will also increase their motivation.

So far we have examined two areas that are related to academic performance, student ability and motivation. In the next section we will turn our attention to the communication processes that occur in the classroom context. First, we will describe the dominant features of instructional communication and then we will explore the communication behaviors that have been linked to academic performance.

Reflection

- Identify and discuss teaching strategies that increase student interest.
- What are your academic goals and how do they influence your motivation in a class?
- Which perspective on motivation best explains your approach to academic tasks?
- Identify and discuss your favorite academic subjects.

Teacher Efficacy

The previous section focused on perspectives on student motivation. We also believe it is important to discuss teacher motivation. A rather substantial body of research has examined teacher efficacy and its impact on instructional outcomes (see Klassen, Tze, Betts, & Gordon, 2011 for an extensive review of the literature on teacher efficacy). Teacher efficacy references the belief that a teacher can impact student learning. The significance of teacher efficacy can be traced to two RAND Corporation studies that were conducted in the seventies (Armor et al., 1976; Berman & McLaughlin, 1977). The authors found that teachers with high-efficacy positively impacted student reading achievement and the number of project goals they accomplished. Following these seminal studies, a number of investigations have examined the impact of teacher efficacy on instructional outcomes.

Gibson and Dembo (1984) identified two primary dimensions of teacher efficacy: personal teaching efficacy and teaching efficacy. Personal teaching efficacy references the belief that the teacher has the skills and abilities to produce student learning. Teaching efficacy is the belief that a teacher's effectiveness is limited because of factors outside of the teacher's control such as home and community influences. Tschannen-Moran and Hoy (2001) refined previous conceptualizations and identified an efficacy measure consisting of three primary dimensions: efficacy for instructional strategies, (the extent to which a teacher uses a variety of assessment strategies), efficacy for classroom management (the extent to which a teacher can control disruptive behavior) and efficacy for student engagement (the extent to which a teacher can get students to believe they can do well in schoolwork).

A number of studies document the positive impact of teacher efficacy. For example, Gibson and Dembo (1984) found that high-efficacy teachers spent more time in whole group instruction and more time checking student work. What was particularly interesting concerned the difference in the feedback given by high- and low-efficacy teachers. Low-efficacy teachers engaged in more negative criticism than high-efficacy teachers. Cousins and Walker (1995) found that high-efficacy teachers use instructional strategies that promote student self-directed learning. Teacher efficacy has been associated with achievement in reading, mathematics and it also has been found to predict final grades (Caprara, Barbaranelli, Steca, & Malone 2006).

Research also indicates that high-efficacy teachers create learning contexts that are conducive to student self-directed learning (Allinder, 1994). They also use strategies that increase student on-task behavior (Onafowora, 2004). They are more willing to experiment with new methods. High-efficacy teachers are more likely to help low-achieving students be successful (Alderman, 1990).

In summary, high-efficacy teachers have a cognitive script and a communication repertoire that can impact student performance. We believe that increasing the communication competence of future teachers will positively influence their beliefs about teaching in diverse classrooms. We will now turn our focus to the third component discussed by Friedrich specifically; we will discuss descriptive patterns of classroom communication and then review research on the communication practices that are predictive of instructional outcomes.

Communication Processes

Thus far, we have discussed the effects of student ability and motivation on learning. We will shift our focus to the third component of the learning model explicated by Friedrich (1982)—the quality of classroom communication. The effects of classroom communication are circular and their impact on learning and achievement are difficult to determine. Further, differences in contexts and the methodological variations used to study communication make comparisons problematic. Nevertheless, there are some trends that have been identified and in the next section we will review the dominant communication patterns occurring in instructional contexts.

Instructional Patterns

Belleck, Kliebard, Hyman, and Smith (1966) characterized classroom interaction as a "game" with rules that teachers and students follow. Four communication moves are used in the game. Structuring moves are used to establish the context for appropriate student behavior. Teachers might say, "This morning we are going to discuss the reading assignment I made yesterday." Soliciting moves seek to elicit a verbal response from the students. "Did you bring your cultural artifacts for today's discussion?" Responding moves follow from soliciting moves. They consist of the responses to student answers. Reacting moves are statements used to modify, or evaluate what students have said. When classroom communication is defined in this fashion, the teacher is expected to do most of the talking. In most classrooms, teachers talk approximately 70 percent of the time.

Haslett (1987) stated that instructional communication entails three language functions. One function involves directing students. This type of communication is concerned with giving students the information necessary to complete an instructional task. A second language function, informing, involves giving students new content. The third language function, eliciting, involves soliciting student responses. Asking students if they understand a task is an example of eliciting.

Cazden (1988) stated that the fundamental pattern of classroom interaction is the three-turn unit called the IRE. In this pattern, the teacher initiates a communication exchange (I), a student responds (R), and then the teacher comments on the response (E). Cazden stated that the initiation usually comes in the form of a question. Teacher questioning, then, is one of the dominant forms of communication used in the classroom.

The research cited above suggests that teachers engage in a limited range of behaviors. They give information, they ask for information, and direct student behavior. These descriptions, while informative, do not provide insight into the effects of these communication patterns on student learning and achievement. Research shows that the use of questions, and teacher clarity, impact learning (Brophy & Good, 2000; Kindsvatter, Wilen, & Ishler, 1996).

Questions

Questions are used by teachers to invite student participation and engage them in learning. Brophy and Good (2000) stated that research spanning 30 years shows that frequent questioning by teachers correlates positively with student achievement. Maximum effects on learning, however, are related to the clarity of the question and the way it is managed. Kindsvatter, Wilen, and Ishler (1996) stated that student achievement is enhanced when teachers ask clearly phrased questions, probe student responses, redirect questions to non-participating students, wait for student responses, and provide feedback on the accuracy of student responses

The type of question also influences learning. Tienken, Goldberg, and DiRocco (2009) reviewed the literature and categorized questions as being either reproductive (i.e., recall of facts,) or productive (i.e., analysis, and evaluation of ideas and information). This is an example of a reproductive question: "Class, who can identify the nine missions founded by Friar Junipero Serra in California?" In contrast, a productive question requires higher-order thinking and problem solving: "Class, what impact did the Mission in Santa Barbara have on the indigenous people who lived there?" Tienken et al. found that 68 percent of the questions asked by experienced teachers were reproductive and 85 percent of the questions of novice teachers were reproductive. These data suggest that most of the questions require students to restate information rather than reflect, critically evaluate, or problem solve. In Chapter 9 we will provide strategies for asking higher-order questions.

Clarity

Teacher clarity has also been linked to academic achievement. Clarity is facilitated when the teacher uses communication strategies to enhance understanding of instructional material. Bush (1977) conceptualized teacher clarity in terms of seven behaviors: (1) gives examples and explains them; (2) explains the work to be done, and how to do it; (3) gives written examples; (4) uses common examples; (5) gives explanations that the students understand; (6) speaks so that all the students can hear; and (7) takes time when explaining. Behaviors that detract from clarity include ambiguity, vagueness, hedging, bluffing, insufficient examples, and mazes (false starts, halts in speech, redundancy in spoken words). Bush, Kennedy, and Cruickshank (1977) used factor analysis to identify the underlying dimensions of teacher clarity. They found that clear teachers: (1) explained ideas; and (2) used ample illustrations while explaining ideas; and giving directions.

Hines, Cruickshank, and Kennedy (1985) examined teacher clarity and its effects on student achievement and satisfaction. Three types of clarity behaviors were examined: (1) teacher stresses important aspects of content; (2) teacher explains content by use of examples; and (3) teacher assesses and responds to perceived deficiencies in understanding. The results indicated that cognitive achievement and satisfaction with the instruction was positively related to teacher clarity.

After a systematic review of the literature, Brophy and Good (1986) stated that achievement is maximized when teachers actively present material, structure it with overviews, provide internal summaries, and signal important main ideas.

These communication strategies require teachers to use examples that connect with the experiences of students.

Although the behaviors reviewed above may facilitate understanding, we want to emphasize that clarity is unlikely to occur when a teacher uses low inference clarity behaviors. Students process information in terms of their own frames of reference and signal their understanding or lack of understanding of the material to the teacher. Ultimately, clarity is the result of these negotiated processes. Think for a moment of the teacher who uses an example the students do not understand. According to research by Darling (1989), students signal their lack of understanding in one of three ways. They provide specific information on what they do not understand and request clarification (focused/directive strategy). Here the student is very direct ("How is self-efficacy different from internal locus of control?"). A second strategy (focused non-directive) signals a lack of understanding but the student does not ask for clarification ("I don't understand what you mean by multiple intelligence"). The third strategy (personally qualified) entails a series of questions or mazes that the teacher must work through to provide clarification ("Why am I wrong, I said the same thing that Lindsey said?").

The research by Darling (1989) and Kendrick and Darling (1990) suggests that clarity is relational. These findings resonate with Civikly (1992a) and Eisenberg (1984) who argued that clarity is embedded in a relational context. Understanding is negotiated between teachers and students in instructional episodes. Teachers or students introduce concepts which are discussed, critiqued, and clarified. Clarity is compromised when closure is not brought to these episodes. The nature of the teacher–student relationship also plays a role in the way these episodes unfold. Some teachers can read the nonverbal behavior of students and recognize that an example does not make sense. From this feedback a new example is introduced and the information continues to be negotiated. In our judgment, then, it is best to consider clarity an episodic and relational process.

Teacher Immediacy

An extensive body of literature has examined the effects of teacher immediacy on learning. After summarizing the literature Rodriguez, Plax, and Kearney (1996) claimed: "No other teacher communication variable has been so consistently associated with increases in both students' affective and cognitive learning in the classroom" (p. 293). This claim, while compelling, may be overstated. The role of immediacy in learning is a bit cloudy.

Teacher immediacy is anchored in the research of Mehrabian (1969a, 1969b, 1970a, 1970b, 1971), who argued that people move toward those they like and away from those they dislike. It is important to emphasize that Mehrabian believed that immediacy was communicated through implicit nonverbal codes. Immediacy is primarily signaled through nonverbal behavior. Andersen (1979) extended the immediacy construct to the instructional setting. She reasoned that the nonverbal behaviors that reduce physical and psychological distance between teachers and students would positively impact learning. Behaviors such as smiling, eye contact, a relaxed body posture, and movement toward students, signal immediacy. Andersen found that nonverbal immediacy positively influenced student affect or their feelings about the teacher and the course but did not influence how well students did on a standardized measure of cognitive learning.

After the publication of Andersen's original article, a number of studies explored the effects of immediacy on learning. These studies have consistently reported positive correlations between measures of immediacy (nonverbal and verbal) and affective learning (e.g., Christensen & Menzel, 1998; Gorham, 1988; Kearney, Plax, Smith, & Sorensen, 1988; Kearney, Plax, & Wendt-Wasco, 1985; Kelly & Gorham, 1988; Moore, Masterson, Christophel, & Shea, 1996; Powell & Harville, 1990; Sanders & Wiseman, 1990). However, this program of research has not been successful in explaining the effects of immediacy on cognitive learning. At best, these studies reveal that students believe they learn more from immediate teachers. However, no study demonstrates that test scores or other cognitive measures are impacted by immediacy in any clear and consistent way.

Hess and Smythe (2001) contended that four models have been used to explain the relationship between immediacy and cognitive learning. The learning model was initially advanced by Andersen (1979) and proposed that immediacy directly influences learning. The teacher who engages in positive immediacy will engender positive student outcomes. Studies testing this assertion have found no association between immediacy and test scores. Andersen's seminal investigation found positive associations between immediacy and affective orientations to the class and teacher but there was no impact on test scores.

The motivation model hypothesized that immediacy facilitates an indirect effect on learning (Christophel, 1990; Richmond, 1990). Immediacy engenders state motivation (how students feel about a particular class and teacher) and as a consequence students study harder, go to class, increase their study time and learn more. Rodriguez, Plax, and Kearney (1996) advanced the affective learning model, which also hypothesized an indirect relationship between immediacy and cognitive learning. In this model, affective learning serves as a trigger or mediator for cognitive learning. Immediacy primes affective learning, which is a precursor to cognitive learning.

The arousal model twists the previous explanations and argues that immediacy creates arousal which increases attention and learning. Comstock, Rowell, and Bowers (1995) proposed that the relationship between immediacy and cognitive learning is curvilinear. They found that moderate amounts of teacher immediacy had the greatest impact on cognitive learning. The teacher who displays no immediacy puts students to sleep and the teacher who has too much immediacy may create anxiety or tension.

According to Hess and Smythe (2001), the studies testing these models have several flaws. First, the studies have not provided cognitive explanations of immediacy. The studies show patterns of association between immediacy and a number of outcomes such as affective learning, but they do not explain why these associations exist.

The measure of immediacy is the second flaw identified by Hess and Smythe (2001). The authors contend that too many studies have relied on self-reports rather than actual teacher behavior. The danger with self-report is that student judgments of immediacy might be confounded with other factors. For example, teachers might be considered immediate because they are an easy grader, bring food to class, or meet student needs. What is driving the student evaluation of immediacy is difficult to determine. In addition, extant instrumentation has departed from the original conception of immediacy. Gorham's (1988) measure of verbal immediacy, for example, is predicated on a presumed relationship between teaching effectiveness and immediacy. Immediacy and teaching effectiveness may be correlated but they are different constructs.

The third flaw concerns the measures of cognitive learning. A number of studies have used student reports of learning. In a typical study, students are asked to estimate what they have learned rather than to specifically measure what they learned. Hess and Smythe (2001) argued that students are not able to accurately measure what they learned. Students may vary in terms of their personal orientations to learning and how the teacher facilitates it. Judgments of learning may also be influenced by the relationship between a teacher and student. Students may inflate what they learn from a teacher they like and may deflate what they learn from a teacher they dislike.

Hess and Smythe contended that previous studies attempting to delineate the relationship between immediacy and cognitive learning have been misdirected. They argued that immediacy's primary function is to promote a positive relationship with the student. To test their contentions, the authors designed a study to assess the impact of teacher immediacy on student affect and cognitive learning. The results indicated that immediacy was positively related with perceived learning and liking for the instructor. A positive relationship between teacher affect and reported learning was also found. However, immediacy did not impact test performance. Finally, the results indicated that students were motivated by self-interest rather than teacher behavior. Grades were the primary motivating factor for the students.

The results of this investigation support the theory advanced by Hess and Smythe (2001). Immediacy played a substantial role in student perceptions about the teacher, the course and their perceived learning. It had little to do with how they performed on tests.

What can we say then about immediacy and its role in classroom learning? We agree that the primary impact of immediacy is to cultivate a positive relationship with the student. In terms of motivation, immediacy probably has its most pronounced impact on situational interest. This interpretation is closest to the arousal model explicated by Comstock, Rowell, and Bowers (1995). Test scores and other standardized assessments have more to do with student skill and academic engagement time (amount of time studying for a test) than with teacher communication behavior.

We are hesitant to completely abandon the role that immediacy plays in cognitive learning. Let's return to Mehrabian's initial contention that people move toward those they like and away from those they dislike and consider its role in cognition. The research clearly indicates that immediacy teachers are perceived to be approachable. Immediacy helps shape an environment where students feel comfortable to seek clarification and help on academic tasks. Students probably do not think much about their teacher at night when they are studying for a quiz or deliberating on the assignments they should complete. Previous research has not found a link between academic engagement time and immediacy (Powell & Aston, 1994; Sine, 1995), self-interest, levels of motivation, parents, and the significance of the assignment will influence how much time students spend on academic tasks.

Reflection

- What role does teacher immediacy play in learning?
- What are some negative aspects of teacher immediacy?

Communication Apprehension

The previous section examined the communication behaviors and processes that are positively associated with learning. We will conclude this chapter by discussing communication apprehension (CA), a construct that has been found to constrain learning in the classroom. Communication apprehension is one of the most researched constructs in the discipline of communication but has not been discussed much in education. Hundreds of studies have been done and the results have been consistent. In terms of the instructional context, the research indicates that students who experience communication apprehension have more difficulty in school than students who do not experience communication apprehension.

McCroskey and McCroskey (2002) identified four major effects of communication apprehension: internal discomfort, communication avoidance, communication withdrawal, and overcommunication. The one universal finding is that individuals with high CA experience internal discomfort and negative arousal when they face an event that requires communication. Frequently these feelings are connected with fear. These states may range from a warm flush to terror. Because individuals have such negative responses to the communication events related to the negative states, they frequently attempt to avoid them. Because an oral report may be terrifying, the apprehensive student will do everything to avoid giving it. If it is impossible to completely avoid the situation, a communication apprehensive student may try to physically or psychologically withdraw from it. The student who is scheduled to do a report may say, "I didn't do it," or may respond to a teacher's question by saying, "I don't know." Both strategies allow the student to step back from communication involvement. According to McCroskey and McCroskey (2002), on rare occasions, a student with communication apprehension may attempt to deal with the negative arousal by over-participating in communication. These students may attempt to "talk" through their anxiety. In these circumstances, the individual may be more concerned with the quantity rather than the quality of the interaction.

There are significant academic consequences for students with high communication apprehension. They obtain lower grade point averages and have poorer attitudes about school (McCroskey & Andersen, 1976). Because of their feelings about communication, apprehensive students are less likely to seek help from teachers and are less likely to articulate their instructional needs. These students also have fewer peer friendships. In a study designed to assess college student retention and academic success, McCroskey, Booth-Butterfield, and Payne (1989) found that high communication apprehensives were more likely to drop out of school than low apprehensives. The effects of communication apprehension had its greatest effect in the first two years of college.

Similar findings have been observed in elementary and middle school. Comadena and Prusank (1988) assessed the relationship between communication apprehension and academic achievement among elementary and middle school students. The findings indicated that students who had high communication apprehension received the lowest scores on all measures of academic achievement. The authors also found that communication apprehension increased with grade level. Communication apprehension increased 17 percent from the second grade to the eighth grade. The data do not indicate if these shifts are related to academic success or other factors. Whatever the reason, communication apprehension seems to increase with grade levels and is negatively associated with academic success.

Chesebro et al. (1992) conducted an extensive study on the potential role of communication apprehension for "at-risk" students. "At-risk" students were those failing to achieve in school or dropping out of school. The authors collected data at 14 urban, large, predominantly minority, middle and junior high schools. A total of 2,793 students participated in the study. The results indicated that "at-risk" students are substantially more apprehensive about speaking in groups and speaking in dyads. The authors noted that these data are troubling because so much of instruction occurs in these contexts.

The results also indicated that "at-risk" students perceived themselves to be less competent in communication. The data indicated that nearly all of the differences were related to communication with acquaintances and strangers.

The "at-risk" students did not feel competent in these settings. Once more, these data are distressing because students frequently work in groups or teams. Their feelings about communication in these contexts may have deleterious effects on their academic performance.

Rosenfeld, Grant, and McCroskey (1995) reasoned that if communication apprehension negatively affects "at-risk" students, it should have the opposite effect for academically talented students. The authors studied 7–10th-grade students who were accepted into a gifted program at Duke University and found that gifted students had lower apprehension than the "at-risk" students assessed by Chesebro et al. (1992). Further, the findings indicated that gifted students had less apprehension in the small group setting than "at-risk" students.

Causes of Communication Apprehension

The data showing the negative effects of communication apprehension are rather consistent. There is controversy about its causes. Daly and Friedrich (1981) stated that communication apprehension might be caused by genetics, social skill acquisition, modeling, and reinforcement.

The genetic explanation proposes that communication apprehension is related to factors such as sociability, physical appearance, body shape, and competence in motor skills. Each of these predispositions are enhanced or constrained by environmental factors.

Another way that communication apprehension may emerge, according to Daly and Friedrich (1981), involves the way in which social skills are acquired. Skills such as language use, sensitivity to nonverbal communication interaction management skills may be lacking in the communication apprehensive student. The protypical "geek" or "nerd" may be the student who lacks social skill and cannot "fit into the flow" of social interaction. As a result, communication is not very rewarding and new skills are not developed.

The third explanation that Daly and Friedrich (1981) discussed is modeling. If the child is around communicatively apprehensive individuals, then these are the behaviors modeled. When the individual is asked to engage in communication behaviors that have no frame of reference, the result will be anxiety and apprehension.

According to Daly and Friedrich, the most frequently advanced explanation of communication is explained through reinforcement theory. An individual who receives positive reinforcement for communication will not develop communication apprehension. The child who is told to be quiet, and not encouraged to communicate may develop negative attitudes about communication. McCroskey and Richmond (1978) found that students from rural areas and small towns reported higher communication apprehension levels than students from medium-sized and urban communities. The authors argued that this finding "is the first theoretically projected relationship between an environmental factor and communication apprehension that has been empirically verified"

(p. 247). When comparing the environmental factors influencing attitudes about communication, urban children face more communication demands than rural children. For example, the rural students studied by McCroskey and Richmond attended small homogeneous schools with little ethnic diversity. A common and narrow set of skills led to communication competence in these communities. In contrast, urban students face a much wider set of communication constraints. As a result, they must develop a broader range of competencies in order to be successful.

A new perspective, one that challenges the reinforcement explanation, is emerging. Some researchers (Beatty, McCroskey, & Heisel, 1998; Beatty, McCroskey, & Valencic, 2001) challenge the reinforcement explanation and contend that neurobiological processes primarily determine communication apprehension. Beatty, McCroskey, and Heisel (1998) state that "communication apprehension is primarily a function of two interrelated neurobiological systems, the thresholds of which are the products of genetic inheritance" (p. 224).

Opt and Loffredo (2000) assessed the relationship between communication apprehension and the Meyers–Briggs personality type preferences. The Meyers-Briggs assessment draws from Jungian psychology, a perspective that anchors personality in inborn traits. The authors argued that communication apprehension is not something to overcome but is a preference not to communicate. The participants were assessed on extraversion–introversion, intuition–sensing, thinking–feeling, and judging–perceiving and on their level of communication apprehension. The results indicated that introverts and sensors scored significantly higher on communication apprehension. The authors concluded that communication apprehension is perceived as a problem when it is viewed through the perspective of extroverts. For the introvert, it is normal to not openly communicate or seek out communication exchanges. The introvert prefers quiet places and solitary activities. The authors conclude by suggesting that one way to deal with a person's apprehension is to help him or her become more complete in their personalities by confronting and expanding less preferred competencies.

The nature–nurture debate of communication apprehension has not been resolved and the reader is encouraged to read additional literature on this topic (Beatty, McCroskey, & Valencic, 2001; Condit, 2000). Whether communication apprehension is rooted in learning or theory or in biology, the teacher must have some strategy for dealing with it. The student who exhibits communication apprehension experiences numerous educational disadvantages. McCroskey and McCroskey (2002) discussed several ways that a teacher can prevent and reduce student apprehension. Specifically, they suggested that teachers:

- Reduce oral communication demands.
    1. Avoid testing through talk.
    2. Avoid grading on participation.

  3 Avoid alphabetical seating.
  4 Avoid randomly calling on students.

- Make communication a rewarding experience.

  1 Praise students when they participate.
  2 Try to avoid indicating that any answer is completely "wrong."
  3 Try not to punish any student for talking.

- Be consistent about communication.

  1 Try to be consistent in how you handle student talk.
  2 Be very clear about any rules you must have regarding talking.

- Reduce ambiguity, novelty and evaluation.

  1 Make all assignments as clear and unambiguous as you can.
  2 Be clear about your grading system.
  3 Avoid surprises.

- Increase student control over success.

  1 Give the student options.
  2 Be certain that the student can avoid communication and still do well in the course.

Reflection

- How would you deal with communication apprehension in your class?

Summary

This chapter has attempted to explicate the relationship between communication and learning. We have proposed that students bring a rich set of experiences, language skills, and interests that play an important role in the learning process. We believe that the relationship between classroom communication and learning is a function of three primary factors: student ability, motivation, and communication processes. The research we have reviewed suggests that instructional strategies building on student strengths positively influence academic performance. We also examined different perspectives on motivation and suggested ways to promote self-efficacy and internality. Finally, we examined the communication processes that shape learning experiences. Teacher questions, clarity and immediacy play important roles in the way instructional material is presented, processed, and understood.

Learning Activities

- Complete an assessment of your multiple intelligences. How do these preferences influence the way you approach learning tasks?
- Several of your students do not seem interested in reading.
- Which perspective on motivation can you use to devise a way to increase their interest in reading?
- Many teachers use external rewards (prizes, stickers, money) to engage students in learning tasks. What can teachers do to increase students, learning goals and internal motivation?

Resources

- Motivating students to engage in class activities
  www.nwrel.org/request/oct00/engage.html
- What do students want and what really motivates them?
  www.middleweb.com/StdntMotv.html
- Encouraging student academic motivation
  www.interventioncentral.org/htmdocs/interventions/motivation/motivation.php

Unit II

UNDERSTANDING DIVERSITY

This unit focuses on three features of diversity: culture, gender, and exceptionalities. As noted previously, we consider diversity to be fluid and multidimensional. Culture, gender, and exceptionalities converge and emerge in different contexts. For purposes of clarity, we will deal with each of these areas separately. We begin with cultural diversity. Demographic changes are affecting education in profound ways. Students from, and who have generational connections to, Latin American, Southeast Asian, African, and Middle Eastern countries are entering the educational system in increasing numbers. Chapter 3 is intended to increase readers' understanding of the ways in which culture influences beliefs about how to communicate in the classroom. Readers are encouraged to interrogate their personal beliefs about culture and education. We begin the chapter by contrasting assimilation and pluralistic viewpoints about culture. We discuss the value dimensions of culture and how those dimensions inform expectations about classroom behavior. We follow this with an explanation of the impact of cultural identity, culture and learning style, and ways to engage in culturally responsive teaching. Chapter 4 examines sex and gender. We begin the chapter by reviewing difference and similarity hypotheses. These hypotheses propose different explanations of male and female brains and behavior. This section is followed with a discussion of vulnerability and empowerment explanations of female beliefs and behavior. We also include a discussion of strategies for teaching males who are at risk for academic failure. In Chapter 5 we explore students with exceptionalities. First, we define risk and then review pertinent legislation on disabilities. In this chapter we also include a discussion of other factors that place students at risk. We address immigrant children, English learners, poverty, and homelessness. We conclude the chapter by discussing practices that promote positive interactions with all students in inclusive classrooms.

3

CULTURE AND CLASSROOM COMMUNICATION

Learning Outcomes

1. Explain the cultural values that define educational contexts.
2. Analyze the way cultural identity impacts classroom communication practices.
3. Describe how culture impacts preferences for learning.
4. Reflect on your attitudes about culture and diversity.
5. Develop strategies for accomplishing culturally responsive teaching.

Classroom Scenario

On the first day of class, LeAnne Young, a first-year teacher, waits enthusiastically for the students in her first-period English class to arrive. They trickle in, some quietly, others engage in heated conversation. The veritable rainbow of student colors impacts Ms. Young considerably. Finally, the students take their seats and look at Ms. Young as she takes out her roll sheet and begins to call out their names: Eduardo Martinez, Shanisha Knight, Teng Her, Sandi Chalensouk, Gabriela Gamino, Markus Tyson, Michael Smith, Azor Singh, Ignacio Vidales, Danny Castanon, Tamika Yosida, and Brian Moore.

Ms. Young faces a daunting task. She recognizes the vast diversity in her class but is unsure how to address this opportunity. The one cultural studies course she took in college focused on the African-American history. Although interesting, the course did not provide Ms. Young with the skills needed to teach in a culturally diverse classroom. In this chapter we examine the role of culture in the instructional process. Our goal is to provide a foundation for culturally responsive teaching.

American schools are experiencing profound demographic shifts. For example, in 2000–2001, 61 percent of the students enrolled in public elementary and secondary schools were White, while 17 percent were Black, 16 percent were Hispanic and 4 percent were Asian/Pacific Islander. In 2007–2008, 56 percent were White, 17 percent were African-American, 21 percent were Hispanic and 5 percent were Asian/Pacific Islanders (Digest of Educational

Statistics, 2012). The trends are more significant in the west where White students represent 43 percent of students enrolled in public schools followed by Hispanics, 38 percent, Asian 6.4 percent and Black, 6.2 percent (Digest of Educational Statistics, 2012).

We must also be mindful that there are substantial differences within the cultural groups identified above. Asians may consist of Chinese, Japanese, Hmong, Vietnamese, Laotian, and Cambodian. Hispanics may consist of Mexican, Cuban, Salvadorian, Mixtec Columbian and Spanish. Blacks consist of African-American, Nigerian, Ethiopian, Haitian, and Jamaican. There are also increasing numbers of students from East Indian and Middle Eastern ethnic backgrounds. Also a large number of students come from blended families where the parents are from different ethnic or cultural backgrounds.

Immigration has dramatically influenced the shifting student mosaic. In the past, immigrant children traced their heritage to Europe. Approximately, 70 percent of recent immigrants with legal status are from Latin America, and Asia (Martin & Midgley, 2006). There are also a large number of immigrants from non- or mixed documentation families (Passel, as cited in Rong & Preissle, 2009).

Indeed the students in today's classroom come from a wide variety of cultural experiences. They bring their languages, customs, religions, attitudes, and abilities. At the same time, 80 percent of the teachers are White and may have limited understanding of the way culture influences the teaching–learning process.

The demographic changes can be challenging and exciting at the same time. Responsible schools and educators must struggle with ways to meet the needs of students with a wide range of experiences, skills, and interests. Understanding the ways in which culture influences educational contexts can empower teachers to reach all of their students. This is no easy task. Teachers must understand not only how culture influences the behavior of students, but also the way that it influences their own perceptions and behaviors. According to Rong and Preissle (2009), there are two perspectives on teaching immigrants and we would say diversity in general. One is to use an assimilation model. Within this perspective education serves to subordinate an ethnic identity so that an American identity can be created. Central to this view is that the immigrant or diverse student develops competence in English, values, individual accountability, and perseverance. Educators embracing an assimilation perspective often view diverse students and new immigrants from a deficit perspective. Teachers embracing this view claim that through hard work and education, everyone can participate in the American Dream. Many White teachers, because of their history and teaching experiences may buy into the assimilation model. Every semester, I place students into diverse groups and ask them to answer a series of questions about culture. One question asks them to identify their country of origin. Many White students state that they have no idea or that they are, "a mutt" or "Heinz 57"—a blended variety. They do not see themselves as cultural or having a cultural identity. They do not see their cultural traditions, such as Christmas, Thanksgiving, Easter, or their norms for dress, or their values and beliefs, as inherently cultural.

In contrast, a pluralistic model does not strive for a homogeneous society but one that recognizes and celebrates heterogeneity. This perspective recognizes that there are a variety of factors influencing an individual's assimilation. Teachers view diversity as a resource that can be used to bolster educational goals and objectives. This perspective also recognizes the institutional and educational structures and obstacles facing students such as racism, prejudice, xenophobia, and socioeconomic status. The perspective advanced in this text is consistent with the pluralistic perspective. We believe that teachers who increase their cultural competence will be in a better position to create a classroom culture where all students can prosper and grow.

Reflection

- How do you define culture?
- To what cultural groups do you belong?
- Do you have friends who are culturally different from you?
- What do you know about your friend's traditions or history?

Culture

Culture is a difficult concept to understand. An examination of some representative definitions might be helpful. Lustig and Koester (1999) defined culture as "a learned set of shared interpretations about beliefs, values, and norms which affect the behaviors of a relatively large group of people" (p. 30). Orbe and Harris (2001) characterized culture as "learned and shared values, beliefs, and behaviors common to a particular group of people; culture forges a group's identity and assists in its survival" (p. 6). Individuals are taught, sometimes implicitly, sometimes explicitly, to view the world in a certain way and to behave in a way that supports this viewpoint. Samovar, Porter, and Stefani (2000) offered the following conceptualization of culture:

> the deposit of knowledge, experiences, social hierarchies, religion, notions of time, roles, spatial relationships, concepts of the universe, and material objects and possessions acquired by a group of people in the course of generations through individual or group striving.
>
> (p. 7)

Culture, then, influences what people know, how they came by that knowledge, what roles they play and how they should play them, what they value, and how they put their values into action. Clearly, culture plays a significant role in the education process.

Dimensions of Culture

A number of scholars have investigated the role culture plays in communication exchanges. The research of Hall (1976) and Hofstede (1980) is particularly relevant to our examination of culture in the classroom. Hall believed that individuals are faced with so many stimuli that they develop mechanisms for filtering and making sense out of them. According to Hall, the context for communication plays a significant role in the way the information is sifted and acted upon (Hall, 1976, p. 86). A communication context has physical, social, and psychological features. The physical feature is the actual setting for the interaction (classroom, principal's office, home). The social feature is the relationship among the participants (teacher/student, teacher/parent, teacher/teacher). Psychological features include the attitudes, sentiments, and motivations of the participants. Culture influences the degree to which communicators focus on these features.

Hall postulated a continuum with high-context messages on one end and low-context messages on the other (1976, p. 91). A high-context message has most of the relevant information in the physical setting or is internalized in the person. Much of the meaning in the message is implied. Japanese, Hmong, Koreans, Chinese, and Latinos are examples of high-context communities. Members of high-context groups have developed similar expectations about how to perceive and respond to a particular communication event. Consequently, explicit verbal messages are not necessary for understanding. Low-context groups, on the other hand require that the message include a great deal of explicit information. Uncertainty is reduced and understandings are obtained through expressed verbal codes.

Most American classrooms are predicated on low-context exchanges. Teachers are expected to be clear, direct, explicit, and linear with their instructions and expectations. Students are expected to be clear, direct, and explicit with their answers. The farther students depart from these communication conventions, the more at risk they become.

Hofstede (1980), another expert on intercultural communication, explained that individuals possess cognitive processes that are shaped by culture and are expressed through the culture's dominant value dimensions. He identified four dominant patterns and each has its own application to classroom exchanges.

The first dimension is *power distance*. This dimension is concerned with the way in which status differences are ascribed and negotiated. Some cultures believe that power should be distributed while others hold that only a few people should possess power and authority. European American students tend to believe that power should be distributed and that everyone has an equal opportunity to possess it. Students from Latin and Southeast Asian cultures tend to believe that power should be held by a select few. As we noted, clan elders possess a great deal of power in the Hmong community and young women possess very little. Some teachers wield a great deal of power in classrooms. They make all classroom decisions and impose their will on the students. Other teachers share power with students and give them an opportunity to make decisions about instructional issues and class activities.

A second dimension is *uncertainty avoidance*. This dimension is concerned with the ways in which a culture deals with change and unpredictability. Some cultures have very little tolerance for circumstances that may threaten the culture's structure and hierarchy. Severe consequences follow for the individual who does not adhere to the culture's expectations. Individuals from cultures high on uncertainty avoidance have very strict rules governing appropriate behavior and there are severe consequences for violating these rules. Schools and classes also establish rules and policies for appropriate classroom behavior. Some teachers may be very strict and intolerant of student "misbehavior." One teacher stated that the problem with Native-American students is that they lack structure at home so he was going to be sure they learned discipline in his classroom. His primary instructional goal was to control student behavior; learning was a secondary goal. Other teachers allow students to make choices, multi-task, and socialize with other students.

A third dimension is *individualism–collectivism*. This dimension is concerned with the degree to which individuals commit to self or community. Competition, autonomy, privacy, personal opinion, and independence are core elements in individualistic societies. The United States is extremely high on this dimension. The school system, with its growing emphasis on grades and test scores, competition, and performance outcomes, strongly promotes individualistic values. Cultures subordinating the needs of the individual to the group are reflective of collectivist societies. Humility and sharing are core values in collectivistic cultures. Thus, focusing attention on the achievements of one individual can bring much stress. For example, it is inappropriate to single out the success of a Native-American individual. Obligation is another core element in collectivist cultures. Some teachers have become frustrated with students who miss class because of family "business." The teachers do not understand that, in some cultures, especially for new immigrants from collectivist societies, family obligation transcends school and education.

The fourth dimension discussed by Hofstede is *masculinity–femininity*. This dimension concerns the degree to which the culture values assertiveness and achievement versus nurturance and social support. Some cultures judge others by their achievements and the manifestations of appropriate masculine behavior. In Mexico, for example, the male is the head of the household, is primarily responsible for the financial security of the family and ultimately makes all the important decisions. Women are expected to tend to home duties such as child rearing and cooking. Attitudes about masculinity and femininity are also revealed in America's classrooms. Boys are often encouraged to be assertive, active, and competitive while females are encouraged to be passive, and cooperative. The issue of masculinity and femininity is complex and we discuss this topic in Chapter 4.

After publishing the first four dimensions, Hofstede (2001) added a fifth dimension which he labeled *long-term and short-term orientation.* According to Hofstede, this orientation is rooted in Confucianism which values thrift, and persistence and a predictable social order. Values of a short-term orientation are a concern for "here and now," a low concern for status and a motivation to protect one's identity. Students from long-term orientation are likely to show great respect for teachers and are concerned with task accomplishment. Students from short-term orientations are more likely to play before work and be more likely to exhibit disrespectful behavior to the teacher.

The perspectives offered by Hall and Hofstede have great application for today's diverse classroom. Recall that culture shapes perceptions, values, and behaviors. The dominant perspective of America's classroom is low-context and individualistic. In most classes, the preferred way of communicating is to be explicit and linear. Yet more and more students are from high-context, collectivistic cultural experiences. For these students, the teacher is considered the expert; knowledge is passed from the teacher to the student. The student's task is to absorb the information. These students are less likely to perceive that knowledge is negotiated. The teacher who is unaware of the way culture informs students of preferences for appropriate behavior may perceive that high-context, collectivist students are disconnected while low-context individualistic students are engaged. Seldom are these issues made clear to the students as they navigate the instructional system.

Cultural Identity

The connection to a culture's values is accomplished through the performance of cultural identity. Cultural identity denotes the ways individuals view themselves and the ways they wish to be viewed by others. Lustig and Koester (2000) noted that cultural identity involves learning about and accepting the traditions, heritage, language, religion, ancestry, aesthetics, thinking patterns, and social structures of a culture (p. 3).

According to Collier (1994), identities are co-created and negotiated through communication exchanges. A person may have different identities, depending on the context. Students may have "home," "playground," and "classroom" identities. A student can be quiet and inattentive in the classroom and loud, boisterous, and aggressive in the school yard. Student identity plays a fundamental role in the groups they move toward and away from. Think about the ways students cluster and the way in which they navigate through the groups in which they participate. "Skaters," "emos," "preps," "schoolboys," "bandos" dress and talk in ways that support their identities.

Goffman's (1959, 1963) dramaturgical perspective is an excellent framework for viewing the cultural identities of students. He claimed that whenever people participate in social interaction, they are engaged in a type of performance. Like actors in a play, they construct an image they want the audience to accept. Goffman (1959) stated that each person constructs a face and uses a line (way of talking) to support it. A successful performance, according to Goffman, requires the individual to look the part they are trying to play and talk in a way that supports the projected image. These performances are not always positive. For example, some students do not perceive that being a good student is "cool" so they slump in their desks, appear bored, and seldom participate in class discussion. Recall our discussion of self-worth theory and motivation. Students construct a social performance that removes them from academic engagement.

In multicultural classrooms, a student may enact a performance that the teacher misunderstands or does not accept. Cupach and Imahori (1993) examined the way individuals from different cultural backgrounds manage the predicaments (a situation that is embarrassing or unpleasant) created by someone else. Even though their research did not focus on instructional contexts, their research has direct application to the topic we are discussing.

The authors claimed that all individuals want to have their identities supported during social interaction. Receiving undue recognition, being criticized or corrected, having their privacy violated, and being caused to look foolish are the types of situations causing individuals to lose face (Cupach & Metts, 1990, 1992). When individuals are confronted with these predicaments they are compelled to invoke a strategy to save face. Examples of the strategies individuals use to restore their identity are: apology (accepting blame and seeking forgiveness), excuse (minimizing responsibility), justification (downplaying harmful consequences), humor (joking or laughing), remediation (actively attempting to repair damage), avoiding (ignoring the transgression), escape (leaving the scene), and aggression (verbally or physically attacking).

Cupach and Imahori (1993) predicted that American and Japanese students would use different strategies to deal with face-threatening situations. The authors predicted that Americans would use humor, accounts (reasons that justify a behavior), and aggression, while Japanese would use apology and remediation. The results supported the hypotheses. The authors concluded from the findings that Americans use strategies which support their own face and Japanese use strategies to support others.

These findings have direct implications for classrooms. Teachers criticize students for the way they dress, for their taste in music, and on their academic performance. Without meaning to, teachers may also threaten the cultural identities of students. Shortly after the bombing of the World Trade Center, Muslim students and students who looked Middle Eastern were criticized, mocked, and challenged by teachers and students. Students create predicaments for teachers when they question grades, tell a teacher assignments are unclear, or challenge the authority of teachers. The way in which these predicaments are managed can dramatically influence the climate of the classroom.

Reflection

- What are some of the cultural labels you use?
- How do you feel about the students who perform these identities?
- How do you respond to face-threatening situations?

Collier (1994) observed that cultural identities are expressed through core symbols, labels, and norms. Core symbols reference beliefs about the universe and people's positions in it. These symbols direct members of a cultural group to perceive the world in a particular way and behave in a way that is consistent with that definition. Core symbols for African-Americans are authenticity, powerlessness, and expressiveness (Hecht, Collier, & Ribeau, 1993). Latino core symbols are obligation to family, respect, and faith.

Labels are important components of cultural identity. Students with ancestors from Mexico may at different times describe themselves as Mexican, Mexican-American, Hispanic, Chicano, or Latino. Some students say they are African-American, and others call themselves Black. White Hmong are different from Green Hmong, and an Afghan is different from an Iraqi.

Tanno (1997) discussed the different labels characterizing her cultural identity. She spent her formative years in New Mexico, where she used the label Spanish to describe herself. She spoke Spanish and practiced some of the traditions that were introduced into New Mexico by the early Spanish settlers. When she moved from New Mexico she was confronted with a different label. Outside of New Mexico the preferred label for her heritage was *Mexican-American*. This label captured the duality of her heritage: the traditions of Mexico and dominant patterns of America. To be too Mexican was to reject the American in her. To reject the Mexican and become too American was to abandon her historical roots. A third label found its way into her vocabulary. Whereas, the label *Mexican-American* captured a dual identity, the new label *Latina* captured her connectedness. The Spanish had captured vast territories and merged with indigenous peoples from Cuba, Mexico, and South America. Language, religion, and numerous daily practices were common among a vast group of people. For Tanno, to be *Latina* was to belong to a broad cultural community.

The final label that Tanno discussed is Chicana. This label is unique because it was created by an ethnic group to describe an ethnic group. With this label came a political consciousness. The label *Chicana* recognizes the marginalization that Americans of Latin descent have experienced and the desire to reconstruct these structures through political action.

Tanno concluded her essay by arguing that each label represents a part of her identity. She noted that all individuals take on multiple roles and believed we should be respectful of this complexity. Teachers might also be mothers, fathers, husbands, wives, uncles, little league coaches, and big sisters. Students may be sons, daughters, soccer players, and goddaughters. Further, these labels are not static, but fluid. Individuals may use different labels to define themselves at different times.

Sometimes teachers inappropriately label students or use a label that students do not prefer, like, or perceive to be insulting or embarrassing. Students from Cambodia are often confused with students from China. It is important for teachers to recognize that the way in which they respond to these labels may indicate acceptance or rejection of the student. While labels may seem helpful, they can be problematic. Every African-American student does not have the same attitudes, possess the same skills, or have the same interests. Group norms also play an important role in cultural identity (Collier, 1994). Norms are the standards for competent participation in a community. There are norms for turning in assignments, participating in class, working individually or in groups. Language performance is a central feature of cultural identity. To competently perform a cultural identity is to use language and behave in a way that sustains and projects that identity. Murrell (2002) draws from the work of Holland, Lachicotte, Skinner, and Cain (1998) and argues that identities are "improvised." That is, identities are tested, negotiated, and reconstructed in each communication context. According to Murrell (2002), identity management is the most significant developmental task facing African-American students.

As we previously discussed, Standard English is the preferred discourse style of the classroom. Some research indicates that students of color assume that in order to be academically successful they must abandon their ethnic identity and assume a White one (Fordham & Ogbu, 1986; Ogbu, 1999). Ogbu (1999) referred to this as a Dialectical Dilemma. In his research in Oakland, California, he found that African-Americans endorsed learning Standard English for education and employment but this mastery also threatened membership in the community. That is, parents and others stated that they did not want students to use Standard English at home or to criticize the use of language styles used in the community. In other words, it appeared to be acceptable to "talk White" at school but not at home. Ogbu's position is that a number of community factors negatively influence the academic performance of minorities. Murrell (2002), a scholar of African-American pedagogy, has a different approach for interpreting the academic performance of African-Americans. He contended that all students experience concern about possible academic failure. Rather than believing that African-Americans must act White to be successful, Murrell (2002) argued they fear that they will confirm negative stereotypes that African-American students and other students of color do not have academic potential. He goes on to contend that schools need to help reshape a construction of African-Americans and we include other groups that require deconstructing a "triple threat." This threat involves teachers, the media, and peers. Many students have teachers who do not expect students of color to be successful (Threat 1). These students face national and local media that reify an achievement gap between White students and students of color (Threat 2). Finally, students of color may see academic achievement as "selling out" (Threat 3).

Other research indicates that African-American students are committed to academic success. In a comprehensive longitudinal study, Eccles, Wong & Peck (2006) studied the impact of African-American ethnic identity, and experiences with discrimination on academic motivation and achievement. Data obtained from the Maryland Adolescents Development in Context Study were used to answer the key questions posed by the researchers. Among the findings were that African-American students placed as much value on education as Euro-American students. The data also indicated that a student with a strong African-American identity was as academically motivated as Euro-American students. About 5 percent of African respondents indicated that academic success was associated with acting White.

The analysis also indicated that the students' anticipated racial discrimination and family experiences with discrimination in the workplace positively impacted student academic motivation and academic performance. This suggests that education is one way to respond to future discrimination. In contrast, day-to-day experiences with discrimination negatively impacted academic performance. Students who experienced discrimination from peers placed less value in school, and discrimination from teachers negatively impacted academic self-confidence and the value they placed in school.

Finally, the authors investigated the impact of cultural group connection to academic performance. The results indicated that cultural group connection positively impacted student grade point average. The more an African-American student had a strong ethnic identity, the better they did in school.

The findings of this study indicate that day-to-day experiences of racial discrimination from peers and teachers has a deleterious impact on the academic identity and performance of African-American students. However, these effects are minimized when the student has a strong connection with his or her ethnic group. Thus cultural identity serves a positive role. Some parents may socialize children to understand the realities of racial discrimination, and that education is an important way to respond to it.

Clearly this is a complicated issue. But we want teachers to think carefully and deeply about their beliefs about students of color, the ways in which they enact their identities, and what this means for their curriculum, evaluative procedures, and relationships.

The research by Rex (2003) illustrates how teachers, even those with good intentions, dismiss and devalue students who do not use mainstream speech. She further contends that high-stakes testing has exacerbated the problem. In one study she observed an exchange between a teacher and an inner city student on the use of topic sentences. In the instructional episode the students were writing sentences about drug use in the community. The student from the inner city wanted to debate the assertion made by the teacher that drug use was a problem. He was from the community and did not use drugs. Rather than engaging the student in the discussion and probing his experience, the teacher moved the focus to the grammatical and syntactical structure of the sentence he was supposed to write. This instructional move was motivated by the desire to help the student improve his writing so that he would score higher on the state test but the effect may have been to disconfirm the student's identity and experiences. Rex (2003) raises several important questions for teachers to consider. For example, she asks, "What if they don't believe they need to talk, read or write in the ways the high stakes tests imply they should?" (p. 39). "What classroom conversations are lost and what opportunities for inclusion disappear when much of the talk is about reading and writing as they appear on the test?" (p. 39).

Godley, Sweetland, Wheeler, Minnici, and Carpenter (2006) offer recommendations for teachers facing dialectically diverse classrooms. The authors argue that teachers need to change their ideology about teaching English. They state "When teachers engage in teaching of Standard English it is important they frame Standard English as an addition to students' linguistic repertoires, rather than as a more prestigious more 'correct' substitution for the varieties that students already speak."

The authors discuss three ways in which teachers can be more responsive to dialectically diverse classrooms:

1 *Dialect diversity is a resource not a deficit.* Godley et al. (2006) contend that teachers, especially when teaching language arts, should build on and use the dialects that students bring to the classroom. They go on to recommend that teachers should not label nonstandard dialects as ungrammatical, illogical, or as slang (p. 35).
2 *Students benefit from learning about dialect diversity.* The authors note that language naturally varies from situation to situation. Helping students analyze and utilize these different forms enriches their understanding of language use. Godley et al. state that programs implemented in middle and high schools have helped students develop a better understanding of regional and social language variation. Teaching about dialectical diversity encourages students to recognize the multiple language forms they use.
3 *Dialect patterns should be distinguished from errors in writing and addressed through a contrastive approach.* This strategy requires teachers to try and understand the underlying patterns of language rather than focusing on correcting errors in language grammar, logic or syntax. Consider the following example of student writing. A student writes, "I seen your buds at the Rodeo Café last night." This sentence has a grammatical structure; there is an object and verb. Godley et al. recommend using a contrasting approach that builds on the student's competence. They suggest that a sentence is "data" that

> can be analyzed and used to facilitate the use of Standard English. Rather than labeling the error, the teacher might ask the student to reflect on the grammatical pattern that was used. The student can be asked to identify circumstances when it is appropriate to write, "I seen" and when it is appropriate to write "I saw."

The recommendations suggested by Godley et al. (2006) are difficult to implement and take time. However, research indicates that the overall writing performance on standardized assessments has improved when these strategies have been implemented (e.g., Fogel & Ehri, 2000; Schierloh, 1991; Taylor, 1989).

In the previous section we have attempted to describe the role that cultural identity plays in the classroom. Students manage multiple identities through their styles of dress, ways of talking, and norms of behavior. Some of these identities are positively received and others are rejected. All, however, impact the way that interaction unfolds in the classroom.

Culture and Learning

The relationship between student culture and preferences for learning has been discussed frequently, but teachers have not been particularly effective in incorporating culture into classroom practice. Kuykendall (1992) suggested that students who find their culture and learning styles reflected in instruction are more likely to be motivated and less likely to be disruptive. The research by Dunn and Griggs (2000) indicates that student academic achievement increases when instructional practices adapt to the learning styles of students. It is important therefore to understand how culture influences learning and how to integrate this knowledge into instructional practice. The following discussion is introductory so we encourage future teachers to continue to investigate this topic.

Learning style is concerned with the characteristic ways of dealing with instructional information and culture influences this process. For example, observational research suggests that Mexican-American students are more comfortable with broad concepts than with isolated facts (Cox & Ramirez, 1981; Vasquez, 1991). African-American students prefer tactile "hands on" learning (Shade, 1989). Native-Americans relate well to instructional tasks requiring skills in visual discrimination, and the use of imagery (Shade, 1989). Mainstream White students value independence, analytical thinking and objectivity.

Cultural differences have been found on self-report measures. Cultural researchers assessing learning styles have found differences in field-independent and field-dependent learning (Gollnick & Chinn, 1994). Field-dependent learners process information holistically and are more concerned with the social context, and are more intuitive. Field-independent learners process information sequentially, do not consider the social situation important, and are rational.

Mainstream White students tend to be field-independent and students from minority groups tend to be field-dependent.

It is important to note, however, that there is not a straightforward relationship between culture and learning style. As Guild (1994) noted, there are as many variations within a group as there are commonalities. Moreover, many conceptualizations on learning style are bipolar. One end is represented by analytic processes while the other end is represented by holistic ones.

Gay (2000), a central figure in multicultural education, argues that learning styles are not "monolithic" or "static traits," but are the "central tendencies" students from different ethnic groups draw upon to engage in learning. According to Gay, teachers can utilize these dimensions to develop culturally compatible instruction for ethnically diverse students.

- *Procedural*—the preferred ways of approaching and working through learning tasks. These include pacing rates; distribution of time; variety versus similarity; novelty or predictability; passivity or activity; task directed or sociality; structured order or freedom; and preference for direct teaching or inquiry and discovery learning.
- *Communicative*—how thoughts are organized, sequenced, and conveyed in spoken and written forms, whether as elaborated narrative storytelling or precise responses to explicit questions; as topic-specific or topic-chaining discourse techniques; as passionate advocacy of ideas or dispassionate recorders and reporters; whether the purpose is to achieve descriptive and factual accuracy or to capture persuasive power and convey literary aestheticism.
- *Substantive*—preferred content, such as descriptive details or general patterns, concepts and principles, or factual information, statistics or personal and social scenarios; preferred subjects, such as math, science, social studies, fine or language arts; technical interpretive, and evaluative tasks; preferred intellectualizing tasks, such as memorizing, describing, analyzing, classifying, or criticizing.
- *Environmental*—preferred physical, social, and interpersonal settings for learning, including sound or silence; room lighting and temperature; presence or absence of others; ambiance of struggle or playfulness, of fun and joy, or pain and somberness.
- *Organizational*—preferred structural arrangements for work and study space, including the amount of personal space; the fullness or emptiness of learning space; rigidity or flexibility in use of claims made to space; carefully organized or cluttered learning resources and space locations; individually claimed or group-shared space; rigidity or flexibility of habitation of space.
- *Perceptual*—preferred sensory stimulation for receiving, processing, and transmitting information, including visual, tactile, auditory, kinetic, oral, or multiple sensory modalities.

- *Relational*—preferred interpersonal and social interaction modes in learning situations, including formality or informality, individual competition or group cooperation, independence or interdependence, peer–peer or child–adult, authoritarian or egalitarian, internal or external locus of control, conquest or community.
- *Motivational*—preferred incentives or stimulations that evoke learning including individual accomplishment or group well-being, competition or cooperation, conquest or harmony, expediency or propriety, image or integrity (Gay, 2000, pp. 151–152).

According to Gay (2000) some ethnic group members display "purer" learning style characteristics than others. The degree of purity is determined by group identification, gender, social class, and level of education. African-American students with a high degree of ethnic identification may relate best to instruction that is based on group activities in procedural, motivational, relational, and substantive dimensions of learning. Traditional Japanese or Chinese students might be bi-stylistic—because of their collectivistic cultural values they may respond well to activities requiring group problem solving. At the same time these students may perform well on mechanistic, technical, and atomistic learning tasks. Teachers need to understand that one set of strategies will not work with all students.

Reflection

- Consider the dimensions discussed by Gay and identify your preferences.
- Share your perspective with a classmate.
- What are the commonalities and differences?
- How could you use this information to develop a math lesson?

For many years educators have acknowledged the relationship between culture and orientations to learning, but few have offered concrete recommendations on how a teacher can integrate culture into classroom practice. Claxton (1990) provided a framework that serves the interests of both minority and non-minority students. He argued that "Recognizing the need to teach minority students well . . . must also involve teaching White students more effectively" (p. 35). Claxton's framework is built on two approaches to learning; the first he called *separate knowing* and this entails the separation of the object of inquiry and the knower. Ideas, facts, and information are isolated from the larger contexts in which they are found. The second approach is *connected knowing*. This implies a relationship with the thing being studied. The closer the relationship, the deeper the understanding.

Claxton advocated developing teaching strategies which integrate the two ways of knowing. The model he develops is called the connected teaching model and consists of five central features. The central metaphor of the connected learning model is the teacher as midwife rather than the teacher as banker. Bankers, according to Claxton, deposit knowledge, whereas midwives help students draw it out. The role of the teacher is to help students build on what they know and connect to what they do not know.

The second feature of connected teaching is a focus on problem posing. Traditional teaching focuses on imparting information through lecture or print. Connecting teaching requires students to solve problems that are significant and relevant. When learning is relevant, students become engaged. Delpit's (1995) work on writing resonates with Claxton's position. She stated, "Actual writing for real audiences and real purposes is a vital element in helping students to understand that they have an important voice in their own learning processes" (p. 33).

The third feature of connected teaching is the insistence that dialogue is not one-way communication. This idea reinforces the points made by Sprague in Chapter 1. Knowledge is not located in the teacher and transmitted to the student; it comes through the interaction between and among learners. In this view, learning is emergent and negotiated between and among participants.

The fourth feature of connected teaching is disciplined subjectivity. In traditional teaching, students are held accountable for the knowledge presented by the teacher. The instructor is the center and students are expected to report what the teacher wants. In connected teaching, the emphasis is on the student. Teachers attempt to view content from where the students stand. Reflect on the study conducted by Rex (2003) discussed earlier in the chapter. The teacher missed an opportunity to view the instructional task from the student's perspective. He wanted to discuss drug use and she wanted him to write a topic sentence. These are not mutually exclusive goals.

The final feature of connected teaching is fostering collaboration and community rather than competition and individualism. Students do not compete for grades but create a community where knowledge is discovered. Cleary and Peacock (1998) reported that such cooperative environments are particularly useful for Native-American students. Similar findings have been identified with other cultural groups.

Culturally Responsive Teaching

We believe that the key to managing cultural diversity is to develop intercultural competence. Wlodkowski and Ginsberg (1995) offered the following definition of culturally responsive teaching:

> Teaching that is culturally responsive occurs when there is equal respect for the backgrounds and contemporary circumstances of all learners, regardless of individual status and power, and when there is a design of learning processes that embraces the range of needs, interests, and orientations to be found among them.
>
> (p. 17)

Gay (2000) outlined the core characteristics of culturally responsive teaching: First, culturally responsive teaching is *validating*. It draws upon the cultural knowledge, traditions, and styles of diverse students, extending and affirming their strengths of competencies. Among its other features, culturally responsive teaching incorporates multicultural information into the instruction of all subjects and uses a variety of instructional strategies.

Second, culturally responsive teaching is *comprehensive*. Teachers use cultural referents to impart knowledge. This requires teachers to be willing to learn about the cultural backgrounds, traditions, and histories of the students represented in the classroom. In addition, teachers must make efforts to enhance connections to the community, maintain cultural identity, and to instill attitudes of success and commitment. Responsibility and commitment to self and others are encouraged. They are expected to internalize the value that learning is a communal, reciprocal, interdependent affair, and manifest it habitually in their expressive behaviors (Gay, 2000, p. 430).

Third, culturally responsive teaching is *multidimensional*. Any topic or issue can be approached from multiple perspectives. Gay describes ways that teachers could collaborate to teach the concept of protest. Students could be encouraged to discover the ways different groups symbolize their issues and concerns. By examining literature, poetry, music, art, interviews, and historical records, students could learn about both what gives rise to protest and how it is exhibited. Assessments should also be multidimensional. In this framework, the teacher does not use one standardized assessment but uses multiple assessments. Howard Gardner's seminal work on multiple intelligence is applicable to culturally responsive teaching (Gardner, 1983, 1993, 1999).

Fourth, culturally responsive teaching is *empowering*. Teachers who successfully implement culturally responsive teaching expect all students to succeed and develop structures that increase the probability of student success. Success is accomplished by "bolstering students' morale, providing resources and personal assistance, developing an ethos of achievement, and celebrating individual and collective accomplishments" (Gay, 2000, p. 32). Culturally responsive teaching shifts the emphasis from external to internal forces, thus engaging students in the learning process.

Fifth, culturally responsive teaching is *transformative*. Instructional practices build upon the students' strengths and extend them further in the learning processes. According to Gay, success is perceived to be a "non-negotiable mandate" for all students. Students are encouraged to give back to their respective communities and participate fully in the national society. Education is transformative when students come to understand the structures and processes that are related to discrimination and prejudice and when they develop skills to combat them.

Finally, culturally responsive teaching is *emancipatory*. Students are given the freedom to move beyond the traditional canons of knowledge and explore alternative perspectives and ways of knowing. Within this perspective, students challenge and question and come to understand that no truth is total and permanent. According to Gay (2000), "These learning engagements encourage and enable students to find their own voices, to contextualize issues in multiple cultural perspectives, to engage in more ways of knowing and thinking, and to become more active participants in shaping their own learning" (p. 35). Consider, for example, the various ways that a lesson on the "discovery" of America could be taught. Loewen (1995) thoughtfully outlined what is omitted from most textbooks about the circumstances, the events and tragedies involving the voyages of Columbus. Allowing students to explore and examine alternative stories may help them find connections that are not possible with dominant interpretations.

Reyes, Scribner, and Scribner (1999) show that culturally sensitive teaching has tremendous payoffs. These authors studied eight high-performing Hispanic schools. These schools were located in lower socioeconomic communities along the border of Texas and Mexico. One of the most significant findings was that the eight schools studied had a strong commitment to culturally responsive teaching. The authors reported:

> Perhaps the most powerful finding pertaining to the classroom learning was the incorporation of the students' interests and experiences, the "funds of knowledge" they bring with them into the learning situation, whether it be reading, writing, mathematics, or other subjects.
>
> (p. 14)

Thus, effective teachers built upon the cultural values of the students and made the classroom a culturally inviting place.

Gay (2002) made specific recommendations on ways to accomplish culturally responsive teaching. She contended that culturally responsive teaching has four primary features. First, the teacher develops a cultural knowledge base. Developing this base requires teachers to understand the cultural characteristics and contributions of different cultural groups. Cultivating a cultural database on the specific contributions of specific cultural groups helps the teacher establish a context for learning. She stated that culturally sensitive teaching deals as much with multicultural strategies as it does with adding specific content into lessons. Weaving this knowledge into instructional practice helps the teacher make the connections necessary for learning.

The second feature involves converting cultural knowledge into relevant curricula. According to Gay, three types of curricula are present in the classroom. The formal curriculum entails the standards approved by state policy boards. Gay recommends that teachers carefully assess the strengths and weaknesses of this curriculum and make the necessary changes to improve overall quality. The second type of curriculum Gay identifies is the symbolic curriculum. This involves the images, symbols, and awards that are used to promote learning and values. Images displayed on bulletin boards, pictures of heroes, and statements about social etiquette are examples of this type of curriculum. Teachers need to ensure that these displays are representative and accurate extensions of what is taught in the formal curriculum. The final type of curriculum is the societal curriculum. This curriculum involves the images about cultural groups that are reflected in the mass media. Culturally responsive teachers ask students to question and challenge the representations that appear on television and in the news.

The third feature of culturally responsive teaching is demonstrating cultural caring. To accomplish this, teachers need to build on the experiences of the students and broaden their intellectual horizons. Understanding the communication styles and knowing how to connect them to learning goals is a crucial feature of culturally responsive teaching. Teachers, thus, must have

> knowledge about the linguistic structures of various ethnic communication styles as well as contextual factors, cultural nuances, discourse features, logic, rhythm, delivery, vocabulary usage, role relationships of speakers and listeners, intonation, gestures, and body movements.
> (Gay, 2000, p. 111)

Culturally responsive teachers must also understand different "protocols of participation in discourse" and different ways that groups engage in task. The IRE pattern we discussed in Chapter 2 is dominant in mainstream classes. Students from groups of color, however, are more active, participative and circular in their interaction patterns. Serious classroom management problems can unfold when teachers do not understand these communication differences. Wlodkowski and Ginsberg (1995) observed: "Probably the area where the dominant perspective in education is in greatest conflict with other behavioral styles is that of language and dialect" (pp. 146–147). It is therefore crucial that teachers increase their communication competency in intercultural exchanges.

The fourth feature of culturally responsive teaching concerns the actual delivery of instruction. Gay argues that teachers need to *multiculturalize* instructional practice. This final feature involves the strategies teachers use to bring the material to life. Cooperative learning strategies follow from a knowledge that some ethnic groups prefer tasks that allow them to work with others. Knowing that some groups do not communicate in a linear analytic fashion allows the teacher to use narrative as a way to present material. Finding ways to integrate diversity into the high-status academic areas (i.e., math, reading, and science) is an excellent way to show a commitment to the world-views of students).

The recommendations advanced by Gay (2000, 2002) can help teachers understand the role of student culture and preferences for learning and what teachers can do. However, this goal is difficult to achieve. Teachers, administrators, school boards and some parents may not support this type of approach. One school board in rural California would not allow students to do projects on Cesar Chavez, even though 90 percent of the students were Mexican-American. Some teachers fight against the goals of these perspectives and school boards may criticize these types of strategies. Even with this information, however, some teachers will favor students whose behavioral and learning styles match their own. When there are language distinctions between teachers and students, teachers may use their own language as an evaluative lens for judging the abilities of the student. The student who uses nonstandard speech may be perceived as less intelligent and less competent. The notion that students with nonstandard English patterns are considered less competent has been documented in research (e.g., Powell & Avila, 1986).

In addition to speech pattern and accent, a teacher may respond negatively to other stylistic features of a student's communication. Latin students may use metaphor and other ornamental forms of speech. These forms depart from linear, reductionistic features of individualistic cultures. Teachers may consider the comments unclear or inappropriate.

Reflection

- How can a teacher develop a cultural knowledge base?
- How do teachers signal their lack of understanding of culture?

Cultural Alignment

We take the position that everyone is cultural, yet teachers, especially teachers whose ancestors are from Europe have difficulty understanding their cultural presuppositions. As a consequence, they may not reflect on the ways in which culture influences their attitudes, behaviors, and beliefs. Orbe and Harris (2001) suggested that Whiteness signals dominance, normalcy, and privilege. Yet many Whites do not accept these descriptions as portraying their lived experience. McAllister and Irvine (2000) argued that in order to be effective, teachers must critically examine their world-views and confront their personal biases. Kumashiro (2000) contended that educators can easily oppress students of color or students from other marginalized groups when those students are seen as the "other." Teachers take important steps toward inclusion when they examine their own world-views. Because the overwhelming majority of teachers are White, we wish to conclude this chapter by exploring "Whiteness" as a cultural construct.

Paley, in her book *White Teacher* (1989), examined the challenges societal values reflected in today's classrooms through an examination of her own prejudices as a White teacher. In her work with African-American children, she stated:

> The black child is Every Child. There is no activity useful only for the black child. There is no manner of speaking or unique approach or special environment required only for black children. There are only certain words and actions that cause all of us to cover up and there are other words and actions that help us reveal ourselves to one another. The challenge in teaching is to find a way of communicating to each child the idea that his or her special quality is understood, is valued, and can be talked about. It is not easy, because we are influenced by the fears and prejudices, apprehensions, and expectations, which have become a carefully hidden part of every one of us.
>
> (p. xv)

Answer the questions posed by Manning and Baruth (2000):

- Are my opinions of parents and families based on myths and stereotypes or on accurate and objective perceptions?
- Have my experiences included positive firsthand contact with people from culturally different backgrounds?
- What means have I employed to learn about the customs, traditions, values, and beliefs of all people?
- Do I understand the extended family concept or do I only think "too many people live in the same house because of poverty conditions"?
- Am I prejudiced, or do I have genuine feelings of acceptance for all people regardless of culture, ethnicity, race, and socioeconomic background?
- Do I hold the perceptions that Native-Americans are alcoholics, that African-American families are headed by single females, that Asian-Americans are the model minority and have achieved what represents the American Dream, or that Hispanic-Americans have large families and live on welfare?
- Can I perceive that aunts, uncles, and grandparents are as important as more immediate family members (i.e., the mother and father)?
- Do I understand the rich cultural backgrounds of families, and am I willing to base educational experiences on this diversity?

- Do I know appropriate sources of information to learn more about parents and families from culturally diverse backgrounds?
- Do I have the motivation, skills, and attitudes to develop close interrelationships with parents and families from culturally different backgrounds?

(p. 284)

Some of these questions are very difficult to answer. Few of the White individuals we know openly state that they have privilege and opportunity because of their ethnicity. Yet as Howard (2000), a White multi-educational scholar, noted:

> White Americans are caught in a classic state of cognitive dissonance. Our collective security and position of economic and political dominance have been fueled in large measure by the exploitation of other people. The physical and cultural genocide perpetrated against American Indians, the enslavement of African peoples, the exploitation of Mexicans and Asians as sources of cheap labor—on such acts of inhumanity rests the success of the European enterprise in America.
>
> (p. 326)

Howard (2000) further contended that daily survival for people of color is related to their knowledge of White America. On the other hand, the survival of White Americans has not depended on an understanding of the structures, institutions, and language of minority groups. One area where this disparity is most obvious is in the area of education. We believe that all teachers should examine their cultural assumptions and consider ways these assumptions may influence their teaching.

McAllister and Irvine (2000) reviewed three process models that have been used to explain the transitions from culturally ethnocentric to culturally sensitive orientations: Helms's (1990) Racial Identity model, Banks's (1994) typology of ethnic identity, and Bennett's (1986) Developmental Model of Intercultural Sensitivity. Each model focuses on a different feature of cultural identity and awareness but each suggests that individuals progress through different stages of awareness and differentiation. In the early stages, individuals have limited and naïve orientations about culture.

White teachers, for example, are not inclined to view themselves as cultural or to see how their "Whiteness" influences their orientation to the world in general or the classroom in particular. In later stages, there is an understanding of cultural norms, expectations, and actions. In these stages, individuals are able to take the perspective of individuals from different cultural orientations and make context appropriate adaptations.

After reviewing the studies conducted on these models, McAllister and Irvine (2000) concluded that the results offer important challenges for those involved in teacher education programs. The first challenge is realizing that individuals are at different places in their level of cultural awareness and understanding. For some, cultural sensitivity is simply an unnecessary waste of time, for others, it is vital to effective pedagogy. The process models reviewed provide a framework for understanding where teachers stand on intercultural issues including resistance and denial.

Second, teacher training programs should be sensitive to the stages individuals experience as they struggle with cultural issues. Teacher training programs cannot assume that after one class, or one workshop, teachers are going to leap into cultural sensitivity. Teachers entrenched in the early stages will need to move incrementally. In addition, individuals must come to understand their own culture before they can begin to understand someone else's. In one professor's class, students are required to give micro lessons on cultural artifacts. White students typically have the most difficulty with this assignment because they do not see themselves as cultural. After a discussion of core symbols and cultural orientation, they "discover" that their world is full of cultural artifacts and symbols. After the lesson, they learn of great connections between themselves and those presumed to be culturally different.

Finally, and perhaps the most difficult challenge, is that teacher education programs need to invite honest conversations about race, racism, privilege, marginalization, and oppression. Frequently these topics invoke hostility, anger, guilt, and confusion. Although difficult, these conversations are necessary if we are going to help teachers face the complexity of today's diverse classroom. A teacher's sentiment about race, culture, and ethnicity will be revealed in both subtle and explicit ways. Teachers' affective posture, the way they teach the "facts" of history, how they ask questions, how they discipline, who they call on and who they talk to outside of class say much about how they view culture and cultural issues. Once teachers acknowledge the role of culture in the instructional process, they are in a better position to meet the needs of all the students in their classrooms.

The goal, then, for all teachers is to strive for culturally responsive teaching. Our teacher, Ms. Young, should start her journey by increasing her knowledge and understanding of the cultural backgrounds of the students enrolled in her classes. But it is not enough to understand the cultures, but to exhibit a genuine respect and interest in them. According to the research, students who feel respected and understood are more likely to connect with the teacher and classroom experiences. Ms. Young also needs to examine her own cultural presuppositions and attitudes. In understanding the way in which culture shapes her orientations, she will be in a better position to understand her students. Additionally, we believe that schools, and school districts should commit to culturally responsive teaching and provide support for all teachers. The end result will be a better learning situation for everyone.

Learning Activities

- Who am I?
  On a piece of paper write the numbers 1–20. For each item provide a description of yourself. These descriptions may be a social role (i.e., father, student) and psychological (i.e., emotional, humorous). After completing this task, form a group and share your lists with the other students.
- Dialectical diversity
  Maintain a journal of different dialects and language styles you observed in a 24-hour period. In your journal explain your impressions of these different language forms. Did you respond positively to some and negatively to others?
- How will you use a "cultural database" to accomplish culturally responsive teaching?

Resources

- Teaching diverse learners
  www.alliance.brown.edu
- Culturally responsive teaching
  www.intime.uni.edu/multiculture/curriculum/culture/teaching.htm
- Geert Hofstede cultural dimensions
  www.geert-hofstede.com
- Multicultural activities
  www.edchange.org/multicultural/activityarch.html
- Teaching multicultural literature
  www.learner.org/workshops/tml/workshop1/commentary3.html

4

GENDER AND CLASSROOM COMMUNICATION

Learning Outcomes

1. Evaluate the difference and similarity hypotheses.
2. Contrast the vulnerability and empowerment perspectives of females.
3. Explain the "boy code."
4. Identify the differences in the academic performance of males and females.
5. Discuss strategies for teaching underachieving males.
6. Explain the impact of sex on classroom interaction patterns.

Classroom Scenario

Leticia and Danny, two sixth-graders, have just returned from school and are greeted at the kitchen door by their dad, Antonio, who asks, "How was school today?" "Good," says Danny as he opens the refrigerator door and forages through each shelf for something to eat. Leticia silently goes to her bedroom and takes out her calendar to check her homework. Antonio notices that Leticia seems bothered by something and follows her to the bedroom and asks her if everything is OK. She sits on her bed and says that everything is fine. Danny bounces down the hallway and asks his dad when soccer practice is. "Don't interrupt; I'm talking to your sister," Antonio barks. Once more Antonio asks his daughter "Are you sure everything is OK, mi hija?" Danny hangs back in the hallway when Leticia opens up and says, "I don't get it. Mr. Hayes never calls on me in class. I work hard and know the answers, but every time I hold up my hand he ignores me and calls on Danny or one of the other guys in the class. Today he told me I was showing up the boys for doing so well in math. I don't think he likes me."

A substantial body of research has investigated male and female differences on a variety of instructional processes and outcomes (Condravy, Skirboll, & Taylor, 1988; Gurian & Stevens, 2005; Hall & Sandler, 1982; Murphy & Gipps, 1996; Nadler & Nadler, 1990; Pollack, 1998; Sadker & Sadker, 1994; Wood, 2001). Some of this research suggests that educational practices have privileged males (e.g., American Association of University Women, 1991). Others argue that current approaches place males at risk for failure (Gurian & Stevens, 2005). The situation is complex and exacerbated by the fact that teachers are not adequately prepared to deal with gender issues and therefore use their personal theories to guide instructional practices. Schools of education typically dedicate only two hours of instruction per semester to gender issues. We agree with Wood (2001), who argued that teachers need to do all they can to understand the way in which gender dynamics influence student and teacher behavior. In this chapter, we will examine the ways that gender impacts the instructional process. Specifically, we will examine the developmental and sociocultural factors that impact attitudes and behavior, intellectual differences between males and females, and the ways males and females are treated by teachers. We will conclude the chapter by exploring ways to create and sustain a more gender responsive classroom climate.

Sex and Gender

Teachers often use the terms sex and gender interchangeably. Sex, however is a biological designation and gender is a social/psychological one. Boys are not made of frogs and snails and puppy dogs' tails but an XY chromosome pair; girls are not made of sugar and spice and all things nice but by an XX chromosome pair. Although there is a prevailing sentiment that "boys will be boys" and "girls will be girls," biology alone does not determine behavior.

There are two perspectives we will address. One is a difference hypothesis. Theorists who embrace this view contend that there are substantial differences in male and female brains that explain their behavior. The second view is a similarity hypothesis. This view argues that there are more similarities than differences between males and females and that context is the biggest factor influencing male and female behavior. First we will review research from the difference perspective.

The Difference Perspective

Gurian and Henley (2001) focused on developments in brain-based learning. They discussed five differences between male and female brains that influence learning and classroom behavior. The first is structural. The authors reported that females have a larger corpus callosum, the bundle of nerves that connects the two lobes of the brain. This allows females to access both sides of the brain during certain tasks. For example, brain scans indicate that when females are listening, both sides of the brain are activated. This is not the case for males. Does this mean that females attend to academic instructions better than males? Or does it mean they add information that may not be directly related to the task? Males, on the other hand, may only listen for the bottom line and not attend to nuances in the instructions. We do not believe females listen better but it appears they listen differently from males.

The second area of difference is chemical. Females secrete more serotonin, vasopressin, and oxytocin. These chemicals are related to impulsivity and the ability to experience empathy. The greater production of these chemicals may explain why females are less fidgety and more able to connect emotionally with others.

The third area is hormonal. Estrogen and progesterone are the dominant hormones in females and testosterone is the dominant hormone in males. The authors contend that hormonal differences play a significant role in the behavior of males and females. Males with high levels of testosterone tend to be aggressive and those with low levels tend to be sensitive and nurturing. Female hormones influence mood and responses to certain academic tasks.

The fourth area is functional. Gurian and Henley (2001) claimed that males are more inclined to use the right hemisphere of the brain whereas females use both. Males tend to access the left hemisphere, which directs analysis and critical thinking. Females are more right-hemisphere dominant. The right part of the brain controls artistic activity and intuitive thinking.

Emotional stimuli for males is channeled from the limbic system to the brain stem whereas emotional stimuli for females is processed in the upper brain, where higher-order processing occurs. Thus females view relationships and interpersonal situations from a more complex perspective. Gurian and Henley (2001) also stated that the female brain has a greater capacity for memory and sensory intake and the male brain is predisposed to special tasks and abstract thinking.

The final area of difference is emotional. According to Gurian and Henley (2001), the female brain processes more data through more senses. The authors speculated that males may be more emotionally fragile because their brains are less able to process a wide variety of emotional stimuli. Consequently they may be more affected by problems at home or with other students.

What do these differences mean in terms of education and academic performance? Jensen (2000) provided a summary of some of the differences. For example, females generally outperform males in:

- fine motor skills
- computation tests
- multi-tasking
- recalling the position of objects
- spelling
- fluency of word generation
- tasks that require being sensitive to external stimuli
- remembering landmarks
- use of verbal memory
- appreciation of depth and perceptual speed
- reading body language/facial expressions.

On the other hand, males generally outperform females in:

- targeting skills working vocabulary
- extended focus and concentration mathematical reasoning and problem solving
- navigation with geometric properties of space
- verbal intelligence
- habit formation and maintenance
- most spatial tasks

The Similarity Hypothesis

Other theorists argue that brain differences are exaggerated and do not adequately explain male and female behaviors. Eliot (2010), for example, noted that males and females differ in many ways but the differences are not as large as implied by those embracing the difference perspective. Neuroscientists have found few reliable differences between male and female brains (Bishop & Whalsten, 1997; Lenroot et al., 2007). Eliot (2010) asserted that females do not have a larger corpus callosum or higher circulating levels of serotonin.

Hyde (2005) conducted an extensive meta-analysis of psychological sex differences. Specifically, she analyzed investigations conducted in six categories: cognitive variables, verbal and nonverbal communication, social personality variables, psychological well-being, psychomotor behaviors, and miscellaneous constructs such as moral reasoning. The results of her extensive analysis showed little support for the difference hypothesis. The largest sex differences were in the area of motor performance. Males throw a ball harder and farther than females.

In interpreting and reflecting on the findings, Hyde (2005) observed that developmental studies may provide more insight. The magnitude of sex difference may change with age. That is, the differences between males and females may fluctuate throughout the life span. Experiences, then, play an important role in how males and females develop.

According to Hyde (2005), context is a major factor in sex differences. She argued that a sex effect may be large or small depending on the social context in which a measure is obtained. A male may be nurturing and a female may be aggressive depending on the situation. Hyde cautioned against accepting the position that males are hardwired one way and females another. She further argued that such positions reify sex stereotypes.

How might these predispositions play out in classroom activities? Females may have better penmanship, may be more proficient in tasks such as coloring between lines, math worksheets, and reading comprehension as well as remembering instructions and perceiving if someone is frustrated or upset. Males, on the other hand, may be better at word problems, drill and rehearsal tasks, gross motor tasks such as throwing and running, and spatial tasks.

Although biology is important, it is not the primary factor that explains the way males and females perform in academic settings. According to Wood (2001), the way we deal with differences is most important to understand. The sentiments, expectations, attitudes, and behaviors are connected to, but not directed by, biological sex or the way in which the brain is hardwired. However, there are deeply rooted cultural expectations about male and female behavior, and school is a place where these attitudes are reinforced. As a consequence, the interaction that occurs in schools can perpetuate and reinforce gender stereotypes to the detriment of the intellectual and emotional development of students. In other words, social context plays a profound role in the academic and social aptitudes males and females develop. In the next section we will explore the way in which communication influences attitudes about males and females and the way they should act and perform in educational contexts.

Reflection

- Do you agree with the difference or similarity hypothesis?
- What other factors influence the behavior of males and females?

Gender

Gender is a social and symbolic construction. Individuals are born male or female but are taught how to be masculine and feminine (Wood, 2001). Ivy and Backlund (2000) argued that the family is the most significant agent of gender socialization. Parents, siblings, and relatives send explicit and implicit messages about what it means to be male and female in the larger culture. In the United States, for example, masculinity is frequently connected with strength, ambition, rationality, and assertiveness. Femininity, on the other hand, is usually associated with physical attraction, emotionality, and cooperation. Little boys are encouraged to roughhouse, to be aggressive, and to explore their surroundings. Little girls are encouraged to be cheerful, gentle, and cooperative. Research suggests that these expectations begin the day of birth and continue as children mature (e.g., Block, 1984; Rubin, Provensano, & Luria, 1974; Stern & Karraker, 1989).

The attitudes and expectations established in the family carry on into the school setting. Messages about gender are communicated in a number of ways. A "tomboy" will be criticized for acting too masculine and a boy who likes to play with dolls is teased and called a sissy. A teacher's attitude about gender will influence the way s/he manages a classroom and will affect his or her expectations about student ability. Finally, the curriculum, the texts students read, and the assignments they do may contain implicit and explicit themes about gender.

In the attempt to maximize the talents, ambitions, and interests of all students it is helpful to understand the way in which the "gendering process" unfolds in schools. In the next section we will examine the forces that influence attitudes about appropriate male and female behavior.

Reflection

- What does it mean to be male in our culture?
- What does it mean to be female in our culture?

Females

Females struggle with a number of factors that influence classroom attitudes and performance. Females are bombarded with a multitude of contradictory messages about what it means to be female. These messages come from the media, family members, peers, and the schools. Research from the American Association of University Women (1991) indicates that females aged 8–9 are comfortable and confident with their identities but their attitudes decline until they leave high school. The largest drop occurs between elementary and middle school. In middle school, many females begin to lose their interest in intellectual ideas and increase their interest in relationships and romance (Bate, 1992). At this stage one of the biggest factors influencing girls' self-esteem is how they look. According to Wood (2001), females who feel they do not meet the cultural standard of attractiveness also believe they are less competent and capable in other areas.

Pipher (1994), the author of *Reviving Ophelia: Saving the Selves of Adolescent Girls*, wrote that young girls feel an enormous pressure to be beautiful and are keenly aware of evaluations about their appearance. Young women perceive that their popularity is connected to physical beauty. The media is powerful in communicating the social significance of attraction. As a consequence, young girls spend a tremendous amount of time focusing on their looks. Pipher (1994) observed:

> Beauty is the defining characteristic for American women. It's the necessary and often sufficient condition for social success. It is important for women of all ages, but the pressure to be beautiful is most intense in early adolescence. Girls worry about their clothes, makeup, skin, and hair. But most of all they worry about their weight.
>
> (p. 18)

Because of the pressure to be thin and attractive, many females, especially European-Americans, start to develop eating disorders in middle school.

Females predisposed to eating disorders embody popular culture's definition of femininity—they are thin, passive, attractive, and eager to please. Although these students may be bright, their identities seem to be tied more to their looks than to their intellect. Schools, teachers, and peers may reinforce this cultural value. Teachers too often comment on how pretty a young girl is and not enough on the quality of her thinking (Sadker & Sadker, 1994).

The preoccupation with looks and the larger culture's ideal about women manifests itself in peer group relations as well. Girls who wear the "wrong" clothes, who do too well in school, who are too large, or who are too athletic may be severely criticized by other girls. Because aggressive behavior is considered unacceptable for females, they learn to develop verbal competencies that serve to chastise, evaluate, and dissect others. Think about conflicts that have occurred among adolescent girls. What were the topics and who were the targets of the conflicts? Over time, these verbal abilities become more refined and sophisticated.

Martin (1989) observed that peer groups are more accepting of individuals who adhere to gender stereotypes. However, peers seem to be more accepting of females who engage in masculine behaviors than males who engage in feminine ones. Girls who play sports and roughhouse are perceived more positively than boys who want to play with dolls.

Peer groups also play an important role in the way values are tested. Young females use communication to test the boundaries of appropriate behavior. "Girl talk," for example plays a role in the construction of normative behavior. Discussions that focus on the behavior, dress, or activities of other girls help shape boundaries and expectations. Consider the following example of the way values are tested in peer communication exchanges. Three middle school females, Elizabeth, Natalie, and Julie, are discussing Natalie's interest in Tony. The focus of Tony's affection is Monica, a girl outside of the clique described above. During their discussion, Elizabeth calls Monica a "skank," a label used to describe someone who is overly sexual and violates the normative expectation for dress and behavior. The girls conclude the session by noting that if Natalie must "stoop" to Monica's level, Tony isn't worth having as a boyfriend. This discussion reveals the group's values and expectations of behavior. Through this interaction the girls establish how far one should go to pursue a boy. Eder and Sanford (1986) stated that gossip, teasing, and humor are other ways to communicate unacceptable behavior without direct confrontation.

The larger society places substantial pressure on females to embrace certain values. They should be physically attractive, feminine, and passive, especially in public contexts. In addition, females are discouraged from maximizing their intellectual abilities.

In contrast to the "vulnerability" narrative represented in books, such as *Reviving Ophelia* (Pipher, 1994), is an "empowerment" one. Kindlon (2006), for example, argues in *Alpha Girls* that females born in the late 1980s are competent, assertive, and internally motivated. They have high grade point averages, assume leadership positions, participate in extracurricular activities, have high achievement motivation, and view themselves as dependable (p. xviii). Kindlon (2006) claimed that the alpha generation is replete with females who feel empowered. He argued that they are the first generation who are benefactors of the women's movement. Kindlon contended that the mothers and grandmothers of "alpha girls" were instrumental in changing policies on reproductive rights (*Roe v Wade*), passing Title IX, and increasing educational access. In addition, he noted that women earned more post-secondary degrees than men and larger numbers are serving in elected office. On a psychological level, alpha girls have high self-esteem and they do well in school. Kindlon acknowledged that not all girls are alphas. Many experience low self-esteem, have eating disorders, experience harassment, and struggle with body image. He suggested that the psychology of many girls is changing in ways that are contrary to the vulnerability perspective.

Pomerantz and Raby (2011) conducted a qualitative analysis of the constructions of females who were academically successful. They conducted two focus groups, one with middle-class White females and the second with working-class females who were White and Arabic. The first group consisted of middle-class White females who attended different high schools but were friends outside of school. The second group consisted of working-class females who attended the same high school. Participants in the first focus group indicated that being academically successful was frowned upon and even though it was important to them, they did not engage in conversations about their success. In contrast, participants in the second group indicated that academic success was perceived positively in their schools.

The authors also found that the respondents in each group felt that success was a result of individual commitment and effort. If the student wanted to be successful she needed to work hard and earn extra credit. The participants reported that academic success was important and self-satisfying. The participants did not indicate that they wanted good grades to please their parents. The respondents also claimed that their hard work was not always rewarded but boys were "over praised" (Pomerantz & Raby, 2011).

The females also believed their futures were in their own hands; hard work and good grades would open up numerous opportunities. They did not see any institutional structures that would constrain their aspirations. According to Pomerantz and Raby (2011), the females embraced an individualistic narrative that involved the belief that girls can do anything that boys can. However, these "super girls" believed that being smart is multifaceted. Smart girls must be book smart, street smart, and socially smart.

Gonick (2006) offered a different viewpoint. She also examined the differences between the Girlpower and Reviving Ophelia narratives. She argued the Girlpower narrative is grounded in a position that females can be assertive, confident and capable—the position advanced by Kindlon (2006)—but they also experience anxiety if they are not successful in all the tasks they attempt.

Gonick raised an important point not adequately addressed by Kindlon. Social class and culture also impact identity in profound ways. Adolescent females reared in middle- to upper-class families see themselves, school, and opportunity differently from students reared in lower, ethnically diverse environments. Gonick explained the tension that can emerge when females receive messages that they can accomplish anything through hard work and at the same time face economic circumstances that limit opportunities.

We believe that many girls are focused, emotionally mature, and academically engaged. Yet there is still a great deal of work to do. Many females do not have the resources that support educational success and extracurricular access. The media still promote gender stereotypes and there remain disparities in wages; women continue to earn less than men for the same job (Bureau of Labor Statistics, 2012). We will close this discussion with an example of a 16-year-old girl from New Mexico. She strives for perfection in several aspects of her life. She wants to excel in the classroom and on the volleyball court and wants to pursue a lucrative professional career. She is popular, attractive, and has excellent communication skills. Yet she does not feel comfortable taking risks and is fearful of failure, which in school means a C in any class. Her attitudes mirror the findings reported by Pomerantz and Raby (2011). Our New Mexico female wants to excel at all she does.

Males

The school setting also influences the gender identity of males. Research indicates that boys account for the majority of behavior problems in schools and represent a large proportion of students in special education classes. Educational difficulties with boys start in elementary school and continue through high school. Expectations about appropriate male behavior are also shaped by the media, families, peers, and schools.

William Pollack (1998), author of *Real Boys: Rescuing Our Sons from the Myths of Boyhood*, addressed many of the factors that place boys at risk. At the core of boys' development is the "boy code," a masculine ethic directing feelings and emotions inward. Boys are encouraged to wear a "mask" that hides or obscures any difficulty or problem. Pollack concluded that boys are quick to state that everything is fine when it is not.

Young boys may be very expressive at birth, but by the time they reach elementary school begin to hide their feelings as their gender identity starts to take shape. Pollack (1998) identified two important processes that influence the gender identity of boys. The first is the use of shame. Little boys are made to feel ashamed of feelings, weakness, vulnerability, anxiety, or fear. The second is the separation process. Boys are encouraged to separate from their primary caretakers before they are emotionally ready.

The use of shame to control boys is significant, according to Pollack (1998). The pressure to "act" like a man comes from many directions. The media idealize men who are strong, aloof, and detached. Peers refer to each other as "woman," "sissy," "faggot," "mama's boy" when emotions are not held in check. Parents communicate concern if a young boy does not act "masculine" enough. Teachers are not tolerant of boys who play "too much" with girls or have a communication style or interests that seem "feminine."

The second contributor discussed by Pollack (1998) is the premature separation from their primary caregiver. In most cases, this is the mother but it can be father, grandmother, aunt, or some other significant person. The 5-year-old who wails after being dropped off at kindergarten is often told to "be a big boy, stop crying." The boy who falls off a swing is not held and comforted but told to "be tough."

Some research suggests that the different emotional struggles that young boys face influence their orientations to learning situations. Hudson and Jacot (1991) suggested that boys must learn to compensate in some way if they are taken from a primary caretaker before they are emotionally ready. Because of their limited social skills, boys are often drawn to material objects not requiring the management of relationships. Interest in science, computers, and math may be related to these social processes.

Pollack (1998) argued that in elementary school teachers see little boys as the feeling-vulnerable beings they are. As they grow older, the emotional core of the boy is lost in a body that appears masculine. Their vulnerability is hidden in faces with growing facial hair, voices that grow deeper, and bodies that sometimes tower over their teachers. In addition, teachers may not understand the "boy code" or be sensitive to the range of messages that inform a boy to be tough, aggressive, and strong. Teachers may in fact reinforce the very behaviors they are critical of in other contexts.

Cleveland (2011) explained why some boys struggle in school and what can be done to engage them in the academic process. She asked educators, administrators, and counselors a number of questions about underachieving boys. Based on their responses she gleaned clues in four areas about male underachievement. The first clue related to nonacademic factors. High-achieving males were confident, enjoyed learning, and had strong support systems (p. 12). The second clue involved experiences with school. High-achieving boys were connected to friends and teachers whereas low-achieving boys had problematic relationships with teachers and did not relate to the instructional strategies that were used (p. 12). The third clue related to attitudes about literacy. Boys who struggled in reading, writing, spelling, grammar, and composition did not work hard to achieve competence in these areas. This relates to our earlier discussion of self-worth theory. Boys who do not do well in language arts or other academic areas may be inclined to self-sabotage rather than put more effort into the task. Finally, Cleveland suggested that the physical environment might constrain some boys more than others. For example, classrooms that limit opportunities for movement or interaction may have a deleterious impact on males.

Cleveland (2011) echoed many of the concerns raised by Pollack (1998). Specifically, she argued that the "boy code" might be particularly influential on lower-achieving males. She hypothesized that literacy, an area in which females outperform males, may be perceived as feminine and therefore males disconnect from this academic area and do not build sufficient competency for academic and professional success. Cleveland also contended that boys are just as emotional as females but the code requires them to be stoic rather than emotive. Rather than understanding their fears or frustrations, boys deny them or push them inward. Finally, Cleveland argued that a lack of positive male role models might reinforce the power of the boy code.

In response to social and educational processes that may constrain the academic success of some boys, Cleveland outlined a framework she labeled Pathways to Re-Engagement. We will briefly outline the six pathways she explained but for a thorough discussion we encourage the reader to review her book, *Teaching Boys*.

- Pathway 1: *Support*. Building trusting relationships is essential to helping an underachieving boy succeed. Boys define support as teachers who care for them, like them even if they mess up, will help them be successful, and do not humiliate them in front of the class.
- Pathway 2: *Guide*. The teacher provides clear instructions, gives feedback and reinforcement as a way to help the struggling boy succeed.
- Pathway 3: *Reinforce*. Teachers help boys develop communication skills that are necessary for collaboration. The author used Cox's pragmatic skills (as cited in Cleveland, 2011), which focus on three specific areas: physical (e.g., maintaining appropriate distance, maintaining eye contact); verbal (e.g., taking turns, giving compliments); and cognitive (e.g., detecting emotions in others, perceiving and expressing humor).
- Pathway 4: *Adjust*. Cleveland (2011) argued that the physical environment intersects with what a boy needs to learn. She discussed four areas that can be incorporated into instructional practice: the need for increased physical activity, the need for social interactions, the need for a reduction in visual and auditory distractions, and the need for physical comfort (pp. 160–161). She offered several ways to address these intersections, such as using study buddies and allowing for standing time. Teachers can also have movement activities to assess understanding.
- Pathway 5: *Ignite*. Instruction ought to be adjusted so boys feel more comfortable and engaged in the class. Cleveland (2011) offered the following recommendations:

    1. *Active involvement*: Encourage the struggling male to make personal connections by applying the information to new situations. The outcome of active involvement is "active construction of his understanding" (p. 176).

2. *Compelling situations*: Stimulate the real-world applications that involve emotions and problem solving. The outcome of compelling situations is "added relevance and personal meaning" (p. 177).
3. *Direct experience*: Direct experience facilitates attention and recall. The outcome of direct experience is "increased attention and memory" (p 177).
4. *Enjoyable setting*: Create opportunities for social interaction and opportunities for relaxation. The outcome of an enjoyable setting is "increased attention and memory" (p. 177).
5. *Frequent feedback*: Informational feedback that guides the struggling student to understand where he needs to go. The outcome for frequent feedback is "belief in the possibility of success" (p 177).
6. *Informal learning*: The boy's reactions, feelings, and perceptions of the learning experience foster a deeper understanding of the learning experience. The outcome of informal learning is "elaboration" (p. 177).
7. *Patterns and connections*: Help the underachieving boy merge prior knowledge and help him combine "disparate ideas" to create meaningful structures. The outcome of patterns and connections is "consolidated learning" (p. 178).
8. *Reflection*: Build on the boy's self-awareness so that he understands how he learns. The outcome of reflection is "insight" (p. 178).

- Pathway 6: *Empower*. According to Cleveland (2011), literacy skill is the linchpin of academic success. Reading plays a significant role in academic learning regardless of content area.

Cleveland's (2011) perspective provides helpful information and strategies for addressing the needs of underachieving boys. At the heart of her model is a teaching strategy that provides an opportunity for boys to have interpersonal connections and self-expression.

Reflection

- How does Cleveland's perspective compare with your observations of underachieving boys?
- Provide examples of the way the "boy code" influences academic engagement.

The previous section outlined various perspectives on the social and psychological factors influencing female and male orientations to school and learning. Next we will examine research that explored sex and learning style.

Sex and Learning Style

A number of studies have investigated the way in which males and females approach learning tasks. Head (1996) argued that males and females could be differentiated on four categories of cognitive style. The first is field independence or dependence. Field-independent learners approach the environment in an analytic fashion. Responses to assessments, such as the Group Embeddedness test, show that males more than females are inclined to extract figures from the backgrounds in which they are embedded. Field-dependent learners consider the larger context and approach learning tasks from a more connected standpoint.

A second category discussed by Head (1996) is impulsiveness and reflection. Males have been found to be more impulsive than females, who exhibit care and deliberation. It is not uncommon, for example, for boys to race through multiple choice items or blurt out answers without carefully evaluating the questions. Head argued that the consequences for an incorrect response are not as high for boys. Think about student responses to questions in the classroom. The research indicates that males are called on in class more often than females. This pattern may unfold because males may leap into the interaction and capture the attention of the teacher. Females may think more about the question because they want to answer it correctly. This pattern of male dominance may create an implicit assumption that the voices of males should be heard and voices of females should be quiet. Wood (2001) argued that classrooms are masculine speech communities that reward students who compete and speak in absolute terms.

The third category discussed by Head (1996) is locus of control. Males tend to attribute academic success to their own efforts and failures to external factors. Females exhibit a different response; females attribute success to luck and failures to internal factors.

When individuals feel they have the skills necessary to complete a task, they will put in the effort to accomplish it. However, if individuals do not feel they can complete a task, they do not expend the necessary effort. This pattern can lead to what Dweck (1986) labeled learned helplessness. Teachers, then, need to develop teaching strategies that require females to take personal responsibility for success and thus build internal locus of control.

The final category discussed by Head (1996) is cooperation versus competition. Much educational philosophy is driven by a competitive system of external rewards. Competition is believed to motivate students to achieve. However, this system may work better for boys, who are socialized through athletics and other activities to be aggressive, assertive, and dominant. Females, on the other hand, may work better on tasks that require cooperation and the management of relationships. A competitive classroom may at the same time motivate and intimidate students. We will explore the benefits of cooperative learning in Chapter 9. The point we want to stress here is that several factors may influence the way a student moves toward or away from a learning goal.

Other researchers have examined differences between males and females. Belinky, Clinchy, Goldberger, and Tarule (1986), for example, investigated the ways females come to know. The authors contended that the traditional educational curriculum is predicated on a masculine way of knowing, in which rationality and objectivity are valued over intuitive and personal knowledge. After interviewing 135 women, the authors identified four ways of knowing: silence, received knowledge, subjective knowledge, and constructed knowledge. These orientations or styles depart from the rational orientation that appears to dominate educational practice. From this research a coding system called Educational Dialectics was developed. The assessment consists of 12 bipolar scales; one choice is masculine, the other is feminine.

Kolb (1976) provided a typology of learning that is based on two dimensions: active experimentation versus reflective observation and concrete experience versus abstract conceptualization. Four styles can be identified with the system. An accommodator is best at a hands-on experience. Divergers are best at learning requiring imagination and brainstorming. Convergers are best when seeking practical solutions, and assimilators are most adept at logic and organization.

Philbin, Meier, Huffman, and Boverie (1995) examined sex differences in educational dialectics and learning styles. The authors asked 45 females and 25 males to complete the Learning Style Inventory (Kolb, 1985) and the Educational Dialectics instrument (Belinky et al., 1986). The results indicated that the preponderance of males used an assimilator learning style. In terms of educational dialectics, the majority of males were more concerned with self than others when it came to educational decisions. The authors contended that the traditional learning environment, one that celebrates rationalism, may not fit the learning style of females. Even though this study was exploratory, the findings and recommendations resonate with authors such as Gilligan (1982), who contended that education does not do enough to find a best fit between educational practice and learning style. The manner in which content is presented and the methods used to assess learning may favor the learning preferences of males.

Although the studies examining the effects of sex on learning style have yielded some noteworthy findings, there is not overwhelming evidence that these results warrant the conclusion that often males are superior in some intellectual endeavors and females are superior in others. Much of the dialogue about the differences between males and females may be exaggerated and driven more by gender expectations than by fact. In the next section we will review research that has systematically analyzed the effect of sex on several important areas. We will begin by examining the findings on math, science, and verbal performance.

Sex and Intellectual Ability

There is a prevailing belief that males are good at math and females are good in language arts. Theorists such as Gurian and Stevens (2005) argued that these differences are a function of brain structure. Scores on standardized tests tend to reflect this commonly held belief. The standardized tests used nationally are the American College Testing Program (ACT), the Preliminary Scholastic Assessment Test (PSAT), and the Scholastic Assessment Test (SAT). Between 1990 and 1997, males outscored females on the verbal and math sections of the SAT. Females outscored males on the verbal section of the ACT but males scored higher than females on the mathematics and scientific reasoning sections of the ACT (American Association of University Women, 1999). With the inclusion of the writing portion of the PSAT, differences in gender showed a "dramatic" shift. The differences between boys and girls were narrowed considerably.

Data from the National Center for Education Statistics indicate that the largest differences between males and females are in the areas of reading and writing. Females have closed the gap in mathematics performance. Tables 4.1, 4.2, and 4.3 report the test scores in these areas.

These data indicate that the greatest difference between males and females is in the area of verbal linguistic competence (reading and writing). Females consistently scored higher in these areas. The largest difference occurred in writing in the 12th grade; females outscored males by 24 points. There were virtually no differences between males and females on mathematical competence. These results appear to support the assertion that females are more proficient in verbal abilities but they do not support the claim that males are superior in math.

We believe it is important to be cautious about drawing hard and fast conclusions about sex differences and academic ability. Hyde and McKinley (1997) reviewed meta-analytic studies conducted on gender differences on a variety of achievement tests. Meta-analysis is a procedure for aggregating results across a series of studies, thus reducing the possibility of error that may result from a traditional review of literature. The aim of their investigation was to determine if some of the findings on gender abilities reported in the literature were supported by the meta-analytic procedures. Four areas were analyzed: verbal ability, mathematics performance, spatial ability, and science achievement.

Table 4.1 Average Mathematics Scores for Students in Grades 4 and 8 in 2011 and 2013

Sex	*Grade 4*		*Grade 8*	
	2011	*2013*	*2011*	*2013*
Male	241	242	284	285
Female	240	241	283	284

Source: U.S. Department of Education, National Center for Education Statistics, National Assessment of Educational Progress, Mathematics Assessment, 2013.

Table 4.2 Average Reading Scores for Students in Grades 4 and 8 in 2011 and 2013

Sex	*Grade 4*		*Grade 8*	
	2011	*2013*	*2011*	*2013*
Male	218	219	261	263
Female	225	225	270	273

Source: U.S. Department of Education, National Center for Education Statistics, National Assessment of Educational Progress, Reading Assessment, 2013.

Table 4.3 Average Writing Scores for Students in Grades 8 and 12 in 2009 and 2011

Sex	*Grade 8*	*Grade 12*
Male	140	143
Female	160	157

Source: U.S. Department of Education Sciences, National Center for Education Statistics, National Assessment of Educational Progress, Writing Assessment, 2011.

In terms of verbal ability, the results of two meta-analysis studies (Hedges & Nowell, 1995; Hyde & Linn, 1988) were examined. The results indicated that any general difference between males and females is extremely small. The authors argued, however, that there are different types of verbal ability that may be lost in traditional testing. Females, for example, may be superior in speech production and males may have more difficulties with verbal performance.

The results of the meta-analyses conducted on mathematical ability did not indicate male superiority. Males obtained higher scores but the amount of the difference was minimal. Similar to verbal ability, there are different types of mathematical competencies that are not frequently discussed in the literature. Mathematical ability entails computation, concepts, and problem solving. Each of these subsets may be lost when scores are summarized. A meta-analysis conducted by Hyde, Finnema, and Lamou (1990) found that females scored higher than males on computation tasks by a small amount in elementary school and junior high but not in high school. There were no differences at any age in understanding mathematical concepts. And there were no differences in problem solving in elementary or junior high. Males did obtain higher scores in problem solving in high school and in college.

The third area reviewed by Hyde and McKinley (1997) was spatial ability. They reviewed a meta-analysis conducted by Linn and Petersen (1985). Three types of spatial ability were analyzed: spatial perception, (the person's sense of horizontality or verticality); mental rotation, (how well one can mentally rotate a three-dimensional object that is depicted in two dimensions and match it to other illustrations); and spatial visualization (visually locating a simple figure within a complex one). The results of the analysis conducted in spatial ability yielded no clear-cut gender differences.

Finally, Hyde and McKinley (1997) analyzed science achievement. Three meta-analytic studies were reviewed (Becker, 1989; Fleming & Malone, 1983; Hedges & Nowell, 1995). Fleming and Malone analyzed the science performance of kindergarten to 12th-grade students. Boys scored higher than girls but the differences were small. The largest gender difference was found in the middle school age group. An analysis conducted by Becker found that the largest gender difference was related to the subject matter tested. Boys received significantly higher scores in physics. Hedges and Nowell investigated high school achievement and found that males outscored females in science. Hedges and Nowell noted that fewer females elected to take science in high school and therefore the findings were subject to bias.

The results of the science performance meta-analyses indicated that males outscored females by a relatively small amount. Further, the findings seem to relate to the particular subject matter examined. Males did best in physics and physical science.

The research reported above does not provide compelling evidence for sex differences in intellectual capacity. This is not to say that there are no cognitive differences between males and females, but it is difficult to ascertain what these differences are and what they mean in actual practice. Numerous methodological problems cloud the research on sex and gender. One problem is that the research tends to focus on biological sex and not on the social-psychological features of gender. This approach makes it difficult to ascertain if any difference found is related to sex, gender, or some other intervening variable. One study that tried to account for the effects of gender was conducted by Kirtley and Weaver (1999). These authors argued that gender conceptions serve as filters that modify cognitions and behaviors. They identified two cognitive schemes. The agentic role construct includes characteristics such as goal-orientation, assertiveness, and self-activation. In contrast, a communal orientation involves characteristics such as selflessness, openness, caring, and kindness. In the classroom an individual with an agentic role identity may positively respond to tasks requiring analytical thinking whereas an individual with a communal identity may prefer verbal learning tasks.

Reflection

- What role does gender play in learning?
- Do you believe that males are naturally inclined to be better than females in math and science?

Interaction Patterns

A rather substantial body of literature indicates that males and females are not treated the same in the classroom (Diller, Houston, Morgan, & Ayim, 1996; Sadker & Sadker, 1994). Diller et al. (1996) summarized the findings by stating:

> Studies on teacher–student interactions indicate that within the coeducational classrooms, teachers, regardless of sex, interact more with boys, give boys more attention (both positive and negative) and that this pattern intensifies at the secondary and college levels. Girls get less attention and wait longer for it. When they do get attention, it is more likely that the teacher will respond to them neutrally or negatively (although this depends some on the girls' race and class). The reinforcement girls do get is likely to be for passivity and neatness, not for getting the right answer.
>
> (p. 52)

Sadker and Sadker (1994) conducted a great deal of research on gender differences and emphasized the following points:

- Teachers typically initiate more communication with boys than with girls in the classroom, strengthening boys' sense of importance.
- Teachers tend to ask boys more complex, abstract, and open-ended questions, providing better opportunities for active learning.
- In class projects and assignments, teachers are more likely to give detailed instructions to boys and more likely to take over and finish the task for girls, depriving them of active learning.
- Teachers tend to praise boys more often than girls for intellectual content and quality of their work. They praise girls more often for neatness and form.
- When boys perform poorly, teachers often blame failure on lack of effort. When girls perform poorly, it is for reasons other than effort.
- All too often teachers discourage girls from courses of study that lead to high-skilled, high-paying careers.

Sadker and Sadker (1994) further noted that when student culture is included in the analysis of interaction patterns, another trend emerges. White males received the most attention, followed by minority males, White females, and minority females. The group of students most impacted by the lack of teacher attention may be minority females. The American Association of University Women (1991) reported that African-American girls, while entering school with high self-esteem, grow increasingly negative about school and their teachers. Hispanic girls show the most negative shifts. Between elementary school and high school the self-esteem of Hispanic girls drops more than any other ethnic group studied.

Sadker and Sadker (1994) identified four types of responses from teachers: praise, ("good job"), remedies ("check your addition"), criticism ("this is not correct"), and accepts ("okay"). Teachers praise only 10 percent of the time and criticize 5 percent of the time. The most frequent form of feedback provided by teachers is a verbal or nonverbal "okay." Boys receive the most praise. Praise is an important educational resource and one that seems to benefit boys the most because it is typically tied to intellectual endeavors.

When females receive praise, it is frequently for the way they look. Teachers compliment hair styles, dresses, smiles. These comments do not come during lectures but in small-group discussions and between-class exchanges. Sometimes, students pull the teacher into this "gendering exchange." Think about how you would respond to the following: "Teacher, what do you think of the dress my dad brought me from his trip to Albuquerque?" The culturally reflective teacher would consider ways to offer a compliment but also to make an intellectual comment as well.

Research also indicates that teachers give males more time to answer questions. Most teachers wait about one second for a student to answer but teachers wait less time for females. Further, boys are more likely to display nonverbal cues that they want to answer a question. Hands leap in the air and some boys may blurt out an answer before being called on. Sadker and Sadker (1994) call students acting this way "green arm" students. Their arms are in the air so long the blood seems to drop from their arms. Females may be more passive and hesitant in the way they signal an answer. Also, knowing the correct answer may be more important to the females so they may be more tentative in their responses.

Houston (1996) summarized the problem:

> If teachers fail to notice the gender of the student who is talking, if they pay no attention to who is interrupting whom, whose points are acknowledged and taken up, who is determining the topic of discussion, then they will by default perpetuate patterns that discourage women's participation in the educational process.
>
> (p. 54)

Jones and Dindia (2004) acknowledged that teachers treat males and females differently but these patterns may not be solely attributable to the sex of the student. The authors identified several possible moderating variables that impact interaction patterns such as teacher's sex, student classroom behavior, student achievement, and student race. The authors also hypothesized that teacher sex role orientation and contextual factors such as school subject might also impact classroom communication.

In the attempt to identify possible moderating variables the authors conducted a meta-analysis of 32 empirical studies. The results indicated that males did not receive more praise than females. Teachers did reprimand males more than females. Jones and Dindia (2004) did not find a moderating variable explaining these findings. The authors concluded by suggesting that student sex is only one factor influencing classroom interaction. They stressed that the social context of the classroom as well as numerous moderating factors shape teacher–student interaction.

Nonverbal Behavior

The nonverbal orientations of the student and the teacher play an important role in the way in which communication is managed in the classroom. Research suggests that males and females develop different orientations to nonverbal behavior. Wood (2001) noted that nonverbal codes are significant in managing identities and interpersonal relationships. She drew from the work of Mehrabian (1981) and identified three features of nonverbal communication that are used differently by females and males. These features are: responsiveness, liking, and power. Understanding these features of communication helps teachers manage the communication exchanges in the classroom.

"Responsiveness" is concerned with how expressive individuals are in interaction. Both females and males are responsive but communicate it in different ways. Generally, males are more expansive in their gestures. Wood contended that males are socialized to command attention. Think about the number of times young boys are told to look at someone in the eye and speak up when asked a question. Females, on the other hand, learn to use nonverbal behavior to manage interpersonal connection. Females learn to read subtle cues such as eye contact, and males learn strategies for getting and holding attention.

A second important dimension of nonverbal behavior is "liking." Some theorists suggest that females are encouraged to put more stock into this feature of their communication and as a consequence develop more skills in communicating liking than males (LaFrance & Mayo, 1979; Wood, 2001). Females tend to sit closer than males, engage in more eye contact, and use affiliative touch more than males. It is not uncommon for middle school females to hug and walk with interlocked arms. Some research suggests that females are much more concerned with how the teacher feels about them.

The final dimension discussed by Wood is "power" or control. Control is concerned with who decides topics, who interrupts whom, who has the most space, who initiates touch. Males tend to engage in more nonverbal behaviors of control than females. Young males wrestle, slap, poke, and push to gain control and authority. Males tend to interrupt females more and command more space in interaction. Look around the classroom and compare how males and females sit.

Minimizing Differences

What can teachers do to create environments that are safe and provide opportunities for males and females to be academically successful? We will close this chapter by discussing some ways teachers can create learning environments that affirm all students. We will begin by examining language processes.

In Chapter 1, we contended that individuals act upon the meanings they construct. Language has a substantial effect on classroom exchanges. Some of the effects are subtle but others are most substantial and significant.

Sexist language can be defined as "words, phrases, and expressions that unnecessarily differentiate between females and males or exclude, trivialize, or diminish either gender" (Parks & Roberton, 1998, p. 455). Many teachers unfortunately see little need or value in being aware of the way in which language creates images and shapes expectations.

It has been consistently documented, for example, that male generic language excludes women (Wood, 2001). Words like "chairman" and "mailman" are not inclusive. What are teachers implying when they say that a young female student is a "hottie" or a young male is a "stud"? It is not enough for teachers to change the pronouns they use to recognize that language shapes deeper expectations about gender. Wood observed that language could be used to devalue and trivialize females. Richmond and Dyba (1982) identified four effects of sexist language: (1) the use of sexist language promotes sexual stereotyping and the adoption of sex-typed attitudes and behaviors; (2) teachers serve as important models for language learning of children; (3) when teachers employ sexist language, their behavior is likely to promote sexism and sexist behavior in their students; and (4) when the use of sexist language on the part of the teachers can be reduced, an attendant reduction in sexism and sexist behavior in their students can be expected.

Richmond and Dyba (1982) tested the effects of modeling on a group of elementary and secondary teachers. They found that teachers frequently engaged in sexist language by using the generic "he" or other masculine pronouns. However, after intervention, teachers learned to reduce the use of these language forms. Similar positive effects on teacher modeling were obtained by Cronin and Jreisat (1995). The authors studied the effects of modeling nonsexist written language and found that students could learn to incorporate nonsexist language into written messages. The research does suggest that teachers can have a positive effect on students' use of sexist language

In addition to modeling nonsexist language, teachers need to select curriculum that stresses accomplishments of women and men and notes their achievements in other ways. In Chapter 3 we discussed the way the social curriculum influences expectations based on ethnicity. In terms of gender, teachers need to utilize curriculum that provides a balanced viewpoint on the contributions of males and females. Further, teachers need to shed the cultural expectation that males are mathematically and logically inclined and that females are verbal and emotional. A safe environment would provide opportunities based more on gender identity than on biological sex. Teachers need to be aware of the larger culture's expectations about intelligence, academic success, physical attraction, beauty, health, masculinity, and femininity. In other words, females who are logical and interested in science should receive as much encouragement as males interested in these areas. Similarly, males who are interested in literature should receive the same support as females interested in these areas.

Teachers need to be sensitive to learning style and try to create activities and assessments that are matched with students' abilities. It may be unreasonable to expect a teacher to abandon multiple choice tests, which seem to favor males, but they can limit how much weight such assessments have in the allocations of grades. Research suggests that there are a number of other instructional strategies that can benefit boys and girls. Cooperative learning and active learning strategies, for example, have been found to be helpful for a wide range of learning styles. Our discussion on multiple intelligences will provide more guidance on these issues.

The powerful effect of peer groups should also be recognized. Research by Ryan (2001) indicates that peer groups have a dramatic effect on male attitudes toward school. Peers who enjoy school create social groups with peers who enjoy school. Similarly, peers who dislike school tend to select friends who also dislike school. Ryan also found that the students who "hung out" with friends who disliked school grew more negative about school over time. This research suggests that peer groups influence attitudes about school and academic achievement. Some peer groups create norms and expectations for success and others create expectations for failure. Additional research suggests that peer groups influence attitudes about gender identity and norms for appropriate behavior (Eder & Sanford, 1986). Although it may be difficult for teachers to influence peer group selection, they can influence the way students group in the classroom. Encouraging connections among a wide range of students with a wide range of abilities may prove helpful. Through these connections, students, especially those who do not like school, may discover new areas of interest. Facilitating new relationships may garner positive academic rewards.

Teachers should help young women filter the multitude of confusing messages they receive about physical beauty, popularity, health, femininity, and intelligence. Helping females understand and embrace the significance of intellect and good health will empower them in important ways. Females need to understand that the world of math and science is not the sole territory of males. Teachers play an important role in the way in which gender messages are processed.

Teachers ought to address the needs of boys as well. Pollack (1998) suggested that schools fail boys in four ways: (1) they do not recognize the problems boys face in certain academic areas such as reading and writing, (2) schools and teachers tend to be poorly versed in the special social and emotional needs of boys and mishandle their difficulties, (3) a good number of schools are not environmentally friendly or warm for boys, and (4) schools do not have curricula and teaching methods designed to meet boys' needs and interests.

One important step teachers can take is to recognize the forces that contribute to the "boy code." In early elementary school, teachers may have difficulty recognizing little boys as vulnerable and feeling. But as Pollack (1998) noted, when they grow older and become adolescents, we start to see them in a different way. Yet underneath their façade of strength is a swirling pool of emotions and feelings. One moment boys may be aloof and the next fighting back tears from a poignant movie. Teachers do much to reinforce gender stereotypes and view boys as the "bad guys" who should be controlled in order to accomplish learning goals.

Summary

This chapter examined the various ways sex and gender intersect in classroom communication. Even though gender expectations run very deep, classrooms can be places where new insights and expectations are shaped and formed. Teachers who understand gender issues can do much to manage curriculum and communicate in ways that build on or extend the talents of all students. We encourage future teachers to incorporate our recommendations for minimizing differences into their instructional repertoires.

Learning Activities

- Identify the various ways gender is communicated through popular culture such as film, music videos, clothing, and television.
- Divide the class into two groups, males and females.
- Ask females to answer the following question: What do males need to know to communicate effectively with females?
- Ask males the following question: What will females say that males need to understand to communicate effectively with females?
- Identify the similarities and differences among the responses.
- What types of strategies can teachers use to increase male interest in reading and writing?
- How can teachers ensure that their class is safe for gay and transgendered students?
- How do beliefs about femininity and masculinity vary by culture?

Resources

- Male and female brains
  http://faculty.washington.edu/chudler/heshe.html
- Neuroscience for kids
  http://faculty.washington.edu/chudler/experi.html
- Brain activities
  www.funbrain.com/

5

STUDENTS WITH DIVERSE LEARNING NEEDS

Learning Outcomes

1. Define the concept of at risk and identify factors that may limit opportunities for learning.
2. Describe the ways in which deficit thinking affects student outcomes.
3. Summarize the major provisions contained in the Individuals with Disabilities Education Act (IDEA), Section 504 of the Rehabilitation Act of 1973, and the Americans with Disabilities Act (ADA).
4. Identify the disability categories served under the Individuals with Disabilities Education Act (IDEA).
5. Summarize and discuss the prevalence and characteristics of students with high-incidence disabilities, learners with low-incidence disabilities, and those students with gifts and talents.
6. Recommend strategies classroom teachers can use to support students with disabilities in the classroom.
7. Summarize and discuss the prevalence and characteristics of immigrant and refugee students and English language learners.
8. Recommend strategies classroom teachers can use to support immigrant students, and specifically English language learners.
9. Recommend strategies that classroom teachers can use to support students and families affected by poverty and/or homelessness.

Classroom Scenario

Cai is a 6-year-old first-grade student at Mark Twain Elementary. His classroom teacher referred Cai to the student study team. His teacher had concerns about Cai's skills in all academic areas. Cai has difficulty attending to task, following directions, and processing and retaining information. Cai's teacher knew he had language delays in Hmong, his first language, and limited English usage. It was difficult to determine whether the problems Cai exhibited were due to the fact he has a learning disability or to the process of language acquisition. His teacher thought he might also have attention deficit/hyperactivity disorder due to his inability to sit still or stay in one place. Cai had been receiving English as a second language (ESL) services for English language learners (ELLs) two hours each morning and spent the remaining time in the general education first-grade classroom. Although he is making progress, Cai is still behind his peers in all academic areas. Despite these challenges, Cai loves being at school. He loves music, art, and socializing with other English learners.

Cai's parents emigrated from Laos to the United States 15 years ago. He lives with his parents and his six siblings. Three of Cai's siblings have special health and academic needs. The family struggles to make ends meet. They live in a small, two-bedroom home in a neighborhood where other Hmong families and relatives live. Cai's brothers and sisters work together, cooking, cleaning, shopping, etc. to support the family. The cultural values of work and education are very strong in Cai's family.

The intervention team, which includes the ESL teacher, Cai's first-grade teacher, the school psychologist, and Cai's parents, met to discuss testing results. His parents do not speak English. The ESL teacher sat next to Cai's parents and translated what the team and the parents said. Cai's mother indicated that he had some of the same problems at home, where Hmong is the primary language spoken. Data based on teacher interviews, parent interviews, and interventions implemented by the ESL specialist and classroom teacher, indicated deficits in receptive and expressive language skills in Hmong and English. A plan for remediation was developed.

Early on, many teachers become disenchanted as they learn they will be responsible for teaching students from differing cultural backgrounds, with different spoken languages, and with varied learning abilities. In this chapter, we begin by considering the term "at risk" as it relates to students who typically do not fare well in school. We talk about the adverse conditions, both in school and out of school, that limit students' opportunities for success in school. We challenge you to consider the negative effects of "deficit thinking" on student outcomes and instead focus on student and family strengths when planning instruction. Prevalence rates, characteristics of learners, and general teaching strategies are addressed for students with disabilities, English language learners, and students struggling in school due to family poverty and homelessness. Finally, pertinent legislation and eligibility criteria that qualify students and their families for special services will be discussed.

Defining "At Risk"

A major challenge in the educational system today is improving the quality of instruction for *all* students. The term "at risk of school failure" is commonly used to describe students who face adversities known to hinder their educational success. The term "at risk" came into use after the 1983 report *A Nation at Risk* was published by the National Commission on Excellence in Education, which found poor academic performance at every level and criticized the educational system in the U.S. for failing to meet the needs of a competitive workforce (Placier, 1993). The commission recommended numerous educational reforms, resources, and incentives for improving the state of education in America (U.S. Department of Education, 2008). Despite the reform movements, a significant number of students continue to remain at risk of school failure.

At any given time in a student's life he/she may exhibit academic or behavioral difficulties due to temporary life circumstances (e.g., divorce, death, illness). However, there are also children who face many difficult life circumstances but fail to evidence problems in the classroom. In other words, the indicators we describe do not necessarily guarantee that problems will emerge. Children enter school environments affected by both positive and negative circumstances that fall within and outside of their control. For example, there are many external factors (e.g., concentrated poverty, family instability, and early exposure to violence) that make children at risk for school failure. There are also many internal factors (e.g., mismatch between teacher expectations and student ability, negative school environment, or inadequate resources). Wells (1990) identified several factors that place students at risk. Some are student related factors (e.g., low ability level, attendance/truancy, non-participation). School related factors include low expectations, conflict between home/school culture, disregard of student learning styles. Wells also identified family related factors (e.g., low socioeconomic status, non-English speaking home, high mobility, ineffective parenting, abuse) and factors related to community (e.g., high incidence of criminal activities, lack of school/community linkages, and lack of community support services or resources). Those who determine the criteria of at-risk status most often focus on students who have a traditional pattern of poor school performance, which includes children who are ethnic minorities, children who are academically disadvantaged, children who are disabled, and children who speak a language other than English (No Child Left Behind, 2001).

The term "at risk" means different things to different people (parents, teachers, policymakers, etc.). Hixson (1993) defined the term "at risk" as follows:

> Students are placed "at-risk" when they experience a significant mismatch between their circumstances and needs and the capacity or willingness of the school to accept, accommodate, and respond to them in a manner that supports and enables their maximum social, emotional, and intellectual growth and development.
>
> (p. 2)

We chose Hixson's definition because the term "at risk" is contextualized within the relationships and interactions among students, parents, teachers, and administrators. The definition encourages educators to move away from a focus on student and family deficits and instead concentrate on what teachers and schools can do to maximize the strengths and attributes of those they serve.

Readers are encouraged to think about the ways in which labels like "at risk" are socially and politically constructed:

> For instance, the term "at risk" can on the one hand work to reproduce inequities by obscuring the sources of risk in social injustices; yet on the other hand, the term becomes a necessary means of support for students at risk when it is used in order to procure resources for high needs schools.
>
> (Portelli, Shields, & Vibert, 2007, p. 6)

Education professor Ladson-Billings (2006) claimed in a speech that the label "at risk" actually contributes to the challenges. For example, when school personnel discuss students at risk, you may hear things like, "These kids' parents just don't care, so why try?" When teachers, administrators, and policy makers try to explain high school dropout rates, poor test scores, and low graduation rates, they often blame the students' backgrounds (e.g., dysfunctional family), individual characteristics (e.g., learning disability), and challenges outside of school (e.g., poverty) as the reasons for these failures.

Deficit Thinking

In education, we use the term "deficit thinking" to describe the practice of placing the educational failure of students on individual and family shortcomings rather than looking at institutional injustices that contribute to students' academic failure. Deficit thinking equates the achievement of students from low-income and culturally and linguistically diverse backgrounds with factors outside the control of the school. Oakes (1995) referred to deficit thinking as assumptions that low-income children, children of color, and their families are limited by cultural, situational, and individual deficits that schools cannot alter. Interventions (e.g., counseling, special education, discipline) are therefore about "fixing" the student and their families to fit the context of the dominant school culture (Ravitch, 2009). Deficit thinking creates obstacles to obtaining a rigorous and equitable education for students deemed at risk of school failure. As a result, these children receive fewer educational and social advantages. This perspective allows schools and social entities to be absolved of responsibility when children do not succeed. This type of thinking leaves parents feeling intimidated and inadequate when opportunities for school involvement do arise (Cooper, 2009). People who succumb to deficit thinking fail to see the positive attributes of the student's life experience and family that make them unique and resilient.

Hixson (1993) suggested that students are not inherently at risk, but rather placed at risk by adults. Building on students' strengths (experiences, skills, talents, interests, etc.) rather than focusing on their deficiencies is the key to helping students succeed in school. Hixson suggested that it is the quality of students' school experience rather than their individual characteristics that will determine their success or failure in school. We support Hixson's perspective. As you learn about varied groups of students with diverse learning needs in this chapter, we encourage you to think past the challenges these students present and instead focus and build upon the knowledge, talents, interests, and family experiences they bring to the classroom experience.

Reflection

- Cai would easily have been considered a student "at risk" of school failure. What external (outside of school) and internal (inside of school) factors place Cai at risk?
- What role do teachers play in promoting/perpetuating deficit thinking?

Students with Disabilities

In the first chapters of the book we discussed different types of diversity—ethnic, cultural, linguistic, sexual, and gender—as they relate to classroom communication. Students with disabilities present another type of diversity challenge for classroom teachers. They are the largest group of diverse learners we discuss. In 1975, the Individuals with Disabilities Education Act (20 U.S.C. §1400, 2004; hereafter IDEA) mandated the provision of a free and appropriate public school education for eligible children and youth ages 3–21. These children and youth with disabilities have skill diversity significant enough to require a specialized program of instruction in order to achieve educational equity. According to the National Center for Education Statistics (2013), the number of children and youth receiving special education services ages 3–21 was 6.4 million in 2010–2011, which is about 13 percent of all public school students. The number and percentage of children and youth served under IDEA have declined each year from 2005–2006 through 2010–2011, which may be due to targeted early identification and intervention efforts designed to assist students and prevent referral to special education. For those students with disabilities enrolled in public school programs, 80 percent spend most of their day in general education classrooms.

Pertinent Legislation for Students with Disabilities

Teachers working with students who have disabilities should understand three major laws—IDEA, Section 504 of the Rehabilitation Act of 1973, and the

Americans with Disabilities Act (ADA). IDEA is a federal law that governs all special education services in the United States. It provides funding to state and local education agencies to guarantee special education and related services to students who meet the eligibility criteria within the categories of disabilities. Each category has specific criteria defining the disabling condition. In each category, the disabling condition must adversely affect the student's educational performance. IDEA ensures that all children, from 3 through 21 years of age, regardless of type or severity of disability, are entitled to a free, appropriate, public education. An individualized education plan (IEP) is developed for every child served under IDEA.

In contrast, Section 504 of the Rehabilitation Act of 1973 is a civil rights law. It prohibits discrimination against a person with disabilities. The statute states, in part, that "No otherwise qualified handicapped individual in the United States . . . shall, solely by reason of his [her] handicap, be excluded from the participation in, be denied benefits of, or be subjected to discrimination in any program or activity receiving federal financial assistance." This means that individuals eligible for accommodations under this law must demonstrate the existence of an identified physical or mental condition (e.g., asthma, attention deficit disorder) that substantially limits a major life activity (e.g., walking, seeing, hearing, breathing, caring for oneself). Section 504 does not require that the student receive special education services—the school district determines eligibility. Both IDEA and Section 504 require that school district personnel develop a plan for eligible students, which includes specialized instruction, related services, and accommodations within the general education classroom.

The Americans with Disabilities Act was signed into law in 1990 and provided that individuals with disabilities not be discriminated against and that such individuals be provided with "reasonable accommodations" in the workplace. This law is an important extension of IDEA in that it provides protections for individuals with disabilities enrolled in colleges and universities, meaning that they are also entitled to appropriate accommodations in the classroom. ADA extends services beyond the high school years. High school teachers are often involved in transition planning for youth with disabilities.

Eligibility for Services

Under IDEA, students who exhibit academic and/or social and behavior problems that negatively affect their education performance may qualify for services under one of 13 disability categories: autism, deaf-blindness, deafness, emotional disturbance, hearing impairment, intellectual disability, multiple disabilities, orthopedic impairment, other health impairment, specific learning disabilities, speech or language impairment, traumatic brain injury, or visual impairment including blindness. Infants and toddlers with disabilities, from birth through age 2, and their families receive early intervention services. These children may need early intervention services because they are delayed in one or more of the following areas: cognitive development, physical development, vision and hearing, communication development, social or emotional development, adaptive development, or have a diagnosed physical or mental condition that has a high probability of resulting in developmental delay. School-aged children and youth aged 3 through 21 receive services through the school system. These children may experience delays in one or more of the following areas: physical development, cognitive development, social or emotional development, or adaptive development. Each child seeking services under IDEA must receive a full evaluation including academic and psychological testing.

Children with attention deficit/hyperactivity disorder can be served under the federal law if they meet eligibility criteria for a learning disability, emotional disturbance, or other health impairment. Students who are gifted and talented are not served under the federal special education law for students with disabilities unless they qualify as learning disabled, emotionally disturbed, or communication disordered. Most states provide for initial screening and adapted instructional programs for gifted students. Special education eligibility provides students with disabilities opportunities for specialized instruction designed to more appropriately meet their needs in general education and/or special education classrooms.

Collaborating to Meet the Needs of Students with Disabilities

Collaboration is voluntary, requires parity among participants, is based on mutual goals, depends on shared responsibility for participation and decision making, and requires shared accountability for outcomes (Friend & Cook, 1996). Collaboration is the process that ensures that students with special needs receive a free, appropriate education mandated by IDEA. For example, a team of individuals, sometimes referred to as a multidisciplinary team (e.g., parents, special education teacher(s), general education teacher(s), administrator, psychologist, the child if appropriate, and an advocate for the family if desired), meets to determine where, when, and how a student with special needs will be educated. The individualized education plan (IEP) indicates educational goals and objectives and services needed to enable each student to maximize his or her potential. IDEA requires that the following be included in the IEP:

1. A statement of the child's present levels of academic achievement and functional performance, including how the child's disability affects his or her involvement and progress in the general education curriculum.
2. A statement of measurable annual goals, including academic and functional goals.
3. A description of how the child's progress toward meeting the annual goals will be measured and when periodic progress reports will be provided.

4. A statement of the special education and related services and supplementary aids and services to be provided to the child or on behalf of the child.
5. A statement of the program modifications or supports for school personnel who will be provided to enable the child to advance appropriately toward attaining the annual goals, to be involved in and make progress in the general education curriculum, to participate in extracurricular and other nonacademic activities, and to be educated and participate with other children with disabilities and nondisabled children.
6. An explanation of the extent, if any, to which the child will not participate with nondisabled children in the regular class and in extracurricular and nonacademic activities.
7. A statement of any individual accommodations that are necessary to measure the academic achievement and functional performance of the child on state and district-wide assessments.

   Note: If the IEP team determines that the child must take an alternate assessment instead of a particular regular state or district-wide assessment of student achievement, the IEP must include a statement of why the child cannot participate in the regular assessment; why the particular alternative assessment selected is appropriate for the child; the projected date for the beginning of the services and modifications; and the anticipated frequency, location, and duration of those services and modifications.

   For students approaching the end of their secondary school education, the IEP must also include statements about what are called *transition services*, which are designed to help youth with disabilities prepare for life after high school (National Dissemination Center for Children with Disabilities, 2010a).

Students with disabilities are entitled to receive a variety of services that enable them to be successful in school. Special education teachers have the primary responsibility for managing and coordinating the services a student receives. Special education teachers must learn to collaborate with other teachers, parents, administrators, and other service providers (e.g., psychologists, social workers, speech/language therapists, interpreters, and paraprofessionals) to provide the best service to students. General education teachers must take responsibility and ownership for the students with disabilities included in their classrooms. They are responsible for identifying students who exhibit suspected disabilities.

IDEA provides definitions for 13 categories of disabilities. Federal definitions guide states in determining who is eligible for a free and public education under special education law. In order to fully meet the definition (and eligibility for special education and related services) as a "child with a disability," a child's educational performance must be adversely affected by the disability. The phrase "adversely affects educational performance" appears in most of the disability definitions. This does not mean that a child has to be failing in school to receive special education and related services. According to IDEA, states must make a free appropriate public education available to "any individual child with a disability who needs special education and related services, even if the child has not failed or been retained in a course or grade, and is advancing from grade to grade" (§300.101(c)(1)). The 13 categories of disabilities are defined below.

We also share evidence-based practices determined to be effective for working with children and youth with different disabilities. Dunst, Trivette, and Cutspec (2002) defined evidence-based practices as those practices that are informed by research in which the characteristics and consequences of environmental variables are empirically established, and an instructional strategy, intervention, or teaching program that has resulted in consistent positive results when experimentally tested, is described. The research must incorporate experimental, quasi-experimental, or single-subject research designs, be replicated multiple times, and be published in peer-reviewed professional journals. It excludes evidence that is supported by anecdotal reports, case studies, and publication in non-refereed journals, magazines, Internet, and other media news outlets (Boutot & Myles, 2011).

Low-Incidence Disabilities

Low-incidence disabilities include autism, visual impairments, hearing impairments, physical disabilities and other health impairments, traumatic brain injury, and severe and multiple disabilities. Lower-incidence disabilities are often present at birth or can be acquired later in life. Many students in this category are served in inclusive settings with general education teachers.

Under IDEA, *autism* is defined as:

> a developmental disability significantly affecting verbal and nonverbal communication and social interaction, generally evident before age three, that adversely affects a child's educational performance. Other characteristics often associated with autism are engaging in repetitive activities and stereotyped movements, resistance to environmental change or change in daily routines, and unusual responses to sensory experiences. The term autism does not apply if the child's educational performance is adversely affected primarily because the child has an emotional disturbance, as defined in IDEA. A child who shows the characteristics of autism after age three could be diagnosed as having autism if the criteria above are satisfied.
>
> (34 CFR §300.8(c)(1))

When children display similar behaviors but do not meet the criteria for autism, they may qualify for one of the other disorders on what is called the autism spectrum. Autism spectrum disorder may be diagnosed after the age of 3, and implies a qualitative impairment of social interaction and communication

(Hallahan & Kauffman, 2003). Included under this umbrella term are several disorders: autism; Asperger's syndrome, Rett syndrome, childhood disintegrative disorder; and pervasive developmental disorder not otherwise specified (often referred to as PDDNOS) (American Psychiatric Association, 2000).

The American Psychiatric Association published the fifth edition of the *Diagnostic and Statistical Manual of Mental Disorders* (DSM-5) in 2013. The definition of autism was updated for the first time since the manual was published in 1994. The diagnosis was called autism spectrum disorder (ASD), and there are no longer sub-diagnoses (autistic disorder, Asperger's syndrome, pervasive developmental disorder not otherwise specified, and disintegrative disorder). In DSM-5, symptoms are divided into two areas: social communication/interaction and restricted and repetitive behaviors. The diagnosis is based on symptoms, current or by history, in these two areas (Hyman, 2013).

Individuals with autism account for approximately 0.55 percent of the school-age population, or 4.9 percent of students served under IDEA (U.S. Department of Education, 2011). Autism spectrum disorders are the fastest growing category of disability in the United States. You cannot have watched the news recently without having heard a story about a child with autism, the challenges for parents and teachers, or numerous ads promising successful treatments or cures for the disorder. There may be many different factors that make a child more likely to have an ASD, including environmental, biologic, and genetic factors. We do know that ASDs occur in all racial, ethnic, and socioeconomic groups but are almost five times more common among boys than among girls. The Centers for Disease Control and Prevention (2013) estimate that about 1 in 88 children have been identified with an ASD. Learn more about the research being done on possible risk factors and causes of ASDs at www.cdc.gov/ncbddd/autism/research.html.

Students with ASDs require individually designed interventions that meet their needs. No one intervention has been universally identified as being effective for all children with ASD. That being said, the National Professional Development Center on ASD (2010) has identified interventions that meet the criteria for evidence-based practices for children and youth with ASD. These strategies have been shown to be effective through scientific research. We describe a few of the practices below.

Prompting is a behavior-based teaching strategy in which learners are assisted in some way to complete a task or activity. There are different kinds or levels of prompting that vary in the amount and type of assistance that is provided. Physical prompts, for example, may be provided by touching learners, usually on the hand, and physically guiding them (Neitzel & Wolrey, 2009). *Task analysis* is a teaching technique that consists of breaking a task down into small steps and teaching each step until the learner can do the complete task. This technique is especially useful with skills that are physical or routine (e.g., self-care, work tasks) (Franzone, 2009).

Computer-aided instruction (CAI) is the use of computers to teach academic skills to promote communication and language development skills (Collet-Klingenberg, 2009). *The Picture Exchange Communication System* (PECS) has been used to help children and youth with ASD develop a system for communicating with teachers, parents, and peers. PECS was initially developed as an alternative communication system and has been demonstrated in the research literature to promote speech development and production. There are six phases of PECS instruction, each phase building on the previous one. The phases are: (1) Teaching the physically assisted exchange, (2) expanding spontaneity, (3) simultaneous discrimination of pictures, (4) building sentence structure, (5) responding to "What do you want?" and (6) commenting in response to a question (Collet-Klingenberg, 2009).

Social narratives are interventions that describe social situations in some detail (highlighting relevant cues and offering examples of appropriate responding) and are aimed at either helping individuals adjust to changes in routine and adapt their own behavior based on the social and physical cues of a situation or teaching specific social skills or behaviors. Narratives are individualized and typically quite short, perhaps including pictures or other visual aids. Sentence types used in constructing social stories include descriptive, directive, perspective, affirmative, control, and cooperative (Collet-Klingenberg, 2009; Franzone, 2009).

Video modeling is a teaching method that uses assistive technology (computers, digital cameras, etc.) as the core component of instruction. Video modeling is a growing evidence-based practice for teaching individuals with ASD and other disabilities. Video modeling has been used to teach a wide range of behaviors, including social/emotional skills, adaptive behavior, life skills, academics, and play skills. Video modeling can be applied in several formats, but each involves the following basic components: (a) the individual being taught or other models are videotaped performing some targeted behavior, (b) the video recording is then played back to the learner, and (c) the learner is prompted or asked to perform the behavior. Variations of video modeling include self-modeling, point-of-view modeling, and video prompting (Collet-Klingenberg, 2009; Franzone & Collet-Klingenberg, 2008). For other evidence-based practices for students with autism, see the resources at the end of this chapter.

Sensory Impairments

Students with sensory impairments may include those who are deaf or hard of hearing, blind or visually impaired, or deaf-blind. According to IDEA, *Visual impairment including blindness* "means an impairment in vision that, even with correction, adversely affects a child's educational performance. The term includes both partial sight and blindness (§300.8(c)(13)). *Partially sighted* indicates some type of visual problem with a need to receive special education. *Low vision* generally refers to a severe visual impairment, not necessarily limited to distance vision. Low vision applies to all individuals with sight who are unable to read the newspaper at a normal viewing distance, even with the aid of eyeglasses or contact lenses. *Legally blind* indicates that a person has less than 20/200 vision in the better eye after best correction (contact lenses or glasses), or a field of vision of less than 20 degrees in the better eye. *Totally blind* means that an individual does not have sufficient sight to learn to read even with magnification and must learn through braille or other nonvisual media (National Dissemination Center for Children with Disabilities, 2012).

Deaf-blindness means concomitant [simultaneous] hearing and visual impairments, the combination of which causes such severe communication and other developmental and educational needs that they cannot be accommodated in special education programs solely for children with deafness or children with blindness (U.S. Department of Education, 2000). According to the U.S. Department of Education (2011), nearly 1,700 students are deaf-blind, having significant impairment of both hearing and vision.

Under IDEA, *hearing impairment* is defined as a loss, whether permanent or fluctuating, that adversely affects a child's educational performance but is not included under the definition of "deafness." *Deafness* refers to a hearing impairment so severe that a child has difficulty processing linguistic information through hearing, with or without amplification that adversely affects a child's educational performance. Hard of hearing describes individuals who have hearing loss but are able to use the auditory channel as their primary mode for perceiving and monitoring speech or acquiring language (Diefendorf, 1996). According to the U.S. Department of Education (2011), about 71,000 students have hearing impairments.

It is important to remember that hearing loss or deafness does not affect a person's IQ or ability to learn. Even so, children may require special education services in order to receive an adequate education. Services may include:

- regular speech, language, and auditory training from a specialist;
- amplification systems;
- services of an interpreter for those students who use manual communication;
- favorable seating in the class to facilitate speech and reading;
- captioned films/videos;
- assistance of a note taker to take notes for the student with a hearing loss so the student can fully attend to instruction; and
- instruction for the teacher and peers in alternate communication methods such as sign language counseling (National Dissemination Center for Children with Disabilities, 2010b).

Turnbull, Turnbull, Shank, Smith, and Leal (2002) recommended the following strategies for inclusion of students with sensory impairments in general education classrooms:

- Remember to have a student's attention before speaking. Look directly at a person with a hearing loss during a conversation, even when an interpreter is present. Speak clearly—no need to shout.
- Utilize activities that allow students to experience concepts, such as role play, experiments, and field trips.
- Make use of collaborative learning and peer tutoring to provide students who are deaf or hard of hearing with opportunities to be equal participants with peers during learning activities.
- Present information visually or in sign language. Use illustrations, semantic maps, graphic organizers, flowcharts, and computer technology.
- If the students use an assistive listening device, use the microphone at all times. Pass the microphone to other students who are talking.
- Always speak with the light on your face, not behind you.
- Speak slowly and distinctly; but do not exaggerate your mouth movements or speak more loudly. Keep your hands away from your face while talking.
- If the child uses a sign language interpreter, provide enough time between asking a question and calling on a student so the interpreter has enough time to interpret the question. Most students who are deaf in general education classrooms will have sign language interpreters and note takers.

Think About This: What is deaf culture? Go to www.deaf-culture-online.com/ to read about different perspectives on the experience of being deaf or hard of hearing. What educational implications does the information have for classroom teachers?

IDEA refers to *physical disabilities* as *orthopedic impairments*, which means a severe orthopedic impairment that adversely affects a child's educational performance. The term includes impairments caused by a congenital anomaly (e.g., clubfoot, absence of some member, etc.), impairments caused by disease (e.g., poliomyelitis, bone tuberculosis, etc.), and impairments from other causes (e.g., cerebral palsy, amputations, and fractures or burns that cause contractures) (§300.7(b)(7)).

Curricular goals for students with physical disabilities vary depending on the specific disability. Teachers will need to work with other service providers (e.g., nurses, occupational and physical therapists) and families to help students improve mobility, increase communication, learn daily living skills, and learn self-determination skills. Special education teachers and students' parents are important resources for general education teachers. They are familiar with adaptive equipment to improve mobilization, technology to improve communication, medical technology assistance (e.g., tracheotomy, colostomy) utilized to replace or augment vital body functions.

Other health impairments, often referred to by educators as physical disabilities, is another category of disabilities covered by IDEA. Other health impairment means having limited strength, vitality, or alertness, including a heightened alertness with respect to the educational environment that is due to chronic or acute health problems such as asthma, attention deficit disorder or attention deficit hyperactivity disorder, diabetes, epilepsy, a heart condition, hemophilia, lead poisoning, leukemia, nephritis, rheumatic fever, sickle cell anemia, and Tourette syndrome; adversely affects a child's educational performance (§300.8(c)(9)).

Students with human immunodeficiency virus (HIV) and students with acquired immune deficiency syndrome (AIDS) are served under this disability category. Students who have cancer, diabetes, or epilepsy are also served under the *other health impairment* category.

The educational needs of students with health impairments are similar to those for students without disabilities. However, the teacher should be willing to make allowances for absences. Keeping in close contact with family members and medical personnel is necessary when working with students with health impairments. Other students in the class may need to be educated as to specific health issues. Peers may be helpful in assisting with a student's care or with classroom and homework assignments.

Under IDEA, traumatic brain injury means:

> an acquired injury to the brain caused by an external physical force, resulting in total or partial functional disability or psychosocial impairment, or both, that adversely affects a child's educational performance. The term applies to open or closed head injuries resulting in impairments in one or more areas, such as cognition; language; memory; attention; reasoning; abstract thinking; judgment; problem solving; sensory, perceptual, and motor abilities; psychosocial behavior; physical functions; information processing; and speech. The term does not apply to brain injuries that are congenital or degenerative, or brain injuries induced by birth trauma.
>
> (§300.7(6)(12))

Of children ages 0–19 years, traumatic brain injury (TBI) results in 631,146 trips to the emergency room each year, 35,994 hospitalizations, and nearly 6,169 deaths (Centers for Disease Control and Prevention, 2010). In every age group, TBI rates are higher for males than for females (Faul, Xu, Wald, & Coronado, 2010). Children with mild to severe TBI often have poor coping and social skills. Traumatic brain injury thrusts them into a situation dramatically different from the one they previously knew. Relationships are often strained as these individuals respond with anger, anxiety, fatigue, and depression (Tyler & Mira, 1999). Tyler and Mira suggested that teachers should obtain as much knowledge as they can about the specific injury and long-term outcomes. Behavior and instructional expectations should be clearly stated. Do not assume the student knows what is expected. Learning to foresee what triggers problem behavior will help both teacher and student to respond appropriately.

According to IDEA *multiple disabilities* means

> concomitant impairments (e.g., intellectual disabilities and seizures; deafness and learning disabilities), the combination of which causes such severe educational problems that they cannot be accommodated in special education programs solely for one of the impairments. The term does not include deaf-blindness.
>
> (§300(b)(6))

Severe disabilities is defined by IDEA as follows:

> The term *severe disabilities* refers to children with disabilities who, because of the intensity of their physical, mental, or emotional problems, need highly specialized education, social, psychological, and medical services in order to maximize their full potential for useful and meaningful participation in society and for self-fulfillment . . . Children with severe disabilities may experience severe speech, language, and/or perceptual-cognitive deprivations, and evidence abnormal behaviors, such as failure to respond to pronounced social stimuli, self-mutilation, self-stimulation, manifestation of intense and prolonged temper tantrums, and the absence of rudimentary forms of verbal control, and may also have intensely fragile physiological conditions.
>
> (§315.4(d))

Many professional organizations find the IDEA definitions to be inadequate, focusing on the negative characteristics of students rather than on the supports necessary to assist students to be successful. The definition of persons with severe disabilities suggested by one professional organization, the Association for Persons with Severe Handicaps, focuses on three factors: (1) adaptive fit: the relationship of the individual with the environment, requiring the individual to cope with the demands of various environments and vice versa; (2) the need to include people of all ages; and (3) extensive ongoing support in life activities. The definition is as follows:

> Persons with severe handicaps include individuals of all ages who require extensive ongoing support in more than one life activity in order to participate in integrated community settings and to enjoy a quality of life that is available to citizens with fewer or no disabilities. Support may be required for life activities such as mobility, communication, self-care, and learning as necessary for independent living, employment, and self-sufficiency." Most multiple disabilities are believed to involve sensory deficits, brain malfunctioning, or genetic disorders that disrupt the normal progression of the development of cognitive, social, and physical skills.
>
> (Alquraini & Gut, 2012, p. 3)

Students who have multiple or severe disabilities are most likely to receive service in self-contained special education classes, separate schools, and home and hospital settings (U.S. Department of Education, 2002). Evidence-based practices indicate that related services are best offered during the natural routine of the school and community rather than by removing the student from class for isolated therapy.

To address the considerable needs of individuals with severe and/or multiple disabilities, educational programs need to incorporate a variety of components, including language development, social skill development, functional skill development (i.e., self-help skills), and vocational skill development. Related service providers and the appropriate therapists (such as speech and language, occupational, physical, behavioral, and recreational therapists) must work closely with classroom teachers and parents.

Teachers must consider students' needs for medication, special diets, or special equipment. Technology advances such as augmentative or alternative communication systems, communication boards, head sticks, and adaptive switches enable students with severe disabilities to participate more fully in integrated settings. Many high school students participate in community-based or school-to-work transition programs. Overall curricular goals for students with severe or multiple disabilities include teaching skills that will help them to be successful at school, at home, and in the community.

Reflection

- Emily is a seventh-grade student with a mild hearing impairment enrolled in your physical education class. Today you will be requiring students to work in teams for basketball practice. What accommodations might be needed to include Emily in this activity?
- What types of information would a general education teacher need to obtain to adequately serve students with other health impairments such as diabetes or epilepsy in the classroom?

High-Incidence Disabilities

The disabilities most commonly identified in schools are high-incidence disabilities, which include learning disabilities, emotional or behavioral disorders, intellectual disabilities, and speech or language disorders. Under the Individual with Disabilities Education Act, these disability areas make up about 90 percent of the total population of students ages 6–21 served. General education teachers will likely serve students with high-incidence disabilities in their classrooms. Under IDEA, the term *specific learning disability* means:

> a disorder in one or more of the basic psychological processes involved in understanding or in using language, spoken or written, that may manifest itself in the imperfect ability to listen, think, speak, read, write, spell, or to do mathematical calculations, including conditions such as perceptual disabilities, brain injury, minimal brain dysfunction, dyslexia, and developmental aphasia. The term does not include learning problems that are primarily the result of visual, hearing, or motor disabilities; of intellectual disability; of emotional disturbance; or of environmental, cultural, or economic disadvantage.
>
> (§300.8(c)(10))

There are several other terms that refer to specific learning disabilities. Dyslexia refers to difficulties in reading. Dysgraphia refers to difficulties in writing, and dyscalculia refers to difficulties in math.

Students with learning disabilities constitute the largest percentage of students, about 50 percent, served in special education. Clearly, the predominant problem for students with learning disabilities is academic. These students achieve at a level far below what is expected, given their intellectual abilities. In fact, students with learning disabilities usually have average or above average intelligence; their brains just process information in a different way. Learning problems may occur in the areas of reading, written language, mathematics, memory, and metacognition. The old adage "you can lead a horse to water but you can't make it drink" applies to learning and students with learning disabilities. As a group they are not risk-takers when it comes to academics. They often avoid asking questions and participating in class activities.

Teachers can best serve these students by varying instruction (e.g., lecture, small group, discussion, video), academic activities (e.g., journaling, storytelling, activity centers, cooperative groups, role play), and evaluation (e.g., presentation, project, portfolio). Refer to Thomas Armstrong's book *Multiple Intelligences in the Classroom* for other suggestions. Explicit instruction is often needed for students to learn main concepts. The student's special education teacher should be consulted for specific educational goals and for recommendations regarding instructional strategies and accommodations. This is, of course, needed when working with any student identified as having a disability and who has an individualized education plan. A 2010 meta-analysis of the effectiveness of various teaching strategies on student learning in different content areas found the following strategies to be effective: mnemonic strategies, spatial organizers, study skills instruction, note-taking strategies, computer-assisted instruction, and peer mediation. Explicit instruction was the most effective of any strategy studied (Scruggs, Mastropieri, Berkeley, & Graetz, 2010).

Students with learning disabilities also lack social and communicative competence. Forness and Kavale (1999) analyzed over 100 independent studies and found that 80 percent of students with learning disabilities are perceived to have deficits in social competence. These children tend to be less accepted and are less socially skilled than their nondisabled peers (Coleman, McHam, & Minnett, 1992; Toro, Weissberg, Guare, & Liebenstein, 1990; Vaughn & Hogan, 1994). Students with learning disabilities exhibit deficits in verbal and nonverbal communication skills and are less able to adjust to changing social situations than are their nondisabled peers (Weiner & Harris, 1997). Other socio-emotional problems presented by students with learning disabilities include low self-esteem, anxiety, depression, and delinquency (Bryan, Pearl, & Herzog, 1989; Scruggs & Mastropieri, 1996). Students with learning disabilities often report feelings of isolation and alienation toward peers and teachers as reasons for dropping out of school (Bryan et al., 1989; Seidel & Vaughn, 1991). Researchers offer varied explanations for these problems from neurological deficits and cognitive processing problems (Mathinos, 1991) to difficulty perceiving the feelings and emotions of others (Stone & LaGreca, 1983).

Reflection

- Go to a website called Misunderstood Minds at www.pbs.org/wgbh/misunderstoodminds/about.html to experience firsthand what it might be like for students struggling with basic skills such as attention, reading, math, and writing. What thoughts and feelings did you experience as you tried to complete the activities?

According to IDEA, the term *serious emotional disturbance* means:

> A condition exhibiting one or more of the following characteristics over a long period of time and to a marked degree, which adversely affects educational performance:
>
> - an inability to learn that cannot be explained by intellectual, sensory, or health factors;
> - an inability to build or maintain satisfactory relationships with peers and teachers;
> - inappropriate types of behavior or feelings under normal circumstances;
> - a general pervasive mood of unhappiness or depression; or
> - a tendency to develop symptoms or fears associated with personal or school problems.
>
> The term includes children who are schizophrenic. The term does not include children who are socially maladjusted unless it is determined that they are seriously emotionally disturbed.
>
> (U.S. Department of Education, 1998)

The report of the American Psychological Association (APA) Task Force on Evidence-Based Practice for Children and Adolescents (2008) found the prevalence of children's behavior disorders in the U.S. to be quite high. Approximately 10 to 20 percent of youth meet the APA diagnostic criteria for a mental health disorder. However, less than 1 percent of the school-age population currently receives services for emotional or behavioral disorders as defined by IDEA. This discrepancy may be due to the stigma attached to having a mental health disorder and to the expense involved in treatment. This unfortunately means that many children and adolescents do not get the services they need (Masi & Cooper, 2006).

Boys are significantly more likely to be identified as having a behavioral disorder than are girls (Klingner et al., 2005: Kauffman & Landrum, 2009). African- American students, especially those from lower socioeconomic backgrounds, are disproportionately referred to and placed in the high-incidence special education categories of mental retardation, emotional or behavioral disorders, and learning disabilities (Zhang & Katsiyannis, 2002). Disproportionality exists when students' representation in special education programs or specific special education categories exceeds their proportional enrollment in a school's general population. In addition to being mislabeled, once placed in special education, many of these students are more likely to receive their instruction in special education classes with little to no access to their nondisabled peers.

There is a wide range of conditions that qualifies students for services under this category. These include (but are not limited to): anxiety disorders, bipolar disorder, conduct disorders, eating disorders, obsessive-compulsive disorder (OCD), and psychotic disorders (National Dissemination Center for Children with Disabilities, 2010a). Children with these conditions may exhibit internalizing or externalizing behaviors. Internalizing behaviors may include social withdrawal, anxiety, or depression. Externalizing behaviors include aggressive, acting-out, and noncompliance behaviors. Students with externalizing behaviors often have difficulty adjusting to the behavioral expectations of their teachers, are often rejected by peers, and have difficulty developing and maintaining friendships (Schonert-Reichl, 1993; Walker & Leister, 1994). Smith (2001) noted that young children without disabilities responded negatively to children exhibiting externalizing types of behavior whereas children with internalizing behaviors were less likely to be noticed. Adolescents rejected their disabled peers who exhibited externalizing and antisocial behaviors. Children with psychological problems were viewed less favorably by their nondisabled peers than were those with medical problems. It is usually social skill deficits, not academic difficulties, that cause these children to be removed from general education settings.

Gresham and Elliot (1989) reference social learning theory to explain social skill deficits in students with disabilities:

> A social skill deficit results from failure to acquire a social skill due to lack of opportunity to learn the skill and/or lack of exposure to models of appropriate social behavior. A social performance deficit results from a lack of opportunity to perform social skills and/or lack of reinforcement for socially skilled behaviors.
>
> (p. 122)

A plethora of evidence exists showing that students with emotional and behavioral disorders can benefit from specific social skills instruction (Forness & Kavale, 1999; Mathur, Kavale, Quinn, Forness, & Rutherford, 1998). Numerous commercial programs are available for teaching social skills to students with mild disabilities. These include: the ACCEPTS Program (A Curriculum for Children's Effective Peer and Teacher Skills, Walker et al., 1983); the ACCESS Program (An Adolescent Curriculum for Communication and Effective Social Skills, Walker, Todis, Holmes, & Horton, 1988); Skillstreaming the Adolescent (Goldstein & McGinnis, 1997). These programs all focus on teaching specific skills (e.g., listening, asking for assistance, resolving conflicts peacefully) rather than global skills (e.g., self-esteem building). All three programs have pre and post assessment measures to determine whether teaching certain skills is necessary and whether students have learned the skills taught.

Several evidence-based strategies have been found effective in educating students with emotional and behavioral disorders. Some of these strategies include increasing behavior-specific praise and student opportunities to respond (OTR) to academic requests. In a review of literature related to the use of OTR with students with emotional and behavioral disorders, Sutherland and Wehby (2001) found that increased rates of OTR resulted in increased student task management, decreased inappropriate and disruptive student behaviors, and improved academic outcomes. They also found that teachers who praise their students frequently also provided high rates of OTR. Opportunities to respond can also include teacher-directed choral response, class-wide peer tutoring, or something as simple as asking students to respond to a question with a thumbs up for "yes" or thumbs down for "no" (Haydon, MacSuga-Gage, Simonsen, & Hawkins, 2012). Increasing students' OTRs can lead to increased student engagement and participation and, ultimately, less teacher time used to respond to disruptive behaviors.

Wehby, Symons, Canale, and Go (1998) recommended establishing effective instructional strategies by:

> providing appropriate structure and predictable routines; establishing a structured and consistent classroom environment; implementing a consistent schedule with clear expectations, and set rules and consequences; fostering positive teacher–student interaction with adequate praise and systematic responses to problem behaviors; promoting

high rates of academic engagement; and encouraging positive social interaction and limited seatwork.

(p. 52)

Reflection

- Why do you think students with emotional and behavioral disorders are disproportionately identified in special education?
- Is this a case where "race matters"? Explain your answer.

Intellectual disability is a new term in IDEA. In October 2010, President Obama signed Rosa's Law into law. Rosa's Law changed the term "mental retardation" previously used by IDEA to "intellectual disability." The definition of the term itself did not change: "*Intellectual disability* . . . means significantly sub average general intellectual functioning, existing concurrently [at the same time] with deficits in adaptive behavior and manifested during the developmental period that *adversely affects* a child's educational performance" (§300.8(c)(6)).

Intelligence refers to a persons' ability to learn, reason, make decisions, and solve problems. Individuals with intellectual disabilities have difficulty with adaptive skills necessary in day-to-day life, such as communicating effectively, interacting with others, and taking care of oneself. They often show low academic achievement in all areas. Basic skills such as memory, attention, and problem solving are generally a weakness for those with intellectual disabilities. Children with intellectual disabilities can and do learn new skills, but they may learn them more slowly than a typical child.

The most common causes of intellectual disabilities are genetic conditions such as Down's syndrome and fragile X syndrome, problems during pregnancy that can affect the child's brain such as malnutrition, and drug or alcohol abuse. Oxygen deprivation at birth, being extremely premature, and illnesses or injuries (e.g., meningitis, whooping cough, head trauma) can all lead to intellectual disability. According to the U.S. Department of Education (2011), less than 1 percent of the school-aged population is classified as having intellectual disabilities. Most of these children spend a portion of their day (40–80 percent) in general education classrooms.

Kennedy (2012) identified some general strategies for teachers working with students with intellectual disabilities: break down learning tasks into small steps; use a multisensory approach to learning; and make sure students have opportunities to revisit learning goals through a variety of activities that keep them engaged and motivated. Kennedy also recommended a range of technologies appropriate for teaching students with intellectual disabilities. For example, digital tools such as iPads now include numerous apps for students with disabilities, allowing them to explore concepts through the use of voice, touch, sound, movement, and music, to name a few. The built-in text-to-speech option on the iPad allows students to type and get immediate voiced feedback from anything they type, paste, or copy from Internet sites.

Teaching life skills and self-determination skills is also an important goal for teachers working with students who have intellectual disabilities (Wehmeyer & Schwartz, 1997). Self-determination is a combination of skills, knowledge, and beliefs that enable a person to engage in goal-directed, self-regulated, autonomous behavior. An understanding of one's strengths and limitations together with a belief in oneself as capable and effective are essential to self-determination. When acting on the basis of these skills and attitudes, individuals have greater ability to take control of their lives and assume the role of successful adults (Field et al., 1998, p. 115). Training is focused on helping students adjust to environments in which they will live, work, and play after they leave school. Instructional strategies are varied from large-group instruction and individual conferences to one-on-one behavioral interventions. Students are taught to set goals, solve problems, and advocate for themselves. Wehmeyer, Argan, & Hughes (1998) proposed that students learn to be "causal agents" or actors in their own lives instead of being acted upon.

Some of the best-intentioned teachers often step in to protect students with disabilities by making their decisions for them. Becoming self-determined also means experiencing the consequences of one's actions. A synthesis of research in the area of self-determination for individuals with disabilities can be found in Algozzine, Browder, Karvonen, Test, and Wood (2001).

Reflection

- Read the publication and view the video *Taking Charge: Stories of Success and Self-Determination* at www.washington.edu/doit/Brochures/Technology/charge.html for insights from successful young people and adults with disabilities.
- How can teachers help students learn self-determination skills?

Speech or Language Impairments

According to IDEA, speech or language impairment means a communication disorder such as stuttering, impaired articulation, language impairment, or a voice impairment that adversely affects a child's educational performance (§300.8(c)(11)). The American Speech-Language-Hearing Association (1993) differentiates between language and speech disorders. A speech disorder is characterized by an inability to deliver messages orally such as an impairment in an individual's production of sounds, rhythm of speech, or voice quality. A language disorder is characterized by difficulty in receiving, understanding, and formulating ideas and information. The most common speech disorders are articulation disorders (distort, substitute, or omit sounds), fluency disorders (e.g., stuttering); voice disorders (changes in pitch, loudness, or overall voice quality); and motor speech disorders (difficulty planning and programming movement sequences for speech production).

A child who has language impairment has difficulty understanding and using words in sentences. This affects both expressive and receptive language skills. Approximately 20 percent of students in special education receive services for speech or language disorders. This does not include students who receive services for speech and language disorders under other disability categories (U.S. Department of Education, 2011).

Smith, Polloway, Patton, and Dowdy (2001) recommended the following classroom accommodations for students with speech and language disorders:

- Work closely with the speech-language pathologist, following suggestions and trying to reinforce specific skills. Also consult with the special education teacher to determine IEP goals and objectives specific to speech and language development.
- Provide opportunities for students to participate in oral group activities.
- Give students lots of opportunities to model and practice appropriate speech.
- Maintain eye contact when the student speaks.
- Increase receptive language in the classroom.
- Teach listening skills for class discussions.
- Encourage students' conversations through story reading.
- Use music and play games to improve language.
- Be a good listener and don't interrupt or finish students' sentences for them.
- When appropriate, educate other students in the class about speech disorders and about acceptance and understanding.

Advances in technology such as communication boards and mechanical or electronic communication devices have allowed students with severe communication disorders to communicate with teachers, peers, and family members. For example, a voice synthesizer is used to produce speech output. Communication boards can be made of paper or a sturdier material and allow students to point to words or pictures to communicate. Computers can be used to make communication boards with programs such as *Boardmaker* from Mayer-Johnson Company. This program contains more than 3,000 picture symbols in black and white or color. The print labels accompanying each symbol are available in more than ten languages. These devices are easy for teachers to program and allow students with communication disorders to participate in classroom activities.

Attention deficit/hyperactivity disorder (ADD/ADHD) is one of the most common behavioral disorders of childhood. It is usually diagnosed early in childhood and often lasts into adulthood. ADHD is not a specific category under IDEA. However, students with ADD or ADHD may be served under IDEA if they meet the criteria under the category of learning disabilities, emotional disturbance, or "other health impairment." Some students with attention problems may be served through Section 504 (Mattox & Harder, 2007).

The definition of ADHD was updated in the fifth edition of the *Diagnostic and Statistical Manual of Mental Disorders* (DSM-5; American Psychiatric Association, 2013). The update reflects decades of research showing the condition to extend through adulthood. According to the American Psychiatric Association, ADHD is characterized by a pattern of behavior, present in multiple settings (e.g., school and home) that can result in performance issues in social, educational, and work settings. As in DSM-4, symptoms are divided into two categories of inattention and hyperactivity and impulsivity that include behaviors like failure to pay close attention to details, difficulty organizing tasks and activities, excessive talking, fidgeting, or an inability to remain seated in appropriate situations. Children can experience an attention deficit disorder with or without hyperactivity. More information about symptoms and criteria for diagnosis can be found in the Diagnostic and Statistical Manual. The American Psychiatric Association (2000) stated in the DSM-4 that 3 percent to 7 percent of school-aged children have ADHD. Parent reports of ADHD are much higher. Boys are far more likely to be identified as having ADHD than girls (Centers for Disease Control and Prevention, 2013). Teacher intolerance of movement in the classroom is often blamed for the over identification of ADHD.

Specific causes for ADHD are unknown; however, international research on twins shows that genetics plays a critical role (Faraone & Mick, 2010; Gizer, Ficks, & Waldman, 2009). In addition to genetics, scientists also look at other factors such as brain injury, environmental exposure (e.g., lead), alcohol and tobacco use during pregnancy, premature delivery, and low birth weight. Refined sugar, food additives, parenting, watching too much TV, etc. do not cause ADHD (Centers for Disease Control and Prevention, 2013).

Students identified as having ADHD are a heterogeneous group. Not one intervention or treatment will work for all students. According to the National Resource Center on ADHD (2009), multimodal treatment (e.g., parent training, behavior management techniques, medication, an appropriate education, and supports) produces the best results for children and adolescents with ADHD. It is the goal of the classroom teacher to determine individual needs and then tailor a plan to meet the needs of each student.

The National Dissemination Center for Children with Disabilities (2013) recommended the following strategies for working with students with ADHD: (1) figure out what specific tasks are difficult for each student (e.g., following directions, sustaining attention, staying on task); (2) clearly define and post rules, routines, and assignments; (3) teach the student to use an assignment book and daily schedule, teach study skills and learning strategies and reinforce them regularly; (4) help students channel their need for movement through regular activity breaks or allow them to stand while working; (5) give students step-by-step directions both in writing and verbally; (6) allow the student to work on the computer; (7) work with the student's parents to create and implement an appropriate education plan; (8) regularly share information as to how the student is doing at home and at school; and (9) maintain high expectations by maximizing the student's opportunities for success, be patient and willing to try new strategies when needed.

Medical management is also an important component in managing students with ADHD. Although controversial, research has found stimulant medication to be the most effective and beneficial intervention for children with ADHD (MTA Cooperative Group, 2004). According to U.S. Surgeon General David Satcher, stimulant medication is highly effective for about 75 to 90 percent of children with ADHD (MTA Cooperative Group, 2004). Although medication has helped many students improve their performance in school, drugs are not the only answer. The National Institutes of Health issued a statement in 2006 indicating that even though stimulant medication improved the core symptoms of students with ADHD, medication alone did not improve students' academic achievement or social skills deficits. For example, many students with ADHD also have learning or other disabilities that require academic and/or behavioral interventions. In any case, teachers need to work closely with parents and physicians to monitor side effects and behavior changes.

Reflection

- ADHD has been the subject of much controversy over the years. For more information Education World has published a five-part series that explores ADHD, research and treatments, and the controversy that surrounds it at www.educationworld.com/a_issues/issues148c.shtml
- After reading the series, answer these questions:
  - Why do you think there has been a rise in childhood ADHD and medication use?
  - Is medication the best ADHD treatment? Explain your answer.

Including Students with Disabilities

Today, students with special needs receive the majority of their education in general education classes with special services provided as needed, either in the classroom or in a learning lab. This has not always been the case. In the early days of education in the United States, students with special needs were placed in general education classes but without the assistance of trained specialists. Students with severe disabilities were often excluded from school. As special education grew, students with severe disabilities were sent to special schools and students with milder disabilities, who presented a difficult challenge to general education teachers, were removed and placed in separate special classes. Concerns regarding such issues as segregation, labeling, and the high incidence of minority students identified as disabled led parents and educators to question current practices. The pendulum swung from segregation of special students in separate schools and separate classes toward inclusion into the mainstream of education. Inclusion is the term most often used today to refer to the placement of students with special needs in general education. Today, students with disabilities are served in general education classrooms with the assistance of specialists including special education teachers, speech and language pathologists, and other service providers deemed necessary for students to succeed in school.

Studies have shown that students with disabilities can benefit both academically (Helmstetter, Curry, Brennan, & Sampson-Saul, 1998; Malian & Love, 1998; Shinn & Powell-Smith, 1997; Waldron & McLeskey, 1998) and socially (Kennedy & Itkonen, 1994; Kennedy, Shukla, & Fryxell, 1997) from being educated alongside their nondisabled peers. Benefits include more opportunities for social interaction, improved communication and social skills, friendships, appropriate models of behavior, and perceived higher standards of performance from teachers. Researchers have found that students without disabilities can also benefit from association with their peers with special needs. They benefit as role models for students with disabilities, thereby improving their social competence and decreasing feelings of loneliness and rejection in inclusive classrooms (Pavri & Monda-Amaya, 2000). Students without disabilities also benefit by learning about tolerance, individual difference and human exceptionality. They learn that students with disabilities have many positive characteristics and abilities.

Academic achievement and improved social competence is most likely to be achieved when instruction is individualized and when support is also provided to teachers (Madden & Slavin, 1983; Schulte, Osborne, & McKinney, 1990). Teachers play a critical role in developing a climate of acceptance through curriculum design, instructional strategies, and activities that encourage positive social interactions among students with special needs and their nondisabled peers.

Although inclusion is a concept typically related to the education of students with disabilities in general education classrooms, we believe that inclusion is not a place, but rather an attitude that requires the building of community support and a strong sense of belonging in all students. Inclusion is a way of thinking and acting that allows every individual child to feel accepted, valued, and safe.

Other Students with Diverse Needs

Not all students with diverse learning needs are classified as having disabilities. Students with other special learning needs include students who are gifted and talented, immigrant and refugee students, students who are English language learners (ELLs), and students who are affected by family poverty and homelessness. In this section, we discuss the prevalence and characteristics of these student groups and recommend ways teachers can assist these students to be successful in school.

Gifted and Talented Students

As defined in the Jacob K. Javits Gifted and Talented Students Education Act of 1988 (PL 100–297), individuals who are gifted and talented are

> students, children, or youth who give evidence of high achievement capability in areas such as intellectual, creative, artistic, or leadership capacity or in specific academic fields, and who need services or activities not ordinarily provided by the school in order to fully develop those capabilities.
>
> (§9101(A)(22))

Although there are many definitions of gifted and talented in the literature, the above definition was reauthorized in 2001 as part of the No Child Left Behind Act. Even though the definition references the need for services, special education is not required to provide services to students who are gifted and talented.

There are various reports as to the prevalence of gifted and talented students in public schools. Some reports indicate that approximately 3–5 percent of school-age students are gifted (Clark, 2008). Other reports indicate a higher percentage; 10–15 percent of students could be considered gifted (Renzulli & Reis, 2013).

Gifted students, although they do not qualify for special education services, often provide challenges, both academic and social, for classroom teachers. Gifted students are often rejected by their peers and feel isolated in school. Classroom teachers must consider the unique needs of these students. Teachers should be aware that many gifted students remain unidentified and therefore may not receive appropriate educational services.

Kennedy (1995, pp. 232–234) offered several inclusion tips for teachers working with gifted learners:

1. Resist policies requiring more work of those who finish assignments quickly and easily. Instead, explore ways to assign different work, which may be more complex and more abstract. Find curriculum compacting strategies that work and use them regularly.

2. Seek out curriculum and supplementary materials that require analysis, synthesis, and critical thinking, and push beyond superficial responses.
3. De-emphasize grades and other extrinsic rewards. Encourage students to learn for learning's sake, and help perfectionists establish realistic goals and priorities.
4. Encourage intellectual and academic risk-taking. The flawless completion of a simple worksheet by an academically talented student calls for little or no reward, but struggling with a complex, open-ended issue should earn praise.
5. Help all children develop social skills to relate well to one another. Help them see things from others' viewpoints. Training in how to "read" others and how to send accurate verbal and nonverbal messages may also be helpful. Tolerate neither elitist attitudes nor anti-gifted discrimination.
6. Take time to listen to responses that may at first appear to be off-target. Gifted students are often divergent thinkers who get more out of a story or remark and have creative approaches to problems. Hear them out and help them elaborate on their ideas.
7. Provide opportunities for independent investigations in areas of interest.
8. Be aware of the special needs of gifted girls. Encourage them to establish realistically high-level educational and career goals, and give them additional encouragement to succeed in math and science.

Immigrant and Refugee Students

During the 1990s, the United States experienced a dramatic increase in refugee resettlement, admitting more than 132,000 refugees in 1992 (U.S. Department of State, 2008). Following the terrorist attacks of September 11, 2001, the number of refugees admitted to the U.S. dropped sharply (Dewey, 2003). However, the number of refugee children as a percentage of all refugees resettling to the U.S. has increased over the past decade. For example, in 1998, only 13 percent of all refugees resettled in the U.S. were children, but in 2008, 37 percent were children (U.S. Department of State, 2008). In this section, we turn our attention to the demographics and characteristics of school-aged immigrants and refugee children, aged 5–18. We also recommend teacher and program supports for children and their families.

The changing demographics in U.S. elementary and secondary schools are largely a result of record-high immigration. Immigrant and refugee children now constitute one of the fastest growing populations in the United States. The changes are driven by immigration from Latin America, Africa, Asia, and the Caribbean. Children of immigrants (both foreign-born and U.S.-born with foreign parents) in K–12 classrooms more than tripled from 6 to 20 percent between 1970 and 2000 (Morse, 2005). Children of immigrants and refugees are now one in five K–12 school-age children (Suarez-Orozco & Suarez-Orozco,

2001). In 2000, almost half of California's K–12 student population consisted of children of immigrants (Fix & Capps, 2005).

The federal No Child Left Behind Act defines immigrant students as individuals aged 3 to 21 who were not born in the United States and who have attended U.S. schools for less than three years. According to United States law, a refugee is an immigrant "outside of his or her country of nationality who is unable or unwilling to return because of persecution on account of race, religion, nationality, or membership in a particular social group, or political opinion. A refugee does not include anyone who ordered, incited, assisted, or otherwise participated in the persecution of any person on account of race, religion, nationality, membership in a particular social group, or political opinion (U.S. Citizenship and Immigration Services, 2013, p. 1).

CHALLENGES

The process of immigrating to the United States is full of challenges that are unique to children of refugee and immigrant families (Pumariega, Rothe, & Pumariega, 2005). Both groups experience leaving familiar surroundings, family, and friends. Families must locate housing, secure jobs, and familiarize themselves with the English language (Strekalova & Hoot, 2008). Those immigrant parents who are well-educated and have professional credentials in their country of origin often experience a drop in their status and earnings while they spend time improving their English skills, take courses, and pass exams needed to practice their profession in this country (Allen, 2005). These challenges take place at the same time families are trying to assimilate into a new society while retaining their own culture and identity.

Unlike many immigrants, refugees are often fleeing from oppression, having endured horrors such as rape, abduction, and trafficking—arriving in the U.S., with few belongings, in order to save their lives (Strekalova & Hoot, 2008). Refugee children are often separated from family members as they flee persecution (Boyden, de Berry, Feeny, & Hart, 2002). These challenges often lead to anxiety and uncertainty. Post-traumatic stress disorder (PTSD) is a major concern in working with many refugee children as they attempt to cope with extreme psychological trauma. Trauma can take many forms, including physical or sexual assaults, natural disasters, the death of a loved one, or emotional abuse or neglect. Students who have been exposed to trauma are at increased risk of academic, social, and emotional problems (Delaney-Black et al., 2002).

Many refugee children come from countries with unstable infrastructures due to extreme poverty, war, or other disasters. Many children become heads of households or are on their own due to the death of their parents or caretakers. According to Boyden et al. (2002), children will likely live with relatives or others who are not related. Many refugee children have had their education interrupted or have had no access to schooling when they arrive in the United States (Boyden et al., 2002). For many older children this can significantly affect their learning when they begin school in the United States. For example, immigrant high school students have to complete in four years what American students have had 13 years to finish.

TEACHER SUPPORT

School is often one of the first contacts many refugee students have in their new homeland. Teachers are therefore in an ideal position to observe, monitor, respond to, and support the students' needs. To meet the needs of immigrant children, it is important to understand the challenges related to their adaptation. We recommend a book, *Children of Immigration*, written by Harvard University immigration experts Carola and Marcelo Suarez-Orozco. The book is "designed to provide an overview of the major themes in the lives of the children of immigrants—the nature of their journey to the United States, their earliest perceptions, and their subsequent transformations" (p. 13). We also recommend *Educating Immigrant Students in the 21st Century: What Educators Need to Know*, written by Xue Lan Rong and Judith Preissle (2009). The authors focus on the unique challenges of immigrant students, primarily those from the Middle East and students of White, non-Hispanic backgrounds. The authors help educators explore evidence-based practices and policies for adapting and improving the learning environment.

It is important to remember that immigrant and refugee children may be behind in basic skills due to circumstances not within their control. Robertson and Breiseth (2008) remind us:

> Refugee students have learned skills in survival and decision-making through intense exposure to dramatic global issues that most of their peers probably have not experienced. They are capable of learning English and the skills necessary to be successful academically: it will just take longer than mainstream students and even other English Language Learners (ELLs) who have had formal education in their own language in their home country.
>
> (p. 4)

Providing consistency in the form of predictable routines and schedules is necessary to help children feel safe. It's important to be aware of activities that may elicit a child's anxiety or regression and try to guard against them. Do not tell a child who talks about or who you know has experienced trauma, to just forget about it. This minimizes their experience and fears and may also make them feel like failures if they can't forget. Teachers should be open to providing the emotional safety these children need by listening and validating their feelings and experiences. The National Child Traumatic Stress Network offers current information and resources to teachers, mental health and medication professionals, community agencies, and refugee families. Connecting students to a positive peer group will help them adjust to their new environment. Finding classroom jobs and responsibilities will help students feel a sense of control and ownership in the classroom. Integrating the students' cultural and country information will also help students feel comfortable in the classroom and will educate and widen the perspective of their mainstream peers. Finally, teachers need to keep open the lines of communication with families, to discuss school related concerns or to recommend school or community resources. Teachers often misinterpret language barriers, transportation issues, and an inability to take time off work as a lack of interest in a child's education (Suarez-Orozco & Suarez-Orozco, 2001). Research indicates otherwise; immigrant parents are a huge motivating factor for their children's academic success (Portes & Rumbaut, 2001).

The Bridging Refugee Youth & Children's Services (2013) has developed *Refugee Children in U.S. Schools: A Toolkit for Teachers and School Personnel* in order to support and assist schools with large numbers of refugee students. The purpose of this toolkit is threefold:

> to facilitate information-sharing among school personnel and others working with refugee children in the schools on a national level; provide information on frequently asked questions in the form of brief "tools" that may be used in the professional development of teachers and other school personnel; and to raise awareness of the needs of refugee children in the schools.
>
> (p. 1)

Numerous other resources exist at the national and state levels.

Think About This: Public discourse is divided over the issue of immigration. Go to the following website to read ten myths about immigration:

www.tolerance.org/immigration-myths

Children of Migrant Workers

Migrant children are those whose families travel across the country seeking seasonal or temporary work in the agricultural, dairy, or fishing industry. They are children who are born outside the United States but live in this country without legal permission of the federal government. Although their numbers are difficult to calculate, the Urban Institute suggests that there are approximately 650,000 migrant children in the United States, most coming from a residence in Mexico to a U.S. residence, and most often in California or Texas (Huddle, 2000). Although most migrant children are Latino, there are other diverse groups, including Southeast Asian, White, Pacific Islander, and Alaska Native. A majority of migrant children do not speak English and have poor language skills in their own language. Many children have little educational experience when entering school in the United States. High rates of mobility, social and cultural isolation, hard work outside school, and poor health and poverty contribute to poor academic achievement and high dropout rates among this student population (Cox et al., 1992). Frequent moves makes it difficult to attend school on a regular basis, maintain grade-level work, and accumulate academic credits to eventually meet graduation requirements (Green, 2003).

Teachers and schools are thus challenged to meet the educational needs of these students. Green (2003) pointed out that Public Law 93–380 requires school personnel to identify the children of migrant workers who are eligible to receive services. Funding is available for school recruiters to go to locations where migrants are working and assist migrant students in enrolling in school (Anstrom, 1997).

Menchaca and Ruiz-Escalante (1995) recommended several instructional strategies to capitalize on the strengths migrant students bring to the classroom. A few of those strategies are as follows:

1. *Build on migrant students' strengths.* Most students have traveled and lived in many states. Their experiences as well as the richness of their cultures and languages can be included in lesson planning. Content can be personalized by using familiar places and names in addition to using analogies to connect new concepts to students' experiences.
2. *Integrate culturally relevant content.* This allows migrant students to develop pride in their culture and learn content from a familiar cultural base. Teachers can read to students, generate discussion, and have them either write or share in groups some similarities and differences between the books' characters and the students' own lives. It helps students learn about and respect other cultural groups' heritage and histories while keeping their own culture instilled in their hearts and minds.
3. *Use cooperative learning.* Migrant students do well in cooperative learning settings because they sense other students are encouraging and supporting their efforts to achieve, it lowers anxiety levels and strengthens motivation, and they get equal access to learning opportunities.

   The No Child Left Behind Act strongly emphasizes family literacy and involvement and requires that it occur "in a format and language understandable to parents." Opportunities for migrant students to succeed can be enhanced through family involvement activities that are sensitive to time constraints, mobility, language barriers, etc. Appropriate activities might include provision of the following:

- Bilingual community liaisons who can bridge language and cultural differences between home and school (i.e., they can train parents to reinforce education concepts in their native language and/or English).
- Curriculum that reflects the culture, values, interests, experiences, and concerns of the migrant family; this can enhance learning. Parents can more easily relate to such "homework" and will be more inclined to help their children with subjects that affirm their experiences.
- Flexible instructional programming that allows students to drop out of school to work or take care of family responsibilities and return and pick up their academic work without penalties; this can increase migrant students' success.
- Multiple, coordinated "second-chance" opportunities for education and training at work sites, community centers, churches, and school sites; these can be made available for both students and families.
- Partnerships with the agriculture industry that can help cultivate potential collaborative activities that allow schools to tap into parents' knowledge, skills, and talents through "flex time" (i.e., allowing parents to attend school activities during work hours.

(Martinez & Velazquez, 2000)

Migrant families may bring challenges to our educational system, but they also enrich it. Teachers need to remember to build curriculum and activities around the strengths of migrant students' experiences and culture to make learning more meaningful. Involving migrant family members can only enhance students' learning experiences

English Learners

Given the dramatic increase in the percentage of immigrants to the U.S., it makes sense that English Language Learners (ELLs) are the fastest growing populations in public schools (Smith-Davis, 2004). Most ELL students, however, are native-born U.S. citizens. In fact, more than half of ELLs are second or third generation U.S. citizens (Capps et al., 2005). Two-thirds of ELLs come from low-income families, and three out of four ELLs are Latino/Latina Spanish-speaking (National Clearinghouse for English Language Acquisition, 2007). Nationally, ELL student enrollment grew from 2.1 million in the 1990–1991 academic year to over 4 million (8 percent of all students) in the 2002–2003 school years. The No Child Left Behind Act uses the term "limited English proficient" to refer to students acquiring English for their education. These students are also known as ESL (English as a second language) students.

However, in recent practice, these students are most often referred to as ELLs (English language learners). We will use the term ELLs to discuss the needs of those students for whom English is not their first language.

PERTINENT LEGISLATION

There exists a substantial body of laws that establish the rights of ELL students and require legal responsibilities of school districts serving these students. These laws also apply to refugee students for whom English is not their first language. In a landmark case, *Lau v. Nichols* (1974), the U.S. Supreme Court ruled that the San Francisco, CA school system violated the Civil Rights Act of 1964 by denying non-English speaking students of Chinese ancestry a meaningful opportunity to participate in the public school system. The decision indicated that just because students had access to the same equipment and materials did not mean that they had equal educational opportunity, especially if they did not speak English. Instruction must be adapted to meet student needs. In another case (*Plyler v. Doe*, 1982), the U.S. Supreme Court ruled that: (1) public schools were prohibited from denying immigrant students access to K–12 public education; (2) immigrant students residing in the U.S. cannot be denied resident status by public schools solely on the basis of their immigration status; and (3) making inquiries that might expose the undocumented status of a student or the parents is prohibited.

There are several laws designed to improve the education of children of immigrants and ELLs. The No Child Left Behind Act (NCLB) calls for quality education and accountability for all students in U.S. schools. Title I of the NCLB ensures that all children, including those in "highest-poverty schools, limited English proficient children, migratory children, children with disabilities, Indian children, neglected or delinquent children, and young children in need of reading assistance," have a fair and equal opportunity to high-quality education (§1001(2)) (U.S. Department of Education, 2002). Title III of the NCLB aims to assist ELLs and immigrant students "to achieve at high levels in the core academic subjects" (Part A, §3102(2)) and do the following:

- Develop and reach English language proficiency
- Attain high levels of academic achievement in core content areas
- Meet the same academic and achievement standards other students are expected to meet.

(U.S. Department of Education, 2002)

Both Title I and Title III hold schools accountable for ensuring that ELLs learn English and academic content. NCLB legislation requires all states to report on the standardized scores of ELL students as well as other subgroups such as students with disabilities, students of color, and economically disadvantaged students. Sanctions may be imposed on states that do not meet adequate yearly progress (AYP) benchmarks for English language learners. The problem remains that achievement data indicate a serious gap between ELLs and students who speak English as their primary language (Abedi & Gándara, 2006; Klingner, et al., 2005). In 2009, only 12 percent of students with limited English proficiency scored "at or above proficient" in mathematics in fourth grade on the 2009 National Assessment of Educational Progress (NAEP) compared with 42 percent of students not classified as English language learners. The gap was much wider in eighth-grade math, where only 5 percent were proficient in math on the NAEP compared with 35 percent of non-ELLs. The reading gap has also widened since 2005 (National Assessment of Educational Progress, 2009). On the NAEP reading test only 3 percent of ELLs met the standard in eighth-grade reading in 2009 compared to 34 percent of non-ELLs. The achievement gap remains.

These issues remain further complicated by the potentially disproportionate numbers of ELL students in special education, a condition that has been a concern for the past 30 years (Donovan & Cross, 2002; Heller, Holtzman, & Messick, 1982). For example, it is assumed that the same proportion of students with disabilities will be found in any population. Based on this assumption, approximately 12 percent of the school population should require special education services (Minow, 2001). However, ELLs are overrepresented in some special education programs. In California, for example, approximately 22 percent of ELLs are also designated for special education services (Minow, 2001). Zehler et al. (2003) found an underrepresentation of ELLs in special education at the national level. Overrepresentation of ELLs in special education may be due to practitioners not being able to distinguish between ELLs who struggle to learn because of a disability and ELLs who struggle to learn because of language acquisition issues (Artiles & Ortiz, 2002). Let's say, for example, that a teacher has just finished a lecture and is now asking clarifying questions to the whole group. Children who are learning English may take longer to respond to teacher questions because they are trying to process between two different languages, not because they have a learning disability. Children with a learning disability may take longer to respond to teacher questions because they need more time to process the question. Assessment bias is also a concern in the overrepresentation of ELLs in today's classrooms.

Effective instruction is key if English language learners are to be successful in meeting the required academic standards and becoming proficient in English. Programs for ELLs fall on a continuum from the bilingual model at one end to the English-only model at the other end. One English-only approach is referred to as *structured English immersion*, in which native-language supports are gradually decreased as learners develop sufficient English language skills. The goal is to increase learners' English fluency quickly by teaching content in English (Moughamian, Rivera, & Francis, 2009). Teachers in content classrooms use clear, direct English that gradually increases in complexity as ELL students' English language proficiency grows (Echevarria & Graves, 2011).

A wide range of *scaffolding strategies* is used to create meaning of multifaceted content in classroom discussion, activities, reading, and writing. A dual-language program is one of the bilingual models. The goal is to develop learners' skills in two languages simultaneously. These programs exist for many languages (e.g., Spanish, French, Chinese) and seek to maintain native languages and cultural backgrounds of English language learners. Research on effective education for ELLs indicates that instruction in a student's first language provides the most positive student outcomes (Thomas & Collier, 2001).

The Institute of Education Sciences (IES) has identified evidence-based programs and strategies for working with ELL students. Following are a few of the programs. *Peer-Assisted Learning Strategies (PALS)* was found to have potentially positive effects on reading achievement for ELL students (Institute of Education Sciences, 2010). The peer-tutoring program was designed for elementary students to improve their proficiency in reading. A more thorough description of the program is in Chapter 7. *Fast ForWord Language* is a computer-based instructional program designed to improve English language proficiency and reading skill. The program was found to have potentially positive effects on language development of ELL students but no discernable effects on reading achievement for elementary ELL learners (Institute of Education Sciences, 2006a). Just the opposite was true for a program called *Enhanced Proactive Reading*. This program was shown to have potentially positive effects on reading achievement but no discernable effects on English language development (Institute of Education Sciences, 2006b). For more information on effective interventions for ELL learners, go to http://ies.ed.gov/ncee/wwc/topic.aspx?sid=6.

Family Poverty and Homelessness

FAMILY POVERTY

In the United States, the Office of Management and Budget (OMB) sets the official poverty thresholds. The federal poverty guidelines in the United States set the poverty level at $22,050 for a family of four and $18,310 for a family of three. Persons with incomes lower than that are deemed to have difficulty providing basic needs such as food, clothing, and shelter for their families. Research indicates that families need about twice the federal poverty level to meet the basic needs (Children's Defense Fund, 2012). For the purposes of this book, we define two different types of poverty. *Generational poverty* occurs in families in which at least two generations have been born into poverty. This is different from *situational poverty*, which is generally caused from a lack of resources due to a particular set of events (i.e., a death, chronic illness, divorce, job loss) and is often temporary. Our discussion pertains to both types of poverty.

The numbers tell a story. According to the U.S. Census Bureau (2011), 23 percent of children (16.4 million) lived in poor families in 2010, up from 22 percent (15.7 million). Even though our national unemployment rate is declining, the number of children living in poverty continues to increase. Today, children are the poorest age group in the United States and are almost two and a half times more likely to be poor than senior citizens ages 65 and older. Among children under age 5, 25.9 percent are poor, compared to 20.5 percent of those ages 5–17, and one in four infants, toddlers, and preschoolers are poor during the years of greatest brain development.

The nation's poorest children (47.6 percent) live primarily in households headed by single females. In fact, children of single moms experience poverty at a rate four times higher than children living with married couples. According to the U.S. Census Bureau (2011), the child poverty rate among African-Americans (39 percent) in 2010 was almost three times the rate for non-Hispanic Whites (14 percent). Only three other countries in the developed world have a higher poverty rate than the United States; Mexico leads all nations with a rate of 25.79 percent, followed by Chile at 23.95 percent, Turkey at 23.46 percent, and the U.S. at 21.63 percent.

CONSEQUENCES

There is much to be learned from those who have experienced poverty. Beegle (2003) interviewed people who grew up living in poverty but were able to achieve success through education. Participants in the study talked about experiencing great shame and humiliation growing up in poverty. They felt that others blamed them for living in poverty. Participants talked about being embarrassed by their appearance or the appearance of family members, not wanting anyone to see their living conditions. One participant stated, "Everyone could tell I was poor by my ragged clothes, horrible shoes, and free lunch tickets" (p.12). Participants talked about not having enough food and being embarrassed by having to use food stamps. Most talked about their families being "sick all the time" (p. 13). They reported having few funds for health and dental care or for prescriptions. Most of the participants reported they felt that without money education would not be attainable. These experiences are important in understanding why education was often a secondary thought to surviving on a day-to-day basis for most of the participants in the study.

Growing up in poverty is one of the most influential factors in a child's development, placing the child at risk for school failure. Cauthen and Fass (2008) contended that poverty and financial instability can impede children's cognitive development and their ability to learn and can contribute to behavioral, social, and emotional problems and to poor health. The risks posed by economic hardship are greatest among children who experience poverty when they are young and among children who experience persistent poverty. When parents are unemployed or their incomes are low, they may struggle to meet their children's most basic needs for food, safe housing, medical care, and quality child care (Yeung, Linver, & Brooks-Gunn, 2002).

Teachers agree that having breakfast improves academic achievement by permitting increased concentration (95 percent), better academic performance (89 percent), and better classroom behavior (Share Our Strengths, 2012). In a survey of public school teachers released by Share Our Strengths, 56 percent of teachers agreed that most of their children relied on school meals as their primary source of nutrition. A lack of health insurance also places children and their families at great risk. In 2011, 9.4 percent (7.0 million) of homeless children were without health insurance. In 2012, the uninsured rate for children living in poverty was 12.9 percent compared to 7.7 percent for children not in poverty.

Research has shown that childhood poverty is linked to underachievement in school (Kellett, 2009). Children often do not have the opportunity to read at home or be read to by a parent or someone else. Reading and math scores in fourth and eighth grade were lower for students attending high-poverty schools between 1998 and 2009 (Aud et al., 2010). Children who live below the poverty line are 1.3 times more likely to have developmental delays or learning disabilities than those who do not live in poverty. The negative effects of poverty also increase the chances of poor outcomes for youth and young adults, such as teen pregnancy, failure to graduate from high school, poor health, and lack of secure employment (Gershoff, Aber, & Raver, 2003). Other long-term outcomes for those living in generational poverty include completing fewer years of schooling, working fewer hours, and earning lower wages as adults (Children's Defense Fund, 2012).

ATTITUDES MATTER

One of the most influential voices in the instructional conversation on poverty and education is Ruby Payne. Her book, *A Framework for Understanding Poverty*, and her other publications have influenced teacher and administrator attitudes about and ways to perceive and teach students who experience poverty. Even though her "framework" is popular, the empirical support for her claims about poverty are woefully inadequate. What is perhaps most problematic is that she argues that there is a "culture of poverty." For Payne, individuals in poverty "share more or less monolithic and predictable beliefs, values, and behaviors" (Gorski, 2008, p. 32). Moreover her viewpoint represents a deficit perspective, which blames the victims for their own circumstances. Critics of Payne's work suggest that students who come from poverty are labeled less capable, less cultured, and not as worthy as other learners (Sato & Lensmire, 2009). Gorski suggested that Payne's framework fails to consider the class inequality that pervades U.S. schools. Gorski further suggested that poverty and its relationship to education couldn't be understood without realizing the ways in which our schools mirror societal classism that keeps many of our students in poverty.

Gorski (2008) identified several myths or stereotypes people use when considering poverty. Think about how these stereotypes mirror societal classism. The first myth is that poor people are unmotivated and have weak work ethics.

The reality is that most students living in poverty have at least one employed parent, who, given the shortage of living-wage jobs, may work several jobs to make ends meet. As a result, many poor working parents work more hours than those who are wealthier.

A second myth is that poor parents are uninvolved in the education of their children, mainly because they don't value education. Nothing could be further from the truth. Gorski (2008) argued that poor families have many of the same values as wealthier parents but have less access to school involvement. For example, it is difficult for a parent working two jobs, one during the day and another late at night, to attend school functions. Parents who work more than one job may not have paid leave. There may be child-care or transportation issues as well. Gorski reminded us that schools need to be accountable to meet the needs of families in these circumstances.

The next myth is that poor people are linguistically deficient. In fact all people use a variety of language forms with sophisticated grammatical structures. This is not to say that language is not important. As we have stressed, language is related to cognition, but teachers may confuse style with competence. For example, a core component of Payne's model is addressing the language differences between poor and non-poor students. She contended that poor students use a casual language register that is used with friends and has a limited vocabulary and incomplete grammar. The task for teachers is to build the formal language register of poor students so they use standard sentence syntax and complete sentences. It is beyond the scope of this text to provide a full critique of Payne's work but we encourage the reader to consult the following authors for more information: Bomer, Dworin, May, and Semingson (2008); Gorski (2007a); and Sato and Lensmire (2009). We will add that Payne's view runs contrary to what we have discussed earlier in regards to language diversity. Increasing the vocabulary of poor students will not be a springboard to the American dream. Review our earlier discussion of teaching in linguistically diverse classrooms.

The final myth discussed by Gorski (2008) is that poor people abuse drugs and alcohol. The author observed that although drug sales may be more visible in poor neighborhoods, they are more prevalent in wealthier ones. Educators are aghast when a star athlete from a prominent family is arrested for armed robbery to support a drug addiction but have no response when a poor African-American student is arrested for selling marijuana. The student who comes from a family with resources can afford legal support and rehabilitation whereas the poor student goes to jail.

Gorski (2008) challenged teachers to examine their attitudes about class and culture. They must understand that access to opportunity is not the same for children from poverty. A study conducted by the National Commission on Teaching and America's Future (2004), found many discrepancies between high-poverty and low-poverty schools that affect opportunities for children to be successful in school. For example, high-poverty schools hire more teachers who are not fully credentialed or who are not licensed in the content areas they teach. High-poverty schools have inadequate materials and supplies and limited access to technology. Embracing these myths allows educators and administrators to place the blame on families and students, to focus on their weaknesses instead of their strengths. In this text we have taken the position that diversity is a resource rather than a deficit.

TEACHER SUPPORT

Many of the changes needed for children currently living in poverty to be successful (e.g., affordable housing) will have to be made at the institutional level. We focus here on what teachers can do to support students to be successful in school. Gorski (2007b) recommended that teachers:

1. challenge ourselves, our biases and prejudices, by educating ourselves about the cycle of poverty and classism in and out of U.S. schools;
2. challenge our colleagues when they stigmatize poor students and their parents, reminding them of the inequitable conditions in our schools and classrooms;
3. assign work requiring computer and Internet access or other costly resources only when we can provide in-school time and materials for such work to be completed;
4. work with our schools to make parent involvement affordable and convenient by providing transportation, on-site childcare, and time flexibility;
5. give students from poverty access to the same high-level curricular and pedagogical opportunities and high expectations as their wealthy peers;
6. teach about classism, consumer culture, the dissolution of labor unions, environmental pollution, and other injustices disproportionately affecting the poor, preparing new generations of students to make a more equitable world;
7. keep stocks of school supplies, snacks, clothes and other basic necessities handy for students who may need them, but find quiet ways to distribute these resources to avoid singling anyone out;
8. develop curricula that are relevant and meaningful to our students' lives and draw on their experiences and surroundings;
9. fight to get our students into gifted and talented programs and give them other opportunities usually reserved for economically advantaged students and keep them from being assigned unjustly to special education;
10. continue to reach out to parents even when we feel they are being unresponsive; this is one way to establish trust; and

11. most importantly, we should never, under any circumstance, make an assumption about a student or parent—about their values, culture, or mindset—based on a single dimension of their identity. (Gorski, 2007b, p. 3)

Reflection

Watch This:

- At a time when one in five American kids lives below the poverty line, Frontline's documentary ***Poor Kids*** explores daily life of living hand to mouth, not having enough, through the eyes of children. The documentary follows three young girls who are growing up against the backdrop of their families' struggles against financial ruin. Watch the documentary at: www.pbs.org/wgbh/pages/frontline/poor-kids/.
- What did you learn from the children telling their stories?
- How does the information inform teachers?

Homelessness

When you think of a person being homeless, what images come to mind? There are many misconceptions or stereotypes about what makes a person homeless. We often hear people say things like, "They're just lazy and don't want to work," "They are drug addicts or mentally ill," or "They choose to live on the streets." There is a perception of homeless people in our society based on stereotypes or assumptions, most of which are wrong. The reality is that people who find themselves homeless come from all walks of life, and no one, given the right circumstances, is immune from the possibility of becoming homeless. Just 20 years ago, single men and women were the most likely to lack permanent shelter, and today, families and children are the fastest growing homeless population in the United States (National Coalition for the Homeless, 2007).

There are multiple causes of homelessness including lack of income, unemployment, extreme poverty, and the inability to find affordable housing. Non-economic factors such as mental illness, substance abuse, drug addiction, alcohol addiction, parent abuse, disease, emotional distress, depression, and other health problems are also major contributors to the growing problem of homelessness in the United States. The National Center on Family Homelessness (2011) reported that a significant spike in child homelessness occurred due to the 2005 hurricanes Katrina and Rita, both unprecedented natural disasters. The storms led to more Americans being displaced than at any other time in the nation's history, accounting for an increase in the number of homeless children in 2006. Between 2007 and 2010, financial speculation sparked the collapse of the housing market and financial institutions and a stock market crash. Escalating foreclosures and job layoffs left many families homeless.

In 2007, 23 percent of all homeless people were members of families with children (U.S. Conference of Mayors, 2004). Today, more than 1.6 million American children, or one in 45 children, are homeless in a year. This equates to more than 30,000 children each week, and more than 4,400 each day (National Center on Family Homelessness, 2011). Recent evidence confirms that homelessness among families is still increasing. From 2011 to 2012, there was a decrease in all homeless subpopulations with the exception of persons in families. In fact, the number of homeless families with children increased by 1.4 percent from 2011 to 2012 (National Alliance to End Homelessness, 2013). Most homeless families are comprised of a single mother in her 20s with two young children. The numbers are likely an underestimate due to the fact that many families double up, living with other family members, and are not counted at the federal level as homeless.

Young children are not the only ones affected by homelessness. There are also many teens living on the streets or in shelters for a variety of reasons, and they are at risk of school failure. Teens who are homeless leave home mainly because of severe dysfunction in their families, situations that put them at risk for being sexually abused, or physical abuse by their parents or other family members (Moore, 2006). Parental alcoholism and family conflict often cause adolescents to run away from home. Between 1.7 and 2.8 million adolescents run away from home each year (Hammer, Finkelhor, & Sedlak, 2002). Some leave home because their parents have disapproved of their sexual orientation or gender identification. In fact, approximately 40 percent of homeless teenagers are lesbian, gay, bisexual, or transgendered (Ray, 2006). Others leave home because of their own alcohol or drug addiction. Regardless the reasons, living on the streets places teens at great risk of being victimized.

Reflection

Watch This:

- We recommend that you watch the CBS 60 Minutes report entitled "Hard Times Generation: Homeless Kids" at www.youtube.com/watch?v=SYCJLiXigPk
- Now go back and revisit the images that came to mind when we asked you to think about a person who is homeless. What did you learn?

Homelessness has a devastating impact on children's and youths' educational opportunities and outcomes. Schools require that parents provide documentation of residency and guardianship when they enroll their children. Delays in the transfer of school records, lack of immunization records, or lack of transportation can prevent children from being enrolled in school. What compounds this issue is the fact that families move frequently; within a single year, 97 percent of homeless children move up to three times (National Center on Family Homelessness, 2009). Frequent moves are often due to limits on the length of time someone can stay in a shelter or other temporary housing arrangements. Families are often separated, with children living with relatives or friends. Some children are moved into foster care (Barrow & Lawinski, 2009). Frequent moves disrupt the education of these children and youth. Hunger is another major factor affecting the educational experiences of children and youth who are homeless. Homeless children experience hunger at twice the rate of other children and are more likely to experience health problems due to inadequate nutrition and shelter (Books, 2004).

According to the National Center on Family Homelessness (2009), children who are homeless are four times more likely to have delayed development and twice as likely to have learning disabilities than children who are not homeless. Further, they are 16 percent less proficient than their peers in math and reading. It makes sense that homeless children are at greater risk for emotional (Morris & Butt, 2003), social (Fantuzzo & Periman, 2007), and behavioral problems (Books, 2004; Knitzer & Lefkowitz, 2006) that contribute to school attendance and performance problems. Homeless children who are enrolled in school still have difficulty with regular attendance: of the 87 percent of homeless children enrolled in school, only 77 percent attend regularly (National Coalition for the Homeless, 2007). The ongoing bombardment of stressful events has a profound effect on a child's ability to learn.

PERTINENT LEGISLATION

What legislation supports children and youth who are homeless? To begin with, teachers should know what defines homelessness and then determine what assistance is available for homeless students and their families. The McKinney-Vento Homeless Assistance Act was first passed in 1987 and was reauthorized with the passage of No Child Left Behind. The act requires states and school districts to furnish homeless children with equal access to the same free education provided to other students. In addition, schools must do their best to eliminate any barriers to the educational success of homeless students. The education subtitle of the McKinney-Vento Act includes a comprehensive definition of homelessness. This statute states that the term "homeless child and youth" means:

> (A) individuals who lack a fixed, regular, and adequate nighttime residence . . . and (B) includes: (i) children and youth who lack a fixed,

> regular, and adequate nighttime residence, and includes children and youth who are sharing the housing of other persons due to loss of housing, economic hardship, or a similar reason; are living in motels, hotels, trailer parks, or camping grounds due to lack of alternative adequate accommodations; are living in emergency or transitional shelters; are abandoned in hospitals; or are awaiting foster care placement; (ii) children and youth who have a primary nighttime residence that is a private or public place not designed for or ordinarily used as a regular sleeping accommodation for human beings . . . (iii) children and youth who are living in cars, parks, public spaces, abandoned buildings, substandard housing, bus or train stations, or similar settings, and (iv) migratory children . . . who qualify as homeless for the purposes of this subtitle because the children are living in circumstances described in clauses (i) through (iii). (*McKinney-Vento Act sec. 725(2); 42 U.S.C. 11435(2).*
>
> (National Coalition for the Homeless, 2007)

Both IDEA and the McKinney-Vento Act require districts to ensure homeless children have access to education and services they need to meet the same academic standards as all students to prevent them from getting left behind in school. The McKinney-Vento Act requires school districts to have a liaison who is responsible for identifying students who are homeless and coordinating with families and other pertinent agencies to make sure students and their families receive the services they are entitled to. Both laws support students in homeless situations by helping them enroll in school immediately, whether or not they have their previous school's records; giving students the right to remain in one school regardless of the changes in their living situations; setting up transportation to school; accessing medical, dental, mental health, or other needed services; and informing their parents/guardians of available programs and services. Transition planning for youth beginning at age 16 is mandated by IDEA.

SUPPORTING HOMELESS CHILDREN AND THEIR FAMILIES

For children and youth who are homeless, school may provide the stability and safety not experienced in their living conditions. So, what can classroom teachers do to support students and families who are homeless? Teachers will need first to set judgments about homelessness aside, and instead attempt to understand the problems these students and their families face. Children don't just choose to be homeless. Families are often embarrassed and reluctant to acknowledge and discuss their circumstances for fear of being judged as parents or for fear that their children will be stigmatized by the thoughtless remarks of others (Driver & Spady, 2004). Teachers must be sensitive to the unimaginable challenges families endure in order to survive and provide for their children.

Knowing the possible signs of homelessness may help teachers identify students who are at risk and for whom supports could be provided. Possible signs of homelessness observed in a classroom look as follows:

- history of attending many schools
- erratic attendance and tardiness
- consistent lack of preparation for class
- sleeping in class
- hostility and anger or extremes in behavior
- needy behavior (seeking attention or being withdrawn)
- poor hygiene and grooming
- clothing inadequate or inappropriate for the weather
- hunger and hoarding food
- resistance to parting with personal possessions.

(Driver & Spady, 2004, p. 1)

Students exhibiting any one of the above signs require further attention. Once teachers know they have a child who is homeless in their classroom, they should coordinate services with the school district's homeless liaison, school nurse, and psychologist as needed. A school liaison or social worker may be available to assist parents with obtaining transportation to shelters and transitional living facilities or to medical appointments and school related meetings or activities. Parents should be welcomed and given assistance to ascertain available in-school and community resources. A child's best chance of succeeding in school depends on a relationship built on mutual trust and open and honest communication with both the child and the family.

It's very difficult for any child to succeed in school when basic needs (e.g., food, water, shelter) are not met. For example, teachers can make sure water and healthy snacks are always available in the classroom. They can also make sure students know they are entitled to receive free breakfast and lunch at school. All students have a need to feel socially connected. If other needs, such as physical, emotional, and social needs, are unmet, it is especially difficult for children to focus and stay on task. Providing opportunities in the classroom to assist other students, to be responsible for certain class jobs, etc. can help students feel a sense of belonging in the classroom.

Extra school supplies and books may need to be provided for students to complete out-of-class assignments. Think about what's reasonable and doable when it comes to homework. Students who are homeless may not have access to computers necessary to complete their work. Homework shouldn't be a barrier to students' success in school. Provide the materials or equipment needed for students to complete homework either before or after school. Check to see if tutoring is available through school or community organizations.

Classroom behavior must also be considered as a lens to the real circumstances homeless children face on a day-to-day basis. What teachers identify as problem behavior may instead be a child's response to inadequate sleep, poor nutrition, or insufficient health care. A homeless child who gets angry because his teacher confronts him for sleeping in class should not be dismissed or reprimanded. Students who are homeless should never be punished for things they have little control over (e.g., tardiness, tattered clothing, lack of school supplies, no money to attend a field trip). Further exploration into the problem is a better response. We recommend that teachers focus on the strengths students bring to the classroom while collaborating with families and other pertinent personnel to provide the services and supports needed to assist in helping children succeed in school.

Summary

Students with disabilities, those who are gifted, English language learners, and students considered at risk of school failure due to family poverty or homelessness represent an extremely diverse group of learners. In this chapter we defined the 13 categories of disabilities eligible for services under IDEA. We discussed what it means to be at risk of school failure. Moving away from deficit thinking to a strengths-based focus is key to helping our students succeed in school. Although evidence-based practices or instructional strategies were recommended for each group of learners, we encourage teachers to focus on the individual needs of each student when planning instruction. The successful inclusion of all students can be accomplished only when we develop an attitude of acceptance and a willingness to promote and celebrate the strengths our students and their families bring to the educational experience.

Learning Activities

- Observe in a classroom or a program designed for ELL students. Describe the program goals. What interventions or strategies were used to increase student engagement in learning?
- Interview a special education or general education teacher (someone who has been teaching for ten or more years) in your neighborhood school. Ask the following questions: Describe the changes you have seen in education over the years. Tell me about the students in your classroom (ethnicity, socioeconomic status, academic and behavior strengths and challenges). Finally, ask the teacher to comment on the future of education (what changes need to be made) to improve outcomes for children and youth.
- Visit or volunteer at a homeless shelter serving children in your community. What types of services and supports are provided to homeless children and their families?

Resources

- http://tash.org: TASH (formerly The Association for Persons with Severe Handicaps) is an international advocacy organization whose mission is to promote the full inclusion and participation of children and adults with significant disabilities in every aspect of their community and to eliminate the social injustices that diminish human rights.
- http://community.cec.sped.org/ddel/home: Council for Exceptional Children: Division for Culturally and Linguistically Diverse Exceptional Learners.
- www.ldonline.org: LD Online is the leading website on learning disabilities, learning disorders, and differences.
- www.chadd.org: Children and Adults with Attention-Deficit/Hyperactivity Disorder (CHADD) is a national organization providing education, advocacy, and support for individuals with ADHD.
- www.ccbd.net: CCBD is an international community of educators focused on the education of children and youth with or at risk of emotional and behavioral disorders.
- www.asha.org: The American Speech-Language-Hearing Association (ASHA) is the national professional, scientific, and credentialing association for more than 166,000 audiologists; speech/language pathologists; speech, language, and hearing scientists; audiology and speech-language pathology support personnel; and students.
- www.autism-society.org: The Autism Society is dedicated to improving the lives of all affected by autism by providing the latest information regarding treatment, education, research and advocacy.
- www.world-gifted.org/aboutus: The World Council for Gifted and Talented Children, Inc. (WCGTC) is a worldwide non-profit organization that provides advocacy and support for gifted children.
- www.ddelcec.org: Division for Culturally and Linguistically Diverse Exceptional Learners advances educational opportunities for culturally and linguistically diverse learners with disabilities and/or gifts and talents, their families, and the professionals who serve them.
- http://center.serve.org/nche: National Center for Homeless Education (NCHE) is the U.S. Department of Education's technical assistance and information center in the area of homeless education.

Videos

A Place at the Table shows how hunger has serious economic, social, and cultural implications for the United States. It shows that the problem can be solved once and for all if the American public decides—as they have in the past—that making healthy food available and affordable is in everyone's best interest. Related resources, news, games, etc. can be found at www.takepart.com/place-at-the-table.

- Children and Adults with Attention Deficit Hyperactivity Disorder, www.chadd.org
- The Council for Exceptional Children: the Division for Diverse Exceptional Learners, www.cec.sped.org/dv/ddel.html
- The Council for Exceptional Children with Behavior Disorders, www.ccbd.net
- The Inclusion Network, www.inclusion.org
- International Society for Augmentative and Alternative Communication (ISAAC), www.isaac-online.org
- LD Online, www.ldonline.org
- The National Information Center for Children and Youth with Disabilities, www.nichcy.org
- TASH Organization, addressing the needs of individuals with significant disabilities, http://tash.org

Unit III

BUILDING AND MAINTAINING COMMUNITIES OF LEARNERS IN DIVERSE CLASSROOMS

Unit III focuses on ways to build and maintain positive relationships between teachers and students. In Chapter 6, we begin by reviewing research documenting the positive impact of quality teacher–student relationships. The second part of the chapter examines the ways teacher–student relationships evolve and change over time. The third section covers constructs that positively influence student feelings about teachers, academic material, and motivation. We conclude the chapter by discussing specific strategies teachers can use to build quality relationships. Chapter 7 moves away from a microscopic focus on teachers and students and looks at the larger classroom community. We begin the chapter by explaining the significance of socio-emotional learning. Research indicates that when students feel part of a community, they learn more and behave more appropriately. Among the topics discussed are the defining features of a learning community and the importance of teacher support, peer tutoring, cooperative learning, peer mediation, classroom meetings, and service learning. Research on classroom management is reviewed in Chapter 8. The chapter begins by reviewing different theoretical perspectives on behavior. Teachers' beliefs about the causes of challenging behavior influence their strategies for managing it. The impact of culture on discipline is also addressed in Chapter 8. We conclude the chapter with a discussion of school-wide positive behavioral supports, a proactive three-tiered model of prevention and intervention aimed at creating safe and effective learning environments for students.

6

BUILDING RELATIONSHIPS

Learning Outcomes

1. Explain the impact of QTSR on student outcomes.
2. Compare the three primary perspectives used to study the role of the teacher–student relationship on academic and social performance.
3. Describe the stages characterizing teacher–student relationships.
4. Identify strategies teachers can use to establish positive relationships with their students.
5. Evaluate Rawlins's perspective on teaching as friendship.
6. Explain the communication behaviors that impact affective learning.
7. Explain the link between parent involvement and students' academic and social success in school.
8. List five ways teachers can encourage family involvement.

Classroom Scenario

Relationships matter. Gabriela lives with her mother, Renata, and two female siblings, one three years older, and one three years younger. The girls' fathers are unknown to them. Renata had drug and alcohol problems but is currently drug and alcohol free. The girls and their mother live in a small, one-bedroom apartment in an area of town considered dangerous due to drugs and gang violence. Gabriela's mother has a difficult time maintaining employment; there are times when she can't pay the bills or buy food or clothing. Family challenges make it difficult for Gabriela and her sisters to focus on schoolwork.

In fourth grade Gabriela was diagnosed with a learning disability in reading. She was initially placed in a special education classroom for most of the day with Ms. Gorena, a credentialed special education teacher. An Individualized Education Plan (IEP) was developed for Gabriela to include supports for her learning challenges. Although Gabriela struggled with reading, Ms. Gorena found her to be quite confident and capable in math, science, and the arts. She spent time each day talking to Gabriela, including her in class discussions, and using the arts to strengthen Gabriela's reading skills. Ms. Gorena also maintained weekly contact with Renata, encouraging her to stay involved in Gabriela's education.

It was during Gabriela's fourth-grade year that Renata contacted Big Brothers/Big Sisters to provide support in helping her take care of her children. Big Brothers/Big Sisters of America is a mentoring program that matches an adult volunteer, known as a Big Brother or Big Sister, to a child, known as a Little Brother or Little Sister, with the expectation that a caring and supportive relationship will develop. Gabriela was matched with a Big Sister named Analee, who was also a teacher. Analee was instrumental in supporting Gabriela through elementary, middle, and high school. She spent time helping Gabriela with homework, took her to community events, and included her in her own family's activities. She attended all of Gabriela's IEP meetings and often met with individual teachers to discuss strategies for supporting Gabriela in core content areas that required a great deal of reading. One teacher in particular, Mrs. Featherstone, was a true mentor to Gabriela throughout the high school years. Ms. Featherstone's interest in the arts inspired Gabriela to use her strengths to express herself in content area assignments. Analee met with Mrs. Featherstone frequently to check in and keep Gabriela on track for graduating. Even though there were many struggles along the way, Gabriela graduated with her class in her senior year.

In today's era of high-stakes testing and accountability, teachers are pressured to meet or exceed state standards and expectations. However, some of the moves teachers make to meet these expectations may in fact be counterproductive. Specifically, teachers may be putting less effort into cultivating positive relationships with their students. This is unfortunate because the interpersonal relationship between a student and teacher has a profound effect on instructional outcomes and activities. Positive teacher–student relationships allow teachers to teach and students to learn. Christopher Knoell (2012) wrote:

> It is in this relationship between teacher and student where learning takes root and begins to grow; and the degree to which a teacher invests in those interactions not only affects learning outcomes and student behavior in the classroom, but also potentially impacts each student's future achievements and success.
>
> (p. 86)

Research consistently shows that interpersonal processes influence how students feel about the content they study and their motivation to study it (Davis, 2003; Fredriksen & Rhodes, 2004; Frymier, 1994; Perry, VandeKamp, Mercer, & Nordby, 2002). Teachers are also affected by the relationships they have with their students. The desires to prepare for class, to give extra attention to students, and to develop creative teaching strategies are related to the types of relationships teachers establish and maintain. This chapter therefore focuses on the interpersonal processes that play a role in the classroom context. We discuss the benefits of positive teacher–student relationships, describe perspectives on the way relationships develop, and review the communication processes found to promote positive teacher–student relationships. We recommend activities for developing positive relationships. Finally, we discuss the importance of developing relationships with families and recommend strategies teachers can use to build on family strengths to encourage involvement.

The quality of the teacher–student relationship has been found to be one of the most important factors influencing student learning outcomes (Hattie, 2009; Roorda, Koomen, Spilt, & Oort, 2011; Rowe, 2001). Positive teacher–student relationships have long-lasting implications for students' academic and social development. Rimm-Kaufman (2011) wrote:

> If a student feels a personal connection to a teacher, experiences frequent communication with a teacher, and receives more guidance and praise than criticism from the teacher, then the student is likely to become more trustful of that teacher, show more engagement in the academic content presented, display better classroom behavior, and achieve at higher levels academically.
>
> (p. 1)

Baker (2006) examined the contributions of positive teacher–child relationships on the school adjustment of 1,310 elementary school-aged children across the period of elementary school. Findings suggest a significant benefit for children across grades, gender, and type of school outcome. One exception was found for students with significant learning problems. A close relationship with a teacher may not be enough to positively affect academic outcomes. Direct instruction focused on remediating deficits is required to improve academic outcomes. Davis (2003) conducted an extensive review of the literature on the influence of teacher–student relationships on cognitive and social development. She concluded that the quality of the teacher–student relationship influences social and cognitive outcomes from preschool to early adolescence. The results of these studies support other findings, which show positive school outcomes for students who have a positive relationship with their teachers (Hamre & Pianta, 2001; Rimm-Kaufman, 2011; Wentzel, 2002). Gettinger and Stoiber (1999) reviewed literature on teaching excellence and highlighted the significance of positive teacher–student relationships. Specifically, they stated that "positive teacher-student social interactions contribute to students' self-efficacy and intrinsic interest in learning, and they foster a sense of identity as a member of a learning community" (p. 940). Deci, Vallerand, Pelletier, and Ryan (1991) found that in classes where teachers encourage autonomy, children were more intrinsically motivated and had higher self-esteem than in classrooms where teachers were more controlling. Students who reported more positive teacher–student relationships also reported greater feeling of belonging and therefore felt more academically effective and less self-conscious (Roeser, Midgley & Urdan, 1996).

Croninger and Lee (2001) argued that a quality teacher–student relationship is a form of social capital that has particular benefits for students who are at risk for academic failure. They analyzed data collected over several years by the National Center for Education Statistics. They found that at-risk students who dropped out of high school had a less positive relationship with teachers than at-risk students who stayed in school. They also found that students who were academically at risk benefited more from a positive relationship with teachers than students who were not academically at risk.

The benefits of positive teacher–student relationships are not confined to academics. Perceived teacher support is related positively to student engagement, liking for school, and motivation (Goodenow, 1993; Skinner & Belmont, 1993). Ryan and Patrick (2001) found that students who perceived their relationships with their teachers to be positive engaged in more self-regulated learning and in less off-task or disruptive behavior. Positive teacher–student relationships often serve as a buffer against developing social and academic problems. Teachers who are nurturing appear to create positive bonds that positively influence a student's orientation to learning tasks. Research suggests that students who have a positive relationship with a teacher also have better peer relationships, and manage their emotions better (Pianta & Steinberg, 1992).

Brewster and Bowen (2004) found that a positive teacher–student relationship positively influenced academic engagement of Latino middle and high school students who were at risk for school failure. The authors stated that school engagement "includes a student's affective, cognitive, and behavioral responses related to attachment, sense of belonging, or involvement in school" (p. 49). They surveyed 699 Latino middle and high school students from the United States and school personnel who identified the students as at risk for school failure. The results indicated that teacher support (e.g., "my teachers really care about me; my teacher is willing to work with me after school") had the greatest impact on the meaningfulness of school. They also found that students who had a positive relationship with a teacher exhibited fewer behavioral problems in school. The authors concluded by positing that teacher support may be more important for at-risk students than for other students.

Characteristics of Positive Teacher–Student Relationships

Many people, from Theodore Roosevelt to John C. Maxwell, have been credited with coining the phrase "People don't care how much you know until they know how much you care." It is an often-used adage that has proven to be true in education. How students feel about school and how well they perform in school are in part determined by the quality of the relationships they have with their teachers. High-quality relationships are characterized by trust, safety, involvement, warmth, and care and support when help is needed (Good & Brophy, 2000; Larrivee, 2005). Some researchers said teachers who have good relationships with their students are caring, friendly, helpful, and understanding (Goodenow, 1993; Rosenfeld & Richman, 1999). Doda and Knowles (2008) asked approximately 2,700 middle school students from diverse communities across North America to respond to the question "What should middle school teachers know about middle school students?" The students said they desired "healthy and rewarding relationships with their teachers and their peers" (p. 27). Most often, they reported, the healthy relationships were "characterized by compassion, respect, personalization, fellowship, and friendship" (p. 27).

Noddings (1995) argued, "We should want more from our educational efforts than adequate academic achievement, and we will not achieve even that meager success unless our children believe that they themselves are cared for and learn to care for others" (pp. 675–676). Teachers demonstrate caring by empathizing with students' feelings and dilemmas and by protecting students with clear boundaries (Elias & Tobias, 1996). They communicate caring in their teaching by showing enthusiasm for the subject, by teaching to students' strengths and abilities, and by providing opportunities for students to be challenged yet successful. Caring teachers express optimism about their students' educational futures. Noddings (1995) argued that spending time developing relationships with students, talking to them about their problems, and guiding them toward sensitivity and competence are significant teaching activities.

Caring teachers are important to the development of classroom communities (Kohn, 1996; Noddings, 1995; Osterman, 2000), which we discuss at length in Chapter 7. Noddings (1995) noted that caring teachers model appropriate behavior, provide dialogue in which students can affect decision making in the classroom, arrange opportunities for students to demonstrate caring through such activities as community service, and validate student growth in their development of caring. These connections are important because they encourage learning that may not occur otherwise.

Kohn (1996) also stressed the role of positive teacher–student relationships when he stated:

> Caring teachers converse with students in a distinctive way; they think about how what they say sounds from the students' point of view. They respond authentically and respectfully rather than giving patronizing pats on the head (or otherwise slathering them with "positive reinforcement"). They explain what they are up to and give reasons for their requests. They ask students what they think, and then care about their answers.
>
> (p. 112)

Bosworth (1995) interviewed middle school students regarding their ideas of what it means to be a caring teacher. Helping with schoolwork was the frequently mentioned characteristic of a caring teacher. Valuing individuality and recognizing different learning styles were important to seventh and eighth graders and among males. Providing guidance and helping with problems outside of school time was the second most frequently mentioned characteristic.

Roorda, Koomen, Spilt and Oort (2011) conducted an extensive meta-analysis of the impact of teacher–student relationships on academic engagement and academic achievement. They analyzed the results from 92 articles that described the results from 99 studies from 1990 to 2011. Overall, their findings indicated that positive teacher–student relationships predicted academic engagement and academic achievement. The effects were stronger for academic engagement. Surprisingly, the results revealed that the impact of a positive teacher–student relationship was larger for older than younger children. Common wisdom would suggest that as children grow older they become more independent and concentrate on peer relationships. It appears that a positive relationship with a teacher in secondary school helps students transition into a new and ambiguous structure and system.

In contrast, negative teacher relationships have a stronger impact on students in primary school. Most students in grades K–6 have one teacher for a 9-month school year. If this experience is negative, students disconnect and do not perform well. This is especially true for poor and ethnic minority students. We also believe that these effects are cumulative. The negative effects can be particularly severe if students have more than one negative experience in primary school and as a result may not develop the academic foundation necessary for success in subsequent grades.

Let's return to the opening scenario in this chapter. It was because of a positive teacher relationship that Gabriela was able to stay academically engaged and become academically successful. Moreover, the most significant relationship she had was in secondary school. As a result of that relationship, she was able to obtain a high school diploma and go to a community college.

Perspectives on Teacher–Student Relationships

According to Davis (2003), three primary perspectives have been used to study the role of the teacher–student relationship on academic and social performance. One approach, attachment theory, suggests that within a child's biological nature there is a need to develop nurturing relationships with a caregiver. An attachment perspective considers the teacher–student relationship to be an extension of the parent-child relationship. The attachments that children form with their primary caregivers can positively or negatively affect future relationships (including those with peers and teachers), their self-concept, their ability to regulate their emotions and behavior, and their ability to learn about the world. The theory posits that teacher–student interaction is driven by students' beliefs about adults, teachers, and adult–child interaction. These beliefs, in turn, influence the processes used to guide students toward academic goals.

A second perspective, reviewed by Davis (2003), focuses on the way a teacher motivates a student to accomplish academic goals. As we discussed in Chapter

2, a significant amount of attention has been given to this topic. Motivational studies examine the communication skills and instructional strategies that impact student motivation to learn. According to Davis, teachers who promote autonomy and help students become self-directed are particularly effective. In contrast, teachers who engage in power struggles have more problematic relationships. For these teachers, the goal has more to do with control than with student learning.

Motivation is impacted by the socio-emotional connections between teachers and students. Research from education and communication studies shows that teachers who exhibit positive affect and promote positive attitudes about instructional material raise students' sense of belonging and increase their self-efficacy (Brophy, 1998; Christophel, 1990; Comstock et al., 1995; Moos & Moos, 1978).

Students are motivated to obtain goals that are not related to academic success. For example, the desire for peer acceptance may in some instances be more important to a student than academic performance. Indeed, the teacher–student relationship is influenced by numerous factors. Teachers have values, beliefs, and expectations about students and course content. Students have attitudes about their teachers, their peers, and themselves. In some cases, teachers and students connect in positive ways, and sometimes they struggle as they attempt to work through the instructional experience.

The third perspective on teacher–student relationships discussed by Davis (2003) is the sociocultural perspective. This perspective views the teacher–student relationship as mutually negotiated. Teachers and students are in a continual process of defining and redefining their relationship. The social-cultural perspective challenges teachers to understand the forces that influence the development and maintenance of interpersonal relationships.

Two approaches are prevalent in the sociocultural perspective: the ecological and the social constructivist views. The ecological view focuses on the physical setup, class size, and the social pressures the student experiences. The effects of class size have received considerable attention. As classes become larger it becomes more difficult for teachers to make connections with their students. Often, teachers and administrators create policies and structures that privilege the test scores at the expense of building positive relationships. As a consequence, students will seek out and develop alternative relationships with classroom aides, student teachers, and peers.

The second approach, social constructivist, considers knowledge as co-constructed between teachers and students. We discussed the constructivist view in Chapter 1. In this perspective learning is considered a social activity. Students must make sense out of both cognitive (learning math) and social (teacher immediacy) material. In order to be effective teachers need to connect with students' sense-making processes. Social constructivists attempt to promote autonomy through cooperative learning, sharing classroom rules, and providing students with the resources to navigate the material. This perspective requires teachers to understand the diverse lived experiences of their students.

Teachers utilize strategies for accomplishing intellectual goals and students create mechanisms for managing their own goals. For example, students who do not want to study math may "act out" or in some way sabotage the lesson. Teachers may refer to these students as "their problem children" or "trouble makers." This relationship may be contentious and difficult. Returning to the discussion in Chapter 3, some teachers may hold negative stereotypes about students of color and project these attitudes in the classroom.

One final point Davis (2003) makes about teacher–student relationships is that relationships change as students move from elementary school to high school. In elementary school, learning is a community enterprise; students have one teacher for a school year and work in numerous cooperative groups and teams. When students advance to middle school and high school, learning becomes more individual. Students have more than one teacher, move from class to class, and have different social relationships. For some, the bonds established in elementary school are broken in middle school. Thus, as the context changes expectations about teacher–student relationships change.

The previous discussion outlines the value of developing positive teacher–student relationships. However, this discussion provides little guidance on ways to obtain these goals. We believe it is helpful to examine the ways the teacher–student relationship develops in the classroom context.

Reflection

- Identify five ways in which teacher–student relationships influence learning.
- In your own experience as a student, identify a teacher you believe developed positive relationships with students. What characteristics did the teacher exhibit that contributed to a positive relationship?
- Which of the above perspectives on teacher–student relationships contributed to the positive relationship you had with the teacher you identified? Explain your answer.
- What effect did the relationship have on your performance in the classroom?

Relationship Development

The teacher–student relationship evolves and changes over the school year. As the school year unfolds, teachers and students share information and experiences and as their understanding of each other increases, the way in which they communicate changes. Two prominent theories that have been used to describe this relationship change are social penetration theory (Altman & Taylor, 1973) and social intercourse theory (Knapp, 1978). Both theories are predicated on a belief that relationships move from superficial to deeper levels. Even though the bulk of research testing these theories has been applied to intimate interpersonal relationships, the theories offer important insight into how teacher–student relationships evolve over time.

Managing two aspects of communication, breadth and depth, are central to relationship development (Altman & Taylor, 1973; Knapp, 1978). Breadth refers to the number of different topical areas available during communication. As teachers get to know students, they learn about their family situations, their extracurricular interests, their academic strengths and weaknesses. Depth refers to how much information a person has about a particular topic. A teacher may learn that a student's mother, who is recently divorced, is starting to date someone the child does not like. When the child reveals how he or she feels about this circumstance, the dialogue involves more depth. It is not uncommon for teachers to learn a great deal from a student when they discuss the reasons homework was not turned in on time, why a student seems lethargic, or why a student misbehaves. Over time the number of topics and opportunities to explore them increase.

Communication changes in other ways over time. Knapp and Vangelisti (1996) stated that communication shifts along eight primary dimensions. Communication in developing relationships becomes more:

- *Broad*—more topics are discussed in more depth.
- *Unique*—people are viewed as unique individuals rather than in stereotyped roles.
- *Efficient*—accuracy, speed, and efficiency of communication increase as a relationship develops.
- *Flexible*—the number of different ways an idea or feeling can be communicated verbally and nonverbally increases.
- *Smooth*—the ability to predict the other's behavior increases so that there is greater synchrony in interaction.
- *Personal*—people reveal more about themselves, such as fears, feelings, likes, and dislikes.
- *Spontaneous*—informality and comfort increase and we feel less hesitant about how to react, what topics to discuss, and how much can be said about a topic.
- *Overt*—praise and criticism are less inhibited as a relationship grows.

According to Knapp and Vangelisti (1996), as relationships start to unravel or deteriorate, communication becomes narrow, stylized, difficult, rigid, awkward, public, and hesitant, and judgments are suspended. Teachers frequently have difficulty with one or more students. Communication at the unraveling stage may be strained, difficult, and awkward. Sometimes, teachers search for ways to reconnect and even start over, but they find that such attempts are difficult if not impossible. Because the relational reservoir is not particularly deep in teacher–student relationships, damage or hurt can have severe consequences.

Knapp (1978) explicated several stages that mark the development of intimate relationships. In his theory, relationships go through a linear progression of stages. His theory can be extended to the teacher–student relationships. The stages we believe are applicable to teacher–student interactions are initiating, experimenting, intensifying, differentiating, and dissolving. It is important to note that teachers and students go through the stages at different rates. Some relationships develop rapidly whereas others trudge along and seem locked in one place.

Initiating

The first relationship stage we enter is initiating. As a popular television ad states, "We don't get a second chance at a first impression." The moment students walk into the classroom, teachers start to form impressions that in many cases are difficult to change. In turn, students develop expectations based on limited data. They respond to the teacher's nonverbal behavior (does he or she smile and seem approachable and enthusiastic?), they respond to the way a teacher explains the academic goals for the semester or year (will they be hard or easy?), and they respond to the organization of the classroom (does it feel inviting?).

Friedrich and Cooper (1999) discussed the importance of the first day of class and provided strategies for managing it. They argued that early meetings play an important role in initiating students to the knowledge and skills they will need to successfully perform the role of student in a particular context. Students also obtain a great deal of information about the teacher's affective orientation to the class. A smiling and expressive teacher is perceived to be friendly and a frowning neutral teacher is considered mean or grumpy. These first impressions play an important role in the trajectories of teacher–student relationships.

Experimenting

A second stage of development is experimenting. During this stage teachers and students try to identify common ground and locate points of difference. In the experimenting stage, teachers start to obtain information about the student that might influence a teaching strategy. For example, teachers may ask students about their favorite hobbies, activities, and family situations. These conversations sometimes occur during class discussion, in a student conference, or during recess. The information obtained in these exchanges provides data that are used to form impressions about students and help shape subsequent communication behavior.

Similarly, students *experiment* with teachers. Students try to sort out teacher likes and dislikes, real rather than professed boundaries (if you give a real good excuse he will let you turn in late work), and their grading biases. In Chapter 3 we discussed ways teachers can gain and use cultural knowledge. Obtaining this information and testing its use relates to the experimenting stage of development. In many ways, elements of experimenting exist throughout the academic year as students and teachers explore ways to manage their relationships.

Intensifying

As students and teachers obtain more depth and breadth in their interactions, their relationship moves to an intensifying stage. This label is most suited for romantic partners, but the communication reflected in this stage is illustrative of teacher–student interactions as well. During this stage participants make communication choices based on psychological rather than sociological information. That is, the communicators make choices based on the individual rather than stereotypic roles. It is in this stage that teachers start to communicate authentic care for the students and the circumstances that enhance and constrain learning.

According to Knapp (1978), there are several features of the intensifying stage. In romantic relationships, forms of address become more informal, use of first-personal plural becomes more common, private jargon may be used, verbal shortcuts built on background information may be used, and more direct expressions of commitment may be employed.

Differentiating

Over time, as participants learn more about each other, they may determine that they really don't care for the other person very much. Even though it is socially inappropriate to admit it, the fact remains that teachers sometimes dislike some of their students and students may come to dislike their teachers. In this stage participants try to distance themselves physically and emotionally. The most obvious indicator of differentiating is conflict. Teachers will sometimes say, "It's like pulling teeth to get her to work" or "He argues about every assignment I give." Students may argue that they do not do well in class because they have a personality conflict with the teacher. Every teacher has a story about a difficult student and every student has had a teacher they felt was Cruella De Ville. Unfortunately, this stage is particularly problematic for learning. The negative feelings accompanying this stage affect students' motivation and willingness to learn. Students avoid the teacher and the teacher avoids the student; as a consequence, learning is compromised.

Dissolving

The final stage is dissolving. In this stage the formal teacher–student relationship is severed. There are several ways this occurs. In some cases, a teacher–student relationship becomes so problematic that the student is removed from the class. A student may be moved because he or she has special learning needs the teacher is not prepared to address or accommodate. A third form of dissolution is matriculation. Each year a class is ushered to the next grade. Even for students who are not passed, it is unlikely that they will have the same teacher.

Even though the formal teacher–student relationship can be dissolved (the teacher no longer has the student in class), the interpersonal relationship does not evaporate. Rather, the teacher–student relationship is redefined. Teachers and students cannot erase the history they shared and the way they affected each other. As students move to the next level or transfer to another school, they take a part of that teacher with them. Many students return to their teachers many years later to praise their efforts. When these relationships rekindle, they do not start from scratch but are based on the history and events that were shared.

The developmental perspective advanced by Knapp (1978) helps teachers understand some of the ways their relationships with students develop and change over time. Teacher–student relationships may not follow the linear progression explicated by Knapp; however, the communication that characterizes these stages does appear in teacher–student relationships. Teachers worry about the ways to start the school year positively (initiating), try different teaching strategies (experimenting), delight when they feel a special connection with a student (intensifying), and obsess when they have conflicts that seem to have no end (differentiating). Knapp's perspective provides one view of the developmental features of the teacher-studentteacher–student relationship; other theorists have looked at this relationship from different perspectives.

Reflection

- Think about a teacher you've had that you had a conflict with. Describe the stages of development in this relationship conflict. How did this conflict affect your performance in the classroom?
- How did your communication with the teacher change over time? Was it more spontaneous and unique?
- What did the teacher do to learn about the interests of his/her students?

Relational Dialectics

Relational dialectics, initially advanced by Leslie Baxter (1987, 1988, 1990, 1992, 1993) and her colleagues (Dindia & Baxter, 1987; Rawlins, 1992, 2000), proposes that in every relationship there are contradictory tensions, and the way individuals deal with these tensions influences the way in which the relationship evolves. The key features of dialectical theory are *contradiction* and *process*. Contradiction is conflict between two opposing forces, such as the desire for closeness and the desire for distance. People in long-term relationships know about the need to "have space" and the need to be close and connected. The need for space finds its meaning through its opposite, the need for connection.

The second feature of dialectical theory is process. Like our theory of communication, relationships are fluid and always in a state of adjustment. Participants continually struggle and work through tensions through communication and other symbolic activities.

Researchers have identified three relational dialectics: *integration/separation*, *stability/change*, and *expression/privacy*. The *integration/separation* dialectic involves the tension between wanting to integrate with another person and wanting to be separate from others. The *stability/change* dialectic involves the tension between wanting predictability and wanting novelty or stimulation. The final dialectic involves the desire to be *open/expressive* on one hand and private and reserved on the other.

William Rawlins (2000) applied the theory of relational dialectics to the instructional context. Specifically, he used a dialectic perspective to explore teaching as a mode of friendship. According to Rawlins, friendship consists of affection, equality, and mutuality.

Affection means caring about and for others. Rawlins (2000) stated, "We can care deeply and significantly about students without desiring an exclusive, intimate connection with them, either as a close friendship that might imply unwarranted favoritism, or as a sexual relationship that involves exploitation and abuse of power differences" (p. 6). Rawlins contended that in the instructional context, affection is concerned with the classical tradition of *philia*, a posture concerned with good will and helping the other prosper. With good will come respect and a concern for the student to do well.

Equality is the second facet of friendship and is more problematic for the teacher–student relationship. Teachers are considered authorities on most issues that touch classroom life. Theoretically they have more knowledge of content and are in positions of power. For Rawlins, however, it is not necessary to exercise these power differences. Rather, teaching as friendship attempts to minimize status differences and create an atmosphere in which all can learn. Teachers can learn a great deal when they open themselves to the world of students.

The final feature of friendship is mutuality. This aspect of friendship follows from the previous ones. According to Rawlins (2000), learning is promoted when teachers and students "create an enterprise of co-learning." Mutuality occurs when teachers and students recognize their interdependency in the pursuit of academic goals. For example, when a teacher acknowledges and thanks a student for proposing a new way of solving a math problem he or she is demonstrating co-learning.

Rawlins (2000) outlined four dialectical tensions that characterize interaction between teachers and students in the context of educational friendship. The first is the dialectic of freedom to be independent and freedom to be dependent. The degree to which educators direct and the degree to which students are allowed to discover have been historical issues. Individuals typically have freedom to choose friendship, but such volition is constrained in the educational context. Teaching as friendship entails cultivating a student's independence in thought and action while being available to provide expertise and guidance when necessary.

Rawlins acknowledged that some students should not be pushed into independence when they are not ready for it. The degree of independence that is appropriate depends on the grade level and the amount of competence the student has to complete the given task. However, the sense of independence and accountability also fosters attitudes of accountability and ownership—important features of academic success.

The second dialectic involves affection and instrumentality. Most teachers will admit they want their students to like them but this is not the only goal that teachers should seek. Rawlins (2000) cautioned teachers not to be too hard on students they like, to guard against the perception of favoritism or being too easy on them because they feel they deserve the benefit of the doubt. Similarly, teachers should not be too hard on students with whom they have not established good will. Teachers ought not give themselves permission to dislike students without giving students permission to dislike teachers. The key here is that the way in which teachers manage this dialectic influences how safe students feel to take risks and develop new competencies.

The third dialectic is concerned with judgment and acceptance. Teachers must balance feedback about how they feel about a student as a person with how the student completes an instructional task. This is perhaps one of the most difficult dialectic tensions to manage. Students may misread the fun, expressive teacher as one who does not have high academic standards and is overly flexible on requirements. Teachers who have the best interests of the student at heart have high expectations but are flexible in how they are obtained.

The fourth dialectic is concerned with expressiveness and protectiveness. On one hand, being open and expressive in pursuing knowledge is important, but so is discretion and respect. One university professor loved to put students on the spot in seminars. He played a game called "shooting fish in a barrel." He required students to give reports on a research article. After the report, the professor would "shoot" question after question at the student with the goal of showing the class that the student did not understand the article, thus requiring the sage professor to explain it. The professor was verbally aggressive as he challenged students to respond to his questions. This strategy did little to foster interest in the topic but much to create anxiety and anger. A thoughtful teacher helps create trust and comfort so students do not feel overly vulnerable about what they do not know nor too smug in what they do.

Relational dialectics provide a useful perspective for understanding the daily strains of interpersonal relationships. Rawlins's notion of teaching as a mode of friendship is particularly interesting. Effective teachers manage relationships that promote the best interests of the students they teach. These teachers recognize that the teacher–student relationship establishes a context that facilitates learning and motivation. The next section of this chapter reviews five major constructs that positively influence the teacher–student relationship. Teacher immediacy, affinity seeking, self-disclosure, humor, and credibility impact the development of a positive teacher–student relationship.

Reflection

- How do you feel about Rawlins's framework?
- In your experience, which dialectical tension was most difficult to manage?
- What did you and the teacher do to resolve the tension?

Teacher Immediacy

Teacher immediacy was introduced in Chapter 2 and has a profound effect on the teacher–student relationship. Immediacy consists of the verbal and nonverbal behaviors that reduce psychological distance. Smiling, eye contact, touch, a relaxed body orientation, and close physical proximity are examples of nonverbal immediacy behaviors. Addressing students by name, using appropriate humor, using personal examples, and referring to the class as "my class" are examples of verbal immediacy behaviors. Although the thrust of research on teacher immediacy has attempted to assess its role in motivation and learning, we agree with Hess and Smythe (2001), who argued that its function is primarily relational.

One consistent finding is that teacher immediacy promotes affective learning—the feelings students have about the instructor and course content. Nonverbal immediacy appears to play a significant role in the feelings the students have about the teacher and the course. Richmond (2002), a leading scholar on teacher immediacy, argued as follows:

> The primary function of teachers' nonverbal behavior in the classroom is to improve affect or liking for the subject matter, teacher, and class, and to increase the desire to learn more about the subject matter. One step toward this is the development of a positive affective relationship between the student and the teacher. When the teacher improves affect

> through effective nonverbal behavior, then the student is likely to listen more, learn more, and have a more positive attitude about the school. (p. 70)

The research conducted on immediacy shows that it is positively associated with a number of affective factors that unfold in the classroom. Students who view a teacher as approachable may feel more comfortable in the learning situation, may be more inclined to listen to instructional material, and may be more comfortable seeking clarification on information they do not understand. Frymier and Houser (2000) found that immediacy was positively correlated with two important communication skills: referential skill and ego support. Referential skill is concerned with explaining content and ego support is how teachers meet student needs. The way in which a teacher explains instructional material is mediated by immediacy. This finding is consistent with Powell and Harville (1990), who found that immediacy was related to teacher clarity, especially for students from Latin and Asian backgrounds. Immediacy may help teachers give form to important instructional contexts. Also, the immediate teacher may be more psychologically connected to students. During instructional episodes immediate teachers may consistently assess student feedback and adjust instructional messages to meet their needs.

Research by Baringer and McCroskey (2000) investigated the effects of student immediacy on teachers. The authors reasoned that using nonverbal behavior is one way students indicate they are accurately receiving information and are positively disposed to it. The authors examined the effects of student immediacy and found that teachers are more positively disposed to students who engage in immediacy behaviors and are more motivated to teach them.

It is important to emphasize that immediacy involves implicit codes. Therefore, maximum effects will occur when teachers interpret the immediacy cues in the same way. Difficulty will arise when implicit codes are misinterpreted, not acknowledged, or inconsistent. An immediate teacher may be perceived as easy or less rigorous. Students may believe a teacher they like will accept late work or give them the benefit of the doubt. Other difficulties can arise when the immediate teacher fails a student or is critical of an assignment. In addition, because most of the studies are correlational, it is difficult to sort out the causal direction of the effects. Do the positive effects start with the student, the teacher, or some combination of both? Our belief is that teachers who exhibit immediacy behaviors will foster positive relationships, which in turn will promote positive attitudes about learning.

Affinity Seeking

As the above research suggests, liking is an important part of a positive relationship. Montalvo, Mansfield, and Miller (2007) have shown that students are likely to exercise more effort and task persistence if they like their teachers.

In addition, their findings indicate that students attain better grades in classes taught by teachers they like. Researchers have examined the strategies teachers use to get students to like them. Bell and Daly (1984) developed a typology of the strategies individuals use to generate liking that have been extended to the classroom context. Richmond (1990), for example, identified five affinity-seeking strategies that influence motivation and affective and cognitive learning in the classroom, such as facilitating enjoyment, assuming control, exhibiting nonverbal immediacy, showing optimism, and confirming the student's self-concept. For a complete list of affinity-seeking strategies, see Table 6.1.

Frymier & Thompson (1992) investigated the relationship between affinity seeking and credibility and found that nonverbal immediacy was significantly related to perceptions of teacher character. This dimension of credibility is concerned with how much a person is liked, respected, and admired. Immediacy appears to increase the positive regard for the teacher, which in turn may influence student attitudes about learning.

Frymier (1994) built on the previous research and proposed a causal model of affinity seeking, liking, and learning. A causal model charts the direction and strength of a set of variables. Frymier (1994) contended that affinity-seeking strategies increase liking, which in turn impacts motivation and learning. Frymier (1994) found that the use of affinity seeking had a significant effect on the degree to which students liked their teachers. The strategies most predictive of liking were *assuming equality* (teacher does not appear superior), *dynamism* (teacher is active and enthusiastic), and *facilitating enjoyment* (teacher develops a classroom environment that is enjoyable). Six other strategies were associated with liking and motivation: *comfortable self* (the teacher is at ease and relaxed), *concede control* (the teacher allows students to control the relationship), *conversational rule-keeping* (teacher is polite and follows rules for appropriate conversation), *elicit other's disclosure* (teacher inquires about student's interests) *nonverbal immediacy* (teacher signals liking and interest), and *optimism* (teacher presents a positive outlook). Frymier (1994) argued that teachers' improved interpersonal relationships help motivate students to work on instructional tasks.

Wanzer (1998) explored the strategies students use to engender liking from an instructor. She also examined how instructors respond to the strategies students use. Students were asked to identify five examples of the ways they get a teacher to like them. Sixty-six percent of the responses fell into five categories: conversational rule keeping (19 percent), nonverbal immediacy (13 percent), eliciting disclosure (13 percent), requirements (11 percent), and self-inclusion (10 percent).

Teacher perceptions of student strategies fell into five categories that accounted for 53 percent of the total responses. Teachers viewed students using self-inclusion (16 percent), conversational rule keeping (14 percent), achievement (8 percent), eliciting other's self-disclosures (8 percent), and self-concept confirmation (7.5 percent).

Table 6.1 Affinity-Seeking Strategies

1. Altruism: The affinity seeker strives to be of assistance to the target in whatever she or he is currently doing.
2. Assume Control: The affinity seeker presents himself or herself as a person who has control over whatever is going on.
3. Assume Equality. The affinity seeker strikes a posture of social equality with the target.
4. Comfortable Self. The affinity seeker ignores annoying environmental distractions, seeking to convey a "nothing bothers me" impression.
5. Concede Control. The affinity seeker allows the target to assume control over relational activities.
6. Conversational Rule Keeping. The affinity seeker adheres closely to cultural rules for polite, cooperative interaction with the target.
7. Dynamism. The affinity seeker presents herself or himself as an active, enthusiastic person.
8. Elicit Other's Disclosures. The affinity seeker encourages the target to talk by reinforcing the target's conversational contributions.
9. Facilitate Enjoyment. The affinity seeker tries to maximize the positiveness of relational encounters with the target.
10. Inclusion of Other. The affinity seeker enthusiastically participates in an activity the target is known to enjoy.
11. Influence Perceptions of Closeness. The affinity seeker engages in behaviors that cause the target to perceive the relationship as closer than it actually has been.
12. Listening. The affinity seeker listens actively and attentively to the target.
13. Nonverbal immediacy. The affinity seeker signals interest in the target through various nonverbal cues.
14. Openness. The affinity seeker discloses personal information to the target.
15. Optimism. The affinity seeker presents himself or herself to the target as a positive person.
16. Personal Autonomy. The affinity seeker presents herself or himself to the target as an independent, free-thinking person.
17. Physical Attractiveness. The affinity seeker tries to look and dress as attractively as possible in the presence of the target.
18. Present Interesting Self. The affinity seeker presents herself or himself to the target as someone who would be interesting to know.
19. Reward Association. The affinity seeker presents himself or herself in such a way that the target perceives the affinity seeker can reward the target for associating with him or her.
20. Self-Concept Confirmation. The affinity seeker demonstrates respect for the target and helps the target to "feel good" about himself or herself.
21. Self-Inclusion. The affinity seeker arranges the environment so as to come into frequent contact with the target.
22. Sensitivity. The affinity seeker acts in a warm, empathic manner toward the target.
23. Similarity. The affinity seeker seeks to convince the target that the two of them share many similar tastes and attitudes.
24. Supportiveness. The affinity seeker supports the target in the latter's social encounters.
25. Trustworthiness. The affinity seeker consistently fulfills commitments made to the target.

Although the data on teacher immediacy and affinity seeking is overwhelmingly positive, there are some additional issues to consider. The bulk of the research has been conducted on young adults in university or college settings. The studies have been based on self-report data. Few observational or experimental studies have been conducted. Status differences and relationship expectations are not the same at this level as they are in elementary, middle, and high school. Although we have reason to believe that immediacy and affinity seeking are also important to younger students, their role in learning and attitudes about instruction may be different from those in older audiences.

Also, the research has not explicated all the consequences of being perceived as approachable. In some cases, a student may perceive that an approachable teacher will accept an excuse for not turning in work on time. An approachable teacher might be expected to give students the benefit of the doubt or not grade as rigorously. Uncertainty is created when the interpersonal behavior does not seem to match the instructional behavior.

Self-Disclosure

One of the processes central to management of interpersonal relationships is self-disclosure. Cooper and Simmonds (1999) argued that self-disclosure is necessary for effective teacher–student interactions. Self-disclosure occurs when someone reveals something of himself or herself that the other person would not know unless disclosed. Through direct comments, stories, and illustrations, teachers reveal themselves to students. These revelations, in turn influence relationships with students, which influence how students feel about the content. Several investigators have explored the effects of self-disclosure in the instructional context. Nussbaum and Scott (1979) were among the first to investigate the role of self-disclosure in instructional relationships; they found that the perception of honesty in disclosure had the most positive effect. Downs, Javidi, and Nussbaum (1988) found that award-winning teachers tended to use moderate amounts of self-disclosure. Further, the disclosures of these teachers were relevant to course content or utilized for the purpose of clarifying course material. When teachers over-disclose or share information that is unrelated to the course, self-disclosure may have more negative consequences. At one university, students frequently complained about a professor who spent an inordinate amount of time discussing the difficulties in her personal life. Although the students did not dislike the professor, they did feel that the class was becoming a waste of time.

Sorensen (1989) investigated how the management of self-disclosure differentiated good and poor teachers. She found that good teachers were more likely to engage in disclosure statements reflecting a concern for students. Evaluative disclosures or ones reflecting a negative outlook were reflective of poor teachers. These types of messages were also related to affective learning. Positive disclosures positively impacted affective learning whereas negative ones did not. Culture plays a significant role in self-disclosure. Individuals from individualistic cultures are the most likely candidates for self-disclosure because explicitness and revelation are part of their cultural experience. Students from Euro-American backgrounds will probably disclose the most in a class. Students from high-context cultures are less likely to engage in self-disclosure. Native-Americans, Asians, and Latinos are less likely to engage in self-disclosure or feel that it is appropriate. Effective use of self-disclosure requires that teachers be attentive to students. When teachers use self-disclosure statements to help illustrate a concept or reveal a struggle or difficulty learning a concept, the disclosure is likely to have positive effects. Disclosures about personal life issues are more problematic and risky.

During class discussions and in individual meetings or conferences, teachers need to be attentive to the role of culture. Students from high-context cultures may be less willing to volunteer information or reciprocate when the teacher discloses. One of the least effective strategies a teacher can use is to demand that students reveal something they are uncomfortable sharing.

Humor

In our judgment a sense of humor is a powerful tool for promoting positive relationships in the classroom. Whether students are in kindergarten or college, they respond positively to teachers who can make them laugh as well as laugh at themselves. Humor appears to be a cross-cultural phenomenon. Kluver (1990) found that a sense of humor was the most frequently ranked characteristic of effective teachers in China. Through humor, important connections, both affectively and cognitively, are made.

Meyer (2000) contended that humor has four major functions. The first two serve to create connections and the second serve to differentiate and create distance. The first connecting function is identification. Humor can be used to link speakers with their audiences, which helps create group cohesiveness. For example, when teachers make fun at themselves, they lower their personal status while raising the status of the students. Humor that reduces tension and reveals that the teacher is also human increases the connection between teacher and student.

A second connecting function is clarification. Humor that is used to encapsulate a view or idea may result in more clarity. Meyer noted that ideas referenced in memorable stories or phrases may lead to greater recall. Humorous stories, because they are frequently presented incongruously or unexpectedly, make the receiver do a bit more cognitive work, which influences recall of information.

A third function of humor, according to Meyer, is enforcement. Humor can be used to level criticisms while maintaining some degree of identification with the audience. Teachers frequently use this type of humor to reinforce class rules and expectations for normative behaviors. Students may ask a teacher to repeat instructions for a task because they were talking to a neighbor and not paying attention. A teacher may use any number of humorous statements to comment on the students' lack of attention.

The final function Meyer discussed is differentiation. People use humor to contrast their views with the views of others. Humor of this kind is frequently revealed in political humor. In the classroom, humor of this type may come in the form of sarcasm or teasing. One professor with a class full of athletes once claimed the phrase "scholar athlete" was an oxymoron. She asked one member of the class if he was a student or an athlete because he did not have the skills to be both. Needless to say, her "humor" did little to connect the student with the teacher or the class. However, when humor is used effectively, positive outcomes can be achieved.

Pollack and Freda (1997) outline six positive effects of teacher humor in the middle school context. Their recommendations apply to a broad range of instructional settings. The first is *building rapport.* Teachers who can laugh at themselves and with their students shape a climate in which students are more willing to work together on instructional tasks. Students like teachers who can laugh. The second is *empowering* learners. Humor helps level status differences and create a culture of learners. Teachers frequently make mistakes and the degree to which these "errors" are dealt with through humor models appropriate behavior for students. Teachers who want to passionately hold on to the mantle of authority do not do much to create positive learning environments. The third is *thinking creatively*. Creative thinking requires individuals to see things from different perspectives. Humor is a way to sort through the incongruous or incompatible, which in turn promotes problem solving.

The fourth is *creating interest.* Humor serves to increase arousal and attention. Students tend to remember content and lessons that are presented in an exciting and humorous way. The fifth is *enhancing self-esteem*. Teachers can help students laugh at themselves, discover realistic expectations, and promote a willingness to work through difficult situations. Teachers with no sense of humor are perceived to be rigid and their students perceive they have little room to make mistakes. The final feature is *emphasizing socialization.* A good sense of humor can help teachers turn a tense situation into a challenging, intriguing one. Humor helps students discover appropriate models of behavior and helps establish a sense of "intellectual humility." Humor can do much to engender the joy of learning.

Several attempts have been made to categorize teacher humor (Bryant, Comisky, & Zillmannn, 1979; Gorham & Christophel, 1990; Nussbaum, Comadena, & Holladay, 1985). Neuliep (1991), for example, developed a taxonomy of high school teachers' humor. He asked high school teachers to assess their humor using the taxonomy developed by Gorham and Christophel. The teachers were also asked to indicate how frequently they used humor and their reasons for using humor. Finally, teachers were asked to describe their last attempt at humor.

Based on the responses, Neuliep (1991) developed a 20-item taxonomy of humor consisting of five major sections: (a) teacher-targeted humor, (b) student-target humor, (c) untargeted humor, (d) external source humor, and (e) nonverbal humor.

- *Teacher-targeted humor.* The teacher is the object of humor. Three types of teacher-targeted humor emerged. One type involves the teacher self-disclosing personal information that may be related to the course content, not related to the course content, or of an embarrassing nature. The second form of teacher-targeted humor involves role playing by the teacher. A teacher imitating a public figure is an example of this type of humor. The final type of teacher-targeted humor is the use of self-deprecating humor through which the teacher pokes fun at himself or herself.
- *Student-targeted humor.* The student is the target of this type of humor. Four types of student-targeted humor emerged. The first involves a teacher making fun of a student's mistake. A second involves teasing in a non-hostile or friendly fashion. The third type of student-targeted humor involves the teacher insulting the student in a non-hostile manner. The final type of humor involves student role playing.
- *Untargeted humor.* The third type of humor is untargeted. The focus of the humor is not a teacher or student, but an issue or topic. Three types of untargeted humor were identified. One involves an awkward comparison or incongruity. For example, one teacher likened the sword fight between Tybalt and Romeo to a WWF wrestling match. The teacher blended Shakespearean language with wrestling jargon to make his point. The second type of untargeted humor is telling a joke. The joke may or may not be related to the topic being studied. A third type of untargeted humor entails a play on words or a pun. The final type of untargeted humor was labeled tongue-in-cheek or facetious humor. This type of humor involves witty remarks by the teacher that are not directed at the student or the teacher.
- *External source humor.* External source humor requires the teacher to draw upon a source other than the teacher or the student. One type of external source humor is to relate some historical event to something the students find humorous. For example, numerous comedians made fun of the ballot counting process during the 2000 presidential campaign. A second type of external source humor is to utilize cartoons, photos, or editorials that have humorous intent. Calvin and Hobbs was a popular comic strip that revealed many of life's difficulties and dilemmas. In the final type of external source humor, the teacher demonstrates some natural phenomenon in a way the class finds amusing. Neuliep (1991) used the example of a teacher releasing a balloon to demonstrate high versus low pressure.
- *Nonverbal humor.* Nonverbal humor entails affect displays and kinetic humor. Using a funny face or other types of gestures to accentuate a point, or

using your body to mock or illustrate something, are examples of this type of humor.

Civikly (1992b) provided five guidelines for the use and assessment of teacher humor:

> 1. Review and assess how humor has been used in the class. Placement of a tape recorder in an unobtrusive location while teaching is simple and review of the tape can provide excellent feedback.
> 2. Analyze and assess the classroom atmosphere. Each class develops distinctive norms and relational bases.
> 3. Identify humor styles comfortable for you. There is a wide range of choices from which to select: stories and anecdotes, puns, riddles, limericks, cartoons and visuals, understatement and exaggeration, impersonation, mime, teasing, satire, witticisms, jokes on oneself, and political humor.
> 4. Work on "planned spontaneity" of instructional humor. This involves doing some preparation of examples and incidents the students see as relevant and humorous and then presenting these in a spontaneous manner.
> 5. Evaluate the humor developed and used. Watch for student reactions and ask for feedback regarding their interest, attentions, liking, and comprehension of the material presented . . . Use this feedback to direct use of humor in class and refine any rough edges that may be identified. (p. 137)

The research indicates that there are numerous advantages to using humor in the classroom. Although we do not advocate that teachers attempt to be stand-up comedians, we do believe humor should be integrated into teaching. Appropriate humor is the key, however. Humor for humor's sake, tasteless and off-color jokes, hostile teasing, and mocking have no place in the classroom. Teachers also need to be aware of the cultural factors influencing humor. Humor is inextricably defined by context (the "I guess you had to be there" phenomenon) and students from some cultures may not have the background information necessary to understand the joke. To test this notion, ask a student from a culture different from yours to tell a story or joke from his or her native orientation. Then ask the student to explain why the example is humorous. This exercise should illustrate how context influences humor.

Teacher Credibility

The last concept we believe is important to the teacher–student relationship is credibility. We typically apply the concept of credibility to political or legal contexts, yet the principles have a great deal of application to instructional settings. Two primary dimensions are related to teacher credibility: competence and character. Competence refers to content knowledge that the teacher possesses. Character refers to the trustworthiness of the person.

The interplay of competence and character appear to be important in the classroom as well. At lower grades, many students are most concerned about the social characteristics of the teacher. One second-grader indicated that she wanted to be placed in Ms. West's class because Ms. West is nice. Even in college, students seek instructors who have positive personal characteristics. Content competence is seldom the only factor influencing the choice to enroll in a particular class. At the same time, students form judgments about how well teachers present instructional information, clarify instructional goals, and criticize student work. These judgments also influence the perception of teacher credibility.

Frymier and Thompson (1992) investigated the relationship between affinity-seeking strategies and credibility and found that affinity seeking was positively related to the character dimension of credibility and moderately related to the competence dimension. The authors acknowledged that it is possible to view someone as competent but not likeable. Teaching effectiveness is enhanced when the teacher is judged highly on both dimensions. Frymier and Thompson identified 12 strategies that relate to both character and competence:

- *Listening*—paying close attention to what the student says and querying to ascertain if the student's intended meaning is the interpreted meaning;
- *Facilitating enjoyment*—developing a classroom environment that is enjoyable, an environment in which learning is both interesting and entertaining;
- *Dynamism*—physically indicating to students that one is dynamic, active, and enthusiastic via physical and vocal animation;
- *Eliciting others' disclosure*—inquiring about students' interests and opinions and providing positive reinforcement for responses;
- *Optimism*—presenting a positive outlook and one's self as someone who is pleasant to be around, someone who will not be self-critical or critical of others;
- *Sensitivity*—communicating empathy, sympathy, and an "I care about you as a person, what you think about" attitude;
- *Conversational rule keeping*—following the cultural norms for socializing, being polite; demonstrating interest in what the student says;
- *Comfortable self*—displaying a confidence in the setting, in oneself, in the students, and presenting self as a relaxed, contented individual;
- *Nonverbal immediacy*—smiling, making frequent eye contact with students, exhibiting forward leans and other nonverbal cues indicating interest;

- *Altruism*—attempting to be of assistance to the student by doing things for her or him and giving advice;
- *Presenting interesting self*—highlighting past accomplishments and positive qualities and demonstrating one's knowledge;
- *Trustworthiness*—letting the student know that as a teacher he or she is responsible, reliable, fair, honest, sincere, consistent in beliefs, and behaviors, and will fulfill promises.

Collectively these behaviors appear to shape a global judgment that a teacher is both knowledgeable and caring.

Teven and Hanson (2004) conducted two studies to assess the effects of teacher caring and teacher immediacy on teacher credibility. Subjects were asked to respond to four hypothetical scenarios that manipulated immediacy and caring: high immediacy/high verbal caring, low immediacy/high verbal caring, low immediacy/low verbal caring, and high immediacy/low verbal caring. They found that credibility was positively related to teacher immediacy. The authors argued that the findings strongly indicate that teachers who display caring and immediacy will be perceived as more competent and trustworthy.

Reflection

- Which affinity-seeking strategies are you likely to use in the classroom?
- What type of humor do you find most effective? Least effective?
- How does self-disclosure promote clarity and understanding?

Strategies for Developing Positive Teacher–Student Relationships

We reviewed literature documenting the significant academic and social benefits for students of positive teacher–student relationships and concluded that it is essential for teachers to find ways to establish positive relationships with their students. Both teachers and students identify positive relationships as the core of what effective teachers do (Good & Brophy, 2000; Larrivee, 2005). There appears to be some agreement among researchers as to best practices for classroom teachers to use to develop relationships with their students. The following section focuses on some strategies that, although not exhaustive, we believe to be effective and that are connected to the literature we have examined.

1. *Know your students as individuals (relationship stages).* Knowing and pronouncing your students' names correctly is first on the agenda. This signifies to each student that he or she is important to you. When you mispronounce students' names or refer to them as "you," they are likely

to believe you don't respect or value them as individuals. Learning all your students' names can be done. Making it a priority is the first step to making it happen. We recommend using roll call to not only learn students' names, but to learn more about each student. Ask students what name they prefer to be called and write it down in your roll book. Some teachers include photos of their students on their personal Web page.

The use of seating charts that require students to sit in the same place each class can help teachers learn names. Using students' names frequently when they ask or answer questions and referring to their comments or questions in a later discussion will help in remembering names and also is affirming to individual students. Learning students' names is an important step toward establishing a respectful teacher–student relationship.

2. *Share information about yourself (positive self-disclosure).* You might begin by introducing yourself through a letter. You can read it aloud to your students and send it home. Share where you're from, where you've lived previously, your educational background, and why you chose the teaching path. Share your vision and expectations for the classroom. End your letter by encouraging your students and their parents to let you know if they have questions or concerns. Let them know how and when they can contact you. Use self-disclosure to support the explanation of academic content.

   You may share information about your family, pets, hobbies, etc. There was a great Calvin and Hobbes cartoon in which Calvin was at the grocery store with his mother over the summer. Calvin saw his teacher, Mrs. Wormwood, one aisle over at the store. Calvin looked surprised and said to his mother, "Look, that's Mrs. Wormwood." Calvin's mother responded, "Why are you so surprised, Calvin?" Calvin says, "I thought she slept in a coffin all summer until school started up again." Students appreciate knowing you have a life outside the classroom, just as they do.

3. *Give students a voice in the classroom.* Giving students a voice in the classroom helps us to help students learn. Dahl (1995) talked about student voice being an expression of a much deeper part of an individual: "Voice is as distinctive as a fingerprint" (p. 125). Recall our earlier discussion about dialogue. When students feel they can add to classroom conversations, they are more likely to be engaged. According to O'Loughlin (1995), students "are storied human beings interpreting their lives through their ethnicity, gender, class and culture" (p. 110). They live their lives as narratives that reflect their upbringing. "Rather than possessing one voice, students construct multiple perspectives on their emerging identities as a result of the social and economic communities" (p. 111). Writing is an excellent way to enable students to use their voices. Read what your students write and give encouraging feedback. Students often tell us about things in their writing that they might not tell us otherwise. Weekly teacher–student meetings and class discussions also allow students to express their feelings and concerns. One teacher asked a student who was in a wheelchair to

explain to the class her experiences and what she needed from her colleagues in the class.

4. *Listen.* Listening to the voice of students provides benefits to both students and teachers. Students develop ownership and responsibility for their education and teachers gain new understandings and insights from listening to students' voices. Listening is a very important and critical skill for understanding, bonding, and supporting students to be successful. Awareness and acceptance of what students have to say leads to student involvement in the curriculum and classroom activities.

   Through listening to the voice of students, we can learn a great deal about what matters to them. In our conversations with students, we hear that they feel important when teachers use their name, when teachers take the time to listen to what they have to say, when teachers ask about their activities outside of school, or when they see the interests they have shared with their teachers acknowledged in the classroom.

5. *Encourage resilience.* Resilience is one's ability to bounce back from adversity. Much has been written about the resilient child who, despite many difficult challenges, is able to bounce back. Sagor (1996) talked about the need for educators to provide all students, and especially those at risk, with a "resiliency antibody." Resilience research in education identifies three protective factors that minimize risks and promote student involvement, interest, and competency, helping students succeed in school. Those protective factors are: establishing caring relationships with students, conveying high expectations, and providing opportunities for meaningful participation in classroom activities (Truebridge, 2010). Werner and Smith (1982) suggested that the most important protective factor for students is a trusting and supportive relationship with an adult who accepts them unconditionally. The adult could be a teacher, counselor, or another adult who serves as a role model. Teachers must provide opportunities in each child's daily routine for the child to experience feelings of competence, belonging, usefulness, potency, and optimism. Sagor suggested that certain activities could help students develop resilience (e.g., mastery learning, authentic assessment, learning style-friendly instruction, cooperative learning, service learning, problem-solving approaches to discipline, and goal setting).

Reflection

- Observe a classroom teacher or, if you have your own classroom, have a peer observe and document your positive and negative comments to students in the classroom. What did you learn from this observation?
- Identify some specific ways teachers can build positive relationships with their students.

Partnering With Families

Establishing a good relationship with parents and/or family members is important to the success of all students. Parents come from varied ethnic/racial and socioeconomic backgrounds. They bring a day-to-day understanding of their children that, as teachers, we may not have. Their perspectives on the goals of education for their children are important for teachers to understand. It is important for teachers to encourage parents/families to be partners in the education of their children.

Research links parent involvement to both academic and social success of children in school. According to Epstein (2005) some of the results of parent involvement include:

> 1. Improved academic achievement
> 2. Improved student behavior
> 3. Greater student motivation
> 4. More regular attendance
> 5. Lower student dropout rates
> 6. A more positive attitude toward homework
> 7. Improved attitudes and better parent ratings for teachers
> 8. More positive parent interaction with children
> 9. More parental cooperation with school personnel in solving children's academic and behavior problems.
>
> (p. 14)

Some of the obstacles to parent involvement involve emotional barriers felt by the parents themselves. Parents may have negative attitudes based on their own bad experiences with school. A level of distrust and anger results when parents pick up the phone only to hear "Your son is causing problems in math class again." Many low-income parents and parents from other cultures see teachers as authority figures and believe educating their children is best left to the schools. Cultural and language barriers often lead parents to maintain a respectful distance from the schools. Educators often misinterpret this choice as a lack of concern for their children's education. Of course, this isn't the case; in fact, many studies have indicated that culturally and linguistically diverse families want to be involved in the decision making regarding their children's education—they are simply not given access to meaningful involvement (Cartledge, Gardner, & Ford, 2009). Dr. Sherick Hughes (2006) reminded educators of the importance of building on the knowledge students bring into the classroom, particularly the knowledge shaped by family, community, and culture. Over a five-year period, Hughes studied multiple generations of Black families in North Carolina. His goal was to search for family knowledge that could transfer to the classroom. His research uncovered the many ways families support their children's education at home and the ways in which families teach their children about hope, challenge, and survival. He referred to such knowledge as "family pedagogy."

Hughes encouraged teachers to find ways to give families a legitimate voice in curriculum and unit planning.

Mostert (1998) recommended that teachers begin by assuming that parents want the best for their children. Teachers need to learn about the families of the children they serve and the communities they live in. Attending community events, eating at local restaurants, shopping at local grocery stores, etc. all give teachers information that can be incorporated into conversations with children and parents as well as included in curriculum development and instruction.

For parents to actively participate in their children's education, parents have to know how the school operates, how to contact teachers and administrators and other pertinent service providers, and how to access available resources. Teachers play an important role in letting parents know about community resources such as museums, boys and girls clubs, sports programs, and organizations that provide tutoring, etc. Family literacy programs can assist parents in acquiring or strengthening their own literacy skills. Through parent education and school supports parents can learn to assist and advocate for their children.

Effective communication is essential for collaboration to be successful. Gordon (1987) identified the following common elements in effective interpersonal interactions: active listening, depersonalizing situations, identifying common goals and solutions, and monitoring progress to achieve goals. Any communication should be in the child's home language. Families should be included in the decision-making processes involving their children's education. Many teachers make home visits, sometimes accompanied by a translator or school colleague. During the visit, teachers introduce themselves, share their goals and expectations, give their contact information, and answer questions family members have. The home visit is an opportunity to make a personal connection with parents and family members. Some teachers prefer to send a letter of introduction providing the same information. Letters should be personalized and translated into the family's native language if it is not English. Ongoing newsletters informing parents of class activities and asking parents to volunteer in the classroom or share their wisdom with students are all examples of ways to show respect to families and encourage their involvement.

Reflection

- Parents wonder if their children will do well in school. They worry about their children's safety, especially given recent reports of school violence. They hope their children's teachers will be kind, knowledgeable, and fair. They wonder if they will be able to help their children be successful in school.
- What can teachers do to alleviate concerns?

Summary

The classroom is a context full of interpersonal challenges. Effective teachers need to understand that learning goals are embedded in relational dynamics. The research suggests that the path to learning is less rocky and contains fewer hairpin turns when there is a positive relational foundation. It is important to stress that at-risk students appear to gain the most from positive relationships with their teachers. We want teachers to reflect on the role of the teacher–student relationship and the approaches they take to build and manage them. We also want teachers to think about the way in which diversity influences their approach to students. Are teachers more willing to display immediacy to students who are similar to them in ethnicity and socioeconomic circumstance? The data on the impact of positive teacher–student relationships is clear. By studying the stages and dialectical processes involved in relationship development and by utilizing the strategies that enhance relationships teachers will be in a better place to accomplish instructional goals and objectives.

Learning Activities

1. The quality of the teacher–student relationship has been found to be one of the most important factors influencing student learning outcomes. Identify five benefits of developing positive relationships with students.
2. Refer back to the scenario on Gabriela at the beginning of the chapter. Identify the external and internal factors (Chapter 5) placing Gabriela at risk of not doing well in school. What are Gabriela's strengths? Discuss the importance of relationship building on Gabriela's success in school.
3. Gabriela showed resilience throughout her school years. What protective factors were involved in encouraging Gabriela to complete school?
4. Analyze the dialectical tensions in a current teacher–student relationship. Which tension do you find most difficult to manage? What strategies do you use to manage the various tensions?
5. Write a five-page position paper on Rawlins's perspective on teaching as a mode of friendship? Explain the pros and cons of this framework.
6. Think about a teacher you currently have. Describe this teacher's verbal and nonverbal immediacy. How does this particular behavior serve the academic goals of the teacher?
7. Which types of teacher humor promote positive teacher–student relationships?

8. Identify three affinity-seeking strategies you typically use. Explain how you would use these strategies to build positive teacher–student relationships?

Resources

Books

- *Teacher–Student Relationships: Toward Personalized Education* by Bernstein-Yamashiro & Noam.
- *The Laughing Classroom: Everyone's Guide to Teaching with Humor and Play* by Loomans & Kolberg.
- *Connecting with Students* by Mendler.

Websites

- Forming Positive Student-Teacher Relationships (www.cedu.niu.edu/~shumow/itt/StudentTchrRelationships.pdf)
- Tips for Developing A Positive Teacher–Student Relationship (www.jamaica-gleaner.com/gleaner/20090518/news/news10.html)
- Robert Marzano has a short and useful article in this issue of Educational Leadership. It's titled "Art and Science of Teaching/Relating to Students: It's What You Do That Counts" (www.ascd.org/publications/educational-leadership/mar11/vol68/num06/Relating-to-Students@-It%27s-What-You-Do-That-Counts.aspx)
- Send in the Clowns (www.reacheverychild.com/feature/humor.html)
- A Funny Thing Happened . . . (www.teachersfirst.com/humor.shtml)

7

BUILDING A COMMUNITY OF LEARNERS IN DIVERSE CLASSROOMS

Learning Outcomes

1. Explain why social and emotional skills are important to learning.
2. Identify four defining characteristics of a classroom learning community.
3. Defend the importance of creating a classroom learning community.
4. List and give examples of three different types of classroom meetings.
5. Discuss the benefits of classroom meetings, peer mediation, and service learning on students' social and emotional growth.
6. Identify five strategies teachers can use to encourage active family involvement in school.

Classroom Scenario

Mr. Naranjo is a second-grade teacher in a large urban community in Central California. He grew up in Mexico and came to the United States with his family when he was 10 years old. He learned English in the United States. He has been teaching at the same school for ten years and has seen many changes and experienced many challenges over the years. Each summer Mr. Naranjo spends hours and hours planning for a new group of students to return or to begin school in the fall. This year he has 22 students in his classroom, 14 boys and eight girls. His students are ethnically diverse: there are ten Hispanic, three Southeast Asian, two African-American, and seven White students. Six students are English learners. For seven students, Spanish is their first language; Vietnamese is the first language for one student. Three male students have ADHD. Eight students come from families who live below the poverty line. These students are eligible for reduced-price or/free lunches. Most of Mr. Naranjo's students live with both parents. Five students live in single-parent families. One student lost her mother over the summer. Two students have fathers in prison.

Mr. Naranjo knows, from previous teachers, that many of his students have social and behavioral challenges. Antonio and Alejandro are best friends; they see themselves as teachers' pets and like telling the other students what to do. They have been disciplined for shoving and calling other students names at recess and during lunch. Calesee has questions about everything; she even has questions about her own questions. Marlena spends most of her time trying to stop Calesee from asking questions. Romeo can't sit still; he's up walking around the room, tapping his pencil or humming during instruction. Marvin is a bit of a class clown, always trying to make a joke about everything. Elizabeth is a very intelligent girl who often gets angry and frustrated when her work is too easy. Tyler has been known to turn over desks when asked to do challenging but doable work. Most of these episodes coincide with domestic disputes in his home.

Each school year Mr. Naranjo wonders if he will be able to reach all of his children and provide an environment that is safe, caring, and engaging. He wonders if the children will like him and if he will like his students. He wonders if he has enough knowledge about classroom management, curriculum development, and assessment to meet the needs of all of his students. He hopes he will be able to connect with the students' families in a way that helps their children grow and thrive at school. Mr. Naranjo's students wonder if their teacher will be nice, caring, and fair. They wonder if he will be fun. They worry about being liked by their peers. And some students worry about being teased or picked on at school. They worry about doing well in school. Some are distracted by their home situations.

As teachers, we are supposed to take a group of diverse students, with many different strengths and challenges, and teach them in ways that meet their academic, social, and emotional needs. Studies indicate that some of the most important skills students need to be successful are the "people skills" of social interaction, communication, collaboration, and problem solving. Research suggests that creating classroom communities where students' academic and social needs are met may improve students' motivation, behavior, and learning. In this chapter, we begin by considering the importance of social and emotional learning. We look at how the classroom community is defined in the literature, discuss core elements found in most classroom communities, and share the many benefits to students involved in programs focused on building community. Classroom meetings, peer mediation, and community service learning will be examined as strategies for increasing students' academic, social, and emotional skills. We believe supporting and encouraging the growth of students' social and emotional skills is every bit as important as the focus on academic achievement.

Social Emotional Learning

According to Elias et al. (1997):

> When schools attend systematically to students' social and emotional skills, the academic achievement of children increases, the incidence

> of problem behaviors decreases, and the quality of the relationships surrounding each child improves. And, students become the productive, responsible, contributing members of society that we all want. (pp. 1–2)

Elias et al. (1997) contended that social and emotional development, and the recognition that learning is relational are often overlooked and replaced by an intense focus on improving students' academic scores. Elias et al. defined social and emotional competence as the ability to "understand, manage, and express the social and emotional aspects of one's life in ways that enable the successful management of life tasks such as learning, forming relationships, solving everyday problems, and adapting to the complex demands of growth and development" (p. 2).

Social and emotional competence includes such skills as self-awareness, understanding communication processes, working cooperatively, self-management, problem solving, and decision making. In Chapter 2 we discussed the work of Gardner (1983) and Goleman (1995), who stressed that emotional and interpersonal competences play dramatic roles in the learning process.

In *A Celebration of Neurons*, Robert Sylwester (1995) also discussed the importance of emotion in student performance: "We know that emotion is very important to the instructional process because it drives attention, which drives learning and memory" (p. 72). Social and emotional issues may very well be at the core of many problem behaviors exhibited by children today. A student who is hungry and traumatized over a recent violent episode at home may not be enthusiastic about a math assignment. Such a student, when asked by the teacher to "get busy," may get angry instead and throw books on the floor. Goleman (1995) referred to this type of response as the thinking brain being "hijacked." A teacher who has very little understanding of the ways that emotions direct learning may respond to the student with harsh discipline. Unfortunately, many students and teachers experience "hijacking" as they attempt to deal with the complex issues presented in today's classrooms. This could very easily be the case if Tyler's teacher didn't understand his circumstances at home.

Defining Community

Much has been written about the importance of developing classroom communities to meet the academic, social, and emotional needs of today's students.

So, what is community? The term "community" has many definitions in the literature.

Dewey (1963) reflected on the social nature of schooling, observing that most children are "sociable." He stated:

> A genuine community life has its ground in this natural sociability. Community life does not organize itself in an enduring way purely spontaneously. It requires thought and planning. The educator is responsible for a knowledge of individuals and for a knowledge of subject-matter that will enable activities to be selected which lend themselves to social organization, an organization in which all individuals have an opportunity to contribute something, and in which the activities in which all participate are the chief carrier of control.
>
> (p. 56)

In this type of community, the teacher maintains the position of leader of group activities instead of boss or dictator.

Alfie Kohn (1996) defined community as:

> a place in which students feel cared about and are encouraged to care about each other. They experience a sense of being valued and respected; the children matter to one another and to the teacher. They have come to think in the plural: they feel connected to each other; they are part of an "us." And as a result of all this, they feel safe in their classes, not only physically but also emotionally.
>
> (pp. 101–102)

McMillan and Chavis (1986) defined community as "a feeling that members have of belonging, a feeling that members matter to one another and to the group, and a shared faith that members' needs will be met through their commitment to be together" (p. 4). The authors identified four elements of community. The first element is membership, which is the feeling of belonging or personal relatedness. The second element is influence, which is present when members make a difference to a group and the group matters to its members. The third element is reinforcement, the feeling that the resources received through their membership in the group will meet each member's needs. The last element is emotional connection, which occurs when members share history, common places and time together, and similar experiences.

According to Watkins (2005), there are four defining characteristics of a classroom learning community: agency, belonging, cohesion, and diversity. Agency means that students make choices and take actions that promote individual and class goals. This requires that students recognize that personal and class goals are accomplished through interdependent actions. A second characteristic is belonging. A sense of community is promoted when students feel respected, liked, supported, and appreciated. The third characteristic is cohesion. As students increase their connection to the class they move away from an "I" to a "we" orientation. The final characteristic is diversity. In a community, diversity is not viewed as threat but as strength. Watkins argued that the ability to embrace differences and positively view diversity leads to reduced stereotypes and more productive interdependent relationships among all members.

Watch This: www.nfb.ca/film/richard_cardinal This is the story of Richard Cardinal, a Métis adolescent who committed suicide in 1984. He was taken from his home at the age of 4 due to family problems; he spent the rest of his life moving in and out of 28 foster homes, group homes, and shelters in Alberta, Canada. He left behind a diary upon which this film is based. What does this story tell us about the importance of belonging to a student's success in school?

Watkins (2005) also explicated several processes that undergird community. One is acting together. Activities in a classroom community require coordinated action that leads to a desired outcome or goal. Two is bridging. This refers to the connections created through interpersonal communication. Through communication, identities and experiences are negotiated and redefined. Individual strengths and limitations are revealed and understood. Three is collaboration. Collaboration is closely related to bridging. Through collaboration, students seek to find common ground or discover new ways of viewing academic and non-academic tasks. The fourth process is dialogue. Students engage in dialogue when they exchange meaningful ideas and thoughts. Dialogue is also central to the creation of new meanings and understandings.

Watson and Battistich (2006) identified six core characteristics common to most community approaches: (a) a positive, developmental view of children; (b) a view of students as imbedded in a social context; (c) a view of community as relational; (d) a view of curriculum as integrated and student-centered; (e) minimal or noncoercive disciplinary strategies; and (f) a common set of classroom activities. Many community approaches also focus on students' need to feel a sense of belonging in school or in the classroom.

Benefits of Classroom Communities on Students' Academic, Social, and Emotional Growth

All students have the basic need to be known, accepted, and competent. Watkins (2005) and other researchers have pointed out that learning communities serve to support the basic social psychological needs of students. For example, several theorists (Baumeister & Leary, 1995; Brendtro, Brokenleg, & Bockern, 1990; Deci & Ryan, 1985; Deci et al., 1991; Solomon, Battistich, Watson, Schaps, & Lewis, 2000) have suggested that an effective school environment supports a student's basic psychological needs to (a) belong to a social group whose members are mutually supportive and concerned; (b) have age-appropriate opportunities to be autonomous, self-directing, and influential; and (c) feel competent and effective in valued activities. Unfortunately, many students, especially those of color and those with learning and emotional or behavioral problems, those who are English learners, or those who live in poverty or who are homeless, continue to feel isolated and lonely as most schools focus on academics and pay little attention to students' affective or socio-emotional needs.

Battistich and Hom (1997) found that increases in school-level sense of community were associated with lowered levels of drug use and delinquent behavior among fifth- and sixth-grade students. Other studies reported positive effects of peer support or acceptance of students' academic behavior and interest in school (Ladd, 1990; Ryan, Stiller, & Lynch, 1994; Wentzel & Asher, 1995). The absence of peer support—feeling rejected or alienated—was linked to students' emotional distress, behavior problems in the classroom, disliking for school, lower achievement, and incidence of dropout.

In an extensive review of literature, Osterman (2000) found many positive outcomes associated with feelings of belongingness. Children who experience a strong sense of belonging or relatedness have more positive attitudes toward school, teachers, and peers. They are more likely to enjoy school and be engaged in learning. Children who experience a lack of belonging, who feel rejected and alienated, are more likely to display problem behavior (aggression or withdrawal) in the classroom, show less interest in school, have lower achievement, and may drop out of school. Other research suggests that many psychological and behavioral problems, such as drug use, eating disorders, depression, dropout, teen pregnancy, etc., exist as a result of "lack of belongingness" (Baumeister & Leary, 1995).

A significant body of literature regarding students' sense of community comes from the Child Development Project (CDP), an elementary to middle school community model that supports a child-centered approach to classroom management, cooperative activities, prosocial values, and classroom problem-solving discussions. In the project, researchers were assigned to help school districts become communities of support that address students' needs for belonging. A goal was to help students experience the classroom as a supportive and caring environment in which students were involved in decision making and goal setting. Family activities offered parents a way to support their children at home. This was the first comprehensive, longitudinal, school-based project that focused on prosocial education.

Solomon, Watson, Battistich, Schaps, and Delucchi (1996) identified teacher interventions utilized in the CDP to enhance students' sense of community. Several elements of this model were found to contribute positively to students' sense of community: (a) cooperative learning, (b) developmental discipline, (c) use of literature to promote interpersonal understanding and discourse about prosocial values, (d) helping/prosocial activity, (e) school-wide and parent activities, and (f) promoting non-exclusionary attitudes. Developmental discipline involved building trusting relationships between teachers and students, providing students with opportunities for autonomy, and teaching appropriate social skills. Students were actively involved in classroom governance. Classroom meetings and discussions encouraged students to take responsibility for their own behavior. Literature was used to help students gain an understanding of not only what they read, but also the needs of others. Inclusion was promoted through various cooperative groupings and noncompetitive science fairs and service projects across grade levels. Most of the research cited suggested many positive academic and social outcomes for students who experience a sense of belonging and community in their schools and classrooms.

Two separate longitudinal studies included more than 5,600 students from grades K–6 in seven school districts across the country. Researchers found a positive relationship between students' sense of community and intrinsic academic motivation (Battistich, Solomon, Kim, Watson, & Schaps, 1995; Solomon et al., 2000). These studies also found that belongingness is associated with positive feelings about school, class work, and teachers.

The CDP was revised and its name changed to the Caring School Community (CSC) program. It is a K–6 school program that seeks to strengthen students' connectedness to school by creating a classroom and school community that fosters academic motivation, achievement, and character formation and reduces drug abuse, violence, and mental health problems. The program, begun in California as the Child Development Project, has been adopted by approximately 1,000 schools in 34 states (National Registry of Evidence-based Programs and Practices, n.d.). The CSC integrates aspects important in children's social development, including supportive teacher–student relationships and opportunities for students to interact and participate in cooperative groups. Elementary school teachers deliver the program, the goals of which are to enrich children's positive behavior without impeding academic accomplishments and advance students' commitment to being fair, empathic, respectful, and responsible.

The program consists of the four original components developed for the CDP. Guidelines for class meetings assist students and teachers to get to know each other and make decisions about classroom rules and goals. *Cross-Age Buddies* pairs classes of older and younger students for academic and recreational activities to help build caring relationships. Buddy teachers meet and plan their lessons together, support their buddy pairs during activities, and meet again to reflect on what worked and what didn't. In *Homeside Activities*, teachers learn how to create lessons that begin in the classroom, are then developed at home through conversations (in both English and Spanish) with their families, and then debriefed back in the classroom. These activities are intended to link family and school experiences and perspectives. The last component, *School-wide Community-Building Activities*, link students, parents, teachers, and the community at large in building connections beyond the classroom. See the National Registry of Evidence-based Programs and Practices (n.d.), a searchable online database for mental health and substance abuse interventions. Implementation evaluations from the CSC program show improvements in student behavior, knowledge, attitudes, values, and academic achievement (Marshall & Caldwell, 2007; Institue of Education Sciences, 2007).

Building Community in the Classroom

In this section we discuss four interventions: classroom meetings, peer mediation, restorative justice, and community service learning. Each is designed to create a classroom environment built on positive relationships and collaboration among students, teachers, family members, and the community at large. Finally, we discuss the importance of family involvement in student learning and community building.

Classroom Meetings

Many teachers use class meetings as a tool for building a sense of community and belonging. Zionts and Fox (1998) noted that the goal of classroom meetings is to teach students to communicate, to solve problems, and to accept and appreciate diversity. Kohn (1996) suggested that classroom meetings are the best places for sharing, deciding, planning, and reflecting on a myriad of issues—from what the students did over the weekend to what kind of place the classroom should be. Kohn (1998) noted that structured opportunities for class members to meet help children feel respected, build a sense of community, and contribute to the development of such skills as perspective taking and problem solving.

Perhaps the guru of classroom meetings is William Glasser. In his 1969 book, *Schools without Failure*, Glasser discussed three types of meetings: (1) social-problem solving, (2) open-ended, and (3) educational/diagnostic. *Social-problem-solving meetings* attempt to solve individual and group problems that involve issues of the class and the school. Students identify problems, propose alternative solutions, and commit themselves to a plan of action. In *open-ended meetings*, children are asked to discuss any topic relevant to their lives including classroom curriculum. Glasser gave the example of an incredible discussion that evolved around the children's interest in what it would feel like to be blind. Glasser noted that in classrooms where children are involved there are fewer discipline problems. The third type of meeting is the *educational/diagnostic*, in which the topic is directly related to what the class is studying. This type of meeting gives the teacher the opportunity to determine students' prior knowledge of a topic and evaluate the extent to which information presented is understood and generalized to other areas. For example, a teacher who is teaching about HIV/AIDS may want to use an initial meeting to determine what students know about the topic. A meeting held after information has been taught could determine whether students would be willing to design a group project focused on HIV/AIDS awareness.

The goals of classroom meetings may vary by grade level. In elementary classrooms teachers often use classroom meetings to teach social skills. In secondary classrooms teachers see several different groups of students and the focus may be more specific to projects or small- and whole-group concerns. One teacher at the middle school level used class meetings to discuss group projects, to identify group roles and rules, and to evaluate process. Another teacher used a "solutions box" to encourage students to identify topics or issues they wanted to discuss during class meetings.

One teacher of a self-contained class for students with emotional and behavioral problems held class meetings three times a week. The meetings usually focused on problem solving for interpersonal issues but were also used to plan field trips and class projects. The teacher described one class meeting that "saved the melodrama." The principal was on her way to the class to see students who were not exactly her favorites perform a melodrama when two students who were involved in a problematic relationship walked out of the class. Several peers were successful at getting the students to return to class. A brief classroom meeting was held to resolve the conflict and the show went on. Students are much more likely to take responsibility when they are allowed to solve their own problems.

ORGANIZATION

Jones and Jones (2007) provided the following guidelines for organizing classroom meetings:

- Class meetings will be held in a tight circle with all participants (including the teacher) seated in the circle. The circle must not be too large or it will detract from students' involvement and encourage off-task behavior.
- All problems related to the class as a group can be discussed. Problems involving two or three individual students may be discussed outside the class meeting unless the problem affects the class as a whole.
- An agenda that is created by students will be written on a clipboard. Students must sign their names behind the agenda item. Students do not list other students' names but merely the issue to be readdressed. The items will be discussed in the order in which they appear on the board. If an agenda item no longer applies when the meeting is held, it will be deleted from the list.
- Discussions during class meetings should be directed toward arriving at a solution that is not a punishment. The goal of class meetings is to find positive solutions to problems and not to criticize people or occurrences in the classroom.
- If an individual student's behavior is on the agenda, the item will not be discussed without the student's permission. If the student

agrees to have a behavior discussed, you (instructor) should emphasize that the goal of the meeting is to help the student. Be sure that students' statements focus on the youngster's behavior and are presented as I-messages rather than as judgmental statements about the youngster or the behavior. The focus should always be on providing the student with sensitive, thoughtful feedback and positive suggestions for altering behavior.

- Students' responsibilities during class meetings include (a) raising hands and being called on to speak; (b) listening to the speaker and not talking while someone else is speaking; (c) staying on the topic until it has been completed; (d) being involved by sharing ideas that will help the group; and (e) using positive, supportive words to discuss the problem and solutions.
- The teacher will initially serve as facilitator for the class meetings.

(pp. 375–376)

Zionts and Fox (1998) identified several basic interpersonal skills that teachers must possess to be effective facilitators. They must be good listeners able to reflect the thoughts, perceptions, and feelings of others. They must seek clarification by asking questions and summarizing concisely. They must be able to give information to the group in order to ensure the flow of the conversation, a sort of "guide on the side," and communicate encouragement and support. They can use self-disclosure, which is leading by example. We caution that teacher self-disclosure should not include too much personal information. The meeting should be focused on students' needs.

Zionts & Fox (1998) also suggested that class meetings be organized ahead of time. Students and the teacher should develop rules. Meetings can be held one to five times a week and last from 30 minutes to 1 hour. Length may depend on the students' attention spans. Glasser (1969) recommended 10 to 30 minutes for the lower grades and 30 to 45 minutes for the upper grades. It is important to determine the purpose(s) of class meetings. For students with emotional and behavioral disorders, a meeting format may include solving problems of a member or members, teaching new skills, and evaluating the results.

Jones and Jones (2001) noted:

> Whenever people live close together for many hours each day, it is mandatory that time be taken to resolve minor conflicts openly. Like an automobile engine that may appear to run smoothly but will suddenly boil over unless properly lubricated, classrooms require proper maintenance checks and minor tune-ups. When implemented in a positive, supportive atmosphere, class meetings serve as the lubricant for a smoothly running classroom.
>
> (p. 342)

Reflection

- How can Mr. Naranjo utilize classroom meetings to build a sense of belonging in his classroom?
- What can Mr. Naranjo do to welcome and provide families with information about school procedures, meetings, and resources?
- How can Mr. Naranjo support and involve parents or caregivers in classroom activities or assignments?

Peer Mediation

Peer relationships are just as important as teacher–student relationships in building a classroom community that promotes socio-emotional learning and growth. Peer mediation, or what is often referred to as conflict resolution programs, are becoming part of school-wide efforts to curb student violence. Students who engage in aggressive behaviors seem to have limited social skills in resolving conflicts in constructive ways (Sim, Whiteside, Dittner, & Mellon, 2006). It is through peer mediation that students learn communication skills to deal with their problems.

The process involves training student volunteers or students who have been nominated by their teachers to mediate conflicts between their peers and to help their peers find reasonable solutions to their conflict. The goal is to provide students an opportunity to share their feelings and their account of the conflict with their peers. The hope is that this process will teach students new ways of handling conflict other than through violence. The mediation process as outlined by Conboy (1994) proceeds as follows:

1. The peer mediator asks all parties involved to agree to listen to the others' points of view without put-downs or name-calling.
2. Conflicting parties are guided to define the problem, what happened, and how they responded or felt.
3. The mediator paraphrases what has been said to ensure that everyone feels their points of view and their feelings about the conflict have been correctly reflected.
4. The mediator asks participants to brainstorm solutions that would be fair to both sides.
5. Once the participants have agreed to a solution, a written contract is developed and signed by both parties.

Conboy (1994) suggested that peer mediation offers administrators and teachers a positive alternative to resolving conflict, prevents conflicts from escalating, helps create a more positive school climate, and encourages students to think of alternative solutions to solving problems with their peers.

PEER MEDIATION PROGRAMS

There are many types of peer mediation programs available. A program developed by Myrick and Erney (1984, 1985) was piloted at Bucholz High School in Gainsville, Florida. Initially the program focused on training high school students in basic counseling skills and providing them with information about substance abuse prevalent in their community. After completing the training, the high school students worked as peer facilitators with children in elementary schools. The program was broadened to include elementary and middle school students in the training. These students learn to be good listeners, group leaders, and role models for one another. Training focused on student achievement, parental issues, making friends, and career choices.

Research points to the effectiveness of peer mediation programs in reducing violence and increasing cooperation among students (Johnson & Johnson, 1996). Students learn alternatives to conflict and become more responsible for their own behavior (Thompson, 1996). When students are involved in solving their own conflicts, teachers report less stress as they have more time to spend on academics. Mediators report improved attitudes toward school and better academic performance. Even after they leave school, mediators report the benefits of their training in solving their own problems (Carruthers, Sweeny, Kmitta, & Harris, 1996). A review of the literature on peer mediation programs affirms the effectiveness of these programs on student-to-student and teacher-to-student relationships, success in teaching peer mediation skills, reducing suspensions and disciplinary referrals, and improving overall school climate (Harris, 2005). Other programs have been effective in teaching assertiveness skills, problem solving and anger management (Johnson & Johnson, 2005).

Reflection

- Today, Marlena, tired of Calesse asking questions, told Calesse, "Shut up and put your hand down." The two girls got into a shoving match. They sit next to each other in class. Mr. Naranjo didn't see who started the shoving.
- How could you use peer mediation to facilitate a workable relationship between these two girls?

RESTORATIVE JUSTICE

One concept that holds great promise for repairing relationships through collaboration is called restorative justice. According to Kidde and Alfred (2011), the concept is "focused on the belief that those affected by harm can work together to repair it and that this collaboration leads to true accountability" (p. 5). School-based restorative justice is implemented for the purpose of building a caring school community by responding to student misbehavior through a process of acknowledging the harm done and repairing relationships. Restorative justice allows students who might otherwise be suspended or expelled an opportunity to participate in a process that helps them become aware of how their actions affect others, to take responsibility for their actions, and to learn how to manage conflicts with peers and adults. We talk more about the effects of punishment in Chapter 8. It is our hope that less time will be spent on disciplinary actions once the main causes of the problem have been addressed.

A core element of most restorative justice programs is a "circle": students and teachers literally sit in a circle as one participant guides the conversation. Those involved in the conflict are the participants. Circles are typically held to discuss disciplinary problems, such as disrespectful behavior, acting out in class, bullying, and more. During the practice, students are taught to show respect, empathy, and compromise. As we discussed earlier, this process could be considered an extension of classroom meetings. See an example of a circle process at www.youtube.com/watch?v=UUKHWhTBNA8.

In California, the state's schools now issue more suspensions to students than diplomas, especially to African-American students. This is particularly true in the Oakland Unified School District. In response, legislative action now requires districts to document disciplinary interventions enacted prior to suspension. District administrators are hoping that restorative justice will reduce the need for disciplinary actions, and instead help students find more productive ways to resolve conflicts.

Reflection

- Read the overview of restorative justice in Oakland Unified School District at www.ousd.k12.ca.us/restorativejustice.
- What are the goals of the program? How does this program relate to the social and emotional goals we discussed in this chapter?
- Watch the video at www.youtube.com/watch?v=RdKhcQrLD1w, showing students at MetWest High School facilitating a community-building circle. What do you think students are learning?
- What is the three-tiered model of restorative justice?
- What programs and services support the restorative justice process? Is it working to meet the stated goals?

Connecting Students to the Community

Students from elementary school through college can benefit from being involved in service-learning projects. They apply what they learn in the classroom to solve real problems in the community. Projects can range from advocating for animal rights to adopting grandparents in a nursing home, planting a garden and donating the food to needy families, cleaning up graffiti, recycling, and raising money for survivors of disasters.

Damon (1995), in his book *Greater Expectations*, described the need for children to experience a sense of purpose. He stated, "The surest antidote to youthful demoralization is a sense of purpose: acquiring, that is, a belief in (and dedication to) something larger than oneself" (p. 240). Damon suggested schools and communities must offer children opportunities to contribute to the welfare of others.

Brendtro et al. (1990) agreed that young people cannot develop a sense of their own value unless they have opportunities to be of value to others. The authors argued that today's youth at risk of school failures have become alienated, discouraged, and self-centered. Service-learning projects bring young people beyond the "narcissism of self-absorption." As young people find that they can make a difference in the lives of others, they validate their feelings of self-worth. Kohn (1996) suggested that schools would best serve students and society by focusing on teaching students to be not only good learners, but also good people. He noted that schools are ideal places to teach children about generosity and caring.

Serving others takes on many forms. Volunteerism, for example, is contributing time without being paid. Community service is helping the community by choice or by court order, also without pay. Volunteerism and community service do not necessarily involve the integration of academics, curriculum, or reflection. Service learning is a philosophy and teaching methodology that integrates service experiences into the curriculum and connects schools with their communities to enrich students' learning and facilitate their academic, social, and emotional growth.

Service learning was defined in the National and Community Service Act of 1990, signed into law by President George Bush and reauthorized in 1993 under President Bill Clinton. America's Promise—the alliance for youth led by Colin Powell—has mobilized the nation to provide young people opportunities to give back through community service. In May 1993, the Alliance for Service Learning in Education Reform defined service learning and set forth standards of quality for its use in school-based programs. Service learning is defined as a method by which young people learn and develop through active participation in thoughtfully organized service experiences that:

1. meet actual community needs;
2. are coordinated in collaboration with the school and community;

3. are integrated into each young person's academic curriculum;
4. provide structured time for young people to think, talk, and write about what they did and saw during the actual service activity;
5. provide young people with opportunities to use newly acquired academic skills and knowledge in real-life situations in their own communities;
6. enhance what is taught in the school by extending student learning beyond the classroom; and
7. help to foster the development of a sense of caring for others.

Types of Service

There are three different types of service-learning experiences: direct service, indirect service, and advocacy. In direct service, students have personal contact with those they are serving. Projects such as mentoring, tutoring, and working with senior citizens in retirement homes are all examples of direct service. Indirect service requires the students to address a problem in the community rather than have direct contact with the beneficiaries of the service. Examples are raising money, sorting clothes at a homeless shelter, and writing letters to hospitalized children. Advocacy service-learning projects allow students to lend their voice to increase public awareness of a problem such as teenage smoking by writing letters to legislators or tobacco companies or by creating fact posters and presenting them to young children.

STEPS IN SERVICE LEARNING

Kaye (2000) identified four steps in service learning. The first step is preparation, which requires the teacher to guide students in identifying a need in the community. Students learn new information and collaborate with community partners. A plan is developed that encourages student responsibility and focuses activities on the integration of service and learning. The project should help students master their subject matter.

In step two, students take action through direct service, indirect service, or advocacy. The integration of action and service provides students with opportunities to actively apply knowledge and skills and simultaneously contribute to the community. A well-known Chinese proverb applies to this step: "I hear and I forget. I see and I remember. I act and I understand."

The third step involves a systematic and ongoing process of reflection through role play, discussion, or journal writing. This is a guided experience in which students are asked to think critically about their service experience. Reflection activities have been found to increase student self-confidence, autonomy, risk-taking, self-respect, and sense of usefulness and purpose (Cairn & Kielsmeier, 1991). In their review of research on service learning, Conrad and Hedin (1991) found that reflection afforded students the opportunity for social and personal development.

The last step requires students to demonstrate their learning through presentations and performances; visual art forms; or written articles or letters to their peers, parents, and/or community members. Students may choose to extend their activities to developing other projects that may be of benefit to the community. Some have added a fourth step: celebration. This component recognizes students for their accomplishments through special assemblies, certificates, parties, and sometimes media coverage. Service providers and recipients may participate.

BENEFITS AND BARRIERS

Service learning has proven to be beneficial to both general education and special education populations. Studies on the effects of service learning for typical children have reported improved academic and social skills (Brugh, 1997; McPherson, 1997; Wade, 1994). Dundon (1999) wrote about the value of service learning: "The most enduring value comes with the connection to our own deepest selves—to the place where empathy and compassion live. Once we have tapped that core being, once we know what that feels like, we will want to go there again" (p. 37).

According to the results of many studies reported by the National Service-Learning Clearinghouse (RMC Research Corporation, 2007), students who participate in quality service-learning experiences are more engaged in learning. Service learning improves interpersonal and social skills; establishes a sense of commitment to school, community, and society; and encourages students to explore varied career paths.

Many students with special needs have significant difficulties in both academic and social domains and have experienced continual failure leading to feelings of inadequacy and helplessness. Students with disabilities are often the recipients of service and seldom have an opportunity to view themselves as valuable to others. Studies that involved students with disabilities pointed to positive gains from service learning in behavior, academics, attitudes, functional skills, social skills, attendance, and relationships with nondisabled peers (Brill, 1994; Malmgren, Abbott, & Hawkins, 1999; Muscott, 2000; Wade, 1994; Yoder, Retish, & Wade, 1996). Curwin (1993) noted the benefits of service learning for at-risk students: "Opportunities to help others may provide a way to break the devastating cycle of failure—to substitute caring for anger and replace low self-esteem with feelings of worth" (p. 36).

Service-learning projects can be labor intensive. According to Rockwell (2001), service-learning projects require (a) an understanding of the benefits, (b) a method of incorporating state standards into the service-learning experience, and (c) an evaluation of resources. She warned of the difficulties in scheduling, integrating curricular content, and acquiring resources (e.g., time, money, and transportation).

Although there are many positive outcomes of service-learning programs, Muscott (2001) suggested we view these outcomes with "cautious optimism." Many of the service-learning programs involving students with emotional and behavioral problems, for example, have been assessed qualitatively using anecdotal information from teacher observation, questionnaires, and students' interviews. Muscott stressed the need for more rigorous research to support the claims of service-learning programs.

Summary

In this chapter we discussed the importance of community building in and out of school, including establishing healthy relationships with peers and adults to promote students' socio-emotional and academic growth. Peer mediation teaches students to view conflict as a natural process in life and as an opportunity for growth and learning. The real-life problem-solving process teaches students skills for dealing with conflict constructively. Classroom meetings and restorative justice also provide opportunities for students to be involved in constructive decision making. Students learn to take ownership and responsibility for their actions. They learn to reflect on the consequences of their own and others' behaviors, to solve problems, and ultimately to take responsibility for their own learning. These are skills that benefit students throughout their lives. Through community service learning, students learn to work together to serve others and solve real problems in the school and the community. Teachers who utilize these practices spend less time disciplining students and more time teaching. The strategies we recommend have the potential to develop the social and emotional skills of students, increase students' connection to school and community, and improve behavior and academic achievement.

Learning Activities

- Bullying is one of the most serious problems today, both in school and on the Internet. Bullying can have devastating effects on bullies, their victims, and bystanders. For some students the fear of bullying is so great they stay home from school or avoid school altogether. In a worst-case scenario, bullying has led to the death of the victim or serious violent or fatal attack of the bully by the bullied. Choose one of the questions below to research. Create a PowerPoint presentation (not more than three slides) to present your answer.
- How can service-learning projects be used to teach students about the negative effects of bullying and encourage students to be proactive in preventing such incidents from occurring?

- What are the pros and cons of using peer mediation to resolve conflicts involving bullying?
- How can classroom meetings or restorative justice be used to resolve school bullying?
- Develop a service-learning project that elementary students could do to resolve issues in the neighborhood or community where you currently live. Identify your goals, resources needed, and plan of action.

Resources

- Kaye (2000) published *The Service Learning Bookshelf*, a collection of book titles to aid teachers and family members in connecting student learning with service to the community. Kaye recommended that books be used as catalysts, allowing readers to consider what they have in common with the characters, to understand how the actions of the characters make a difference in the lives of others, and to identify and address problems in the neighborhood and community. *The Service Learning Bookshelf* lists categories commonly selected for service-learning experiences, from AIDS awareness and education to special needs and disabilities.
- The National Service-Learning Clearinghouse supports the service-learning community in higher education, kindergarten through Grade 12, community-based organizations, tribal programs, and all others interested in strengthening schools and communities using service learning.
  www.servicelearning.org
- The Conflict Resolution Education Connection is a website devoted to the promotion of conflict resolution education throughout the world.
  www.creducation.org/
- Collaborative for Academic, Social, and Emotional Learning is the nation's leading organization advancing the development of academic, social, and emotional competence for all students. Its mission is to make evidence-based social and emotional learning an integral part of education from preschool through high school.
  www.casel.org/social-and-emotional-learning

8

POSITIVE BEHAVIOR SUPPORTS

Learning Outcomes

1. Define classroom management.
2. Identify teacher- and school-related factors that can affect student behavior.
3. Describe the etiology of behavior and the educational application of each theoretical perspective (i.e., behavioral, psychodynamic, biophysical, and ecological).
4. Discuss the impact of punishment on student behavior.
5. Give examples of the ways in which culture influences teachers' responses to student misbehavior.
6. Distinguish the characteristics of each tier in the implementation of School-Wide Positive Behavior Interventions and Supports (SWPBIS).

Classroom Scenario

Professor Donovan's students are studying to be teachers. In one assignment he asked his students to observe in a classroom with children who have been identified with emotional and behavior problems. Four students zeroed in on Julius, a 12-year-old African-American boy enrolled in Ms. Zimmer's seventh-grade history class. The students observed Julius' behavior over a 30-minute period. After a brief discussion, together, students noted the following:

Julius walked in after the class period started and announced, "I'm here, let the party begin!" Most of the students in the class laughed and then continued their work. Students were working on a map activity at their desks. Written instructions were on the board. Julius began tapping his pencil on his desk and rapping a song, inappropriate for the classroom. Several students decided to rap with him. Ms. Zimmer asked the students in class to get back to the assignment.

Under the pretense of sharpening his pencil, Julius strolled down the aisle, greeting each of his buddies with "Wasssup!" and a high-five. Ms. Zimmer commented, "Julius, you are always moving. Get back to your seat."

Julius rolled his eyes and muttered under his breath, "I'll show you a few moves." A few minutes later, with a smile and a wink, Julius shouted out, "Ms. Zimmer, this class is boring and not exactly meeting my needs."

Ms. Zimmer made the mistake of asking Julius how she could meet his needs. He muttered a few explicit sexual suggestions under his breath. Ms. Zimmer replied, "Julius, your smart mouth is not going to help you pass this class."

Julius then got up from his seat and headed toward the front of the class. With the entire class focused on him, Julius said, "Why don't we have a discussion about why this class is so boring?" Ms. Zimmer, looking quite flustered, responded, "Julius, I need to talk to you privately." Julius shouted a few obscenities, overturned a desk, and left the classroom.

After class ended, Ms. Zimmer explained that Julius lives with his grandmother and two younger siblings. His mother left the family when Julius was 2 years old. His father's whereabouts are unknown. Julius's achievement scores place him at approximately fifth-grade level in reading and comprehension. His verbal scores, however, are quite high. Julius has been diagnosed as inattentive, easily distracted, and hyperactive. His peers admire him because of his quick wit. He is very athletic but misses too many classes to be involved in any team sport.

Professor Donovan asked each student in his classroom management course to reflect on why Julius misbehaved. Some comments about Julius's behavior were as follows:

- "Julius is behaving poorly because he has an attention problem. He needs to be on medication. That would probably rein him in."
- "Julius has a definite anger problem. It's important to help Julius find out what's driving his anger."
- "Julius doesn't know how else to behave. He needs to be taught appropriate classroom behavior, not just told to get back to work."
- "I think there's a lot going on with Julius. His family situation, his learning problems, and the fact that the teacher's instructional style doesn't fit his need for activity all contribute to his acting out behavior."

With an increased focus on accountability in our schools in the United States, teachers and school administrators are concerned that students be provided with an environment in which teaching and learning can take place without unnecessary disruptions. Students want to be in classrooms where they feel safe to navigate their intellectual and social worlds. Parents want to send their children to schools that are free from violence and other forms of harassment. In the scenario above, Julius's behavior challenged his teacher, Ms. Zimmer. Her response to Julius is not at all uncommon. Teachers have historically ranked classroom management as one of their main concerns (Evertson & Weinstein, 2006; Sugai & Horner, 2002). Understanding the reasons students act out and responding in a way that is supportive and informative is a key factor to students' success in school.

In Chapter 5 we defined "at risk" and described many out-of-school factors (e.g., disability, minority status, language, family poverty, and homelessness) that have become significant predictors of school behavior, making the teaching and learning process far more difficult for teachers and school personnel. In Chapters 6 and 7 we talked about the importance of positive teacher–student and student–student relationships. We also discussed the value of building a community of learners in school and connecting students through service to the community at large. Class meetings and peer mediation were described as ways to help students resolve conflicts.

Even with important components in place, some students will still challenge their teachers by behaving inappropriately. In Chapter 8 we define classroom management. Several theoretical perspectives and needs theories are described along with the educational application of each as a way of understanding students' unproductive behavior. Cultural influences that may relate to interpreting problem behavior in the classroom are addressed. We explore the negative effects of punishment and suggest positive behavior supports and interventions for preventing and responding to disruptive behavior.

Classroom Management

Many think of classroom management as organizing the classroom, developing rules, or as a response to student misbehavior. Elias and Schwab (2006) defined classroom management as follows:

> All of the teacher's practices related to establishing the physical and social environment of the classroom, regulating routines and daily activities, and preventing and correcting problems. Nearly everything a teacher does, aside from communicating the content of the academic curriculum, is part of classroom management. Indeed, even the mode of instruction (e.g., frontal lecturing, worksheets, creative group work projects) is a component of classroom management.
>
> (p. 309)

This definition addresses the many tasks involved in managing a classroom. Nothing is more important to student success than a teacher's ability to provide students with a safe, well-organized environment in which to learn and grow.

Discipline, on the other hand, can be defined as "the actions that facilitate the development of self-control, responsibility, and character" (Savage & Savage, 2010, p. 8). In addition to helping students succeed academically, teachers are also responsible for helping students develop socially and emotionally. Savage and Savage stressed the importance of classroom management as a preventative measure. Discipline is a reactive measure that teachers and school personnel use to help students develop the self-control needed to be successful in school.

Theoretical Perspectives on Behavior

Educators' perceptions about the behavior children exhibit affect the way they instruct and manage students in their classrooms. Teachers constantly struggle with understanding the factors influencing behavior. For novice and experienced teachers, making sense of student behavior is critical to the teaching and learning process. If we think children are acting out because they have poor skills in reading, we may react in one way; if we think they are acting out to be defiant, we may react another way. If we believe certain children are unable to perform because they come from a low socioeconomic background or from a culture other than our own, we may not be willing to find strategies that will help them be successful. Being able to draw upon a wide range of theories helps teachers make decisions about classroom behavior and justify those decisions to administrators, parents, colleagues, and the students they teach. Theories lead to a more thorough understanding of behavior and to evidence-based best practices.

Although numerous theoretical models have been developed to explain problem behavior, five major theories prevail: behavioral, biophysical, psychodynamic, behavioral, ecological, and needs-based theories. "For purposes of explanation and control of behavior, humans have been variously conceptualized, for example, as spiritual beings, biological organisms, rational and feeling persons, and products of their environments" (Kauffman, 1997, p. 193). The descriptions of these perspectives on behavior presented here are cursory; much additional reading is required to fully understand each theory.

Behavioral

The roots of behaviorism can be traced to a philosophical movement called "positivism" popular in the nineteenth century (Maag, 1999). Positivism supported the notion that the only real knowledge is observable. The behavioral model includes a number of theories and points of view about human behavior (Bandura, 1977a; Skinner, 1971; Wolpe, 1961). Problem behaviors are considered learned and maintained by interactions within the environment. Events in the environment can reinforce behavior either positively or negatively (Cullinan, Epstein, & Lloyd, 1991). Finally, because behavior is learned, it can be "unlearned" and new behaviors can be taught.

Behavioral techniques are the most commonly used interventions in classrooms today and are based on the use of positive reinforcement, negative reinforcement, and punishment. Before we explain these principles it is important to understand why challenging behaviors occur according to a behavioral perspective. There are two major reasons for misbehavior. Students either try to obtain something that is desirable or escape from something that is undesirable (Chandler & Dahlquist, 2010; Hardin, 2008).

Positive reinforcement serves to strengthen a behavior. Teachers who give rewards such as tokens, tickets, and extra time on the computer believe these reinforcements will encourage students to stay on task or engage in socially desirable behavior. Negative reinforcement involves removing something to strengthen a behavior. A teacher may take recess away from students who do not have their work done. In order to effectively use positive and negative reinforcement, it is important for teachers to consider the student. What is positive for one student may be negative for another. For many students, academic instruction is negative. Inappropriate behavior is displayed to avoid the task. To illustrate, Nu is a second-grade student who has difficulty with the simple math concepts of adding and subtracting. Every time the teacher asks him to work at the board, he resists and becomes angry. Nu's behavior is likely to be an attempt to avoid doing math. The teacher sends him to time-out to think about his behavior. In this case the student has managed to escape the task he feared. If avoiding the task is the purpose of Nu's behavior, the teacher needs to spend time teaching him math skills. Nu needs to experience some level of comfort and competence with the math concepts before being asked to work at the board. Teachers must have an understanding of the function of the student's behavior in order to respond in a way that helps the student learn to behave appropriately.

The third principle of the behavioral paradigm is punishment. According to Hardin (2008), punishment is the application of something unpleasant or the removal of something rewarding. For many teachers, controlling children seems to be the focus of their entire day. This "control mentality," says Maag (2001), is pervasive throughout education. Knitzer, Steinberg, and Fleisch, in their 1990 book *At the Schoolhouse Door: An Examination of Programs and Policies for Children with Behavioral and Emotional Problems*, used the term "curriculum of control" to characterize classrooms for students labeled emotionally or behaviorally handicapped. They reported that in such classrooms, the traditional curriculum is not about academics, thinking and problem solving, but rather about controlling children's behaviors. Brophy and Rohrkemper (1981) found that when teachers felt threatened, angry, or frustrated by student behavior, they selected more punitive interventions (e.g., reprimand, time-out, detention, suspension, or expulsion). Problems with student behavior are among the main sources of teacher stress and often given as a reason for leaving the profession.

Unfortunately, punishment has not proven effective in addressing problem behavior in the schools (Skiba & Peterson, 2000). Nevertheless, punishment is common, especially with minority students. African-American and Latino students are more likely than their White peers to be suspended or expelled from school for the same or similar problem behavior (Raffaele Mendez & Knoff, 2003; Skiba, Horner, Chung, Rausch, May, & Tobin, 2011). African-American students are suspended for physical aggression, noncompliance, and insubordination. African-American students are also overrepresented in office referrals, suspension, and expulsions (Skiba, Michael, Nardo, & Peterson, 2002). Other related data indicate that African-American male students with disabilities are also more likely to be suspended at an earlier age and for a longer period of time than White students with disabilities (Forness & Kavale, 1988). These practices exclude African-American students from opportunities to learn and often result in students being disengaged from school and ultimately to academic failure (Cartledge & Talbert-Johnson, 1998).

Let's return to our scenario about Julius. Remembering that Julius is an African-American male student with learning disabilities and an attention deficit disorder, how do you think most teachers would have responded to his behavior? Chances are they would respond with some type of punishment.

Miltenberger (2007) identified a number of undesirable side effects associated with punishment:

- Punishment may produce elicited aggression or other emotional side effects.
- The use of punishment may result in escape or avoidance behaviors by the person whose behavior is being punished.
- The use of punishment may be negatively reinforcing for the person using punishment and thus may result in the misuse or overuse of punishment.
- When punishment is used, its use is modeled, and observers or people whose behavior is punished may be more likely to use punishment themselves in the future.
- Punishment is associated with a number of ethical issues and issues of acceptability.

(p. 114)

Although punishment has many undesirable side effects, it may be an appropriate response when the undesirable behavior is physically dangerous or when, along with punishment, an alternate behavior is taught to replace the negative behavior. A student who is suspended for fighting will likely continue fighting to resolve conflicts. The student may need to learn more appropriate ways of dealing with anger. If a student shouts out answers during classroom discussions, he needs to be taught to raise his hand and wait to be called upon. Reprimanding the student in front of the class, ignoring the student, or taking away privileges do not teach the student what you want him to do. Although punishment may bring about an immediate change in behavior, that change is usually temporary. Punishment teaches children what *not* to do, not what to do.

So, why the overreliance on punishment? The choice of punishment over other strategies may be more of a symbolic gesture to appease administrators, parents, and other teachers. It suggests that strong action is being taken in response to a perceived breakdown of order in the schools (Noguera, 1995). Teachers feel they are expected to have good classroom control. A quiet classroom is regarded highly by administrators and parents. Maag (2003) suggested that punishment continues to be used because it works for about 95 percent of students attending public schools. Mild forms of punishment, such as verbal reprimands, loss of privileges, or removals from the classroom, control most students' behaviors.

Many teachers, ill-prepared in the area of classroom management, choose an authoritarian approach when dealing with students with problem behaviors. This may be because being controlling is part of their personality or it may be because they are afraid of the student(s). Kohn (1996) suggested that we punish because it makes us feel powerful; we think we need to win the battle. In any case, this approach often leads to power struggles that escalate the problem. Brendtro et al. (1990) observed that "when adult strategies are in vogue, two opposing cultures arise: controlling adults and counter-controlling youth. Adult control becomes self-perpetuating: the more one controls the more one needs to control" (p. 103).

Teachers use punishment because it is quick and easy and works in the short term. For example, a teacher sends a student to the principal's office for talking back and refusing to read aloud. The teacher is reinforced because the student is no longer disrupting the class and the teacher is able to return to the reading assignment. If this student has low reading skills and is afraid to read aloud, getting out of class has reinforced the student. This is referred to as negative reinforcement.

These strategies do not work for the 5 percent of students who display the most challenging behaviors. Maag (2003) cautioned that teachers start to think that the 5 percent need to be punished using the same strategies more severely and more often. Schools have moved toward tougher policies such as zero tolerance and expulsion, which have little impact on changing behavior (Skiba & Peterson, 2000). Of course, if the punishment worked in the first place, it would be used less rather than more frequently. Schools use punishment instead of finding ways to involve students and teachers in a rich curriculum of thinking and problem solving.

SOCIAL LEARNING THEORY

In the 1970s and 1980s behavior theories moved away from the focus on environmental factors to cognitive theories that focused on the influence of one's emotions and thinking on learning and behavior. Social learning, or modeling, is one principle proposed by behaviorists. Learning occurs within a social context. According to Bandura (1977a, 1977b) children learn behaviors by observing the actions of siblings, parents, teachers, friends, and others. Behaviors, both negative and positive, can be learned through exposure to a model. An individual's identification with the model, his thoughts and feelings about an event, may override reinforcements in the social environment. Let's say, for example, Julius has an opportunity to work with another student who he looks up to. Social learning theory would surmise that Julius would have less need to act out if allowed to work with a peer he respects and who is respected by the teacher. It is important for teachers to make sure that small groups include students who can model appropriate social skills.

COGNITIVE-BEHAVIOR MODIFICATION

The melding of behavioral and cognitive research has brought about intervention strategies called *cognitive-behavior modification* (Bandura, 1986; Meichenbaum, 1977, 1980). These strategies support the notion that how individuals think and feel about events as well as environmental influences must be taken into consideration when modifying behavior. According to Zirpoli and Melloy (2007), interventions common to this approach include self-management strategies such as self-instruction, self-monitoring, self-reinforcement, and cognitive-interpersonal problem solving. Self-management interventions are all focused on giving more control and opportunities for learning to the student. Alberto and Troutman (2006) identified some advantages to using self-management: responsibility for change is placed on the student, newly learned behaviors are more likely to generalize to other settings, and students learn to be more independent. The goal of cognitive-behavior modification interventions is to help individuals become more aware of their reactions to difficult events and to actively engage them in taking control of their own responses. Proponents of this model believe that externally oriented behavior interventions do not teach students new behavior, but instead make students overly dependent on a teacher to monitor their behavior.

Understanding behavioral psychology is critical to implementing these strategies appropriately. Teachers need to learn how to observe behavior, collect data, design interventions, and evaluate results. For a thorough understanding of principles and procedures of behavior modification see Alberto and Troutman (2006), Maag (2003) and Miltenberger (2007).

Biophysical

The biophysical theory is basically a medical model placing an emphasis on organic origins of behavior. According to this perspective, problem behavior lies within the individual. Proponents of this model believe that physical defects, malfunctions, and illnesses directly affect an individual's behavior. Disorders such as autism, schizophrenia, hyperactivity, and depression are considered to have biophysical causes.

Biophysical interventions (e.g., drug therapy, surgery, biofeedback, and nutrition therapy) require the services of physicians, psychiatrists, neurologists, etc. The role of the teacher is that of liaison to the specialists and parents. For example, a teacher may have a student who is depressed and on medication. A goal of the medication may be to help the student be more alert and receptive to the classroom environment. Another goal, less often discussed, may be to move the student to behavior of a normative expectation. Teachers should be aware of the purposes and benefits of various medications prescribed to students and the potential side effects these drugs may have on academic performance and behavior. A teacher's observations can provide valuable information to parents and physicians. For example, Walker & Shea (1999) suggested the supportive role of the teacher might also include referral, modifying the classroom environment and curriculum to meet students' unique needs, and obtaining permission for administering medication to the child in school.

Psychodynamic

The psychodynamic approach evolved from the original theoretical formulations of Freud (1935). Proponents of the psychodynamic approach (Glasser, 1969; Gordon, 1974; Long, Morse, & Newman, 1965) stressed the importance of teachers understanding the meaning of children's behavior. Behavior is seen as a symptom of inner thoughts and feelings learned from unconscious conflicts in early childhood. Attachment patterns that are formed in early childhood can have an impact on learning in school and later in life.

A teacher or other adult may be identified as a substitute attachment figure to help children deal with the thoughts and feelings that motivate their disruptive behavior. The education process should be less repressive, more encouraging of children's emotional expression, and more sensitive to crisis situations (Rezmierski & Kotre, 1974). Helping students gain control over their own behavior is seen as a long-term goal rather than a quick-fix solution. Teachers might use conferencing and good communication skills, such as reflective listening and questioning, to help students solve problems. Other creative activities (e.g., play therapy, puppetry, role playing, dance and physical activities, music, art, photography) are interventions that encourage students to express their feelings and emotions (Walker & Shea, 1999).

Understanding problem behavior from this perspective helps educators discern the importance of providing a supportive, caring environment that encourages students to express their feelings openly and appropriately. This theory highlights the influence of socio-emotional issues as they relate to learning. It also emphasizes the resource that counselors, psychologists, psychiatrists, and social workers provide outside the school setting.

Ecological

From an ecological perspective, behavior is seen as the expression of the relationship between an individual and physical-spatial and social environments in which that individual functions (Bronfenbrenner, 1979). In order to understand inappropriate behavior one must understand the context in which the behavior occurs. The ecological approach considers many variables in the family, classroom, school, and community. It is meaningless to discuss problem behaviors in isolation from the contexts in which the behaviors exist, especially since it is the contexts that define the behavior as a problem. From an ecological perspective, problem behavior is viewed as a problem within the system; therefore, the child can be viewed as part of the problem rather than the sole owner of the problem. Ecological interventions focus on changes not only in the child, but also in systems in the child's environment.

According to Rhodes (1967, 1970), problem behavior often lies in the expectations of those with whom the child interacts. Kauffman, Pullen, and Ackers (1986) identified several factors teachers contribute to students' problem behavior: inconsistency in management strategies, reinforcement of inappropriate behavior, unrealistic expectations of students, a lack of responsiveness to individual differences, irritability with children, and reliance on punishment to manage behavior. Montgomery and Paul (1982) also noted conditions within the classroom that may contribute to problem behavior: unfair competition, autocratic or permissive teaching style, excessive structuring or lack of structure, over-stimulation or under-stimulation. Teachers can have a major influence on the way students approach their academic work and the way they behave in the classroom.

Peer groups are also a major influence on students' behavior in school. Children are likely to imitate the behavior of those who are socially popular, physically powerful, attractive, and in command of important reinforcers (Bandura, 1986). Students who act out are likely to gravitate toward peers who are also disruptive (Kauffman, 1997). Rejection by peers can cause aggression or depression in some students. Teachers need to be aware of peer influence when planning seating arrangements, assigning cooperative projects, and designing behavioral consequences or rewards.

In addition to classroom pressures, students may be dealing with problems at home (e.g., divorce, illness, death, or loss of employment) that make it difficult for them to attend to school tasks. A student who is angry over a family dispute the night before may not be emotionally available for math instruction. We must remember that parents and teachers hold certain values and beliefs and set behavioral expectations based on the cultures in which they live and work. Students come to school with their own beliefs, values, skills, and expectations about how things should happen. They may react negatively or withdraw when things do not go as expected.

From an ecological perspective, the classroom must be organized to facilitate student learning and behavior management. Among the factors that must be considered are the use of space, materials, and equipment; procedures for classroom routines; and rules for guiding student behavior. Classroom interventions may include the use of group discussion and class meetings to support students working through conflicts and seeing those conflicts from another's point of view.

Understanding problem behavior from an ecological perspective requires teachers to consider their own behaviors, classroom routines, and other factors that may influence a child's behavior. The teacher's role is that of liaison among the numerous individuals and agencies that are involved in the lives of the students. All systems must be analyzed for factors that may contribute to a child's problem behavior and, then, possible solutions can be determined and implemented.

Needs-Based

Another approach to understanding children's behaviors suggests that problems occur when children's needs are not met in the classroom environment. Many times students act out because they did not understand the instructions, the work is too hard or too simple, or peer or teacher interactions are difficult. Some may not have the academic or social skills to be successful. Students may have problems at home that interfere with their ability to concentrate on schoolwork. Some students would prefer to act out rather than look stupid. Teachers may be able to minimize problem behavior by determining student needs, modifying instructional strategies, and/or teaching new skills.

A number of researchers have written about students' basic psychological needs and how those needs influence behavior in the classroom (Brendtro et al., 1990; Coopersmith, 1967; Dreikurs & Cassel, 1972; Glasser, 1969, 1990; Kohn, 1993; Maslow, 1968). Each of these authors resonates with our discussion of culturally responsive teaching. For example, Brendtro et al. (1990), drawing on European tradition and Native-American philosophies of child rearing, indicated that students need to feel a sense of belonging, experience mastery and interdependence, and have an opportunity to be generous to others in order to be successful in school. Native-American child-rearing practices focus on educating and empowering children.

Maslow (1968) suggested that students' needs fall within a hierarchy beginning with the basic physiological needs for shelter, sleep, food, and water. Many children come to school with these basic needs unmet. Problem behavior is viewed as a child's reaction to the frustration of not getting his/her needs met. It is difficult to focus on math when you have not eaten or have not had adequate sleep. Physiological needs are followed by safety needs (e.g., freedom from danger), love needs (e.g., acceptance from teachers, peers), esteem needs (e.g., competence, mastery), and ultimately the need for self-actualization (e.g., creative self-expression, satisfaction of curiosity).

Glasser (1969) maintained that all behavior is an attempt to meet five basic needs: survival (food, shelter, freedom from harm), belonging (security, comfort, group membership), power (sense of importance, consideration by others), fun (enjoying emotional and intellectual endeavors), and freedom (exercising choice and responsibility). In his book *The Quality School*, published in 1990, Glasser further identified the needs for love and self-worth. Glasser (1969) further suggested that our current school system is based on a philosophy of non-involvement and a limited emphasis on thinking, which is a formula for school failure. In order to achieve self-worth, students must learn to think and solve problems. Love and self-worth lead to the most important need: self-identity. It is the responsibility of schools and teachers to help children find a successful identity.

Other theorists argue that teachers need to understand the underlying goals students seek to achieve in the classroom. Research (Albert, 1996; Hardin, 2008) has identified four goals: attention seeking, power seeking, revenge seeking, and failure avoiding. According to Hardin, most student misbehavior is a function of attention seeking. For attention-seeking students, self-worth is connected to the attention they receive from significant others, positive or negative. These students may be very participative and attentive in class but if these behaviors do not produce sufficient attention, they may act out in more problematic ways.

A second goal is to gain power. Students with this goal may react very negatively when a teacher tries to redirect their behavior. The locus shifts from gaining attention to controlling the adult. This student may throw a temper tantrum, claim the teacher is picking on him or her, and/or challenge classroom assignments or activities.

Revenge seeking is a third goal underlying student misbehavior. According to Hardin (2008), revenge seeking results from a series of discouragements that lead students to believe they are not capable of attaining positive attention. The anger the students have may be a function of exogenous factors such as a broken home or endogenous factors such as prejudice, bullying, or academic failure. The way to get attention, then, is to get back at students and teachers. The most striking example of revenge seeking occurred at Columbine High School in 1999. Since that time, school shootings and student suicides related to bullying continue to plague this country.

The final goal is avoiding failure. Failure-avoiding students are discouraged and do not believe that any amount of effort will result in academic success. These students may not act out, but they often give up trying to be successful. Our discussion of self-worth theory in Chapter 2 is relevant here. Some students would rather fail as a result of low effort than put forth effort and fail. These students may not be disruptive; they tend to remove themselves from investing much energy in academic tasks.

Kohn (1993) suggested that to be motivated to learn, students need what he called the three Cs: content, community, and choice. Students need to be taught content that has meaning to their lives. Kohn believed that cooperative learning helps children feel they are part of a safe community. Kohn felt that kids don't learn by just following directions but rather by making choices. Kohn argued that teachers spend too much time manipulating student behavior instead of providing students with an engaging curriculum and a caring atmosphere.

In summary, the perspectives discussed provide a way for educators to think about, understand, and manage student behavior. The theories focus on different issues, emphasize different etiologies, and arrive at different conclusions regarding interventions or best practices. No one theory will suffice to fully explain student misconduct. Rather, we hope teachers will draw upon the theoretical approaches, their own experience, and the experiences of others to diagnose behavior problems and choose interventions that best meet the needs of individual students.

Reflection

- Discuss the cause of Julius's behavior from each theoretical perspective and needs theory.
- What interventions would you choose for Julius and why?
- Which theoretical perspective(s) best fit your view of problem behavior?
- Brainstorm activities to meet each of these basic needs of students in a classroom: Safety, belonging, power, fun, and freedom.

Cultural Influences on Discipline

Zirpoli and Melloy (2001) contended that cultural influences on behavior have been largely ignored in the field of behavior management and must be addressed. Teachers must understand that selected behavioral interventions can be influenced by the students' cultural backgrounds and by their own beliefs and backgrounds (Ishii-Jordan, 2000). As we review research related to cultural influences in classroom management, it is important to avoid stereotyping and to remember that within any cultural group there is a great deal of diversity and individualism.

Grossman (2004) pointed out that:

> Educators don't have to be prejudiced to use biased classroom management techniques with students. Even well-meaning teachers who are not aware of the different behavioral, disciplinary, and communication styles of the various ethnic groups in their classrooms can misperceive and misunderstand students' behaviors when they interpret them from their own perspective. They can perceive behavior problems that don't exist, not notice problems that do exist, misunderstand the causes of students' behaviors, and use inappropriate techniques to deal with students' behavior problems.
>
> (p. 151)

Culturally and linguistically diverse students are likely to experience conflicts when schools and teachers are not sensitive to their culture, language, family background, and learning styles (Baca & Cervantes, 2004), and Cartledge and Talbert-Johnson (1998) noted:

> We are all products of our environment, and [our] experiences greatly determine how we perceive the world and respond to environmental events. With a largely White female teaching force, cultural discontinuities enter in when the student population consists of racially/

> ethnically diverse youngsters who are disproportionately impoverished. When teachers and students are out of sync, they clash and confront each other, both consciously and unconsciously in matters concerning proxemics (use of interpersonal distance), paralanguage (behaviors accompanying speech such as voice tone and pitch and speech rate and length), and verbal behavior (gesture, facial expression, and eye gaze). Examples of these transactions are the ways status in the classroom is determined, the degrading connotations attached to the use of other languages and dialects, and the ways we differentially affirm group membership and cultural identity. The resulting dissonance in communicative processes contributes to the development of communication gaps and misunderstandings.
>
> (pp. 8–9)

Grossman (1991, 1995) reported that educators tend to maintain more prejudicial behavioral expectations for minority students than for non-minority students. For example, teachers tend to have lower expectations for poor African-American students, criticize them more often, and use more punitive disciplinary strategies with them. Townsend (2000) identified several cultural conflicts in the classroom that may pose a threat to African-American students. One is the ability of African-American students to engage in multiple tasks simultaneously. For example, the need to socialize while working on assignments may be perceived as defiance when tasks require individualized work. African-American students also have a need to "prepare" to work, which has been referred to as "stage-setting" behavior. This entails socializing with others, sharpening pencils, and getting out the right notebook before beginning a task. Townsend also identified language differences that lead to misinterpretation. He referred to the use of nonstandard English and slang spoken by African-American students as unfamiliar to most school personnel. Nonverbal communication is also misinterpreted. The example Townsend gave is of African-American girls who act in a very "impassioned" and "emotive" manner. Teachers may choose to punish students for what they perceive as combative or argumentative behavior.

Many African-American students prefer being able to respond out loud when the teacher is talking to show that they acknowledge, agree with, or disagree with what is being said. Although students may be impulsive in their attempt to be involved, this behavior can be viewed as rude and disrespectful (Gay, 2000). We have to remember that socializing and being able to converse is a priority for many students who come from highly verbal environments. Most teachers, however, see these behaviors as threatening, make numerous attempts to control the behavior, and eventually conclude that the child is not manageable. The student escalates the behavior by refusing to work or becoming more verbally aggressive; at the same time, the student gets behind in his or her work and eventually gives up. You can see that this damaging and unproductive cycle happened very quickly with Julius.

Students with disabilities, students from lower socioeconomic backgrounds, and students speaking minority languages or nonstandard dialects of English tend to be disciplined more harshly. For example, African-American students with disabilities are suspended from school at twice the rate of their nondisabled peers. Data collected by the U.S. Department of Education during the 2009–2010 school year (Snyder & Dillow, 2012) indicated that 13 percent of students with disabilities in K–12 programs were suspended, compared to 7 percent of students without disabilities. Quite alarming was the finding that in ten states including California more than 25 percent of Black students with disabilities were suspended. Chicago schools suspended 67.5 percent of its African-American students in 2009–2010.

Irivine (1998, as cited in Evertson & Weinstein, 2006) shared culturally responsive strategies that African-American teachers use:

> They perceive themselves as parental surrogates and advocates for their African-American students. They employ a teaching style filled with rhythmic language and rapid intonation with many instances of repetition, call and response, high emotional involvement, creative analogies, figurative language, gestures and body movements, symbolism, aphorisms, and lively and spontaneous discussions. They use students' everyday cultural and historical experiences in an effort to link new concepts to prior knowledge. They spend classroom and non-classroom time developing a personal relationship with their children, and often tease and joke with their students using dialect or slang to establish this personal relationship. They teach with authority.
>
> (p. 510)

Banks and Banks (1989) cautioned that, "although membership in a gender, racial, ethnic, social class, or religious group can provide us with important clues about individuals' behavior, it cannot allow us to predict behavior" (p. 13). The information gleaned from a person's group affiliation allows teachers to begin thinking about their own beliefs, values, and prejudices and their effects on the teachers' responses to behaviors exhibited by children from cultures other than their own. Teachers are encouraged to recognize cultural diversity as a strength on which to build a positive educational foundation for students.

Utilizing effective instructional strategies can produce positive academic and social outcomes for nearly all students, minimizing the occurrence of problem behavior. Generally, teachers who use a variety of approaches in instruction and assessment will meet children's needs. Banks (1999) recommended implementation of a multicultural curriculum

> with teaching strategies that are involving, interactive, personalized, and cooperative. The teacher should listen to and legitimize the

> voices of students from different racial, cultural, and gender groups. Multicultural content is inherently emotive, personal, conflictual, and interactive. It is essential that students be given opportunities to express their feelings and emotions, to interact with their peers and classmates, and to express rage or pride when multicultural issues are discussed. (p. 111)

Effective teaching involves recognizing one's biases, developing positive teacher–student relationships, building a caring classroom community in which students feel respected and valued before students are able to focus on academic tasks. We recommend that instruction involve active learning, including opportunities for physical movement and opportunities to work collaboratively with peers.

Reflection

- As Julius's teacher, what cultural considerations might influence your planning to include him in classroom activities?
- What are some ways teachers could make the classroom environment inviting to students from different cultural backgrounds?

Positive Behavioral Supports

As we discussed earlier, teachers and administrators are concerned about the amount of time spent dealing with school discipline issues, which takes away from the time spent educating students. There has been a dramatic increase in student referrals for noncompliance, disrespect, and insubordination as well as for more serious behaviors such as threats, bullying, and other forms of harassment that lead to an increase in suspensions and expulsions. We know that the traditional responses to problem behavior don't reduce problem behavior or increase academic achievement.

We begin by introducing you to a school-wide program that, when implemented correctly, has already proven to effectively reduce inappropriate behaviors (as measured by decreases in discipline referrals, suspensions, and expulsions) and increase prosocial behavior and academic success (Simonsen, Sugai, & Negron, 2008). School-wide Positive Behavior Supports (SWPBS) is defined as:

> a proactive, team-based framework for creating and sustaining safe and effective schools. Emphasis is placed on prevention of problem behavior, development of pro-social skills, and the use of data-based

> problem solving for addressing existing behavior concerns. School-wide Positive Behavioral Supports increases the capacity of schools to educate all students utilizing research-based school-wide, classroom, and individualized interventions.
>
> (p. vii)

SWPBS is not a curriculum but rather a collection of evidence-based practices and interventions and systems change strategies that school administrators and teachers agree to use to minimize problem behavior and increase instruction time. What makes this system different from traditional approaches to discipline (e.g., punishment, suspension) is that the focus is on changing the classroom or school environment rather than changing individual students (Evers & Spencer, 2011). Teachers realize that student behavior is as much influenced by environment as it is by individual student characteristics. Teachers thus respond proactively, not reactively, to minimize problem behavior.

There are three tiers of support known as positive behavior interventions and supports (PBIS). Tier 1 is usually referred to as the *universal* or *primary* tier and provides supports for all students (e.g., establishing and teaching school-wide rules and procedures, teaching acceptable social skills, and designing a school-wide system for reinforcing and acknowledging positive behavior) across all settings school-wide. Tier 1 includes consistent consequences for problem behavior. The primary tier provides supports for a majority of students (85 percent). Tier 2, also referred to as *secondary* or *targeted* interventions, supports a targeted number of students who have not sufficiently responded to Tier 1 interventions. This group represents approximately 15 percent of the student population. Several office referrals might indicate a need for Tier 2 interventions. At this level a student's behavior is not considered to be dangerous to self or to others. Interventions at Tier 2 include increased behavior and academic support, instruction on targeted academic or social skills needed to be successful, and ongoing feedback on students' progress. Some students may need an individualized intervention plan, developed after a functional behavior assessment has been conducted by team members involved with the student. Tier 3 interventions, referred to as *tertiary* or *intensive*, are designed to support a small portion (5 percent) of the student population, whose behaviors are chronic and frequent, dangerous, and/or highly disruptive, impeding the learning of others. Students receiving support at this level require individualized interventions tailored to meet their specific needs. Students receiving support at this level are required to have a functional behavior assessment and an individualized behavior plan. At each tier, data are collected to determine intervention effectiveness and changes are made accordingly. Next, we provide detailed information about interventions appropriate for each level. Play the video at www.pbis.org/ to see SWPBS basic features.

Tier 1 Interventions and supports

Establishing and Teaching Positive Rules and Procedures

One of the most important roles the teacher plays is that of classroom manager, fulfilling the many tasks we described earlier. Learning is difficult to achieve without a well-organized classroom. Research on teacher effectiveness indicates that effective teachers organize their classrooms so as to prevent disruptive behavior (Jones & Jones, 2007). Spending time at the beginning of the year designing the physical environment and teaching and clarifying classroom rules and procedures minimizes the occurrence of problem behavior later. The overall physical arrangement of the classroom (e.g., wheelchair access, furniture, schedules, activities, lighting, bulletin boards, materials and supplies, learning centers) is strategically arranged to improve student learning and behavior (Stronge, Tucker, & Hindman, 2004). The physical environment should reflect those who teach and those who learn there. Go to http://behavioradvisor.com/ClassroomDesign.html for guidelines for arranging the physical classroom environment. Then, go to http://iris.peabody.vanderbilt.edu/casestudies.html and complete the activities related to management of students and classroom design.

Rules and procedures are necessary if students are to work in a safe, caring environment. The way the rules are selected and implemented can impact students' classroom behavior greatly. In fact, the extent to which students know the rules and follow them is directly correlated with appropriate behavior (Brophy & Good, 1986).

Developing classroom rules requires, first, knowing the district and school rules in which you work. The rules you develop in your class may be different from, but should not contradict, the rules of your local campus or school district. Rules should tell students what to do and what not to do. Scheuermann and Hall (2007) suggested some guidelines for developing rules:

1. State rules in positive terms. Tell the students what you want them to do. "Walk in the classroom and halls" as opposed to "Don't run in the classroom or hallways." "Use indoor voices" instead of "Don't yell."
2. Keep the number of rules to a minimum, no more than five. When you have too many rules students tend to ignore them.
3. Set rules that cover multiple situations. For example, "Come to class prepared with all required materials."
4. Keep the rules appropriate for students' ages and developmental levels. "Keep your hands, feet, and objects to yourself," may be appropriate for elementary students but not for high school students.

5. Teach your students the rules. Demonstrate what the behavior should and shouldn't look like. This can be done through modeling or role play every day over the first few weeks of class.
6. Set an example for rule-following behavior. A teacher might have a rule stating "Students must turn their work in on time" but then not return their graded papers in a timely manner. Or the teacher may have a rule, "Cell phones, iPods, laptops are not to be used during circle time" and then turn around to answer a cell phone call during circle time.
7. Be consistent in enforcing the rules. Perhaps the teacher has the rule "Raise your hand for permission to speak or leave the classroom" but ignores the rule during a lively class discussion.

(pp. 175–177)

Teachers should remember to respond positively when the rules are followed: "Thank you for raising your hand." Glasser (1990) discussed the importance of students having a voice in determining the curriculum and the rules of their school. He believed that democracy and responsibility are learned by "living" them. Consequences should be developed for noncompliance.

Students are involved in numerous classroom activities that require specific procedures if the classroom is to run smoothly. There are procedures related to equipment (desks, storage areas, learning centers, pencil sharpener), individual seat work (asking for help, participation, assignments, make-up work), group work (student roles, expected behavior), and out-of-class activities (lining up, fire drills, playground, cafeteria, library, bus). For example, students going back and forth to the pencil sharpener can be quite noisy and distracting. A procedure that would cut down on the noise and distraction might be as follows: (1) raise your hand for permission to leave your desk, (2) walk quietly to the counter, (3) place old pencil in the container and pick up a sharpened pencil, (4) return to your desk quietly and begin working. Teachers usually complain that most problem behavior occurs during transition periods, changing from one activity to another. Students who finish assignments early and have nothing to do are likely to find something to do, not usually something the teacher had in mind. Planning for "down time" is critical to effective classroom management.

Procedures need to be clearly defined and taught to students using the same guidelines we described for teaching classroom rules. Again, the time spent clarifying classroom procedures and teaching those procedures to students will lessen opportunities for problem behavior to occur. Asking for student input in creating classroom rules and procedures empowers students and allows teachers to teach and monitor student learning.

Acknowledge and Reinforce Positive Behavior

As Good and Brophy (1973) pointed out, an effective approach to classroom management involves rewarding desirable behavior and utilizing techniques that prevent problems from emerging. Positive reinforcement, such as praise, increases the probability that the behavior it follows will recur. Wielkiewicz (1995) noted that the effectiveness of positive reinforcement is a universal principle that is in effect regardless of gender, age, culture, or disability of a child.

Teacher praise has been found to be one of the most empirically sound teacher competencies (Brophy, 1981; Conroy, Sutherland, Snyder, Al-Hendawi, & Vo, 2009; Maag & Katsiyannis, 1999). Unfortunately, strategies using positive reinforcement such as praise are rarely used, or used correctly, to manage students' behavior. Teachers respond more often to disruptive behavior than to on-task behavior. The expectation is that students will behave well, and when they do, they are ignored. By acknowledging students' positive behavior, teachers encourage them to take responsibility for their own learning. Students are drawn to teachers who are encouraging and supportive, recognize effort and achievement, and show genuine enthusiasm when students are successful.

Brophy (1981) outlined several characteristics of effective praise:

- Effective praise is delivered contingently. Praise must immediately follow desired behaviors. One teacher said, "I can't find anything to praise this student for." She finally started with, "Jacob, it's great to see you here on time today." Students with disabilities and other at-risk students have already experienced failure and may need to be encouraged for small steps toward their goals.
- Another teacher was observed praising a student for sitting down, not talking, putting his pencil on the paper, and for just about everything else the student did that day. Teachers need to be careful not to praise inappropriate behavior and not to praise every desired behavior. The key to using praise effectively "lies in its quality rather than its frequency" (Good & Brophy, 1984, p. 193).
- Effective praise specifies the particulars of the accomplishment. "Good job" does not always tell students what they did to receive praise. "Your project report was well-written and addressed the critical issues of inclusion and implications for teacher training." This statement more clearly identifies the specifics of the accomplishment.
- Effective praise shows spontaneity, variety, and other signs of credibility. "I like the way you chose to solve that problem—very creative." Most secondary students know whether you are genuine in praising them. They may perceive praise given for easy tasks as an indication that the teacher had low expectations of them.
- Effective praise rewards attainment of specified performance criteria, including effort criteria. "You followed all of the steps to get the right answer. Your persistence paid off."
- Effective praise provides information to students about their competence or the value of their accomplishment. "Your presentation showed me that

you have a good understanding of the impact of smoking on pregnancy. I would like to display the posters you developed in the library."

- Effective praise orients students toward better appreciation of their own task related behavior and thinking about problem solving. "I observed your hard work on this project, especially the way you brought your group members together. Great collaboration."
- Effective praise uses students' own prior accomplishments as the context for describing present accomplishments. "This is the second week in a row that you've gotten 100 percent on your spelling test. Using mnemonics is really paying off."
- Effective praise attributes success to effort and ability. Research indicates that students who link effort and achievement will become more internally motivated and academically engaged (Lam, Yim, & Ng, 2008).
- Effective praise gives students immediate and specific feedback about their performance.

Conroy et al. (2009) noted that praise is a "complex, reciprocal process" (p. 18). Effective praise is influenced by a number of factors such as the student's individual and cultural differences, the circumstances under which praise was previously given, and the characteristics of the praise that is given. When utilized appropriately and effectively, praise can be a practical means of affecting students' motivation to engage in behaviors associated with learning.

Positive reinforcement, including special privileges or tangible rewards, should always be accompanied by positive comments such as praise for a specific behavior. Offering students rewards (e.g., extra points, food, stickers and stars, free time) for achievement gains can be positive for some students and counterproductive for others. What is reinforcing for one student may be punishing for another. For example, a student who is low in reading may prefer to have extra computer time as a reward for the successful completion of work. Another, who is reluctant to use the computer, may prefer reading as a reward. What matters is what the student finds rewarding.

In his 1993 book, *Punished by Rewards*, Kohn argued that rewards are ways of manipulating student behavior. He cautioned teachers that rewards could be most damaging when the task that is being rewarded is already intrinsically motivating to the student. Students who are praised every time they complete their math facts may lose interest in the task, especially if math comes easily for them.

Good and Brophy (1987) commented, "The quality of task engagement and of ultimate achievement is higher when students perceive themselves to be engaged in a task for their own reasons rather than in order to please an authority figure, obtain a reward, or escape punishment" (p. 227). We recommend that rewards be used sparingly, perhaps for end of the year celebrations or for individual and group successes that involve challenging tasks.

As discussed, students will be more likely to display fewer problem behaviors when the classroom is well-organized and when rules and procedures are clearly defined. Effective managers involve students in classroom processes such as developing rules and procedures, teaching them about learning styles, engaging them in productive work, and providing feedback that is informational.

Reflection

- Think about the grade level you teach or are interested in teaching and identify several rules you think would be appropriate for your students. Describe how you will teach the rules to your students.
- Write a classroom procedure for each of the following activities: entering the classroom, participating in a small-group activity, and working independently. Be sure the steps can be easily followed.

Designing Predictable Consequences for Behavior Infractions

Sometimes students' disruptive behaviors require intervention. Levin and Nolan (2007) presented a hierarchy of strategies to deal with what Redl and Wineman (1952) called "surface behaviors." Surface behaviors include verbal interruptions (talking, giggling, whispering), off-task behavior (day dreaming, sleeping, doodling), "busy" physical movement (roaming, fidgeting, touching others), and disrespect toward teachers and other students (arguing, yelling, profanity). The hierarchy consists of three stages of intervention: nonverbal, verbal, and the use of logical consequences. Teachers are encouraged to move through stages beginning with nonverbal interventions to more directive actions when earlier interventions have not led to appropriate student behavior.

The first stage in the hierarchy is nonverbal intervention: planned ignoring, signal interference, proximity interference, and touch interference. Planned ignoring means intentionally not responding to problem behavior. Planned ignoring is most successful with behaviors that do not necessarily disrupt the teaching/learning process such as whistling, humming, and pencil tapping. Students may not even be aware of some of these behaviors. One teacher recalled a time when a female student expelled gas at the end of a class period and laughter exploded in the classroom. This was in a psychiatric school program, where points were deducted for such behavior. The teacher, with a blank face, simply deducted the points from the student's point sheet. The teacher waited until the classroom was vacant to have a good laugh and breathe a sigh of relief that the incident had not happened during a lecture. If it had occurred earlier in the period and if the student was intent on getting attention, ignoring may not have worked. Ignoring is also not appropriate with behaviors that may be dangerous, such as threatening other students or fighting. Generally, planned ignoring works when you are sure others in the classroom will also ignore the behavior.

Signal interference provides nonverbal cues to the student that certain behavior is inappropriate. Providing cues to individual students or to the class can be an effective way of obtaining expected behaviors. Hoover and Collier (1986) suggested using nonverbal signals and cues that do not draw attention to individual students. Facial expressions, gestures, eye contact, ringing a bell, and clapping hands are examples of nonverbal signals. A teacher once said she practiced for hours in the mirror trying to perfect the "evil eye." She had a chance to try it out when a student in her class was caught eating a candy bar from his pocket. She started laughing when she tried to use the "evil eye," acknowledging to the student that she had been practicing her look at home and it was not working. The student laughed too and threw away the candy. This is an example of how signal interference and a little humor took care of a problem.

Proximity interference, moving toward the vicinity of the student or standing at the side or behind the student, is sometimes all that is necessary to reduce student distraction or to interrupt misbehavior. Teachers who frequently walk around the room, checking in with students, are practicing proximity control. Teachers who stand at the door, greeting students in the morning or during transition periods, minimize opportunities for problem behavior to occur.

Touch interference is described as physical contact with a student that is nonaggressive. A teacher may take the hand of a wandering student to guide him back to his desk or may use a hand on the shoulder to redirect a student's attention or reassure a student who is frustrated. Hoover and Collier (1986) cautioned that touch interference can be a culturally sensitive form of nonverbal communication. Standing behind students to monitor behavior can convey messages different from those intended. Tapping a student on the head or shoulder could violate accepted norms of interpersonal contact for some students. Teachers need to be sensitive to the responses of students. Some students may find touch reassuring and others may respond with anger and aggression. Physically aversive strategies, such as hitting or grabbing students, are unacceptable.

The second stage consists of verbal interventions. Verbal interventions fall into three categories: hints, questions, and requests or demands. A hint is usually a public commendation of a student's appropriate behavior to call tacit attention to another student's inappropriate behavior. If the teacher is angry with Melissa for shouting out the answer and not raising her hand, she can commend another student for displaying the appropriate behavior: "Marc, I really appreciate you remembering the rule to raise your hand." This strategy probably works best at the elementary level and when the teacher is highly regarded by most students. At the secondary level, when peer influence is generally more powerful, teacher praise may not be effective. Levin and Nolan (2007) suggested that reinforcement of the group as a whole may be a more appropriate intervention at the secondary level. Verbal interventions should be private and brief. Stooping down right next to the student or asking someone to come to your desk is less embarrassing to students than criticizing or confronting them in front of the class. The teacher needs to tell the student what the teacher wants the student to do. Using sarcasm, preaching, judging, and yelling are examples of verbal interventions that do not work. Conferencing with the student's parents to determine a home/school plan or what is often referred to as a written contract may also be appropriate.

Questions are used to determine if students are aware of how they are behaving and how their behavior is affecting others. For example, a teacher who is frustrated with Samuel for loudly humming a tune might say, "Samuel, that's a great tune but some students are complaining that they can't concentrate on their work. Could you keep it down?" This is best done privately at Samuel's desk so as not to embarrass him. Students often misbehave because they do not understand the assignment or they find the work too easy, too difficult, or not interesting. Asking questions gives the teacher information about what the student needs to complete the task.

Requests/demands are more direct responses to inappropriate behavior. A student who calls out answers instead of raising a hand may be responded to by the following request: "Roberto, what is the rule about raising your hand?" Another demand that might be used would be: "Roberto, I will call on you as soon as you raise your hand."

Finally, the third stage involves the use of logical and natural consequences, the goal of which is to teach students to think about their behavior before they act and to make decisions based on the consequences of their actions. Natural consequences result directly from the student's misbehavior. A student who fails to turn in a homework assignment receives no grade (a natural consequence). The natural consequence of forgetting lunch money is not eating lunch. Logical consequences require teacher intervention and are more closely related to student misbehavior. A student who continues to blurt out answers instead of raising his or her hand should be reminded that he/she has a choice: "Michael, you have a choice, you can either raise your hand and continue to participate in the discussion or choose not to participate by remaining quiet.

According to Elias and Schwab (2006), three conditions must be met if logical consequences are going to have maximum effect. In order to be effective, the consequences must be related, reasonable, and respectful. A consequence is related when it is connected to the misbehavior. If a student throws paper on the floor, asking him/her to clean the floor is appropriate. A consequence is reasonable when it is "mild." If a student takes another student's crayons, he/she may be asked to buy a new box of crayons for the student. A consequence is respectful when it is delivered calmly without demeaning the student. A student who has a temper tantrum that disrupts the class may in a classroom meeting apologize to the class for the disruption. A temporary time-out (at student's desk or in another part of the room) might be needed for the student to calm down and think about a solution for the behavior. One of the potential benefits of implementing logical consequences is the promotion of social skill development. Our discussion of natural and logical consequences is introductory; we encourage you to read further on this topic (Albert, 1996; Dreikurs, Grunwald, & Pepper, 1982; Hardin, 2008; Nelson, Lott, & Glen, 1993).

Levin and Nolan (2007) also discussed what they call "contrived" consequences. These consequences are imposed by the teacher but have no real connection to student misbehavior. Here's one we've all heard: "Michael, you continue to not raise your hand, so I want you to write 100 times, 'I will raise my hand to be called on.'" Students rarely see the connection between their behavior and such consequences and often develop resentment toward the teacher. The use of contrived consequences is not effective and not recommended by Levin and Nolan.

Tier 2 Interventions and Supports

Students receiving Tier 2 supports typically exhibit behavior that is not dangerous to themselves or others but is disruptive to their learning or the learning of others. Students receiving support at this level can benefit from daily monitoring, additional feedback from an adult mentor, and an in-school or home/school behavior plan. Interventions for individual students should be based upon a functional behavioral assessment done in collaboration with other team members. Although there is no current legal definition of functional assessment, most researchers would agree that it is a problem-solving process for determining why a student exhibits inappropriate behavior, and selecting interventions to address individual student needs; the goal is to teach the student acceptable replacement behaviors.

Tier 2 interventions provide individual or small groups of students who have not responded to Tier 1 strategies with additional supports. Tier 2 interventions are designed according to specific needs of students. An individual student who refuses to work and is considered to be depressed due to a recent family event may be scheduled for individual counseling. Tier 2 interventions may be implemented for small groups of students who exhibit similar behavior problems and are likely to benefit from the same type of intervention. Students who exhibit deficits in social competence (e.g., problem-solving skills) might participate in a skills group in which all students in the group receive additional instruction in the skills needed to resolve conflicts appropriately.

Several small-group interventions have been successful across age and grade levels. One such intervention is called Check in–Check out (CICO) (Crone, Horner, & Hawken, 2004). This is an individual monitoring system that provides daily positive adult contact, reminders of expectations, and feedback to students on their behavior. The cycle begins with a morning check in with an assigned adult mentor. The student picks up a daily progress report that includes a checklist of established behavioral goals. Student goals are reviewed each morning. The adult mentors help the students organize their materials and encourage the student to do their best. The progress reports are presented to teachers at the beginning of each period. Each teacher completes the progress report. At the end of the day, students return to the adult mentors they checked in with at the beginning of the day. Progress reports are reviewed and acknowledgment given when appropriate. A copy of the report goes home, is signed by parents, and is returned the next morning. The program is set up to support the student throughout the day with positive and/or corrective feedback when necessary. Interventions are monitored through data collection (e.g., points earned on an intervention such as CICO, in-class participation, office discipline referrals, etc.) to determine effectiveness. See how this program works at Henry Wadsworth Longfellow Elementary School at www.youtube.com/watch?v=ERX8yLRKs48. If a student does not meet determined Tier 2 goals, the student is referred for Tier 3 interventions.

Tier 3 Interventions and Supports

Tier 3 interventions are considered when a student exhibits behaviors that are chronic or frequent, dangerous, disruptive to the point of impeding the learning of the student or peers, or when problem behavior results in social or educational exclusion (Dunlap, Goodman, McEvoy, & Paris, 2010). Tier 3 interventions require that a functional behavior assessment be conducted and an individualized behavior support plan be developed and implemented. The assessment is usually conducted by a psychologist or classroom teacher and includes an in-depth look at what is causing the problem behavior by individuals who know the student best (e.g., teachers, psychologist, parents). Interventions are developed and implemented based on the results of the assessment and student's needs. The goal is to decrease problem behavior and increase prosocial behavior. Data are collected to determine intervention effectiveness.

Teaching is not just about eliminating or suppressing problem behavior. Teaching involves giving children the skills and knowledge they need to be successful socially and academically. Instructional approaches to management that teach appropriate behavior rather than punish misbehavior provide alternatives to exclusionary discipline. Darch, Miller, and Shippen (1998) observed that teaching appropriate behavior is instructional and proactive. They viewed student behavior problems as failures of learning rather than purposeful misconduct. Correcting a behavior after it has occurred is reactive, not proactive. The authors encouraged teachers to strategically teach what is required so students have the skills necessary to behave appropriately.

Reflection

- Develop your own management plan including theoretical perspective(s) of behavior, strategies for preventing problem behaviors from occurring, and strategies to respond to minor and more severe disruptions.

Summary

Numerous factors, such as teacher perception, student characteristics, and cultural and environmental influences, affect students' learning and behavior. Effective teachers are aware of their own beliefs and biases regarding students' academic and behavioral goals. They have an understanding of research and theory in classroom management. They provide a classroom environment that is safe, nurturing, and engaging, and they utilize proactive strategies to minimize problem behavior. Classroom rules and procedures are developed by students and teachers and are clearly defined and consistently reinforced. Academic and social goals are developed according to individual students' learning styles and needs. Effective teachers use various teaching and assessment methods to engage students in learning and minimize problem behavior. When problems do occur, they are seen as opportunities for learning. Students are encouraged to take responsibility for their own behavior through guided instruction and self-management, not through teacher control. A goal, then, of classroom management is to create a community of learners in which students feel they belong, a place where they have opportunities to actively participate with peers and adults in the learning process. One author remembered the advice of her mentor: "Becoming a culturally competent classroom manager is a journey, not a destination, and the effective educator is always on that road."

Learning Activities

Plan to observe a minimum of five hours in a local school classroom at a grade level you plan to teach. Contact the administrator at the school to arrange your observation visits. Respond to the following questions.

- What are the classroom rules? Are they posted? Do the rules follow the guidelines listed in this chapter? Are students reinforced positively for following the rules?

- Are procedures for transitions and changes in activities clearly defined? Give an example.
- Identify ways students are encouraged and reinforced for appropriate behavior?
- What strategies did you observe the teacher use to respond to inappropriate behavior? Do you believe the strategies were appropriate? Why or why not?

Resources

- Reclaiming Youth Network: Reclaiming Youth is an organization dedicated to transforming education and human services by creating respectful ways of dealing with youth. This work is based on the Circle of Courage that addresses the universal needs of belonging, mastery, independence, and generosity.
  www.reclaiming.com
- Positive Behavior Support
  http://myweb.usf.edu/~aheindel/PBSwebsite.html
- Behavior Advisor
  www.behavioradvisor.com/715HomePage.html
- Center for Positive Behavioral Interventions and Supports
  www.pbis.org
- The Safe and Responsive Schools Project
  www.indiana.edu/~safeschl
- Intervention Central
  www.interventioncentral.org

Books

- *Crossing Over to Canaan: The Journey of New Teachers in Diverse Classrooms* by Gloria Ladson-Billings
- *The Dreamkeepers: Successful Teachers of African American Children* by Gloria Ladson-Billings
- *Educating Everybody's Children* by Robert W. Cole

Unit IV

BEST PRACTICES FOR COMMUNICATION IN DIVERSE SETTINGS

The final unit reviews research examining best practices for the delivery and discovery of academic material. Chapter 9 begins with a discussion of the importance of planning. It is essential that teachers understand the standards they are expected to meet. We have therefore included a brief discussion of the focus of Common Core standards in language arts, literacy, and mathematics. Following this we explain three frameworks for designing curriculum. First, we discuss differentiated instruction and Response to Intervention, and contend that these frameworks are especially helpful in designing instruction for diverse learners. Second we highlight a traditional lesson plan. The next part of the chapter addresses ways to use communication to put curriculum design into action. We move from teacher-focused strategies, such as the lecture, to a discussion of student-centered strategies such as small groups and cooperative learning. We conclude the chapter by discussing the effective use of questions and how to appropriately provide feedback on student work. The final chapter focuses on the role of technology in learning. This chapter is divided into three sections. The first section reviews different ways to use technology to accomplish instructional goals. The second section explores problems with the use of technology. Specifically, we discuss the digital divide and the potential impact of technology on literacy. The final section provides guidelines on how to effectively use technology in the classroom.

Unit [illegible]

BEST PRACTICES FOR COMMUNICATION IN DIVERSE SETTINGS

9

INSTRUCTIONAL PRACTICES

Learning Outcomes

1. Explain the focus of Common Core state standards.
2. Describe differentiated instruction, universal design for instruction, and Response to Intervention.
3. Identify the features of an effective lecture.
4. List the different ways to use small groups.
5. Discuss ways to create cooperative learning groups.
6. Explain the differences between convergent and divergent questions.
7. Provide examples of effective feedback.

Classroom Scenario

Ms. Johnson peers over the top of her horn-rimmed glasses in a futile attempt to make eye contact with the blurry-eyed students trying to pay attention as she begins her lesson on the California Missions in the unit on California History. Her body seems frozen to the computer station where she reads the first slide on her PowerPoint presentation. Her voice is monotone and has a numbing effect on the students. Steven is in the back of the class, eyes shut, with his head precariously perched on his hand. Several snickering students in the class are watching to see if his hand will slip, causing his head to crash on the desk. Another student is sending a text message to his girlfriend in another class. Ana and Esperanza are flirting with Carlos, the star athlete at the school, who sits in the desk next to them. Desia is sitting straight, grinning and nodding, pretending to listen while he rehearses football plays for Friday's game. Once more, Ms. Johnson has not engaged her students in her lesson.

This chapter focuses on ways to design curricula and use effective communication to accomplish instructional goals in diverse classrooms. We begin the discussion with a brief overview of the new Common Core state standards. Second, we discuss ways to plan and organize lessons. This is followed with a review of specific communication strategies that are at the center of instructional discourse. The final section focuses on the instructional strategies that promote understanding.

Common Core State Standards

Preparation requires an understanding of state standards and how to meet them. Common Core standards in English language arts, literacy, and mathematics have been adopted voluntarily by 46 states, 3 U.S. territories, and the District of Columbia. The impetus for creating Common Core standards came from the desire to better prepare students for college, career, and life. The architects of Common Core believe it is a framework that creates a coherent set of expectations for students regardless of where they live. Previously, each state developed its own standards, thus creating the possibility that what a student learns in California is different from what a student in Oklahoma learns. When achievement measures are collected across different states, they reveal a great deal of variability in what students are expected to know.

Language Arts and Literacy Standards

The English language arts and literacy standards shift the focus of instruction in three ways (Common Core State Standards Initiative, n.d.):

REGULAR PRACTICE WITH COMPLEX TEXTS AND ACADEMIC LANGUAGE

Students focus on complex texts and the development of academic language. The standards call for a staircase of increasing complexity so students are ready for college and career reading by the end of high school.

In order for students to deconstruct texts, they need to increase their academic vocabulary. The standards are reinforced through conversation, reading, and direct instruction. The standards do not use reading lists but include an examination of classic myths, foundational U.S. documents, classic American literature, and writings from Shakespeare.

READING AND WRITING GROUNDED IN EVIDENCE FROM TEXTS, BOTH LITERARY AND INFORMATIONAL

The standards require students to use evidence from texts to present careful analysis, well-defended claims, and clear information. Previously, students could draw from their past knowledge to answer questions rather than demonstrate a deep understanding of the material they read. The standards require students to answer text-dependent questions that demand a careful and thoughtful analysis of the text that is being studied.

The focus of writing instruction also shifts under Common Core standards. Previously, K–12 writing focused extensively on student experiences and opinions. The new standards also emphasize narrative writing, but they also expect an understanding of sequencing and argumentative writing that require details and evidence.

BUILDING KNOWLEDGE THROUGH CONTENT-RICH NONFICTION

In order to be prepared for college, career, and life, students must have knowledge about the world around them. Reading content-rich information in history, science, social studies, and the arts is essential for later learning.

The standards in grades K–5 require a 50–50 balance between informational and literary reading. Informational reading includes content-rich nonfiction in history/social studies, sciences, technical studies, and the arts.

In grades 6–12, there is a greater emphasis on a specific category of nonfiction. Significant attention is still dedicated to literature; however, the standards call for students to build knowledge in history/social studies, science, and technical subjects through reading and writing.

Mathematics Standards

The concern about U.S. performance in mathematics has existed for many years. Test scores of U.S. students are well below those of their international peers. According to Alberti (2013), the new standards are more focused and coherent. Rather than focus on breadth, the new standards require more depth. Following are the shifts in the Common Core standards in mathematics.

GREATER FOCUS ON FEW TOPICS

Teachers will be expected to narrow the scope of content and increase the time and energy devoted to the following topics:

- In grades K–2, concepts, skills, and problem solving related to addition and subtraction.
- In grades 3–5, concepts, skills, and problem solving related to multiplication and division of whole numbers.
- In grade 6, ratios and proportional relationships and early algebraic expressions and equations.
- In grade 7, ratios and proportional relationships and arithmetic of rational numbers.
- In grade 8, linear algebra.

LINKING TOPICS AND THINKING ACROSS GRADES

The standards are anchored in systematic progressions from grade to grade. For example, in the fourth-grade students extend their understanding of multiplication by multiplying a fraction by a whole number; in the fifth-grade students build on this skill by multiplying a fraction or a whole number by a fraction; in Grade 3 students learn how to display data on bar graphs and use this information to solve problems.

RIGOROUS PURSUIT OF CONCEPTUAL UNDERSTANDING, PROCEDURAL SKILL, AND APPLICATION

Rigor is not defined by making math harder or by increasing the number of topics covered in each grade. Three aspects of rigor are woven into the standards: conceptual understanding, procedural skill and fluency, and application:

- *Conceptual Understanding*
  The standards require students to develop a deep authentic command of mathematical concepts. Students are not taught tricks to obtain a correct answer, but they learn why an answer is correct.
- *Procedural Skill and Fluency*
  The standards require speed and accuracy in calculation. Students will develop skill in core concepts such as single digit multiplication in order to respond to higher-order problems. Some students will learn these skills more quickly than others, therefore teachers must provide instructional time and resources so students can be successful.
- *Application*
  The standards are designed so that students can use mathematical knowledge to solve real-world problems. Application occurs at each grade level and is not reserved for the end of the learning progression.

The adoption of Common Core standards is not without controversy. Some claim it has too much of an emphasis on testing and that those who created common core standards do not have credentials in educational reform and instructional practice. There is also a concern about the role of textbook publishers and the financial windfall they may gain from selling books and support materials. Finally, there is an underlying assumption that college is for everyone, but as we have discussed, there are significant income disparities that make it difficult for a growing population of students to attend college.

We will not weigh in on the political debate but rather focus on teacher agency. The specific standards identified in Common Core standards are in place. It is important for future teachers to understand them and design instructional tasks and use instructional strategies that will ensure that the standards are met. In addition, the new standards recognize the significance of communication in the learning process.

Differentiated Instruction

Differentiated instruction is one way to plan with student diversity in mind. Tomlinson and McTighe (2006) explained that the primary goal of differentiated instruction is "ensuring that teachers focus on processes and procedures that ensure effective learning for varied individuals" (p. 3). Tomlinson (2003) indicated that differentiated instruction requires a teacher to proactively plan the varied approaches that students need to learn the information, how they will learn it, and/or how they can express what they have learned in order to increase the likelihood that each student will learn as much as he or she can as efficiently as possible (p. 151).

Differentiated instruction is characterized by the modification of three key elements of a lesson plan: content, process, and product. Modifying a "one-size-fits-all" lesson plan is necessary to meet the diverse learning styles and abilities of all students. *Content* refers to what students need to learn or how they might access the information they need. Content is principle- and concept-focused. All classes have state-mandated content standards that must be met. Tomlinson and McTighe (2006) ask teachers to consider ways to meet standards and be responsive to individual students (p. 24).

Process refers to what activities the student is involved in to make sense of the content or to master the content presented. Process concerns the instructional communication strategies used to put the learning into action. Teacher and student communication strategies are central to differentiated instruction and culturally responsive teaching. These communication strategies range from teacher-centered, such as lecturing, to student-centered, such as cooperative learning groups. As we have emphasized throughout this text, effective communication is central to academic engagement. We will discuss these strategies in more detail later in the chapter.

The final concept defining differentiated instruction is *product*—the learning outcomes. Product is measured by initial and on-going assessments. Pre-assessment is critical because it gives teachers and students a sense of where they are with the instructional material and where they need to go to meet the state standards. Assessment is a central feature of differentiated instruction.

Experts recommend that teachers follow the five guidelines presented below for incorporating differentiated instruction into instructional practice (Gregory & Chapman, 2002; Tomlinson, 1999, 2001; Tomlinson & Kalbfleisch, 1998):

1. Clarify and focus on key concepts.
2. Use assessments as teaching tools before, during, and after the learning takes place.
3. Emphasize critical and creative thinking.
4. Utilize a variety of learning tasks to engage the learners.
5. Balance teacher- and student-selected tasks.

Tomlinson and McTighe (2006) argued that teachers need to understand the relationship between curriculum design (understanding by design) and differentiated instruction. Understanding by design focuses on what to teach and what assessments to use. An elegant curriculum design or a clearly organized lesson plan that does not account for student diversity will not lead to effective learning for all students. Figure 9.1 is a planning template that can be used when designing lessons.

<table>
<tr><td colspan="2">Stage 1 – Desired Results</td></tr>
<tr><td colspan="2">Established Goal(s)
What relevant goals (e.g. or content standards, course program objectives, learning outcomes) will this design address?</td></tr>
<tr><td>Understanding(s)
Student will understand that …
What are the big ideas?
What specific understandings about them are desired?
What misunderstandings are predictable?</td><td>Essential Question(s)
What provocative questions will foster inquiry, understanding, and transfer of learning?</td></tr>
<tr><td colspan="2">Students will know …   Students will be able to …
What key knowledge and skills will students acquire asa result of this unit?
What should they eventually be able to do as a result of such knowledge and skill?</td></tr>
<tr><td colspan="2">Stage 2 – Assessment Evidence</td></tr>
<tr><td>Performance Task(s)
Through what authentic performancetask(s) will students demonstrate the desired understandings?
By what criteria will "performancesof understanding" be judged?</td><td>Other Evidence
Through what other evidence (e.g. quizzes, tests, academic prompts, observations, homework, journals) will students demonstrate achievement of the desired results?
How will students reflect upon and self-assess their learning?</td></tr>
<tr><td colspan="2">Stage 3 – Learning Plan</td></tr>
<tr><td colspan="2">Learning Activities:
What learning experiences and instruction will enable students to achieve desired results?
How will the design:
W =Help students know Where the unit is going and What is expected help the teacher know Where the students are coming from (prior knowledge interests)?
H = Hook all students and Hold their interest?
E = Equip students, help them Experience the key ideas, and Explore the issues?
R =Provide opportunities to Rethink and Revise their understandings and work?
E =Allow students to Evaluate their work and its implications?
T =Be Tailored (personalized) to the different needs, interests, and abilities of learners?
O =Be Organized to maximize initial and sustained engagement as well as effective learning.</td></tr>
</table>

Figure 9.1 Planning Template

Source: McTighe & Wiggins (2004, p. 30).

Santamaria (2009) argued that differentiated instruction can also be used to accomplish culturally responsive teaching. Her research is grounded in the work of Ladson-Billings (1994) and Gay (2000). She argued that differentiated instruction is a way to modify instruction based on the knowledge, prior experiences, and performance styles of students from diverse backgrounds. She conducted a qualitative study in two culturally and linguistically diverse elementary schools in San Diego County. She collected data over five years from teachers, administrators, and parents. She developed codes for evidence of differentiated and culturally responsive teaching. She concluded from her analysis that academic gains occurred when teachers attended to differences in students' academic, cultural, linguistic, and socioeconomic status. As a result of her analysis she argued that blending differentiated and culturally responsive teaching provides a framework for meeting the academic needs of all students.

The preceding discussion provides important information on how to plan lessons for culturally diverse classes.

RTI and Universal Design

Response to Intervention (RTI) and universal design for learning (UDL) are problem-solving frameworks that address the needs of students at risk and students with disabilities. According to Fox, Carta, Strain, Dunlap, and Hemmeter (2009), RTI is a systematic, data-driven process that attempts to resolve students' academic and/or behavioral challenges using scientific, research-based interventions in the educational environment. Response to Intervention integrates assessment and intervention within a multi-level prevention system to maximize student achievement and reduce behavioral problems. RTI seeks to prevent academic failure through early intervention, frequent progress monitoring, and increasingly intensive research-based instructional interventions for children who continue to have difficulty. This model is intended to reduce referrals to special education while allowing children in the general education setting to have access to a high quality of curriculum and instruction matched to their level of need.

Fox et al. (2009, pp. 2–3) identified several features of RTI that allow school programs to identify students who are at risk or who have delays in learning and behavior and provide them with the supports they need to be successful. Those features include the following:

1 *Universal screening*: In RTI approaches, the performance of all students is evaluated systematically to identify those who are (a) making adequate progress, (b) at some risk of failure if not provided extra assistance, or (c) at high risk of failure if not provided specialized supports.
2 *Continuous progress monitoring*: In RTI approaches, student progress is assessed on a regular and frequent basis in order to identify when inadequate growth trends might indicate a need for increasing the level of instructional support to the student.

3 *Continuum of evidence-based interventions*: RTI approaches assume multiple levels, or a "cascade," of interventions that vary in intensity or level of support and are derived from scientifically validated research. An individualized intensive curriculum is implemented for students who do not show adequate growth in response to the modified curriculum.
4 *Data-based decision making and problem solving*: At the heart of the RTI approach is instructional decision making based on student performance or growth on curricular outcomes and modifications when insufficient growth is noted.
5 *Implementation fidelity*: RTI requires specific procedures for regular documentation of the level of implementation of each of the features of the model (e.g., were the modifications of the teaching practices implemented consistently and with a high degree of accuracy?).

RTI is conceptualized as a multi-tiered service delivery model including primary, secondary, and tertiary levels of support. RTI is broken into multiple tiers of instruction with various levels of intervention that increase in intensity as you progress up the pyramid (see Figure 9.2). What distinguishes this approach is that the interventions occur within the classroom and are individualized to the student. The focus on individual instruction is based on the belief that no single intervention will be successful for all students. All tiers include a four-step process: (1) problem identification, (2) problem analysis/ selection of intervention, (3) implementation of intervention, and (4) progress monitoring (Fuchs & Fuchs, 2006).

The primary, or first, tier is focused on all students receiving high-quality, scientifically-based instruction in the core curriculum. Ongoing progress

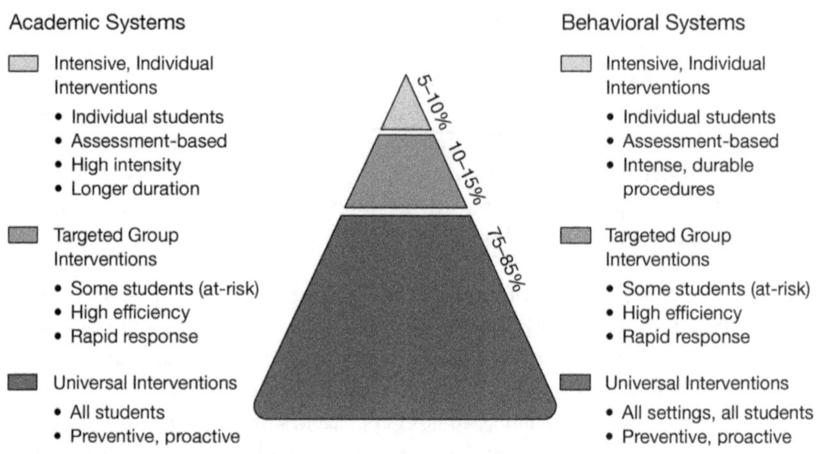

Figure 9.2 RTI, A School-Wide System for Student Success
Source: North Star Educational Tools, www.northstaret.com/rti_01.shtml

monitoring allows for identification of students who are struggling learners and need additional support. In this tier approximately 75–85 percent of the general student body should be able to meet grade-level norms without additional assistance.

The 10–15 percent of students who are not showing progress in the regular classroom are provided with increasingly intensive instruction matched to their needs. Instruction is provided in small-group settings in addition to instruction in the general education curriculum. Students who continue to show little progress at this level of intervention are then considered for more intensive interventions at Tier 3.

Tier 3 will provide services to 5–10 percent of students, the students who continue to show resistance to intervention provided at Tier 2. Hence, the intensity of intervention increases as the severity of the problem increases. At this level, students receive individualized instruction that targets specific skill deficits. Students who do not achieve at this level are referred for a comprehensive evaluation and considered then for eligibility for special education services under the Individuals with Disabilities Education Act (IDEA). The data collected in all three tiers are used to make the eligibility decision.

Universal Design for Learning (UDL) is a framework for designing curriculum (goals, materials, methods, and assessment) that is grounded in the belief that every learner is unique and brings different strengths and weaknesses to the classroom (Rose & Meyer, 2002). UDL is designed to enable all students to learn by reducing barriers to the curriculum and providing additional supports for learning. Rose and Meyer identify three UDL principles that guide the design of a flexible curriculum:

1 Information should be presented in multiple and flexible formats and media to give students with diverse learning styles ways of acquiring information and knowledge.
2 Multiple and flexible pathways should be provided for students' action and expression.
3 Multiple and flexible means of engaging students' interest and motivation to learn should be provided.

The new age of digital multimedia, adaptive technologies, the Internet, and other advancements make it possible to individualize education for all students, not just students with disabilities. Developers and practitioners of UDL apply the intrinsic flexibility of digital media to individualize educational goals, classroom materials, and instructional methods and assessments. Thus, each student has an appropriate point-of-entry into the curriculum—and a pathway toward attainment of educational goals.

New curricular materials and learning technologies should be designed from the beginning to be flexible enough to accommodate the unique learning styles of a wide range of individuals, including children with disabilities. Some examples of UDL are: accessible Web pages, electronic versions of textbooks and other curricular materials, captioned and/or narrated videos, word processors with word prediction, speaking spell checkers, talking dialog boxes, voice recognition, and picture menus. Some students with disabilities will still need assistive technology devices such as communication aids, visual and hearing aids, wheelchairs, etc. However, using UDL will help to ensure that all students will have access to core curriculum and new technologies. The Center for Applied Special Technology (CAST) is a great resource for teachers to learn how to customize instruction using the above-mentioned principles of UDL.

A major goal of both RTI and UDL is to improve educational outcomes for all students. Strangeman et al. (2006) identified three common goals of RTI and UDL. First, both RTI and UDL recognize that poor achievement does not necessarily reflect disability, but rather may reflect poor instruction. Both support the notion that curriculum may need to be adapted to meet the individual needs of students. Second, RTI and UDL both reflect the understanding that one size does not fit all. In other words, what works for one student does not necessarily work for another. Third, both RTI and UDL support the use of multiple assessments to guide instruction. Ongoing progress monitoring is used to guide decision making regarding the appropriate instruction and intervention. The authors suggested that "by simultaneously implementing RTI and using UDL to build the capacity of the general education curriculum, it may be possible to realize broadly effective general education curricula that anticipate students' difficulties and eliminate the need for intervention" (pp. 7–8).

Lesson Plans

Orlich, Harder, Callahan, and Gibson (2001) argued that planning is key to effective teaching. They contended that the teaching of master teachers is characterized by well-organized lesson plans, clear communication, and high expectations for all students. Lesson plans can vary by the experience of the teacher, grade level, the content being discussed, and the characteristics of the learner. Orlich et al. also noted that some teachers, especially experienced ones, may not write out formal lesson plans; rather after many years of constructing plans they may have them etched in their head or stored in teaching files on their computers. We believe it is essential for teachers to formalize their plans and continually adapt them to better meet the needs of their students. Figure 9.3 contains one format that is commonly used.

Classroom Communication in Diverse Classrooms: The Lecture

The instructional strategies with the longest history are the lecture and its derivative, the lecture/discussion. Unfortunately, many teachers lecture like

Component	Description
Objective	The explicit purpose for the lesson. The objective specifies what students are expected to demonstrate after the lesson is completed.
Standards	The state-adopted curriculum standards which align subject matter and grade level requirements.
Anticipatory set	A strategy for grabbing interest and focusing on what is supposed to be learned?
Presentation/communication	Input: The teacher provides the information needed to accomplish the objective. Modeling: The teacher uses the new information to illustrate what students are expected to demonstrate. Checking for Understanding: Determining if the students are clear on what they are expected to do.
Guided practice	Under the supervision of the teacher, students practice their new knowledge or skill.
Closure	Communication strategies which bring the lesson to an appropriate conclusion.
Independent practice	Strategies for reinforcing or "hard wiring" the new skill or knowledge. The may be accomplished through homework, group work, or a subsequent project.
Adaptations	Identify an accommodations or modifications needed for students with disabilities, diverse learning styles, and/or English learners.

Figure 9.3 Components of a Lesson Plan
Source: Adapted from Hunter (1984).

Ms. Johnson. They stand up in front of the class and impart information with little concern about making the content interesting or exciting. Book (1999) stated that people learn best when they:

> (a) actively participate in the learning, (b) have knowledge or specified feedback of the results of learning, (c) know what they are expected to learn, (d) know the purpose of what they are learning, and (e) find the learning to be meaningful to them.
>
> (p. 333)

Incorporating these concerns into the lecture format is challenging but necessary.

One of the first decisions a teacher should make is when to lecture. Not all instructional goals are suited to this instructional strategy. McKeachie (1986) contended that lecturing is not appropriate when the information is available in printed form. Too many teachers lecture on material students have already read. Ms. Johnson could have taken the time to distribute handouts for the students to read, thus leaving time in class for other learning activities. Lecturing is most appropriate when it is used to give students the most up-to-date information or unique insight from a teacher. There frequently is a lag in time between the information that is in textbooks and new developments in an academic area. Lectures can help bridge these gaps. Lectures are also appropriate for synthesizing material collected from a wide range of sources. Finally, lectures can be used to adapt material to a particular audience. Instructors can take information that is written for one type of audience and adapt it to another.

Book (1999) outlined other practical reasons for using the lecture method. Lectures require few materials or equipment, thus giving the teacher a great deal of flexibility. A teacher can go from room to room or place to place to deliver the information. A lecture is not dependent on the size of room or size of class. A good lecture can be presented to two or 102 students. Studies investigating the effects of lectures indicate that when measures of knowledge are used, lectures appear to be as effective as other modes of instruction. When the measures are concerned with problem solving, delayed recall of information, transfer of learning, or attitude change, discussion methods are more effective (McKeachie, 1986).

According to Book (1999), an effective lecture arouses student interest about the content, organizes key concepts, and provides an opportunity for students to apply the information to their own experiences. The centerpiece of the lecture is the instructor's knowledge and understanding of the content. The inability to provide explanations, examples, and illustrations are reflective of an instructor who does not have a good working knowledge of the content and does not know how to adapt the information to the students.

An effective lecture does not attempt to cover too much information. Book (1999) stated that a good lecture covers two or three main points with appropriate elaboration to make them meaningful and memorable. One way to highlight important points is to provide an organizational pattern that complements the lecture material. Table 9.1 contains examples of frequently used organizational patterns. Teachers should select the pattern that matches their goals and objectives.

According to Book (1999), an effective lecture will establish a learning set that helps students focus on important concepts and principles. Several strategies can be used to create a learning set. One strategy is to use the techniques for starting a speech such as posing a significant problem, telling a story, or using an activity that brings focus to the content. Another strategy is to use an advance organizer. Orlich et al. (2001) stated that an advance organizer is a frame of reference that presents the main facts, concepts, or ideas to be learned. The advance organizer can be a study guide, a chart, or a list of ideas students have prior to the lesson. Teachers and students are better able to focus on relevant information when the main ideas are known in advance. Consider the following example:

In this lesson we will focus on:

- ways to organize a lecture;
- strategies for making lectures more exciting;
- how to write an advance organizer.

Instructors can also reinforce the learning set by using strategies to emphasize important points. Statements such as "Think about this" or "This is very important to understand" help frame important concepts and ideas.

Table 9.1 Organizational Patterns

Topical: The lecture is divided into discrete topics that are developed and explained. A topical organizational pattern works well when the goal is to explain the components of a topic.

I. The First Continental Congress was convened in Philadelphia.
   A. Twelve colonies were represented.
   B. The representatives produced the Declaration of Rights and Grievances.

Chronological: This pattern follows a time sequence. History lessons frequently report on the sequence of events that occurred. This pattern can also be used to explain how to do or make something.

I. Two meetings were convened to deal with grievances against England.
   A. On Sept 5, 1774, the Continental Congress was convened in Philadelphia.
   B. On Oct 26, 1774, a second meeting was convened.

Problem–Solution Organization: In this pattern a particular problem is posed and solutions are identified and discussed.

I. The colonies believed the British policies were unacceptable.
   A. The British created the Intolerable Acts.
   B. The British levied inappropriate taxes.

II. Several solutions were implemented.
   A. Boycott trade with England.
   B. Committees of Safety were created to enforce actions against England.

Cause and Effect/Effect to Cause: In this pattern, the causes of certain conditions are proposed and explained.

I. The British tax on tea created several problems.
   A. The Boston government refused to pay for tea that was shipped from England.
   B. Several Bostonians, dressed as Native-Americans, dumped the tea into Boston Harbor.

A good lecturer must also attempt to actively engage students in the learning. Unlike Ms. Johnson, the effective lecturer checks for student understanding of the new material that has been provided in the lecture. Book (1999) suggested that teachers engage students by asking them to summarize the content in their own words.

Sitler (1997) advocated the use of the "spaced lecture" to increase student comprehension of material. In the spaced lecture the instructor pauses for two to three minutes throughout the lecture and gives the students an opportunity to write information in their own words. The instructor can collect this material to check student learning or use pauses to give students an opportunity to ask for clarification or further explanation. This strategy is designed to connect listening, note taking, and learning.

The final feature of effective lecturing discussed by Book (1999) is delivering the information in a stimulating fashion. McKeachie (1986) argued that teacher enthusiasm is an important component of effective teaching. Patrick, Hisley, and Kempler (2000) demonstrated that enthusiasm positively influences student intrinsic motivation. Their findings indicated that a lesson delivered with high energy leads students to experience greater interest in and enjoyment of the instructional material.

Studies examining communication style indicate that dramatic teaching is related to judgments of effective teaching. Norton and Nussbaum (1980) tested the proposition that effective teachers are optimally dramatic. They found that effective teachers were entertaining, told good stories, were humorous, and used double takes. Javidi, Downs, and Nussbaum (1988) studied the classroom behaviors of award-winning teachers. They found that award-winning high school and mid-high school teachers used humor, self-disclosure, and narratives during lectures, primarily in relation to course content. These teachers, however, tended to use humor less frequently than award-winning college teachers.

Dramatic teachers do more than entertain; they increase arousal and interest in the content being discussed. A humorous story or the use of expressive and animated nonverbal behavior reinforces and complements content. One professor used a puppet named Cecelia to explain the processes involved in relationship development. Another professor taught an entire lesson dressed as Mrs. Doubtfire, a character Robin Williams played in a popular film. Although there are instructional benefits to a dramatic teaching style, we don't equate good instructional practice with entertainment. Our goal is for teachers to consider ways to help students attend to and remember important concepts. In the context of the lecture, teacher enthusiasm and expressiveness facilitate learning.

Technology can also complement and enhance lecture materials. More and more teachers are using PowerPoint or other software programs to outline and highlight important lecture content. Some teachers integrate video clips, websites and other graphics into the lecture material. An overdependence on technological tricks and gimmicks can work against learning goals. We explore technology further in Chapter 10.

Before writing a lecture, a teacher needs to consider the background information the students have about the intellectual material. The teacher must consider what the students know and what they need to know. Based on this, the teacher can determine the most appropriate organizational structure.

Reflection

- Describe the characteristics of an effective lecturer you have had.
- How can a teacher use a lecture to accomplish culturally responsive teaching?
- Can a teacher be too dramatic? Explain.

Small Groups

In our judgment, the use of small-group discussion is an underemployed teaching strategy. One of the principal reasons is that a teacher must feel comfortable in shifting responsibility to students. Teachers who have a high need for control and believe that a good class is quiet and attentive have a difficult time assigning group projects. The research, however, suggests that small groups are an effective instructional tool (McKeachie, 1986; Orlich et al., 2001; Stahl & Clark, 1987). Group discussion moves students from passive to active modes of learning. In addition, as we indicated in Chapter 3, groups are a preferred mode of learning for females, Native-Americans, African-Americans, and Latinos.

Throughout this text, we have supported building on the competencies that students bring to the learning situation. Students come to class with a good deal of experience in groups. They belong to primary groups whose fundamental goal is to provide basic needs, and emotional and social support. Families, clans, cliques, and gangs are examples of this type of group. Students also belong to secondary groups, whose purpose is to complete a task or solve a problem or participate in some function. Church, community, and classroom groups are examples of secondary groups.

Schutz (1966) identified three basic needs individuals have; each need is connected to group participation. One need is inclusion. Group participation helps individuals feel they are a part of something. Students who are isolated and disconnected are less likely to be interested in school and are more likely to experience failure. A second need is affection. Care, concern, and support are frequently expressed in group settings. Being liked and loved is a fundamental need; individuals feel better about themselves when they are in a context in which this need is communicated. The final need is control. This need is concerned with the degree to which individuals have some power over themselves, others, and tasks. Many students feel that no amount of classroom effort will make any difference, so they stop trying. These same students, however, may exercise a great deal of control and power on the playground or in other contexts where their skills matter. Clearly, academic success can be better accomplished when educators build upon the natural needs students desire and seek out.

Why Small Groups are Effective

Small-group instructional practices are effective because they engage the learner in active learning processes. As the old adage goes, "Two heads are better than one." The act of talking about a topic or issue engages the student in cognitive processes that are not stimulated in passive learning situations. Students must articulate, defend, plan, criticize, and analyze issues and problems. Some research suggests that through the process of collaboration, students are able to solve difficult problems they would be incapable of solving alone (Forman & Cazden, 1985). Using groups is considered a best practice for differentiated instruction and culturally responsive teaching. The following are some positive outcomes for using groups:

- increased problem solving
- creative thinking
- critical thinking
- social skill development
- increased cultural sensitivity.

There are two primary ways to use small groups in the classroom. The first is small-group discussion and the second is cooperative learning groups. In small-group discussion, groups are created and given a topic or issue to discuss. The topic should be related to classroom content and be able to hold student interest (Orlich et al., 2001). It is important for teachers to give groups an essential or provocative question for their deliberation. For example, one teacher designed a lesson to meet the state standard on visual and performance arts by asking students to discuss how television and film have influenced the perception of people of color. This assignment resonates with the indicator of sociopolitical consciousness discussed by Ladson-Billings (2001). Orlich et al. (2001) provided a taxonomy of discussion groups varying in the amount of control required of the teacher. These discussion groups are: *brainstorming*, *tutorial*, *task group*, *role playing*, *simulation*, and *inquiry group*.

Brainstorming groups are designed to stimulate creative thinking. The purpose of brainstorming is to generate many ideas on a topic. Discussion and criticism of the ideas generated are discouraged. Brainstorming is usually an initiating activity. The information obtained can be used in other discussion formats or classroom activities. For example, brainstorming is an effective way to identify topics for research projects.

A second type of group, the *tutorial*, is utilized to help students who are having difficulty mastering or understanding certain subject material. The tutorial leader assumes a great deal of control by identifying the learning problems, providing feedback on the skills needed to achieve mastery, and encouraging students to use other students as resources. The use of tutorials can be an effective way to remediate learning problems. Cohen, Kulik, and Kulik (1992) found that students can learn as much from other students as they learn from teachers. Students share experiences and language forms that teachers may not know or understand. New insight and understanding can be obtained by drawing upon the expertise of peers.

The third type of group is the *task* group. Each participant in a task group is expected to make a specific contribution to the group. For example, one student may be responsible for computer graphics, another for library research, a third for typing a final report. Task groups can be effective in facilitating student cooperation and accountability. It is important to make students responsible for the tasks they have been assigned. Teachers should also discourage students from taking over the tasks assigned to other members. In our experience, some students have strong control needs and as a consequence can literally take over the group. The behavior of autocratic participants can be very divisive and counterproductive. Teachers need to help students understand that there is always more than one way to complete a task.

The fourth type of group involves *role playing*. In role-playing groups, students are asked to simulate real-life situations. An elementary school teacher in Nebraska can ask students to play the roles of J. Sterling and Caroline Morton, who moved to Nebraska from Michigan. They missed the trees and shrubs of the northeast and started planting some each year. When J. Sterling was in the state legislature, he proposed that one day be set aside to plant trees in the barren plains. This was the beginning of Arbor Day. The focus of role playing is to dramatize the behaviors or symbols under investigation. Teachers should provide clear instructions on the roles students are supposed to play, discuss how the roles were played, and reflect on what was learned as a result of the exercise.

The fifth type of group involves *simulation*. The purpose of a simulation is to re-create a real object, problem, or event. Business organizations and the military have used simulations as a central feature of their training programs. Teachers can also take advantage of this instructional strategy. For example, a fifth-grade history teacher in Madera, California, annually takes his students on a covered wagon trip to complement their study of California history. This activity gives students a genuine feeling and understanding of frontier life.

The final type of group format is *inquiry-centered* discussion. The purposes of the inquiry group is to simulate scientific thinking, develop problem-solving ability, and promote the discovery of new perspectives and insights. Students are given a problem or question to examine. They collect and analyze data and then draw conclusions or make recommendations based on their efforts. This format is appropriate for the investigation of civil rights or other social issues. One of the values of this approach is that it gives students an opportunity to challenge and test their implicit theories and beliefs.

Teachers need to be aware of how their own ideology can influence their response to this type of assignment. Teachers sometimes develop assignments to promote their own beliefs. Although difficult, teachers must maintain a facilitative role and help students make their own connections.

Cooperative Learning

Cooperative learning is an extension of the discussion methods discussed above. The research on cooperative learning is extremely positive (e.g., Johnson & Johnson, 1999; Johnson, Johnson, & Holubec, 1993; Kagan, 1994; Morton, 1998; Sharan, 1994; Sharan et al., 1984; Stevens & Slavin, 1995). Kagan identified three benefits of cooperative learning: (1) academic gains, especially for minority and low achieving students; (2) improved race relations among students in integrated classrooms; and (3) improved social and affective development among all students. Teachers genuinely interested in culturally reflective teaching should give serious attention to cooperative learning methods.

Johnson et al. (1993) identified six essential features of cooperative learning:

1. *Positive interdependence.* The success of the group is dependent upon the cooperative activities of the members. Positive interdependence is achieved when students believe that one cannot succeed unless all succeed. Without positive interdependence, cooperation is impossible.
2. *Individual and group accountability.* There are two types of accountability. At one level, the group must be held accountable for achieving its goal and each individual must be held accountable for his or her contribution to the group goal. Individual accountability is achieved when the performance of each individual is assessed and the results are given to the group. Cooperative learning strengthens individual performance through continuous feedback and the opportunity to take corrective action.
3. *Face-to-face interaction.* Students need to do real work in which they promote one another's achievements, share resources, and encourage learning. The importance of face-to-face communication cannot be overstated. Learning and understanding are facilitated when students orally explain, correct, and re-explain ideas, processes, and concepts. In cooperative learning situations, students interact, assist one another in learning tasks, share diverse ideas and beliefs, and work as a team to accomplish instructional goals.
4. *Interpersonal and small-group skills.* In cooperative learning, students are required to learn not only academic subject matter, but also the social skills necessary to work in a group. Cooperative learning requires students to simultaneously engage in task work and teamwork. Among the skills necessary for successful group participation are leadership, decision making,

conflict management, and trust building. These skills must be taught as precisely as academic skills.

5. *Group processing.* Group processing exists when group members monitor their progress on tasks and working relationships. Improvement requires an analysis of what works and what creates problems in the group. Each student is held accountable for his or her academic work. The final evaluations come from teachers, peers, and self.
6. *Development of social skills.* Cooperative learning helps students develop the types of interpersonal skills necessary to succeed at work, school, and home. Students enhance interpersonal skills, develop conflict management skills, and increase critical thinking.

Cooperative learning groups should be comprised of students from different academic, social, ethnic, physical, religious, sexual, and attitudinal orientations. The benefits of peer interaction are increased in heterogeneous groups. Cooperative groups provide an excellent opportunity to celebrate diversity, so instructors must be willing to create diverse groups. Our experience is that some teachers don't want to take the risk and contend that "the students can't handle it," so they create homogeneous groups.

Depending on the instructional goals, several types of cooperative groups can be structured. There are several excellent texts available on ways to use cooperative learning in the classroom (Kagan, 1994; Johnson & Johnson, 1999; Johnson et al., 1993).

One type of cooperative procedure is called student teams-achievement divisions (STAD). First, the instructor presents a lesson, frequently using the lecture mode we discussed earlier. Second, student teams are created that are designed to prepare the students for quizzes or other evaluation procedures. Third, students take individual quizzes. The content for the quizzes comes from the course content the students studied in the groups. Fourth, students receive a team score on how much each student improved over his or her previous score. Fifth, team scores are publicized in a newsletter or other publication.

Another type of cooperative group is called teams games tournament (TGT). This procedure is very similar to STAD. In TGT, quizzes are replaced with a system of academic game tournaments in which teams of students compete against other teams of students. Odyssey of the Mind and academic decathlons are some examples of this type of group. Kagan (1994) cautioned against this type of cooperative format for classes that have a great deal of ethnic and academic diversity. There is a danger that these competitive scenarios may provide a structure in which students from individualistic-value orientations will excel. Students from cooperative-value orientations are less likely to be successful in this type of format. Academic tasks can play an important role in how academic ability is displayed and measured, and teachers need to give attention to these issues.

Teams-assisted individualization (TAI) combines cooperative teams with individualized instruction. Students work in four- to five-member teams on self-instructed materials at their own rate and level. Students are responsible for checking and managing the assignments. Teams are rewarded if they achieve preset standards.

In the original jigsaw procedure (Aronson et al., 1978), students were assigned to six member heterogeneous teams to address an academic task. Each member studies the information given to him or her. Members from different groups who received the same information meet in expert groups to deliberate on their understanding of the material. The students then return to their groups to teach the material to their group members.

Slavin (1995) modified the jigsaw procedure to more closely match the student team learning format. In Jigsaw II, students work in four- to five-member teams. All students are assigned some material but each member is assigned a subtopic to master. Students discuss their topics in expert groups and then teach their teammates. Quiz scores are summed to form team scores rather than individual scores.

Kagan (1994) provided a number of ways to adapt jigsaw procedures. For group investigation, students can be placed into small groups and select a topic from a unit being investigated by the class. The group reports to the class the findings of its investigation. Among the skills reinforced in this group are cooperative inquiry, group discussion, and cooperative planning.

Teachers can adapt any of the methods we have described to a cooperative learning context. Educators have applied cooperative learning to mathematics, language arts, social studies, critical thinking, history, and physical education. In order to gain maximum rewards, however, it is crucial that students be held accountable for the product the team produces. Cooperative learning does not work if teachers choose to place students in groups and grade them only on individual achievement or participation. Teachers interested in cooperative learning are encouraged to consult a number of the texts dedicated to this pedagogical practice and develop cooperative learning activities for their classrooms.

The previous section outlines different ways teachers can organize and present instructional material. Lectures are appropriate for some instructional goals and cooperative learning groups are best for others. There are some communication practices that must be understood regardless of the approach. Teachers must explain material and ask questions in lectures and in group settings. In the next section, we will examine these communication practices.

Teacher Clarity

Because students want to understand a lesson, teacher clarity is essential to effective teaching. Clarity is concerned with the message strategies used to increase the fidelity of instructional messages. As we stated in Chapter 2, there are several characteristics of teacher clarity. Hines et al. (1985) argued that clarity behaviors consist of: (1) stressing important aspects of content, (2) explaining by the use of examples, and (3) assessing and responding to perceived deficiencies in understanding.

Book and McCaleb (1985) characterized teacher clarity as the quality of being comprehensible. They argued that teacher clarity entails the use of the following types of communication behaviors: (1) definition of major concepts, (2) accuracy of examples, (3) sufficiency of examples, (4) sufficiency of explanation, (5) checking student understanding, (6) connective discourse, and (7) specific examples. Powell and Harville (1990) stated that the behaviors detracting from clarity include ambiguous terms, vagueness, hedging, bluffing, insufficient examples, mazes, and vague language. Other behaviors used to define the lack of clarity are nonfluencies, false starts, and vocal fillers.

Enhancing Explanations

Rowen (1999) provided a useful framework for examining teacher explanations, a central feature of teacher clarity. She stated that one of the principal responsibilities of teachers is to provide explanations that promote understanding of subject matter. There are typically three areas in which confusion occurs in instructional discourse. One source of confusion involves explaining unfamiliar concepts or using language in unfamiliar ways. A second source of confusion involves difficult-to-picture processes. The final sources of confusion involve counterintuitive explanations.

Rowen discussed three types of explanations that can be used to facilitate understanding. The first type is called elucidating explanations. Elucidating explanations are designed to help students understand the meaning of a term or concept. According to Rowen, good elucidating statements contain "(a) each concept's critical features, (b) an array of examples, and (c) opportunities to practice distinguishing examples from nonexamples by looking for critical features" (p. 321).

The second type of explanation is quasi-scientific. When teachers try to help students understand complex processes such as osmosis, evolution, open systems theory, life cycles, or math formulae, they are engaging in quasi-scientific explanations. Several strategies can be used to facilitate the discussion of quasi-scientific material. Signaling devices, which focus on main points; figurative language; analogies (the San Joaquin Valley is California's bathtub); and graphics are effective tools for bringing focus to important points.

Rowen recommended an instructional technique known as *elaborative interrogation* for quasi-scientific explanations. Students are asked to read an explanatory passage about how some phenomenon occurs and then explain it in their own words. This process requires students to construct their own mental models for difficult-to-understand processes. In lectures, elaborative interrogation could be used in a number of ways to engage students in the material under investigation.

The third type of explanation Rowen discussed is *transformative explanation*. Transformative explanations help students deal with circumstances or events that do not resonate with their personal theories. Rowen stated that the best transformative explanations: (1) state the "implicit" or "lay" theory about the phenomenon, (2) acknowledge the plausibility of the theory, (3) demonstrate its inadequacy, (4) state the more accepted account, and (5) demonstrate the greater adequacy of the alternative theory. Engaging students in these alternative views promotes critical thinking and shapes new insights and understandings.

In Chapter 2 we emphasized that clarity does not occur simply because a teacher uses examples or illustrations. If the examples do not relate to the student's experiences, they are not likely to have much of an effect. We also explained the different ways students signal their lack of understanding. Darling (1989) and Kendrick and Darling (1990) observed that the point a teacher is trying to make during a lesson influences the strategies students use to seek clarification. We also believe that the relationship between the teacher and student influences clarity and the way it is managed. For example, the teacher who criticizes students for asking dumb questions or demonstrates impatience nonverbally (rolling eyes, sighing) sends a clear message to students—don't ask questions. On the other hand, the teacher who is open and willing to address students' lack of understanding sends a different message—let's stay with this idea until we get it. The relationship between the teacher and student also is related to clarity. As teachers develop an understanding of their students, they are more attentive to language and nonverbal cues that indicate understanding. Just as intimates grow more competent in assessing implicit messages, teachers and students grow more able to understand each other as their relationship develops. A look, a glance, a smile may say a great deal about student understanding. Finally, the culture of the student will influence how students signal their lack of understanding. Students from high-context, collectivistic cultures (Japanese, Hmong, Chinese) are unlikely to signal their lack of understanding because such a behavior would threaten the face of the instructor (he or she did a bad job of explaining the idea) and of self (I am embarrassed because I don't understand). Students from these orientations may ask for clarification after class or may ask another student for an explanation.

Reflection

- In what ways do you signal that you don't understand a teacher?
- How do teachers indicate that they do not want to clarify information?

Questions

Asking and managing questions are essential components of classroom interaction. Questions play an important role in both lectures and small-group discussions. Research suggests that teachers spend a tremendous amount of time asking and processing student questions (Cleg, 1987; Hoetker & Ahlbrand, 1969). Effective discussions and lectures require thoughtful attention to questions. However, many teachers often fall into a pattern of asking the same types of questions over and over again. Teachers could better manage questions if they possessed an understanding of what they want a question to accomplish and how the question is related to learning.

There are a variety of ways to use questions. Some are used to glean unknown information whereas others are used to check student knowledge. Pseudo questions, for example, are used to determine if students understand concepts or know certain facts. During a discussion of the Puritans, a teacher may ask, "Who gave the sermon, 'Sinners in the Hands of an Angry God?'" The teacher knows the answer is Jonathon Edwards and is using the pseudo question to get students to recall this fact. Questions may also serve as directives. A misbehaving student may be asked a question to get him or her back on task. A teacher may ask a student who is not paying attention to an instructional task, "Johnny, have you finished your worksheet?" Upon hearing this question, Johnny is likely to stop what he was doing and get back to work.

Research by Gall (1984) indicated that teachers seldom ask questions that require higher levels of thinking (application, analysis, synthesis, or evaluation). Teachers tend to ask questions requiring students to recall facts. This is unfortunate because higher-order questions stimulate critical thinking. Recall that a central aspect of differentiated instruction is asking essential questions that require high levels of thinking.

Bloom, Englehart, Furst, Hill, and Krathwohl's (1956) taxonomy of learning is a classic framework for conceptualizing cognitive questions. Krathwohl (2002) explained the revision to the original taxonomy. The revised taxonomy (see Table 9.2) consists of a hierarchy of objectives that represent different levels of thinking. The six classes of objectives are remember, understand, apply, analyze, evaluate, and create.

Cunningham (1987) argued, "For every cognitive operation, there is a complementary affective operation" (p. 69). In the cognitive area, Cunningham identified three levels of questions (Figure 9.4). The first level consists of *factual recall* questions. These questions are concerned with student recall and recognition. Key processes are naming, recalling, identifying, writing, listing, and distinguishing.

The second level consists of conceptualization questions. According to Cunningham (1987), convergent and divergent questions characterize this level. Questions vary on how open-ended they are. Low-convergent questions are used when the teacher is looking for the "right" answer but they are more complex than questions about the recall of facts. For example, the question

Table 9.2 Bloom's Revised Cognitive Domain of Learning

Level of Learning	*Example*
Remember—Retrieving relevant knowledge from long-term memory	Who developed the teacher immediacy scale?
Understand—Determining the meaning of instructional messages, including oral, written, and graphic communication	What are examples of teacher immediacy?
Apply—Carrying out or using a procedure in a giving situation	How can you increase your immediacy behavior?
Analyze—Breaking material into its constituent parts, detecting how the parts relate to one another and to an overall structure or purpose	In what ways does immediacy influence constituent parts and student learning?
Evaluate—Making judgments based on criteria and standards	Identify three limitations of the immediacy research
Create—Putting elements together to form a novel, coherent whole or make an original product	Use the Hunter Lesson Plan and write a lesson plan on a language arts state standard

Source: Krathwohl (2002)

"What type of state government is used in Nebraska?" requires students to sort through the various definitions of state government and select the one that applies to Nebraska.

High-order convergent questions require students to demonstrate their comprehension of a concept or principle. These types of questions require students to provide evidence and reasons for their responses. At this level students must be able to differentiate facts from opinions. Here is an example of this type of question: "Does exposure to media violence cause viewers to act violently?" To adequately answer this question, students must understand causal reasoning.

Divergent questions give students the freedom to wrestle with a variety of issues without the constraint of searching for a correct answer. In order to respond to divergent questions, students should have a reasonable information base for their responses. Low-divergent questions require students to create new or different ideas. An example of a low-divergent question is: "What are some ways of dealing with school overcrowding?" High-divergent questions call for creative thinking. Students are expected to think in new and novel ways. Cunningham (1987) contended that only 5 percent of classroom questions are of this type. An example of a high-divergent question is: "What role should schools play in fighting racism?" Table 9.3 shows the key words for divergent and convergent questions.

Table 9.3 Key Words for Divergent and Convergent Questions

Convergent		
Understand		comprehend
Translate		explain in your own words
State the problem		what are the main points?
Identify the thesis		what is the explicit theme?
Example: Donny, what is the main idea of the story?		
Divergent		
Apply	use	relate
Utilize	employ	assume
Hypothesis	manipulate	build
Construct	predict	compose
Formulate	create	design
Operate	make	wonder
Find another way	invent	try
Example: Anita, predict what will happen next in the story.		
Key words for value questions		
Rate	determine	assess
Appraise	critique	award
Criticize	prioritize	weigh
Accept/reject	critique	explain why
Grade	judge	censure
Example: Shen, do think this was a well-written story?		

Source: Cunningham (1987)

The third level concerns evaluative questions. These questions are based upon the other levels. This level of question requires students to judge the validity of materials and argue a position. Reponses to these types of questions allow the teacher to probe for additional support and reasoning. The following is an example of an evaluative question: "What are the problems with the death penalty?"

Affective Domain

Students do not process information neutrally; therefore, questions have affective consequences. Some ideas connect and resonate with their experiences and others seem distant and irrelevant. Frequently, teachers miss the affective implications for the questions they ask, however. Cunningham (1987) discussed three levels of questions that are influenced by the affective domain.

The first level is *perceiving and initiating action*. This level of question is concerned with perceptual awareness. This level is concerned with how much attention a student needs to dedicate to the situation. For example, in a history class, a teacher may simply ask who in the class is aware of Cesar Chavez, the founder and leader of the United Farm Workers Union. Questions at this level are not designed to make assessments or evaluations, but simply to note awareness.

The second level, *valuing questions*, addresses the worth or merit of the objects under examination. One role of the teacher is to help the students scrutinize and assess the values they hold. On some issues, students are aware of the topic under consideration but hold no strong attitudes about it, whereas others feel a great sense of commitment and ego involvement in the topic. As values become more internalized, students are more likely to seek out information that is affirming. Questions can be used to facilitate an examination of the value. Let's go back to our example of Cesar Chavez and consider the following question: Did Cesar Chavez act in a heroic fashion? Students viewing Chavez as a champion of the rights of farm workers will respond one way and students viewing him as a threat to agribusiness will view him in another. Teachers facilitating a discussion on this topic might face a lively debate that would increase student awareness on both sides of the issue. Unfortunately, many teachers avoid such discussions because they perceive them as too controversial.

The third level, *actualizing questions*, is designed to challenge existing values and consider the merit of competing ones. At this level, students are exposed for what they believe in and stand for. Through this exploration, the total development of the learner is exposed. Teachers attending to the affective domain must remember that, unlike with cognitive questions, the teacher's role is not to direct the responses but to help students understand how they view the world (Cunningham, 1987).

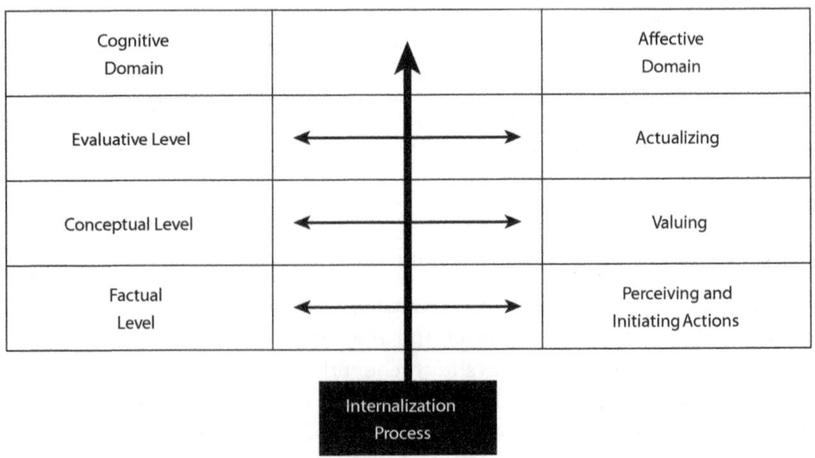

Figure 9.4 Question Types

After discussing the civil rights movement, students might be asked the following: "Who had the greatest impact on the civil rights movement, Martin Luther King or Malcom X?" This type of question taps into student's ideas about racism, non-violence, religion, justice, and communication style.

Teachers need practice and guidance on asking a variety of questions. Effective questions engage students in learning and help them shape the direction of classroom discourse. Further, it is through the management and negotiation of questions that important meanings emerge.

Another dynamic that is related to teacher questions involves wait time. Teachers seldom wait more than one second to answer their own questions. Students quickly learn that if they sit quietly, the teacher will provide the necessary information. One rule for teachers to follow is to wait three seconds before answering a question or calling on a student to respond. The extra time will help students to formulate better answers and give teachers an opportunity to connect student responses to important content. Competency in using questions takes time and effort. Several theorists offer important insight on questions in the classroom (Andersen, Nussbaum, Pecchioni, & Grant, 1999; Brophy & Good, 1986; Hunkins, 1976).

Reflection

- What type of questions do you prefer that teachers ask?
- Which type of questions lead to class discussion?

Feedback

Eptisam goes to her teacher and makes the following statement: "I don't understand why I got a C on my paper." The teacher responds by saying, "Look at my feedback and you will see that you had too many misspelled words." Eptisam picks up her paper and walks dejectedly back to her desk. Scenarios similar to this happen every day because many teachers confuse feedback with an evaluation (Wiggins, 2012). The information given to Eptisam was not feedback; rather it was an evaluation that occurred after the fact. Wiggins contended that feedback is information about how students are doing toward reaching a goal. For example, if I want to run a mile in under four minutes, I will need information on my time at each quarter mile. Or my goal may be to create an assignment that will engage the students in a learning task; if they look confused and do not do what I expect, I have received information about progress toward my goal. This information can be used to make an adjustment to my instructions so I am more successful in accomplishing the goal.

Hattie (2009) conducted extensive research on feedback and argued that for feedback to be effective, teachers need to be clear on the instructional goal they desire students to achieve. In addition they should provide examples of what success looks like. When students understand the goals they are more likely to attend to and use the feedback provided by teachers.

According to Hattie (2009), there are three levels of feedback. Task feedback focuses on how well a student performs a given task. For example, a student may be asked to identify the explicit and implicit themes in a story. A student may receive the following feedback: "The goal was to identify the implicit and explicit theme in the story. You correctly identified the explicit theme but the discussion of the implicit theme is not clear. Remember, an implicit theme is implied, so go back and look for themes not specifically stated."

The second level is process feedback. This level focuses on the processes used to complete the tasks. A student may ask a teacher what a word means and, rather than defining it for the student, the teacher may say, "Can you infer the meaning of the word by comparing it with the other words in the paragraph or can you use your computer tablet to look up a definition?"

The third level is self-regulated feedback, which describes how learners manage their own actions as they work on the learning goal. This type of feedback is designed to reinforce internal motivation and self-regulation. A student may demonstrate an understanding of a math formula but not obtain the right answer. The teacher may encourage the student to review each step they are using to see if they are able to identify an error and correct it. In this case the student may discover he or she is inverting numbers. Armed with this knowledge, the student can self-manage to check for inversions in other mathematical tasks.

Wiliam (2012) argued that teachers need to understand how students respond to feedback. What could the teacher say to Eptisam so that she would not feel dejected and instead would work harder on her spelling?

According to Wiliam (2012), there are eight possible responses to feedback, and six of them are negative (see Table 9.4). Therefore, teachers should use feedback so that students increase their effort to reach their academic goals and also aspire to higher goals. Wiliam asserted that effective feedback:

Table 9.4 Responses to Feedback

Recipients respond to feedback in four basic ways	*If feedback indicated that performance has fallen short of the goal, the recipient may*	*If feedback indicates that performance has exceeded the goal, the recipient may*
By changing behavior	Increase effort*	Exert less effort
By modifying the goal	Reduce aspiration	Increase aspiration*
By abandoning the goal	Decide the goal is too hard	Decide the goal is too easy
By rejecting the feedback	Ignore the feedback	Ignore the feedback

* Effective feedback increases student effort and aspiration.

Source: Wiliam (2012)

- *Focuses on the task at hand rather than the recipient's ego.* Wiliam observed that when students receive scores and comments from their teachers their attention is first drawn to the grade and secondly to the scores their peers received. These comparisons are more about identity management than learning. We encourage teachers to focus on process and ask students to reflect on how they prepared to accomplish a task, how they completed the task, and what they learned from completing the task. We explicitly tell students that comparing grades without understanding that students use different processes to accomplish a task is problematic.
- *Focuses on things that are within the recipient's control.* It is not helpful to tell students to work harder on a task. Rather, help learners identify what they can do to impact their learning
- *Requires more work from the recipient than from the giver.* If feedback only focuses on what is wrong, the student can be overwhelmed and give up. If students solved some equations correctly but missed others they can be asked to find the ones they missed and fix them. If students solved all of them correctly, they can be asked to make up equations for another student to solve or work on more challenging equations.

Wiliam (2012) concluded his essay by arguing that classrooms are complex and teachers cannot provide effective feedback without having an understanding of their students, their experiences with previous teachers, their attitudes about the subjects they are learning, and how they perceive their teacher.

Summary

The purpose of this chapter was to present ways to design lessons and explain how to use communication strategies to engage students in learning. We began the chapter by discussing Common Core state standards and followed with explanations of differentiated instruction, universal design for learning, Response to Intervention, and lesson planning. The next section focused on specific instructional strategies such as lecturing and the use of small groups. We concluded the chapter by discussing communication strategies for managing meaning. The research viewed in this chapter indicates that academic performance is enhanced when teachers connect with and build on the lived experiences of students. There is no perfect method. The selection of a strategy should be based on the goals of the instructor, the teaching strengths of the instructor, student strengths, and the availability of resources. The greater the repertoire of strategies available to a teacher, however, the greater the opportunity to adapt to the needs of the students.

Learning Activities

- Write a 5- to 7-minute lecture on a Common Core standard in language arts and literacy or mathematics. Use the lesson plan discussed in the chapter to plan your lecture.
- Based on the lecture, write questions reflecting each part of Bloom's taxonomy of learning.
- Use brainstorming groups to generate a list of famous people to investigate for a group project. After identifying a person, the groups will develop a way to present their information, such as oral presentations, role-playing skits, a musical.

Resources

www.corestandards.org

10

TECHNOLOGY AND INSTRUCTIONAL COMMUNICATION

Learning Outcomes

1. Identify different ways technology has influenced instructional communication.
2. Explain the digital divide and discuss strategies for reducing it.
3. Design an assignment using a social media site.
4. Explain the attributes of meaningful learning using technology.
5. Identify the components of TPACK.

Classroom Scenario

Lee Harrison, a seventh-grade teacher at Kennedy Middle School, is on his way to a special meeting for all faculty and staff. Rumors have been flying around the school about a major curriculum change about to take place. After everyone is seated, the principal, Mrs. Vera Shoals, steps to the microphone and makes the following announcement:

> Today I am happy to announce that we are creating a partnership with Hyperspeed Learning Systems to create an integrated technological learning community here at Kennedy. We will begin by using tablets in our advanced classes, and in the next 5 years we will phase in several additional supports, including smart boards. Hyperspeed will provide the tablets for the students and train the teachers. We believe this new partnership takes us to where we need to go in the new millennium.

Several faculty members raise their hands and bombard the principal with questions: "Why was this decision made?" "How do we know it will positively affect learning?" "What is Hyperspeed and what's in this for us?" "What's going to happen to students who can't afford a computer or those who don't have computers at home?" "Why weren't we consulted?" Other teachers seem rather content and smug. One was heard to say, "It's about time. Technology is revolutionizing education and it is time to jump on board or stay in the dark ages."

Mr. Harrison leaves the meeting a bit overwhelmed. He is unsure about how this technological revolution will impact him, his teaching, and his students. No single educational development is more dramatic than the technological advancements of the last decade. Because these developments have occurred so quickly, there are few data to determine the educational consequences. Some educators are blindly committed to the benefits of technology. Others resist technology, believing it threatens the human core of the educational enterprise. We can say this: technology will continue to be a significant force and education will be served best by understanding the way in which the teaching/learning process is influenced by it. The focus of this chapter is how technology influences the communication process and learning in the classroom.

Technology and Education

It is an understatement to claim that technology is pervasive. Many students use cell phones, smart phones, laptops, and tablets for a variety of tasks such as talking, texting, taking pictures, sending e-mails, tweeting, connecting to webpages, playing games, skyping, using an assortment of apps, and the list goes on. Classrooms have doc cams, Promethean or smart boards, and LCD projectors. Technology has become an important part of the social fabric and is having a profound impact on education. However, the infusion of technology precedes the research on how to use it to best meet the needs of all students.

Technology includes the mechanisms that are used to facilitate or mediate the teaching/learning process. Although teachers have used videos, TV programs, films, audiotapes, and filmstrips for a number of years, it is the computer that has had the most substantial impact. No other teaching tool has been mandated to become a central part of the educational process. In their Report to the Nation on Technology and Education (U.S. Department of Education, 1996) the Clinton administration issued an initiative to make all students computer literate by the twenty-first century (Getting America's Students Ready). Literally millions of dollars have been committed to this goal. Let's turn our attention to the ways computer technology influences instructional practice.

Whenever technologies are employed, the roles of teachers and students change. According to Chizmar and Walbert (1999), technology allows the teacher to move from the "sage on the stage" to the "guide at the side." When technologies become infused into the curriculum, the teacher's role shifts from being primarily an information source to a facilitator, a coach, a guide, and a co-learner. Jones, Valdez, Nowakowski, and Rasmussen (1995) outlined the way in which these teacher roles are enacted in technologically rich classrooms. They contended that teachers are facilitators when they provide environments and opportunities for students to work collaboratively and solve authentic problems. When they act as guides, teachers mediate, model, and coach. Teachers model when they competently demonstrate the use of technology. They coach by giving hints and encouraging students to refocus and practice their skills. Finally, teachers are co-learners when they participate with students in the discovery and management of new information and insight.

Clearly, the technological developments in the last few years have dramatically influenced classroom interaction patterns. Public school access to the Internet has increased substantially, from 65 percent in 1996 to 100 percent in 2005 (U.S. Department of Education, 2008). Access to the information highway has the potential to alter the types of assignments that are developed, the form in which the assignments are presented, the competencies the students must possess to complete the assignments, the type of learning that will occur, and the kinds of problems, behavioral and technological, that will arise.

Some advocate that technological developments offer limitless opportunities; others are more circumspect about the use of technology. Bransford et al. (2000) argued that technology is not an educational panacea:

> Technologies do not guarantee learning but ineffective use of technologies can hinder learning—for example, students may spend most of their time picking fonts and colors for multimedia reports instead of planning writing and revising ideas. And everybody knows how much time students can waste on surfing the Internet.
>
> (p. 206)

Effective Use of Technology

The authors offered five ways to effectively use technology:

- Bring real-world problems into the classroom.
- Provide scaffolds and tools to enhance learning.
- Give students and teachers more opportunity for feedback, reflection, and revision.
- Build local and global communities that include teachers, administrators, students, parents, practicing scientists, and other interested people.
- Expand opportunities for teacher learning.

A brief discussion of these areas may help teachers and prospective teachers develop a working paradigm for instructional technology.

Real-World Learning

There are several ways to utilize technology to provide new types of learning opportunities for students. Employing a problem-solving orientation is not a new concept, but technology does offer the potential to change the boundaries of the typical classroom. Computer software can be used to simulate problems and give students a variety of ways to work through them.

One way to facilitate real-world problem solving is to connect students with communities examining significant problems. For example, a fourth- through sixth-grade class in Bakersfield, California, used the Internet to connect with students across the country and collaborated with a team of researchers conducting archaeological research in the Four Corners area of the Southwest (Revenaugh, 2000). Another example is to utilize a digital learning platform such as Project WISE. Teachers can log on to the website (http://wise.berkeley.edu) and select lessons on a variety of topics. One available lesson for sixth graders is to study the impact of climate change. Students observe, analyze, experiment, and reflect as they work through a series of learning activities. A third example is tele-mentoring (O'Neil, Wagner, & Gomez, 1996). Students collaborate with practicing professionals, university faculty, or graduate students and through e-mail help the students as they investigate a significant problem.

Providing Scaffolds

Vygotsky (1962/1981, 1978) argued that learning is facilitated when learners are provided models and guidance until they are able to perform tasks alone. Without this help, which he called scaffolding, students are often overwhelmed and do not know how to determine what is important and what is not. Computer-aided instruction can provide valuable scaffolding tools (Oliver, Omari, & Herrington, 1998). Bransford et al. (2000) likened computer scaffolding with using training wheels to teach someone to ride a bike. The training wheels help the learner master some of the mechanics of bike riding without falling. Similarly, computer scaffolding allows learners to perform tasks and solve problems they could not do without this skill. With a coach or tutor, the learner receives hints and guidance in solving problems. Once competency is established, the learner has a foundation to move on to solve tasks without help.

There are several ways to develop scaffolded experiences. One option is to use an apprenticeship model. In this approach, an expert (such as the teacher) models a learning function and guides learners in practice until they can perform the task alone. Another approach is to allow individuals to work collaboratively because in most real-world applications, individuals frequently work with others.

Even though there is potential for scaffolding technologies, there are some potential pitfalls. Because of time constraints and a lack of patience, teachers and mentors may be inclined to do the work for the novice. The goal of scaffolding is to teach new skills, however; new skills are not taught when the teacher or mentors lose sight of their role—to help the novice use the skill independently. Over time this pattern can lead to learned helplessness; that is, the novice sits back and waits for someone else to take over the task.

Feedback, Reflection, and Revision

Feedback to students can be facilitated through the use of Internet technology. In addition to traditional e-mail and websites, new software allows for a more interactive educational environment. Blackboard, for example, is a Web-based program with a number of interactive features that allow teachers to post course outlines, announcements, and assignments; provide feedback to students on projects; answer questions from parents; and use interactive tests. Traditional websites provide information and a certain amount of interactivity but students cannot receive immediate feedback on their work. Innovations such as Blackboard were developed to meet this need. Many teachers may use social media such as Twitter and Facebook to connect with students and provide feedback to them. We discuss the use of social media networks later in the chapter.

Tele-Web integrates server-side software and plug-ins with a Web server. Zhao, Englert, Chen, Jones, and Ferdig (2000) discussed the way this tool can be used to teach literacy. With this technology, teachers develop multimedia learning materials and conduct collaborative learning projects. Teachers can use this tool to archive student assignments and track performance. Students are encouraged to explore independent ideas and collaborate with others. The curriculum focuses on four primary environments: Writing Room, Reading Room, Library, and Publishing Room. Each environment allows teachers and students to create projects and comment on progress.

Not only do these technological developments have the potential to link students with teachers, but they also provide a way for students to conduct research. Say, for example, student teams are asked to examine "problems in their community." Warner-Burke (2014) recommended that students conduct a 5-minute google search to identify credible sources to use in their investigation. Students can also use SurveyMonkey to assess attitudes and opinions from individuals in their communities. As students work through their projects they can e-mail drafts to their instructor for feedback and improvement.

Finally, technology provides tutorial opportunities. For example, tutorial software is available in algebra and writing. In algebra, computer software programs guide students through simple to complex tasks, and the writing software provides students with guidance on grammar and style.

Connecting the Classroom to the Community

There are numerous ways technologies can link the school to the home and the larger community. For example, every school in Clovis Unified School district in California has a home page website with links to extracurricular and curricular activities. Some faculty members have websites with course assignments and grading criteria. The old student response "I don't have any homework tonight, Dad" can be verified by connecting to the website and checking the assignments that are posted.

One common complaint from parents is that they do not know what is going on in the school. This is particularly problematic for divorced families in which announcements may go to only one household. Many schools provide announcements on telephone message systems so that a parent can find out the time of a Frosh football game or open house. The same system can be used to leave voice mail with an instructor or administrator. The time has passed when the school newsletter was the primary tool for disseminating information.

Teacher Learning

The final area that Bransford et al. (2000) addressed is teacher learning. Technology has dramatically changed the teaching and learning process. The authors contended that technology influences classroom instructional practices and affects the professional development of the teacher.

Teachers effectively using technology in the classroom model ways to use these tools to advance learning. For example, when teachers guide students through an instructional task, they may explore and experiment with different ways to solve a problem. This collaborative process helps students and teachers discover new insights and perspectives. Also, there may be occasions when a student understands more about the use of a particular technology than the teacher. On these occasions, the learning event unfolds into a collaborative venture in which the roles of teacher and student are blurred or redefined. The student takes the lead as instructor and the teacher becomes the student.

Obtaining access to new teaching strategies and sharing information with other teachers can also be facilitated because of new technological developments. Teachers can explore teaching websites, read articles in virtual libraries, and download information pertaining to teaching standards. The traditional role of teacher as expert is changed to teacher as facilitator.

One of the more exciting developments is the way in which technology can be used to help teachers prepare for their teaching responsibilities. Teachers can go online to obtain information on teaching standards, download examples of lesson plans, watch YouTube videos of teaching lessons, and participate in chat rooms where teachers can obtain information from other professionals. Edutopia, for example, is an online journal dedicated to improving K–12 education. The journal is dedicated to providing research-based practices that improve student learning.

Reflection

- How does technology facilitate learning?
- Select a website from the back of this chapter and discuss the way it influences learning.

Concerns About Technology

The research reviewed above suggests that technology impacts education in a number of positive ways. But before we accept all of these benefits at face value, we must also understand that many of these benefits do not reach all students and are not applicable to all educational goals. Narrative arguments may exceed the objective data on the positive effects of technology on learning (Selfe, 1999). Healy (1998) observed, "Unfortunately, the political pressures to toss computers into classrooms and to get internet connections before people even know what to do with them is an attempt to run around the teaching profession" (p. 8). We agree and want to emphasize that technology will not be a substitute for an effective teacher.

In this next section we explore the problems that are associated with the infusion of technology. We frame this discussion in terms of the daily practices of a teacher such as Mr. Harrison, who we described in opening this chapter.

Access To and the Use of Technology

Several years ago access to computers and the Internet was considered a significant problem. "The digital divide" was the metaphor used to describe the disparity between those who had access to the computer and the Internet and those who did not. In 1997, for example, 42.8 percent of elementary and secondary students had access to a home computer. In 2010 this number increased to 75 percent (U.S. Census Bureau, 2011). There have also been changes in access to schools. In 1997, 78 percent of all public schools had Internet access but 100 percent of schools had Internet access by 2003 (National Center for Education Statistics, 2006). Even though these data indicate that Internet access has increased, it is not clear how the Internet has been incorporated into classroom practice. We do not know if all schools have access in all classrooms and grade levels.

Access continues to be influenced by ethnicity. According to the U.S. Census Bureau (2011), 86 percent of Asians, 81 percent of Whites, 63 percent of Latinos, and 63 percent of African-Americans live in homes with Internet access. Not surprisingly, income impacts Internet access as well. In homes with household incomes of $25,000 or less, 54 percent have Internet access whereas in homes with incomes of $100,000 or more, 96 percent have access to the Internet (U.S. Census Bureau, 2011).

What is not described in these data is that the number of computers that are accessible also increases with income. Families with incomes in the $20,000 range may have one computer that is shared among family members whereas wealthier families may have two or three computers.

Family occupation is a third factor that influences computer and Internet access (Fairlie, London, Rosner, & Pastor, 2006). Individuals who work in occupations that do not require a computer are less likely to own one. Families who work in agriculture, construction, service, or transportation may be less likely to own a computer, whereas families who work in education or law or own farms or construction companies may be more likely to have computers.

The fourth factor, which is related to occupation and income, is education. As family education levels increase, the amount of access to computers increases. More educated families have careers that require computer access, have the skills to manage and use computers, and see their value. This is true for immigrant and non-immigrant families. Thus an immigrant who went to college or graduated from high school is much more likely to have a computer than an immigrant or non-immigrant who has little education (Fairlie et al., 2006).

The final factor influencing computer and Internet access is language. Fairlie et al. (2006) reported that the majority of Web pages are in English. Even when accounting for education and family income, Spanish speaking Latino immigrants have very low access rates. Language also influences the content of Internet sites and software programs. Unfortunately, little data is available on language and its role in computer access and use.

The data we have reviewed indicate that substantial members of society have limited access to computers and the Internet. This creates a larger burden on educators to address this issue. Teachers in grades K–12 will have students who come from low-income families who do not have computers at home. Because schools have increased their access, teachers need to think carefully about the ways they will provide technological access and opportunity for all students.

According to Brown, Higgins, and Hartley (2001), questions of access reveal themselves in different ways. Some schools with diverse student bodies restrict access to technology. In many schools, computer stations are placed in labs with restricted access. By placing computers in labs, schools are sending two messages: one, the computer is not an integral part of the learning processes, and two, students from poverty or diverse backgrounds cannot be trusted with computers in the classroom. Together these messages indicate that technology is not central to the learning experiences of students from diverse cultural backgrounds (Swain & Pearson, 2001).

The type of computer instruction delivered in schools is often different for students from diverse backgrounds. Research indicates that culturally diverse students receive instruction in which the computer directs the learning whereas White students receive instruction that encourages problem solving and student initiative (Anderson Welch, & Harris, 1984; Crist-Whitzel, 1985; Kozma & Croninger, 1992). Technology for some students is considered a tool to facilitate and explore learning and for others it is a tool to complete repetitive tasks such as word processing or data entry. One type of student is given freedom to use the computer to explore ideas and another is limited to working on remedial competencies.

Access therefore presents difficult problems for teachers whose students live in lower socioeconomic conditions. The first obstacle is financial. Teachers don't have the power to change the financial circumstances of families. They can, however, think through the ways in which they teach about the use of technology.

Brown et al. (2001) offered an extensive list of recommendations. Following are ones we believe teachers should consider:

1. Have roving computer stations that stay in classrooms for extended periods of time.
2. Offer and allow typically underserved students opportunities to take technology courses and earn extra credit for graduation.
3. Have girls' technology day, use female students, and students from diverse ethnic backgrounds as technology monitors, and have more sign-up slots for female students during free time.
4. Lend laptop computers to students, much as band students receive musical instruments.
5. Ensure equal technology use, regardless of gender, ethnicity, or achievement level, by removing some of the biases and stereotypes associated with technology use.
6. Consider summer school courses that meet at atypical times to accommodate students who work after school.
7. Blend technology into the daily routine to promote learner-center learning.
8. Make computers available to the public through schools, libraries, and community centers.
9. Encourage students to use public library technology for after-school homework assistance and to take advantage of mentoring and tutoring programs.

The recommendations above can help teachers reduce the gaps between the technological haves and have-nots. Other researchers offered other recommendations on the digital divide (e.g., Becker & Sterling, 1987; Crist-Whitzel, 1985; Kozma & Croninger, 1992; Swain & Pearson, 2001; Yoder, 2001).

Reflection

- What are additional ways to narrow the digital divide?
- Should educational programs such as laptops for learners be implemented in public schools? Defend your answer.

Technology and Learning

The significance of the digital divide is predicated on the strong belief that technology positively influences learning. Many people don't even question its value as they search for a bigger, faster, and more sophisticated machine. The objective data showing the effects of technology on learning, however, are less than straightforward. Some theorists go as far as to claim that technology has a minimal effect on learning (Cuban, 2001; Roschelle, Pea, Hoadley, Gordon, & Means, 2000). Other research has been more positive.

Park (2008) conducted an extensive study on the role of technology on the mathematics achievement scores for English- and Spanish-speaking Hispanics. The author analyzed data from the 2002/2004 Education Longitudinal Study and found, after controlling for external factors that impact academic performance (i.e., family socioeconomic status, parental support, attendance, delinquency), that individual computer use positively influenced mathematics performance. This effect was even larger for Spanish-speaking Hispanics.

Boster, Meyer, Roberto, Inge, and Strom (2006) studied the effects of video streaming on learning outcomes. The authors conducted a series of studies on third and eighth graders from three school districts in the Southeast. Students were randomly assigned to either an experimental group that was exposed to video streaming or a control group that did not receive exposure to video streaming. Students took standardized tests to determine if video streaming had an impact on learning. The results indicated that video streaming had a positive effect on third-grade science and social studies performance. For the eighth-grade experiment, video streaming did not affect science performance but did affect social studies performance. Thus the data generally supported the proposition that video streaming positively impacts learning. However, the authors identified a number of factors that may have affected the outcomes and they recommended additional research at other grade levels and in other content areas.

Researchers have also examined whether computer technology can be used to effectively teach about diversity. Lee and Bertera (2007) designed a study to determine if participation in an online diversity forum would influence students' perceptions of their cultural competency and positively influence their relationships with students, family members, and neighbors. The researchers also wanted to identify the specific benefits of using instructional technology to support a multicultural course. The authors surveyed students who took a multicultural course in their master of social work program. The participants completed a survey that assessed how the instructional technology influenced their cultural competency. The researchers also conducted a content analysis of student online postings.

Based on the postings, two groups were identified. The positive group believed they appreciated the opportunity to share with other students and reported that they learned from the experience. The negative group criticized the appropriateness of the online forum and felt it was a nuisance. Interestingly, the negative group posted more anonymous messages on the forum. The results, although generally positive, did not support the claim that instructional technology always enhances learning. It may be that the participants' initial attitude about multicultural education and beliefs about online instruction clouded the results. Students who are open to multicultural issues and competent in the use of online instruction may have responded differently from students who were negative about multicultural education and did not feel competent in online instruction (Lee & Bertera, 2007).

Kulik (1994) conducted a meta-analysis of a set of 97 studies examining the effects of technology on learning. A meta-analysis is a procedure that compares the effects of a relevant variable across a range of studies. Kulik argued that in order to understand the effects of computers it is necessary to identify how they are used. For example, a computer can be used as a tutor, to manage information, for simulations, or for programming. Each of these uses may influence learning in a different way. Kulik's results indicated that the most positive and consistent effect concerned tutoring. Elementary and high school students generally learned more in classes that used computer tutoring. No other computer application had a consistent effect. In another meta-analysis, Bayraktar (2001) investigated the effects of computer-aided instruction using science achievement. The results indicated that the effect of the computer varied by the way it was used. The most effective mode of instruction was simulation, followed by tutorial. The findings of Kulik and Bayraktar suggest that the computer may be best used for some instructional goals and not for others.

Student Learning Style and Technology

Student learning style may also influence the effects of computer technology on learning. Ross, Drysdale, and Schulz (2001) examined learning style and performance in a computer applications class. Students were measured on the Gregorc Style Delineator (Gregorc, 1982). This assessment categorizes learning in four ways: concrete sequential (practical, thorough, well-organized, analytical); abstract sequential (evaluative, analytical, logical, and orderly); abstract random (focus on the world of feeling and emotion); and concrete random (organize information in three-dimensional patterns, think intuitively and impulsively). The authors assessed whether learning style influenced the grades obtained in class. The results indicated that abstract-sequential and concrete-sequential learners performed better in the computer course than abstract-random and concrete-random students. The authors argued that students with abstract-sequential and concrete-sequential learning styles are suited to computer tasks such as programming because these activities require linear processing and logical reasoning skills. These findings suggest that learning style mediates the positive effects of computer-aided instruction. The positive effects of computer application are not equivalent for all learners.

Research has also identified differences between males and females on attitudes about computer use. Weber and Custer (2005) studied the preferences of male and female middle and high school students enrolled in technology classes. The results indicated that females preferred designing activities that involve a focus on problem solving or using technology for communication. Males preferred utilizing activities in which they could build or construct items. These findings suggest that gender mediates the way in which technology is used.

Healy (1998), a more vocal critic, explicated other problems with computer technology and education. One problem is that computers will not turn bad teachers into good ones. A teacher's philosophy and orientation is not likely to be changed as a result of technology. Teachers are likely to select software and assignments that fit into their existing ideologies. If teachers believe they should feed facts to students, the technology will be used to collect and categorize facts. If teachers believe they should facilitate problem solving and collaboration, they will use technology to accomplish these goals.

Additionally, teachers may not be adequately trained to take full advantage of technological opportunities. Selfe (1999) stated that when teachers are not adequately trained they resort to commercial programs written by programmers who do not have substantial educational training. Programs designed to teach composition, for example, may be little more than electronic versions of a printed grammar textbook. Prepackaged programs simply do what has always been part of the curriculum: drill, memorization, and word processing. How these tasks prepare students for the twenty-first century is not clear.

One argument that is often advanced in support of technology is that it makes learning fun. Healy (1998) countered that just because something is fun does not mean it has educational value. Learning can be fun but it also is hard work. Technology can short circuit the process of cultivating a work ethic that is vital to academic and real-world success. Advocates may contend that technological competence helps individuals work smarter, not harder. Yet there is a rather compelling database on the positive effects of diligence and effort on academic success (e.g., Covington, 2000; Dweck, 1986). Much computer software, however, allows students to develop impulsive, trial and error responses that simply do not facilitate higher-order thinking.

Healy (1998) also observed that newer technologies emphasize rapid processing of visual symbols such as computer icons and minimize verbal fluency fostered through reading, interaction, and argument. Westby and Atencio (2002) raised similar concerns. They observed that printed texts require readers to read left to right and top to bottom. Computers, on the other hand may use hypertext that includes graphics, animation, video, and digitized sound. With this medium, readers move rapidly from one text chunk to another, non-sequentially. Visual and aural texts have taken the place of the written and spoken word. Watch how students "surf" through different websites. They may be drawn to images that are aesthetically appealing rather than cognitively challenging.

Some have argued that social media sites are positive because they provide increased opportunities to write. However, as Jago (2014) argued, the typewriting used to post information on Facebook or tweeting in 140 characters does little to develop skill in academic writing. She encouraged teachers to promote writing in all classes but she also stressed that it is essential to provide meaningful feedback so students have an opportunity to revise and refine their work.

The computer may be more than just a tool to promote decision making and problem solving. Shovels, lawnmowers, and brooms are tools we use to complete certain tasks, but they do not have much of an effect on the way the brain processes information. Westby and Atencio (2002) observed, "The ways that children access information on a computer, the manner of its presentation, and the ways it can be manipulated all alter children's perceptions of knowing and doing" (p. 74).

Technology influences socio-emotional development and relational competency. Think for a moment about students who are labeled "computer geeks." These students may be viewed as socially awkward, isolated, and immature. The computer does not tell these students to blow their noses when they drip, how to take turns in conversation, to "get a grip" when they don't get their way, or feel shame when they hurt someone's feelings. These competencies are only developed and refined through face-to-face communication with significant others. Think about the way these students react when their computer "goes down," or freezes. Do they become agitated, unsure of what to do, unable to decide on alternative activities?

Authors such as Goleman (1995) and Gardner (1993, 1999) contended that emotional and interpersonal skills are extremely important to academic and personal success but are often neglected in the instructional process. The emotionally mature individual can take the perspectives of others, read emotional states, and suspend immediate gratification. Excessive time spent watching television or connected to a computer limits the amount of time a child is engaged in meaningful social interaction. Technology, according to Healy (1998), cannot develop "feeling" centers of the brain.

Mobile Phones and Instructional Communication

Mobile technology, specifically cell phones, is dramatically influencing the instructional landscape. More and more students bring cell phones or personal digital assistants into the classrooms. Some school districts view cell phones as a problem and ban their use, but these policies are difficult to enforce. After the school shootings in Columbine, Colorado, and the terrorist attacks in New York, Pennsylvania, and Washington, DC, parents have pressured schools to permit students to have cell phones.

There is a growing trend to use mobile technology to meet academic goals. Katz (2005), for example, discussed various uses of cell phone technology. He stated that cell phones could be used for tutoring. Cell phones can be used to access Internet experts who can provide help on definitions and reference information; connect students with faculty, students, administrators, and coaches to find out about assignments; adjust schedules; and get help on academic and personal matters.

Administrators can use cell phones to manage attendance, adjust schedules, and set up meetings. Parents can use cell phones to monitor the activities of their children, to e-mail teachers, and to stay connected to their students.

Even though there are some positives, there are a number of problems with cell phone use. Katz (2005) identified four specific problems: class disruption, delinquency, chicanery, and teacher autonomy. There are several ways cell phones cause class disruption. It is not uncommon for students to receive and respond to phone calls or text messages during class. Students will also use their phones to send text messages, play games, or engage in other non-academic activities. Katz reported a case in which a student who missed lunch used his phone to order a pizza.

A second problem is delinquency. Katz (2005) observed that mobile phones might be targets of theft or phone piracy (demanding to use someone else's cell phone for personal use). Perhaps the most disturbing problem is cyber-bullying. Smith et al. (2008) defined cyberbullying as "an aggressive, intentional act carried out by a group or individual, using electronic forms of contact, repeatedly and over time against a victim who cannot easily defend him or herself" (p. 376). Smith et al. (2008) stated that cyberbullying may include phone calls, text messages, video clip bullying, and e-mails. There are no clear boundaries when or where these events occur. A student can receive a bullying message at home, in class, or on the playground.

A third problem identified by Katz (2005) is chicanery such as truancy and cheating. Students who skip school use cell phones to contact friends and find out when it is safe to return to school without being detected. Cell phones can also be used to cheat. Pictures of a test can be taken and sent to other students who will take the test later in the day. It is also possible for a student in class to text an answer to another student in the same class.

The final problem with cell phones is the erosion of teacher autonomy. More and more schools are implementing policies about cell phones. Some schools want to ban them altogether. Some require students to turn off the phones before coming to class. Others penalize students by lowering their grade if their cell phone rings, vibrates, or plays a song during class. Monitoring these policies takes teachers and students away from academic engagement.

Mobile phone technology will continue to challenge educators. The number of cell phones and the functions they perform will increase. It is unlikely that school authorities will be successful in banning cell phones. Not having any policy, however, allows the student who may not like what is happening in a given instructional moment to surf the web, text friends, or play games. Rather than viewing cell phones only as a source of irritation, crime, and disruption, teachers can consider thoughtful ways to utilize them to support instructional goals.

Social Media and Instructional Communication

We conclude this section by discussing social media and its increasing presence in instructional communication. One of the innovations impacting instructional practices is the use of social networking sites (SNSs). Teachers are using Facebook, Twitter, and blogs to deliver, create, and manage instructional material. The website EmergingEd Tech provides links to the types of assignments and activities teachers have used to create Facebook campaigns on historical figures, conduct surveys, and create collaborative groups. Even though there is burgeoning interest in SNSs, their efficacy as a pedagogical tool has not been established (Manca & Ranieri, 2013).

Although promising, there are limitations to using SNSs for academic purposes. Halverson (2011) discussed three tradeoffs that must be considered when integrating social media into curriculum. The first is privacy versus redundancy. Instructors are required to protect the rights of students and their work. SNSs, on the other hand are designed to provide a platform to publicly display information. Students may not see the value of connecting to an academic network that provides few social benefits. The second is endogenous versus exogenous learning goals. Instructional environments function with specific goals such as designing assessments to meet learning outcomes. However, the instructional goals of a teacher may not resonate with, and in fact may be inconsistent with, the social goals of learners. Students may be more motivated to participate in the social network that exists outside of the classroom community. The third is identity versus identity. As we noted previously, identity plays a significant role in learning. Social networking sites are specifically designed to manipulate and present identity in multiple ways. For example, in Facebook the user makes choices on what they post and highlight. The choice of what to post on an academic site is constrained by the instructor, the assignment, and the student's investment in his or her academic identity. Halverson concludes the essay by offering suggestions on ways to manage these tradeoffs.

Reflection

- Identify three ways teachers can use cell phones to meet academic goals.
- What is an effective way to use Facebook for meeting literacy standards?

Technology will continue to be a ubiquitous force in education. It is unreasonable to believe that technology will not have an important place in education. Moreover, education will always lag behind technological innovations. Postman (1995) made an insightful observation about technology and teaching:

> To be against technology makes no more sense than to be against food. We can't live without either. But to observe that it is dangerous to eat too much food, or to eat food that has no nutritional value is not to be "anti-food." It is to suggest what may be the uses of food. Technology education aims at students' learning about what technology helps us do and what it hinders us from doing; it is about how technology uses us, for good or ill, and about how it has used people in the past, for good or ill. It is about how technology creates new worlds, for good or ill.
>
> (p. 192)

Attributes of Meaningful Learning Using Technology

In order to deal effectively with technology in its many forms, teachers have a clear idea on what they want to accomplish. Ashburn (2006) discussed six attributes of meaningful learning using technology (MLT). The first is *intentionality*. Teachers and students should be directed toward achieving specific learning objectives. Teachers provide the context for learning by identifying the curriculum standards and designing learning activities that facilitate the accomplishment of the desired outcomes. This attribute presupposes that teachers are able to design the learning activities or have access to support providers who can help teachers create the experiences appropriate to accomplishing their goals.

The second attribute of MLT is *content*. The goal here is to use technology to foster the exploration of "big ideas," or essential questions. Ashburn (2006) contended that challenging students to examine big ideas provides the "connective tissue" that binds classroom learning to their personal lives. For example, we might ask future teachers to examine how technology impacts literacy. What does someone need to know to be a literate user of technology? This question can take students in several directions. They can explore different types of technologies or they can categorize different competencies that are needed.

Authentic work is the third attribute of MLT discussed by Ashburn (2006). Students must be challenged to engage in tasks that require complex thinking and problem solving. This is a major departure from an orientation that encourages students to memorize facts or work on worksheets. For example, students may be challenged to closely investigate the effects of immigration patterns, legal and illegal, on the economy. This requires students to move past personal bias, examine sources, and evaluate them on their relevance and credibility. Authentic work encourages students to use technology to do the work that historians and scientists do. Teachers must be willing to design learning tasks that are real to students and as a result may challenge the teacher's belief systems. They also need to understand the orientations of students. Our discussion of culturally responsive teaching in Chapter 3 is an essential criterion for developing authentic work for students.

The fourth attribute of MLT identified by Ashburn (2006) is *active inquiry*. This feature of MLT encourages students to think deeply and purposefully about the types of questions they want to answer, analyze the information used to answer the questions, and think critically about the degree to which the evidence they collect appropriately answers their questions. Let's return to the example about examining the question "How does immigration, legal and illegal, impact the economy?" The students need to consider where they will obtain information on this question. Will the data come from U.S. government statistics that are available on Web pages? Will they collect reports from independent agencies, local and state? What criteria will the students use to assess the value of the information they collect? Once they analyze the data they must draw conclusions, form their analyses, and communicate their findings.

Ashburn (2006) identified five obligations teachers must meet in order to engage students in active inquiry. First, teachers need to know how to create a "culture of inquiry" in which learning units are connected to relevant standards. Second, teachers need to be skillful in using student questions to connect to the curriculum standards. For example, the teacher must know how to link the student questions to an appropriate Web-based resource. This presupposes that the teacher is competent in navigating the Web. Third, teachers must model the inquiry method and assess student understanding of the process. Teachers cannot just turn students loose and expect them to locate information that solves the problem. Teachers must be skillful in helping students generate questions they will own and connect them to the standards they are trying to meet. Teachers need to model the inquiry process by showing students how to use the appropriate technologies to work through the inquiry process. Fourth, teachers need to help transform student identity. Students must see themselves as principled investigators rather than as passive regurgitators of what the teacher deems important. Finally, teachers need skills in using the technological tools that undergird the inquiry process.

Mental model construction is the fifth attribute of MLT discussed by Ashburn (2006). Mental models are constructions of how the world works. Ashburn contended that teaching for meaningful learning requires the teacher to help students unpack, or make visible, their implicit theories. All students come to class with notions about the way the world works. Teachers can help students understand the way they make sense out of instructional material by cognitive mapping, metaphor analysis, or idea webbing. In the technology classroom, software programs can be used to identify student constructions. Ashburn suggested that technologies such as the MLToolbox Inquiry Station can be used to scaffold the development of student constructions of the content they are exploring. Technology can be used, therefore, to help students understand how they think and organize material. Think about the way a PowerPoint presentation illustrates how students make connections among important ideas. We stressed in Chapter 3 that different cultures have preferred ways of organizing and sequencing information. Technology can be used to help students and teachers understand how material is stored, organized, and retrieved.

The final attribute of MLT discussed by Ashburn (2006) is *collaborative work*. In this approach, students work collaboratively on common tasks to accomplish common goals. In Chapter 9 we discussed the importance of collaboration and cooperative learning. Teachers need to design learning tasks that take advantage of technology and fulfill the obligations of collaborative learning. For example, student investigative teams can be developed to explore an important question. In these groups students need to discuss, argue, deliberate, reflect, and share their ideas on the question under consideration.

The recommendations discussed above may seem complex and difficult, but technology is here to stay. We challenge teachers to learn as much as they can so they can make the most out of technological advances. We would like to close this discussion by referencing Postman (1995), who offered the following insights:

1. All technological change is a Faustian bargain. For every advantage a new technology offers, there is always a corresponding disadvantage.
2. The advantages and disadvantages of new technologies are never distributed evenly among the population. This means that every new technology benefits some and harms others.
3. Embedded in every technology there is a powerful idea, sometimes two or three powerful ideas. Like language itself, a technology predisposes us to favor and value certain perspectives and accomplishments and to subordinate others. Every technology has a philosophy, which is given expression in how the technology makes people use their minds, in what it makes us do with our bodies, in how it codifies the world, in which senses it amplifies and in which of our emotional and intellectual tendencies it disregards.
4. A new technology usually makes war against an old technology. It competes with it for time, attention, money, prestige, and a "worldview."
5. Technological change is not additive; it is ecological. A new technology does not merely add something; it changes everything.
6. Because of the symbolic forms in which information is encoded, different technologies have different intellectual and emotional biases.

> 7. Because of the accessibility and speed of their information, different technologies have different political biases.
> 8. Because of the physical form, different technologies have different sensory biases.
> 9. Because of the conditions in which we attend to them, different technologies have different social biases.
> 10. Because of their technical and economic structure, different technologies have different content biases.
>
> (pp. 192–193)

Mishra and Koehler (2008) explicated a framework for effective teaching with technology (TPACK). Three components form the core of this framework: content knowledge, pedagogical knowledge and technological knowledge. Each of these intersect in significant ways. Technologies can be used to manage the way instructional material is presented and discovered. Technology also impacts pedagogical practices such as assessing the use of collaborative work, or the structure of assignments. Moreover, how technology is used depends on an understanding of students, the school, the system infrastructure and the larger community.

Mishra and Koehler (2008) argued that the TPACK framework suggests that teachers develop a new literacy. The authors stated:

> Viewing teachers' use of technology as a new literacy emphasizes the role of the teacher as a producer (as designer), away from the traditional conceptualization of teachers as consumers (users) of technology. When teachers are able to flexibly navigate the landscape of technology, pedagogy, and content, they become responsible for the total curriculum.
>
> (p. 11)

In this chapter, we have explored the conundrum evolving around educational practice and technological development. Mr. Harrison, the teacher in the opening of this chapter, faces and will continue to face some very difficult decisions. New technologies will continually be developed. Just as one is mastered, a new one will come along. Some of these developments will contribute to classroom goals, others will amount to bells and whistles that on the surface look good but don't have much of a direct influence on learning. Sorting out these differences will not be easy. School districts, publishing houses, and families will put pressure on Mr. Harrison to make the right choice.

The digital divide will not go away. Students from privilege will continue to have increased access that may or may not prepare them academically. Access to some of the exciting developments we reviewed earlier in this chapter will not be available for all students. Yet, Mr. Harrison has an obligation to teach all students assigned to his class. He will be well aware of the substantial role interpersonal communication plays in the classroom, but also that technology will not help him create empathy, caring, and character. The way in which he will balance and manage these differences will have a major impact on student affective orientations to learning and academic outcomes.

Reflection

- How would you advise Mr. Harrison to best use technology?
- How should schools accommodate students who cannot afford computers?
- What type of training will help Mr. Harrison accomplish his goals?

Learning Activities

- Design a research assignment around an essential question (e.g. What is the impact of global warming on the environment? What are the effects, social and economic, of undocumented immigration?). Ask students to contact experts who are studying these problems. Once the research is completed, ask students to develop a PowerPoint presentation to report their findings to the class.
- Design a problem-solving task that requires students to participate in "virtual groups" through the use of mobile technology. Upon completion of the assignment have students write a reflection paper on the quality of the solution and the challenges of working in virtual groups.
- Identify a contemporary controversial topic. Ask students to create a "blog" on Twitter. Select a group of students to content analyze the blogs. What were the common themes or perspectives that were posted by the students?

Resources

Online Safeguards

- The International Society for Technology in Education http://cnets.iste.org
- Parents guide to the Internet www.ed.gov/pubs/parents/internet
- www.stopcyberbullyg.org

Instructional Learning Sites

- www.khanacademy.org
- www.edutopia.org
- www.schooltube.com
- www.think.com
- www.wise.berkeley.edu

BIBLIOGRAPHY

Abedi, J. & Gándara, P. (2006). Performance of English language learners as a subgroup in large-scale assessment: Interaction of research and policy. *Educational Measurement: Issues and Practice*, 25 (4), 36–46.

Albert, L. (1996). *Cooperative discipline*. Circle Pines, MN: American Guidance Service.

Alberti, S. (2013). Making the shifts. *Educational Leadership*, 70, 24–27.

Alberto, P. A. & Troutman, C. A. (2006). *Applied behavior analysis for teachers* (7th ed.). Upper Saddle River, NJ: Merrill/Prentice Hall.

Alderman, M. K. (1990) Motivation for at-risk students. *Educational Leadership*, 48, 27–30.

Algozzine, B., Browder, D., Karvonen, M., Test, D. W., & Wood, W. M. (2001). Effects of interventions to promote self-determination for individuals with disabilities. *Review of Educational Research*, 71(2), 219–277.

Allen, J. P. (2005, October). How successful are recent immigrants to the United States and their children? Presidential address presented at the annual meeting of the Pacific Coast Geographers, Phoenix, AZ.

Allinder, R. M. (1994). The relationship between efficacy and the instructional practices of special education teachers and consultants. *Teacher Education and Special Education*, 17, 86–95.

Alquraini, T. & Gut, D. (2012). Critical components of successful inclusion of students with severe disabilities: Literature review. *International Journal of Special Education*, 27(1), 1–18.

Altman, I. & Taylor, D. (1973). *Social penetration*. New York, NY: Holt.

American Association of University Women (1991). *Shortchanging girls, shortchanging America*. Washington, DC: Greenberg-Lake Analysis Group.

American Association of University Women (1999). *Gender gaps: Where schools still fail our children*. New York: Marlow & Company.

American Psychiatric Association (2000). *Diagnostic and statistical manual of mental disorders* (4th ed.) (DSM-4). Arlington, VA: Author.

American Psychiatric Association (2013). *Diagnostic and statistical manual of mental disorders* (5th ed.) (DSM-5). Arlington, VA: Author.

American Psychological Association Task Force on Evidence-Based Practice for Children and Adolescents (2008). *Disseminating evidence-based practice for children and adolescents: A systems approach to enhancing care*. Washington, DC: Author.

American Speech-Language-Hearing Association (1993). Definitions of communication disorders and variations. *AHSA*, 35(Suppl. 10), 40–41.

BIBLIOGRAPHY

Andersen, J. F. (1979). Teacher immediacy as a predictor of teaching effectiveness. In D. Nimmo (Ed.), *Communication yearbook 3* (pp. 543–559). New Brunswick, NJ: Transaction Books.

Andersen, J., Nussbaum, J., Pecchioni, L., & Grant, J. A. (1999). Interaction skills in instructional settings. In A. Vangelisti, J. Daly, & G. W. Friedrich (Eds.), *Teaching communication* (2nd ed., pp. 359–374). Mahwah, NJ: Lawrence Erlbaum.

Anderson, R., Welch, W., & Harris, L. (1984). Inequities in opportunities for computer literacy. *The Computer Teacher*, 11, 10–12.

Anstrom, K. (1997). Academic achievement for secondary language minority students: Standards, measures and promising practices. Washington, DC: National Clearinghouse for Bilingual Education. In P. E. Green (2003). The undocumented: Educating children of migrant workers in America. *Bilingual Research Journal*, 27(1), 51–71.

Arends, R. I., Winitzky, N. E., & Tannenbaum, M. D. (2001). *Exploring teaching* (2nd ed.). Boston, MA: McGraw-Hill.

Armor, D., Conroy-Oseguera, P., Cox, M., King, N., McDonnell, L., Pascal, A., et al. (1976). *Analysis of the school preferred reading programs in selected Los Angeles minority schools* (Report No. R-2007-LAUSD). Santa Monica, CA: Rand Corporation.

Armstrong, T. (2000). *Multiple intelligences in the classroom* (2nd ed.). Alexandria, VA: Association for Supervision and Curriculum Development

Aronson, E., Blaney, N., Stephan, C., Sikes, J., & Snapp, M. (1978). *The jigsaw classroom.* Beverly Hills, CA.: Sage.

Artiles, A. J. & Ortiz, A. (Eds.) (2002). *English language learners with special needs: Identification, placement, and instruction.* Washington, DC: Center for Applied Linguistics.

Ashburn, E. (2006). *Meaningful learning using technology: What educators need to know.* New York: Teachers College Press.

Aud, S., Hussar, W., Planty, M., Snyder, T., Bianco, K., Fox, M., Frohlich, L., Kemp, J., & Drake, L. (2010). *The Condition of Education 2010* (NCES 2010-028). Washington, DC: National Center for Education Statistics, Institute of Education Sciences, U.S. Department of Education.

Azmitia, M. (1998). Peer interactive minds: Developmental, theoretical, and methodological issues. In D. Faulkner, K. Littleton, and M. Woodhead (Eds.), *Learning relationships in the classroom* (pp. 207–234). New York: Routledge.

Baca, L. M. & Cervantes, H. T. (2004). *The bilingual special education interface* (4th ed.). Upper Saddle River, NJ: Merrill/Prentice Hall.

Baker, J. A. (2006). Contributions of teacher–child relationships to positive school adjustment during elementary school. *Journal of School Psychology*, 44, 211–229.

Bandura, A. (1977a). *Social learning theory.* Morristown, NJ: General Learning Press.

Bandura, A. (1977b). Self-efficacy: Toward a unifying theory of behavioral change. *Psychological Review*, 84, 191–215.

Bandura, A. (1981). Self-referent thought: A developmental analysis of self-efficacy. In J. H. Flavell & L. Ross (Eds.), *Social cognitive development: Frontiers and possible futures.* Cambridge: Cambridge University Press.

Bandura, A. (1986). *Social foundations of thought and action: A social cognitive theory.* Englewood Cliffs, NJ: Prentice Hall.

Bandura, A. (1991). Social cognitive theory of self-regulation. *Organizational Behavior and Human Decision Processes*, 50, 248–287.

Bandura, A. (1997). *Self-efficacy: The exercise of control.* New York: W. H. Freeman.

Banks, J. A. (1994). *Multiethnic education: Theory and practice.* Needham Heights, MA: Allyn & Bacon.

Banks, J. A. (1999). *An introduction to multicultural education* (2nd ed.). Boston, MA: Allyn & Bacon.

Banks, J. A. & Banks, C. M. (1989). *Multicultural education: Issues and perspectives.* Boston, MA: Allyn & Bacon.

Baringer, D. K. & McCroskey, J. C. (2000). Immediacy in the classroom: Student immediacy. *Communication Education*, 49, 178–186.

Barnlund, D. C. (1970) A transactional model of communication. In K. K. Sereno and C. D. Mortensen (Eds.), *Foundations of Communication Theory* (pp. 83–102). New York: Harper & Row.

Barrow, S. M. & Lawinski, T. (2009). Contexts of mother–child separations in homeless families. *Analyses of Social Issues and Public Policy*, 9(1), 157–176.

Bate, B. (1992). *Communication and the sexes.* Prospect Heights, IL: Waveland Press.

Battistich, V. & Hom, A. (1997). The relationship between students' sense of their school as a community and their involvement in problem behaviors. *American Journal of Public Health*, 87(12), 1997–2001.

Battistich, V., Solomon, D., Kim, D., Watson, M., & Schaps, E. (1995). Schools communities, poverty levels of student populations, and students' attitudes, motives, and performance: A multilevel analysis. *American Educational Research Journal*, 32(3), 627–658.

Baumeister, R. F. & Leary, M. R. (1995). The need to belong: Desire for interpersonal attachments as a fundamental human motivation. *Psychological Bulletin*, 117(3), 497–529.

Baxter, L. (1987). Symbols of relationship identity in relationship cultures. *Journal of Social and Personal Relationships*, 4, 261–279.

Baxter, L. (1988). A dialectical perspective on communication strategies in relationship development. In S. W. Duck, D. F. Hay, S. E. Hobfoll, W. Iches, & B. Montgomery (Eds.), *Handbook of personal relationships* (pp. 257–273). London, UK: Wiley.

Baxter, L. (1990). Dialectical contradictions in relationship development. *Journal of Social and Personal Relationships*, 7, 69–88.

Baxter, L. (1992). Forms and functions of intimate play in personal relationships. *Human Communication Research*, 18, 336–363.

Baxter, L. (1993). The social side of personal relationships: A dialectical perspective. In S. Duck (Ed.), *Understanding relationship processes, 3: Social context and relationships* (pp. 139–165). Newbury Park, CA: Sage.

Bayraktar, S. (2001). A meta-analysis of the effectiveness of computer assisted instruction in science education. *Journal of Research on Technology in Education*, 34, 173–189.

Beatty, M., McCroskey, J. C., & Heisel, A. D. (1998). Communication apprehension as tempermental expression: A communibiological paradigm. *Communication Monographs*, 65, 197–219.

Beatty, M., McCroskey, J. C., & Valencic, K. (2001). *The biology of communication: A communibiological perspective.* Cresskill, NJ: Hampton Press.

Becker, B. J. (1989). Gender and science achievement. A reanalysis of studies from two meta-analyses. *Journal of Research in Science Teaching*, 26, 141–169.

Becker, H. & Sterling, C. (1987). Equity in school computer use: National data and neglected considerations. *Journal of Educational Computing Research*, 3, 289–311.

Beegle, D. M. (2003). Overcoming the silence of generational poverty. *National Council of Teachers of English: Talking Points*, 15(1), 11–20. Accessed September 15, 2013 at www.combarriers.com/pdf/TP0151Overcoming.pdf.

Belinky, M., Clinchy, B., Goldberger, N., & Tarule, J. (1986). *Woman's ways of knowing*. New York: Basic Books.

Bell, R. A. & Daly, J. A. (1984). The affinity-seeking function of communication. *Communication Monographs*, 51, 91–115.

Belleck, A., Kliebard, H., Hyman, R., & Smith, F. (1966). *The language of the classroom*. New York: Columbia Teachers College Press.

Bennett, M. (1986). A developmental approach to training for intercultural sensitivity. *International Journal of Intercultural Relations*, 10, 179–196.

Berlo, D. (1960). *The process of communication*. New York: Holt Rinehart and Winston.

Berman, P. & McLaughlin, M. (1977). *Federal programs supporting educational change, Vol. II: Factors affecting implementation and continuation* (Report No. R-1589/7-HEW). Santa Monica, CA. Rand Corporation.

Bernstein, B. (1990). *The structuring of pedagogic discourse*. London: Routledge.

Bishop, K. M. & Whalsten, D. (1997). Sex differences in the human corpus callosum: Myth or reality? *Neuroscience and Biobehavioral Reviews*, 21, 581–601.

Block, J. H. (1984). *Sex role identity and ego development*. San Francisco, CA: Jossey Bass.

Bloom, B., Englehart, M., Furst, E., Hill, W., & Krathwohl, D. (1956). *Taxonomy of educational objectives: Cognitive domain*. New York: Longmans, Green.

Bomer, R., Dworin, J. E., May, L., & Semingson, P. (2008). Miseducating teachers about the poor: A critical analysis of Ruby Payne's claims about poverty. *Teachers College Record*, 110(12), 2497–2531. Accessed September 23, 2013 at www.tcrecord.org.

Book, C. (1999). Lecturing. In A. Vangelisti, J. Daly, & G. Friedrich (Eds.), *Teaching communication* (2nd ed., pp. 333–347). New Jersey, NJ: Lawrence Erlbaum.

Book, C. & McCaleb, J. (1985). *Teacher clarity and student awareness and achievement*. Paper presented at the annual meeting of the Speech Communication Association, Denver.

Books, S. (2004). *Poverty and schooling in the U.S.: Contexts and consequences*. Mahwah, NJ: Erlbaum.

Boster, F. J., Meyer, G. S., Roberto, A. J., Inge, C., & Strom, R. (2006). Some effects of videostreaming on educational achievement. *Communication Education*, 55, 46–62.

Bostrom, R. (1983). *Persuasion*. Englewood Cliffs, NJ: Prentice Hall.

Bosworth, K. (1995, May). Caring for others and being cared for: Students talk caring in school. *Phi Delta Kappan*, 76, 686–693.

Bourdieu, P. & Passeron, J. C. (1990). *Reproduction in education, society and culture*. Trans. Richard Nice. Newbury Park: Sage.

Boutot, E. A. & Myles, B. S., (2011). *Autism spectrum disorders: Foundations, characteristics, and effective strategies*. Pearson Education: Upper Saddle River, NJ.

Boyatzis, C. J., Baloff, P., & Durieux, C. (1998). Effects of perceived attractiveness and academic success on early adolescent peer popularity. *Journal of Genetic Psychology*, 159, 337–345.

Boyden, J., de Berry, J., Feeny, T., & Hart, J. (2002). *Children affected by armed conflict in South Asia: A review of trends and issues identified through secondary research*. Refugee Studies Centre, RSC Working Paper No. 7, University of Oxford. Accessed September 4, 2013 at www.rsc.ox.ac.uk/publications/working-papers-folder_contents/RSCworkingpaper7.pdf/view.

Bransford, J. D., Brown, A. L., & Cocking, R. R. (2000). *How people learn: Brain, mind, experience, and school.* Washington, DC: National Academy Press.

Brendtro, L., Brokenleg, M., & Van Bockern, S. (1990). *Reclaiming youth at risk: Our hope for the future.* Bloomington, IN: National Educational Service.

Brewster, A. B. & Bowen, G. L. (2004). Teacher support and the school engagement of Latino mddle and high school students at risk of school failure. *Child and Adolescent Social Work Journal*, 21, 47–67.

Bridging Refugee Youth and Children's Services (2013). Refugee children in U.S. schools: A toolkit for teachers and school personnel. Accessed August 10, 2013 at www.brycs.org/publications/schools-toolkit.cfm.

Brill, C. L. (1994). The effects of participation in service learning on adolescents with disabilities. *The Association for Professionals in Service for Adolescents*, 17(4), 369–380.

Bronfenbrenner, U. (1979). *The ecology of human development.* Cambridge, MA: Harvard University Press.

Brooks, J. G. & Brooks, M. G. (1993). *The case for constructivist classrooms.* Alexandria, VA: Association for Supervision and Curriculum Development.

Brophy, J. (1981). Teacher praise: A functional analysis. *Review of Educational Research*, 51, 5–32.

Brophy, J. (1998). *Motivating students to learn.* Boston, MA: McGraw-Hill.

Brophy, J. & Good, T. (1986). Teacher behavior and student achievement. In M. C. Witrock (Ed.), *Handbook of research on teaching.* New York: Macmillan.

Brophy, J. & Good, T. L. (2000). *Looking in classrooms* (8th ed.). New York: Harper & Row.

Brophy, J. & Rohrkemper, M. (1981). The influence of problem ownership on teachers' perceptions of and strategies for coping with problem students. *Journal of Educational Psychology*, 73, 295–311.

Brown, M., Higgins, K., & Hartley, K. (2001). Teachers and technology equity. *Teaching Exceptional Children, 33*, 32–39.

Brugh, M. (1997). Teaching character education through service learning. *Social Studies Review*, 37(1), 68–72.

Bryan, T., Pearl, R., & Herzog, A. (1989). Learning disabled adolescents' vulnerability to crime: Attitudes, anxieties, experiences. *Learning Disability Quarterly*, 5, 51–60.

Bryant, J., Comisky, P., & Zillmann, D. (1979). Teacher's humor in the college classroom. *Communication Education*, 28, 110–118.

Bureau of Labor Statistics (2012). *Women's earnings as a percent of men's.* Washington, DC: U.S. Department of Labor.

Burgoon, J. K. (1985). Nonverbal signals. In M. L. Knapp & G. R. Miller (Eds.), *Handbook of interpersonal communication* (pp. 344–390). Newbury Park, CA: Sage.

Burleson, B. & Sampter, W. (1990). Effects of cognitive complexity on the perceived importance of communication skills in friends. *Communication Research*, 17, 165–182.

Bush, A. (April, 1977). *An empirical investigation of teacher clarity.* Paper presented at the annual meeting of the American Educational Research Association.

Bush, A. J., Kennedy, J. J., & Cruickshank, D. R. (1977). An empirical investigation of teacher clarity. *Journal of Teacher Education*, 28, 53–58.

Cairn, R. W. & Kielsmeier, J. (1991). *Growing hope: A sourcebook on integrating youth service into the school curriculum.* Roseville, MN: National Youth Leadership Council.

Caplin, P. J., Crawford, M., Hyde, J. S., & Richardson, J. T. E. (1997). *Gender differences in human cognition.* New York: Oxford University Press.

Capps, R., Fix, M., Murray, J., Ost, J., Passel, J., & Herwantoro, S. (2005). *The new demography of America's schools: Immigration and the No Child Left Behind Act.* Washington, DC: The Urban Institute.

Caprara, S. C., Barbaranelli, C., Steca, P., & Malone, P. S. (2006). Teachers' self-efficacy beliefs as determinants of teachers' job satisfaction and students' academic achievement: A study at the school level. *Journal of School Psychology*, 44, 473–490.

Carrozza, C. (1996). Using learning styles and multiple intelligences to differentiate instruction and assessment. In R. W. Strong & H. F. Silver (Eds.), *An introduction to thoughtful curriculum and assessment* (pp. 145–152). Woodbridge, N.J: The Thoughtful Education Press.

Carruthers, W. L., Sweeny, B., Kmitta, D., & Harris, G. (1996). Conflict resolution: An examination of the research literature. *The School Counselor*, 44, 5–17.

Cartledge, G. & Talbert-Johnson, C. (1998). *African American males and serious emotional disturbance (SED): Genetic disposition versus social bias.* Paper presented at the American Education Research Association, San Diego, CA.

Cartledge, G., Gardner, R. III, & Ford, D. Y. (2009). *Diverse learners with exceptionalities: Culturally responsive teaching in the inclusive classroom.* Upper Saddle River, NJ: Pearson Education.

Cauthen, N. K. & Fass, S. (2008). 10 important questions about child poverty & family economic hardship. National Center for Children in Poverty. Accessed September 9, 2013 at www.nccp.org/pages/pdf/page_131.pdf.

Cazden, C. (1988). *Classroom discourse: The language of teaching and learning.* Portsmouth, NH: Heinemann.

Centers for Disease Control and Prevention. (2010). Traumatic brain injury in the United States: Emergency department visits, hospitalizations and deaths, 2002–2006. Available online at www.cdc.gov/traumaticbraininjury/pdf/blue_book.pdf.

Centers for Disease Control and Prevention (2013). Attention-deficit/hyperactivity disorder: Data and Statistics. Accessed August 11, 2013 at www.cdc.gov/ncbddd/adhd/data.html.

Chandler, L. K. & Dahlquist, C. M. (2010). *Functional assessment: Strategies to prevent and remediate challenging behaviors in school settings* (3rd ed.). Upper Saddle River, NJ: Merrill.

Chesebro, J. L., McCroskey, J. C., Atwater, D., Bahrenfuss, R., Cawelti, G., Gaudino, J., & Hodges, H. (1992). Communication apprehension and self-perceived communication competence of at-risk students. *Communication Education*, 41, 345–360.

Children's Defense Fund (2012). *The State of America's Children Handbook.* Washington, DC: Author.

Chizmar, J. & Walbert, M. (1999). Web-based learning environments guided by principles of good teaching practice. *The Journal of Economic Education*, 30, 248–259.

Christensen, L. & Menzel, K. (1998). The linear relationship between student reports of teacher immediacy behaviors and perceptions of state motivation and of cognitive, affective, and behavioral learning. *Communication Education*, 47, 82–91.

Christophel, D. M. (1990). The relationship among teacher immediacy behaviors, student motivation, and learning. *Communication Education*, 39, 323–340.

Civikly, J. (1992a). Clarity: teachers and students making sense of instruction. *Communication Education*, 41, 138–152.

Civikly, J. M. (1992b). *Classroom communication: Principles and practices.* Dubuque, IA: Wm C. Brown.

Clark, B. (2008). *Growing up gifted* (7th ed.). Upper Saddle River, NJ: Pearson Education.

Claxton, C. S. (1990). Learning styles, minority students and effective education. *Journal of Developmental Education*, 14, 6–8.

Cleary, L. M., & Peacock, T. D. (1998). *Collected wisdom: American Indian education.* Boston, MA: Allyn & Bacon.

Cleg, A. (1987). Why questions? In W. W. Wilen (Ed.), *Questions, questioning, techniques, and effective teaching* (pp. 11–21). Washington, DC: National Education Association.

Cleveland, K. P. (2011). *Teaching boys who struggle in school.* Alexandria,VA: ASCD.

Cohen, P. A., Kulik, J. A., & Kulik, C. C. (1992). Educational outcomes of tutoring: A meta-analysis of findings. *American Educational Research Journal*, 19, 237–248.

Coleman, J. M., McHam, L. A., & Minnett, A. M. (1992). Similarities in the social competencies of learning disabled and low achieving elementary school children. *Journal of Learning Disabilities*, 25, 671–677.

Coleman, J. S., Campbell, E. Q., Hobson, C. J., McParland, J., Mood, A. M., Weinfeld, F. D., & York, R. L. (1966). *Equality of educational opportunity.* Washington, DC: U.S. Government Printing Office.

Collet-Klingenberg, L. (2009). *Overview of computer-aided instruction.* Madison, WI: National Professional Development Center on Autism Spectrum Disorders, Waisman Center, University of Wisconsin.

Collet-Klingenberg, L. & Franzone, E. (2009). *Overview of social narratives.* Madison, WI: National Professional Development Center on Autism Spectrum Disorders, Waisman Center, University of Wisconsin.

Collier, M. J. (1994). Cultural identity and intercultural communication. In L. Samovar & R. Porter (Eds.), *Intercultural communication: A reader* (7th ed., pp. 36–45). Belmont, CA: Wadsworth.

Collier, M. J. & Powell, R. G. (1990). Ethnicity, instructional communication and classroom systems. *Communication Quarterly*, 38, 334–34.

Comadena, M. & Prusank, D. (1988). Communication apprehension and academic achievement among elementary and middle school students. *Communication Education*, 32, 185–193.

Common Core Standards Initiative (n.d.). Preparing America's students for success. Accessed April 2, 2014 at www.corestandards.org.

Comstock, J., Rowell, E., & Bowers, J. W. (1995). Food for thought: Teacher nonverbal immediacy, student learning, and curvilinearity. *Communication Education*, 44, 251–266.

Conboy, S. M. (1994). *Peer mediation and anger control: Two ways to resolve conflict.* St. Paul, MN: University of St. Thomas.

Condit, C. M. (2000). Culture and biology in human communication: Toward a multi-causal model. *Communication Education*, 49, 7–24.

Condravy, J., Skirboll, E., & Taylor, R. (1988). Faculty perceptions of classroom gender dynamics. *Women and Language*, 21, 18–28.

Conrad, D. & Hedin, D. (1991). School-based community service: What we know from research and theory. *Phi Delta Kappan*, 72(10), 743–749.

Conroy, M. A., Sutherland, A, S., Snyder, A. L., Al-Hendawi, M., & Vo, A. (2009). Creating a positive classroom atmosphere: Teachers' use of effective praise and feedback. *Beyond Behavior*, 18, 18–26.

Cooper, B. (2009). Deficit thinking: Bridging Spanish language barriers in southern schools, Learn NC Editions. Accessed September 4, 2003 at www.learnnc.org/lp/people/118.

Cooper, P. J. & Simmonds, C. (1999). *Communication for the classroom teacher* (6th ed.). Boston, MA: Allyn & Bacon.

Coopersmith, S. (1967). *The antecedents of self-esteem*. San Francisco, CA: W. H. Freeman.

Cousin, J. & Walker, C. (1995). Predictors of educators' valuing of systemic inquiry in schools. *Canadian Journal of Program Evaluation*, Special Issue, 25-35.

Covington, M. V. (2000). Goal theory, motivation, and school achievement: An integrative review. *Annual Review of Psychology*, 51, 171–200.

Cox, B. & Ramirez, M. (1981). Cognitive styles: Implications for multiethnic education. In J. Banks (Ed.), *Education in the 80s*. Washington, DC: National Education Association.

Cox, J. L., Burkheimer, G., Curtin, T. R., Rudes, B., Iachan, R., Strang, W., Carlson, E., Zarkin, G., & Dean, N. (1992). Final report: Descriptive study of the Chapter 1 Migrant Education Program, Vol. I: Study findings and conclusions. Prepared under contract for the U.S. Department of Education By Research Triangle Institute, Research Triangle, N.C.

Crist-Whitzel, J. (1985). *Computers for all children: A literature review of equity issues in computer utilization*. San Francisco, CA: Far West Laboratory for Educational Research and Development (ERIC Document Reproduction Service No 419–512).

Crone, D. A., Horner, R. H., Hawken, L. S. (2004). *Responding to problem behavior in schools: The behavior education program. The Guilford Practical Intervention in the Schools Series*. New York: Guilford Press.

Cronin, C. & Jreisat, S. (1995). Effects of modeling on the use of nonsexist language among high school fresh persons and seniors. *Sex Roles: A Journal of Research*, 33, 819–831.

Croninger, R. G. & Lee, V. E. (2001). Social capital and dropping out of high school: Benefits to at-risk students of teachers' support and guidance. *Teachers College Record*, 103, 548–581.

Cuban, L. (2001). *Oversold and underused: Computers in the classroom*. Cambridge, MA: Harvard University Press.

Cullinan, D., Epstein, M. H., & Lloyd, J. W. (1991). Evaluation of conceptual models of behavior disorders. *Behavioral Disorders*, 16(2), 148–157.

Cunningham, R. (1987). What kind of question is that? In W. W. Wilen (Ed.), *Questions, questioning, techniques, and effective teaching* (pp. 67–93). Washington, DC: National Education Association.

Cupach, W. P. & Imahori, T. (1993). Managing social predicaments created by others: A comparison of Japanese and American facework. *Western Journal of Communication*, 57, 431–444.

Cupach, W. P. & Metts, S. (1990). Remedial processes in embarrassing predicaments. In J. A. Andersen (Ed.), *Communication Yearbook 13* (pp. 353–364). Newbury Park, CA: Sage.

Cupach, W. P. & Metts S. (1992). The effects of types of predicament and embarrassability on remedial responses to embarrassing situations. *Communication Quarterly*, 40, 149–161.

Curwin, R. L. (1993). The healing power of altruism. *Educational Leadership*, 51(3), 36–39.

Dahl, K. (1995). Challenges in understanding the learner's perspective. *Theory into Practice*, 43(2), 124–130.

Daly, J. A. & Friedrich, G. (1981). The development of communication apprehension: A retrospective analysis of contributory correlates. *Communication Quarterly*, 29, 243–255.

Damon, W. (1995). *Greater expectations: Overcoming the culture of indulgence in America's homes and schools*. New York: NY: Free Press.

Dance, F. E. X. (Ed.) (1982). *Human communication theory*. New York: Harper & Row.

Darch, C., Miller, A., & Shippen, P. (1998). Instructional classroom management: A proactive model for managing student behavior. *Beyond Behavior*, 9(3), 18–27.

Darling, A. (1989). Signaling non-comprehensions in the classroom: Toward a descriptive typology. *Communication Education*, 38, 34–40.

Davis, B., Clarke, A. R. B., Francis, J., Hughes, G., MacMillan, J., McNeil, J., & Weshaver, P. (1992). Dress for respect: The effect of teacher dress on student expectations of deference behavior. *Alberta Journal of Educational Research*, 38, 27–31.

Davis, H. A. (2003). Conceptualizing the role and influence of student-teacher relationships on children's social and cognitive development. *Educational Psychologist*, 38, 207–234.

Deci, E. L. & Ryan, R. M. (1985). *Intrinsic motivation and self-determination in human behavior*. New York: Plenum.

Deci, E. L., Vallerand, R. J., Pelletier, L. G., & Ryan, R. M. (1991). Motivation and education: The self-determination perspective. *Educational Psychologist*, 26(3/4), 325–346.

Delaney-Black, V., Covington, C., Ondersma, S. J., Nordstrom-Klee, B., Templin, T., Ager, J., Janissee, J., & Sokol, R. J. (2002). Violence exposure, trauma, and IQ and/or reading deficits among urban children. *Pediatric Adolescent Medicine*, 156(3), 280–285.

Delpit, L. (1995*). Other people's children: Cultural conflict in the classroom*. New York: The New York Press.

Dewey, A. E. (2003). Immigration after 9/11: The view from the United States. Remarks to the American Society for International Law, April 3, 2003. Accessed September 6, 2013 at www.state.gov/g/prm/rls/2003/37906.htm.

Dewey, J. (1963). *Experience & education*. New York: Macmillan.

Diefendorf, A. O. (1996). Hearing loss and its effects. In T. E. C. Smith, E. A. Polloway, J. R. Patton, & C. A. Dowdy, *Teaching students with special needs in inclusive settings* (7th ed., p. 229). Boston, MA: Allyn & Bacon.

Digest of Education Statistics (2012). National Center for Education Statistics: Washington, DC: Department of Education Statistics.

Diller, A., Houston, B., Morgan, K. P., & Ayim, M. (1996). *The gender question in education: Theory, Pedagogy, & Politics*. Boulder, CO: Westview Press.

Dindia, K. & Baxter, L. A. (1987). Definitions and theoretical perspectives on maintaining relationships. *Journal of Social and Personal Relationships*, 4, 143–158.

Doda, N. & Knowles, T. (2008). Listening to the voices of young adolescents. *Middle School Journal*, 39(3), 26–33.

Donovan, S. & Cross, C. (2002). *Minority students in special and gifted education*. Washington, DC: National Academy Press.

Downs, V. C., Javidi, M., & Nussbaum, J. (1988). An analysis of teachers' verbal communication within the college classroom: Use of humor, self-disclosure, and narratives. *Communication Education*, 37, 127–141.

Dreikurs, R. & Cassel, P. (1972). *Discipline without tears: What to do with children who misbehave*. New York: Hawthorn.

Dreikurs, R., Grunwald, B. B., & Pepper, F. C. (1982). *Maintaining sanity in the classroom*. New York: HarperCollins.

Driver, B. L. & Spady, P. M. (2004). *What educators can do: Children and youth experiencing homelessness*. Information Brief No. 2. Williamsburg, VA: Project Hope Virginia.

Dundon, B. L. (1999/2000). My voice: An advocacy approach to service learning. *Educational Leadership*, December/January, 34–37.

Dunlap, K., Goodman, S., McEvoy, C., & Paris, F. (2010). *School-wide positive behavioral interventions and supports: Implementation guide*. Lansing, MI: Michigan Department of Education.

Dunn, R. & Griggs, S. A. (Eds.) (2000). *Practical approaches to using learning styles in higher education*. Westport, CT: Bergin & Garvey.

Dunst, C. J., Trivette, C. M., & Cutspec, P. A. (2002). Toward an operational definition of evidence-based practice. Centerscope: Evidence-based approaches in early childhood development. Accessed August 19, 2003 at www.evidencebasedpractices.org/centerscope/centerscopevol1no1.pdf.

Dweck, C. (1986). Motivational processes affecting learning. *American Psychologist*, 41, 1040–1048.

Eccles, J., Wong, C. A., & Peck, S. C. (2006). Ethnicity as a social context for the development of African-American adolescents. *Journal of School Psychology*, 44, 409–426.

Echevarria, J. & Graves, A. (2011). *Sheltered content instruction: Teaching English learners with diverse abilities* (4th ed.). New York: Pearson.

Eder, D. & Sanford, S. (1986). The development and maintenance of interactional norms among early adolescents. In P. Adler & P. Andler (Eds.), *Sociological studies of child development, Vol. I*, (pp. 283–300). Greenwich, CT: JAI.

Eisenberg, E. M. (1984). Ambiguity as strategy in organizational communication. *Communication Monographs*, 51, 227–242.

Ekman, P. & Friesen, W. V. (1969). Nonverbal leakage and clues to deception. *Psychiatry*, 32, 88–108.

Elias, M. J. & Schwab, Y. (2006). From compliance to responsibility: Social and emotional learning and classroom management. In C. M. Evertson & C. S. Weinstein (Eds.), *Handbook of classroom management: Research, practice and contemporary issues* (pp. 309–342). Mahwah NJ: Lawrence Erlbaum.

Elias, M. J. & Tobias, S. E. (1996). *Social problem solving: Interventions in the schools*. New York: Guilford.

Elias, M. J., Zins, J. E., Weissberg, R. P., Frey, K. S., Greenberg, M. T., Hanyes, N. M., Kessler, R., Schwab-Stone, M. E. & Shriver, T. P. (1997). *Promoting social and emotional learning: Guidelines for educators*. Alexandria, VA: Association for Supervision and Curriculum Development.

Eliot, L. (2010). The myth of pink. *Educational Leadership*, November, 32–36.

Epstein, J. L. (2005). Developing and sustaining research-based programs of school, family and community partnerships: Summary of five years of National Network of Partnership Schools (NNPS) research, September. Accessed September 20, 2013 at www.csos.jhu.edu/p2000/pdf/Research%20Summary.pdf.

Evers, R. B. & Spencer, S. (2011). *Planning effective instruction for students with learning and behavior problems*. Columbus, OH: Merrill/Pearson.

Evertson, C. M. & Weinstein, C. S. (2006). *Handbook of classroom management: Research, practice, and contemporary issues*. New York: Routledge.

Fairlie, R. W., London, R. A., Rosner, R., & Pastor, M. (2006). *Crossing the divide: Immigrant youth and digital disparity in California*. Santa Cruz, CA: Center for Justice, Tolerance, and Community, University of California–Santa Cruz.

Fantuzzo, J. & Periman, S. (2007). The unique impact of out-of-home placement and the mediating effects of child maltreatment and homelessness on early school success. *Children and Youth Services Review*, 29(7), 941–960.

Faraone, S. V. & Mick, E. (2010). Molecular genetics of attention deficit hyperactivity disorder. *Psychiatric Clinics of North America*, March 33(1), 159–80.

Faul, M., Xu, L., Wald, M. M., & Coronado, V. G. (2010). *Traumatic brain injury in the United States: Emergency department visits, hospitalizations, and deaths*. Atlanta, GA: Centers for Disease Control and Prevention, National Center for Injury Prevention and Control.

Field, S., Martin, J., Miller, R., Ward, M., & Wehmeyer, M. (1998). Self-determination for persons with disabilities: A position statement of the division on career development and transition. *Career Development for Exceptional Individuals*, 21(2), 113–128.

Fix, M. & Capps, R. (2005). Immigrant children, urban schools, and the No Child Left Behind Act, Migration Information Source (November 1, 2005). Accessed August 19, 2013 at www.migrationinformation.org/Feature/display.cfm?id=347.

Fleming, M. L. & Malone, M. R. (1983). The relationship of student characteristics and student performance in science as viewed by meta-analysis research. *Journal of Research in Science Teaching*, 20, 481–495.

Fogel, H. & Ehri, L. C. (2000). Teaching elementary students who speak Black English Vernacular to write in Standard English: Effects of dialect transformation practice. *Contemporary Educational Psychology*, 25, 212–235.

Fordham, S. & Ogbu, J. U. (1986). Black students' school success: Coping with the burden of "acting White." *The Urban Review*, 18, 176–206.

Forman, E. A. & Cazden, C. (1985). Exploring Vygotskyian perspectives in education: The cognitive value of peer interaction. In J. V. Wertsch (Ed.), *Culture, communication and cognition: Vygotskian perspectives*. New York: Cambridge University Press.

Forman, E. & Cazden, C. (1998). Exploring Vygotskian perspectives in education: The cognitive value of peer interaction. In D. Faulkner, K. Littleton, & M. Woodhead (Eds.), *Learning relationships in the classroom* (pp. 189–206). London: Routledge.

Forness, S. R. & Kavale, K. A. (1988). Planning for the needs of children with serious emotional disturbance: The National Mental Health and Special Education Coalition. *Behavior Disorders*, 13, 127–133.

Forness, S. R. & Kavale, K. A. (1999). Treating social skill deficits in children with learning disabilities: A meta-analysis of the research. *Learning Disability Quarterly*, 19, 2–13.

Fox, L., Carta, J., Strain, P., Dunlap, G., & Hemmeter, M. L. (2009). *Response to intervention and the pyramid model*. Tampa, FL: University of South Florida Technical Assistance Center on Social Emotional Intervention for Young Children.

Franzone, E. (2009). *Overview of task analysis*. Madison, WI: National Professional Development Center on Autism Spectrum Disorders, Waisman Center, University of Wisconsin.

Franzone, E. & Collet-Klingenberg, L. (2008). *Overview of video modeling*. Madison, WI: The National Professional Development Center on Autism Spectrum Disorders, Waisman Center, University of Wisconsin.

Fredriksen, K. & Rhodes, J. (2004). The role of teacher relationships in the lives of students. *New Directions for Youth Development*, 103, 45–54.

Freud, S. (1935). *A general introduction to psychoanalysis*. NewYork: Liveright.

Friedrich, G. (1982). Classroom communication. In L. Barker (Ed.), *Communication in the classroom* (pp 55–76). Englewood Cliffs, NJ: Prentice Hall.

Friedrich, G. W. & Cooper, P. (1999). The first day. In A. Vanglisti, J. A. Daly, & G. W. Friedrich (Eds.), *Teaching communication* (2nd ed., pp. 287–298). Mahwah, NJ: Lawrence Erlbaum.

Friend, M. & Cook, L. (1996). *Interactions: Collaboration skills for school professionals* (2nd ed.). White Plains, NY: Longman.

Frymier, A. B. (1994). The use of affinity-seeking in producing liking and learning in the classroom. *Applied Communication Research*, 22, 87–105.

Frymier, A. B. & Houser, M. L. (2000). The teacher–student relationship as an interpersonal relationship. *Communication Education*, 49, 207–219.

Frymier, A. B. & Thompson, C. A. (1992). Perceived teacher affinity-seeking in relation to perceived teacher credibility. *Communication Education*, 41, 388–399.

Fuchs, D. & Fuchs, L. S. (2006). Introduction to response to intervention: What, why, and how valid is it? *Reading Research Quarterly*, 41, 93–99.

Gall, M. (1984). Synthesis of research on teachers' questioning. *Educational Leadership*, 2, 40–47.

Garcia, E. (1999). *Student cultural diversity: Understanding and meeting the challenge* (2nd ed.). Boston, MA: Houghton Mifflin.

Gardner, H. (1983). *Frames of mind: The theory of multiple of intelligences*. New York: Basic Books.

Gardner, H. (1993). *Multiple intelligences*. New York: Basic Books.

Gardner, H. (1999). *The disciplined mind*. New York: Simon & Schuster.

Gay, G. (2000). *Culturally responsive teaching: Theory research and practice*. New York: Teachers College Press.

Gay, G. (2002). Preparing for culturally responsive teaching. *Journal of Teacher Education*, 53, 106–116.

Gershoff, E. T., Aber, J. L., & Raver, C. C. (2003). Child poverty in the U.S.: An evidence-based conceptual framework for programs and policies. In F. Jacobs, D. Wertlieb, & R. M. Lerner (Eds.), *Handbook of applied developmental science: Promoting positive child, adolescent and family development through research, policies and programs Vol. II* (pp. 81–136). Thousand Oaks, CA: Sage.

Gettinger, M. & Stoiber, K. C. (1999). Excellence in teaching: Review of instructional and environmental variables. In C. R. Reynolds & T. B. Gutkin (Eds.), *The handbook of school psychology* (3rd ed., pp. 993–958). New York: John Wiley & Sons.

Gibson, J. (1982). Do looks help children make the grade? *Family Weekly*, June 2, 9.

Gibson, S. & Dembo, M. (1984). Teacher efficacy: A construct validation. *Journal of Educational Psychology Psychology*, 76, 569–582.

Gill, M. M. (1994). Accent and stereotypes: Their effect on perceptions of teachers and lecture comprehension. *Journal of Applied Communication Research*, 22, 348–362.

Gilligan, C. (1982). *In a different voice: Psychological theory and women's development*. Cambridge, MA: Harvard University Press.

Gizer, I. R., Ficks, C., & Waldman, I. D. (2009). Candidate gene studies of ADHD: a meta-analytic review. *Human Genetics*, July, 126(1), 51–90. Epub 2009 June 9. Review. PubMed PMID: 19506906.

Glasser, W. (1969). *Schools without failure*. New York: Harper & Row.

Glasser, W. (1990). *The quality school: Managing students without coercion*. New York: Harper Collins.

Glassman, M. (2001). Dewey and Vygotsky: Society, experience, and inquiry in educational practice. *Educational Researcher*, 30, 3–14.

Godley, A. J., Sweetland, J., Wheeler, R. S., Minnici, A. & Carpenter, B. D. (2006). Preparing teachers for dialectically diverse classrooms. *Educational Researcher*, 35, 30–37.

Goffman, I. (1959). *The presentation of self in everyday life*. Garden City NJ: Doubleday Anchor.

Goffman, I. (1963). *Behavior in public places*. New York: Free Press.

Goldstein, A. P. & McGinnis, E. (1997). *Skillstreaming the adolescent: New strategies and perspectives for teaching prosocial skills*. Champaign, IL: Research Press.

Goleman, C. (1995). *Emotional intelligence*. New York: Bantam.

Gollnick, D. M. & Chinn, P. C. (1994). *Multicultural education in a pluralistic society* (4th ed.). New York: McMillan College.

Gonick, M. (2006). Between girl power and reviving Ophelia: Constituting the neoliberal girl subject. *NWSA Journal*, 18, 1–23.

Good, T. & Brophy, J. E. (1973). *Looking in classrooms*. New York: Harper & Row.

Good, T. & Brophy, J. E. (1984). *Looking in classrooms* (3rd ed.). New York: Harper & Row.

Good, T. & Brophy, J. E. (1987). *Looking in classrooms* (4th ed.). New York: Harper & Row.

Good, T. & Brophy, J. (2000). *Looking in classrooms*. New York: Longman.

Goodenow, C. (1993). Classroom belonging among early adolescent students: Relationships to motivation and achievement. *Journal of Early Adolescence*, 13, 21–43.

Gordon, T. (1974). *Teacher effectiveness training*. New York: Peter H. Wyden.

Gordon, T. (1987). *T.E.T.: Teacher effectiveness training* (2nd edition). New York: David McKay.

Gorham, J. (1988). The relationship between verbal immediacy behaviors and student learning. *Communication Education*, 37, 40–53.

Gorham, J. & Christophel, D. M. (1990). The relationship of teachers' use of humor in the classroom to immediacy and student learning. *Communication Education*, 39, 46–62.

Gorham, J., Cohen, S. H., & Morris T. L. (1997). Fashion in the classroom II: Instructor immediacy and attire. *Communication Research Reports*, 14, 11–23.

Gorski, P. C. (2007a). Savage unrealities: Uncovering classism in Ruby Payne's framework. *Rethinking Schools*, 21(2), 16–19.

Gorski, P. C. (2007b). The question of class. *Teaching Tolerance*, 40 (31). Accessed September 23, 2013 at www.tolerance.org/magazine/number-31-spring-2007/feature/question-class.

Gorski, P. C. (2008). The myth of the culture of poverty. *Educational Leadership*, 65(7), 32–36.

Grant, C. A. & Sleeter, C. E. (2011). *Doing multicultural education for achievement and equity*. New York, NY: Routledge.

Green, P. E. (2003). The undocumented: Educating children of migrant workers in America. *Bilingual Research Journal*, 27(1), 51–71.

Gregorc, A., (1982). *Gregorc style delineator*. Columbia, CT: Gregorc Associates.

Gregory, G. H., & Chapman, C. (2002). *Differentiated instruction strategies: One size doesn't fit all*. Thousand Oaks, CA: Corwin Press.

Gresham, F. M. & Elliott, S. N. (1989). Social skills deficits as a primary learning disability. *Learning Disability Quarterly*, 22, 120–124.

Grossman, H. (1991). Special education in a diverse society: Improving services for minority and working-class students. *Preventing School Failure*, 36, 19–27.

Grossman, H. (1995). *Special education in a diverse society*. Boston, MA: Allyn & Bacon.

Grossman, H. (2004). *Classroom management for diverse and inclusive schools* (3rd ed.). Lanham, MD: Rowman & Littlefield.

Guild, P. (1994). The culture/learning style connection. *Educational Leadership*, 51 (8), 16–21.

Gurian, M. & Henley, P. (2001). *Boys and girls learn differently*. San Francisco, CA: Jossey Bass.

Gurian, M. & Stevens, K. (2005). *The minds of boys: Saving our sons from falling behind in school and life*. San Francisco, CA: Jossey-Bass.

Hall, E. T. (1976). *Beyond culture*. New York: Doubleday.

Hall, R. & Sandler, B. (1982). *The classroom climate: A chilly one for women? Project on the status and education of women*. Washington, DC: Association of American Colleges.

Hallahan, D. P. & Kauffman, J. M. (2003). *Exceptional learners: Introduction to special education* (9th ed.). Boston, MA: Allyn & Bacon.

Halverson, E. R. (2011). Do social networking technologies have a place in formal learning environments? *On the Horizon*, 19, 62–67.

Hammer, H., Finkelhor, D., & Sedlak, A. J. (2002). Runaway/thrownaway children: National estimates and characteristics. *National Incidence Studies of Missing, Abducted, Runaway and Thrownaway Children*. U.S. Department of Justice. Office of Justice Programs. Office of Juvenile Justice and Delinquency Prevention. Washington, DC: Author.

Hamre, B. K. & Pianta, R. C. (2001). Early teacher–child relationships and the trajectory of children's school outcomes through eighth grade. *Child Development*, 72, 625–638.

Hardin, C. J. (2008). *Effective classroom management* (2nd ed.). Upper Saddle River, NJ: Pearson Education.

Harris, R. D. (2005). Unlocking the learning potential in peer mediation: An evaluation of peer mediator modeling and disputant learning. *Conflict Resolution Quarterly*, 23(2), 141–146.

Haslett, B. (1987). *Communication, strategic action in context*. Hillsdale, NJ: Lawrence Erlbaum Associates.

Hattie, J. (2009). *Visible learning, a synthesis of over 800 meta-analyses relating to achievement*. London: Routledge.

Haydon, T., MacSuga-Gage, A. S., Simonsen, B., & Hawkins, R. (2012). Opportunities to respond: A key component of effective instruction. *Beyond Behavior*, 22(1), 23–31.

Head, J. (1996). Gender identity and cognitive style. In P. F. Murphy & C. V. Gipps (Eds.), *Equity in the classroom: Towards effective pedagogy for girls and boys* (pp. 59–70). London: Falmer Press.

Healy, J. (1998). *Failure to connect*. New York: Simon & Schuster.

Heath, R. W. & Nielson, M. A. (1974). The research basis for performance-based teacher education. *Review of Educational Research*, 44, 463–484.

Hecht, M., Collier, M. J., & Ribeau, S. (1993). *African American communication: Ethnic identity and cultural interpretation*. Newbury Park, CA: Sage.

Hedges, L. V. & Nowell, A. (1995). Sex differences in mental test scores, variability and numbers of high-scoring individuals. *Science*, 269(5220), 41–45.

Heider, F. (1958). *The psychology of interpersonal relations*. New York: Wiley.

Heidi, S. & Harackiewicz, J. M. (2000). Motivating the academically unmotivated: A critical issue for the twenty-first century. *Review of Educational Research, 70*, 151–180.

Heller, K. A., Holtzman, W. H., & Messick, S. (Eds.) (1982). *Placing children in special education: A strategy for equity*. Washington, DC: National Academy Press.

Helms, J. E. (1990). *Black and white racial identity: Theory research and practice*. New York: Greenwood.

Helmstetter, E., Curry, C. A., Brennan, M., & Sampson-Saul, M. (1998). Comparison of general and special education classrooms of students with severe disabilities. *Education and Training in Mental Retardation and Developmental Disabilities*, 33(3), 216–227.

Hensley, W. E. (1981). The effects of attire, location, and sex on aiding behavior: A similarity explanation. *Journal of Nonverbal Behavior*, 6, 3–11.

Hess, J. A. & Smythe, M. J. (2001). Is teacher immediacy actually related to student cognitive learning? *Communication Studies*, 52, 197–220.

Hines, C. V., Cruickshank, D. R., & Kennedy, J. J. (1985). Teacher clarity and its relationship to student achievement and satisfaction. *American Educational Research Journal*, 22, 87–99.

Hixson, J. (1993). *Redefining the issues: Who's at risk and why*. Revision of a paper originally presented in 1983 at "Reducing the Risks," a workshop presented by the Midwest Regional Center for Drug-Free Schools and Communities. Accessed September 5, 2013 at www.ncrel.or/sdrs/areas//issues studentsatrisk/at5def.htm.

Hoetker, J. & Ahlbrand, W. P. (1969). The persistence of recitation. *American Educational Research Journal*, 6, 145–167.

Hofstede, G. (1980). *Culture's consequences: International differences in work related values*. Beverly Hills, CA: Sage.

Hofstede, G. (2001). *Culture's consequences: International differences in work-related values* (2nd ed.). Beverly Hills, CA: Sage.

Holland, D., Lachicotte, W. Jr., Skinner, D., & Cain, C. (1998). *Identity and agency in cultural worlds*. Cambridge, MA: Harvard University Press.

Hoover, J. J. & Collier, C. (1986). *Classroom management through curricular adaptations*. Lindale, TX: Hamilton.

Houston, B. (1996). Gender freedom and the subtleties of sexist education. In A. Diller, B. Houston, K. Morgan & M. Ayim (Eds.), *The gender question in education: Theory, pedagogy, & politics* (pp. 50–63). Boulder, CO: Westview Press.

Howard, G. (2000). Whites in multicultural education: Rethinking our role. In J. Banks (Ed.), *Multicultural education: Transformative knowledge* (pp. 323–334). New York: Teachers College Press.

Huddle, D. (2000). *Fiscal impacts of undocumented aliens*. Washington, DC: Urban Institute Press.

Hudson, L. & Jacot, B. (1991). *The way men think*. New Haven, CT: Yale University Press.

Hughes, S. A. (2006). *Black hands in the biscuits not in the classroom: Unveiling hope in a struggle for Brown's promise*. New York: Peter Lang.

Hunkins, F. P. (1976). *Involving students in questioning*. Boston, MA: Allyn & Bacon.

Hunter, M. (1984). Knowing, teaching, supervising. In P. Hosford (Ed.), *Using What We Know About Teaching* (pp. 169–203). Alexandria, VA: Association for Supervision and Curriculm Development.

Hyde, J. S. (2005). The gender similarities hypothesis. *American Psychologist*, 60, 581–592.

Hyde, J. S. & Linn, M. C. (1988). Gender differences in verbal ability: A meta-analysis. *Psychological Bulletin*, 104, 53–69.

Hyde, J. S. & McKinley, N. (1997). Gender differences in cognition: Results from meta-analysis. In P. J. Caplan, M. Crawford, J. S. Hyde & J. T. E. Richardson (Eds.), *Gender differences in human cognition* (pp. 30–51). New York: Oxford University Press.

Hyde, J. S., Finnema, E., & Lamou, S. J. (1990). Gender differences in mathematics performance: A meta-analysis. *Psychological Bulletin*, 107, 139–155.

Hyman, S. L. (2013). New DSM-5 includes changes to autism criteria. AAP News: American Academy of Pediatrics Downloaded from http://aapnews.aappublications.org/ at Calif State Univ Fresno on August 7, 2013.

Institute of Education Sciences (2006a). *English language learners intervention report: Fast ForWord Language*, September. Accessed April 10, 2013 at http://ies.ed.gov/ncee/wwc/pdf/intervention_reports/WWC_Fast_ForWord_092806.pdf.

Institute of Education Sciences (2006b). *English language learners intervention report: enhanced proactive reading*, September. Accessed April 10, 2013 at http://ies.ed.gov/ncee/wwc/pdf/intervention_reports/WWC_Proactive_Reading092806.pdf.

Institute of Education Sciences (2007). *Caring school community: what works clearing-house intervention report*. U.S. Department of Education. Accessed October 30, 2013 at http://ies.ed.gov/ncee/wwc/pdf/intervention_reports/WWC_Caring_School_042307.pdf.

Institute of Education Sciences (2010). *English language learners intervention report: peer-assisted learning strategies*, September. Accessed May, 2, 2013 at http://ies.ed.gov/ncee/wwc/pdf/intervention_reports/wwc_pals_092910.pdf.

Ishii-Jordan, S. R. (2000). Behavioral interventions used with diverse students. *Behavioral Disorders*, 25(4), 299–309.

Ivy, D. & Backlund, P. (2000). *Exploring genderspeak: Personal effectiveness in gender communication*. San Francisco, CA: McGraw-Hill.

Jago, C. (2014). Writing is taught not caught. *Educational Leadership*, 71, 17–21.

Javidi, M., Downs, V., & Nussbaum, J. (1988). A comparative analysis of teachers' use of dramatic style behaviors at higher and secondary educational levels. *Communication Education*, 37, 278–288.

Jensen, E. (2000). *Brain-based learning*. San Diego, CA: The Brain Store.

Johnson, D. W. & Johnson, R. T. (1986). Mainstreaming and cooperative learning strategies. *Exceptional Children*, 52, 553–561.

Johnson, D. W. & Johnson, R. T. (1999). *Learning together and learning alone: Cooperative competitive and individualistic learning* (5th ed.). Boston, MA: Allyn & Bacon.

Johnson, D. W. & Johnson, R. (2005). *Teaching students to be peacemakers* (4th ed.). Edina, MN: Interaction Book Company.

Johnson, D. W., Johnson, R. T., & Holubec, E. J. (1993). *Circles of learning: Cooperation in the classroom*. Edina, MN: Interaction Book Company.

Johnson, R. T. & Johnson, D. W. (1996). Conflict resolution and peer mediation programs in elementary and secondary schools: A review of the research. *Review of Educational Research*, 66, 459–473.

Jones, B. F., Valdez, G., Nowakowski, J., & Rasmussen, C. (1995). *Plugging in: Choosing and using education technology*. Oak Brook, IL: North Central Regional Educational Laboratory.

Jones, E. E. & Davis, K. E. (1965). From acts to dispositions. In L. Berkowitz (Ed.), *Advances in experimental and social psychology, Vol. II*. New York: Academic Press.

Jones, S. M. & Dindia, K. (2004). A meta-analytic perspective on sex equity in the classroom. *American Educational Research Association*, 74, 443–471.

Jones, V. F. & Jones, L. S. (2001). *Comprehensive classroom management: Creating communities of support and solving problems* (6th ed.). Boston, MA: Allyn & Bacon.

Jones, V. F. & Jones, L. S. (2007). *Comprehensive classroom management: Creating communities of support and solving problems* (8th ed.). Boston, MA: Allyn & Bacon.

Kagan, S. (1994). *Cooperative learning resources for teachers*. San Juan Capistrano: Resources for Teachers.

Katz, J. E. (2005). Mobile phones in Educational Settings. In K. Nyiri (Ed.), *A sense of place: The global and the local in mobile communication* (pp. 305–317). Vienna: Passagen.

Kauffman, J. M. (1997). *Characteristics of emotional and behavioral disorders of children and youth* (6th ed.). Upper Saddle River, NJ: Merrill.

Kauffman, J. M. & Landrum, T. J. (2009). *Characteristics of emotional and behavioral disorders of children and youth* (9th ed.). Upper Saddle River, NJ: Prentice Hall.

Kauffman, J. M., Pullen, P. L., & Ackers, E. (1986). Classroom management: Teacher-child peer relationships. *Focus on Exceptional Children*, 19 (1), 1–10.

Kaye, C. B. (2000). *The service learning book shelf* (2nd ed.). Los Angeles, CA: Association of Supervision and Curriculum Development (ASCD) Books.

Kearney, P., Plax, T. G., Smith, V., & Sorensen, G. (1988). Effects of teacher immediacy and strategy type of college student resistance. *Communication Education*, 37, 54–67.

Kearney, P., Plax, T. G., & Wendt-Wasco, N. J. (1985). Teacher immediacy for affective learning in divergent college classes. *Communication Quarterly*, 33, 61–74.

Kellett, M. (2009). Children and young people's voices. In H. Montgomery and M. Kellett (Eds.), *Children and young people's worlds: Developing frameworks for integrated practice*. Bristol: Policy Press.

Kelley, H. H. (1967). Attribution theory in social psychology. *Nebraska Symposium on Motivation*, 15, 192–240.

Kelly, D. H. E. & Gorham, P. (1988). Effects of immediacy on recall of information. *Communication Education*, 39, 198–207.

Kelly, G. (1955). *The psychology of personal constructs*. New York: North.

Kendrick, W. L. & Darling, A. L. (1990). Problems of understanding in classrooms: Students' use of clarifying tactics. *Communication Education*, 39,15–29.

Kennedy, C. H. & Itkonen, T. (1994). Some effects of regular class participation on the social contacts and social networks of high school students with severe disabilities. *Journal of the Association for Persons with Severe Handicaps*, 19(1), 1–10.

Kennedy, C. H., Shukla, S., & Fryxell, D. (1997). Comparing the effects of educational placement on the social relationships of intermediate school students with severe disabilities. *Exceptional Children*, 64, 31–47.

Kennedy, D. M. (1995). Plain talk about creating a gifted-friendly classroom. In R. B. Lewis & D. H. Doorlag (Eds.), *Teaching special students in general education classrooms* (pp. 379–380). Columbus, OH: Merrill/Prentice Hall.

Kennedy, G. (2012). Using iPads with students with intellectual disabilities, May 15. Spectronicsinoz.com. Accessed August 10, 2013 at www.spectronicsinoz.com/blog/tools-and-resources/using-ipads-with-students-with-intellectual-disabilities/?print.

Kidde, J. & Alfred, R. (2011). Restorative justice: A working guide for our schools. Illinois Criminal Justice Information Authority. Accessed June 10, 2013 at http://healthyschoolsandcommunties.org/Docs/Restorative-Justice-Paper.pdf.

Kindlon, D. (2006). *Alpha girls*. New York: Rodale.

Kindsvatter, R., Wilen, W., & Ishler, M. (1996). *Dynamics of effective teaching*. White Plains, NJ: Longman.

Kirtley, M. D. & Weaver, J. B. III. (1999). Exploring the impact of gender role self-perception on communication style. *Women's Studies in Communication*, 22, 190–201.

Klassen, R. M., Tze, M. C., Betts, S. M., & Gordon, K. M. (2011). Teacher efficacy research 1998–2009: Signs of progress or unfilled promise? *Educational Psychological Review*, 23, 21–43.

Kleinke, C. L. (1977). Effects of dress on compliance to requests in a field setting. *The Journal of Social Psychology*, 101, 223–224.

Klingner, J., Artiles, A. J., Kozleski, E., Harry, B., Zion, S., Tate, W., Durán, G. Z., & Riley, D. (2005). Addressing the disproportionate representation of culturally and linguistically diverse students in special education through culturally responsive educational systems. *Education Policy Analysis Archives*, 13(38).

Kluver, R. (1990). *A cross-cultural analysis of instructional immediacy*. Unpublished master's thesis, California State University, Los Angeles.

Knapp, M. L. (1978). *Social intercourse. From greeting to goodbye*. Boston, MA: Allyn & Bacon.

Knapp, M. & Hall, J. A. (1992). *Nonverbal communication in human interaction* (3rd ed.). San Diego: Holt Rinehart & Winston.

Knapp, M. L. & Vangelisti, A. (1996). *Interpersonal communication and human relationships* (3rd ed.). Boston, MA: Allyn & Bacon.

Knapp, M., Cody, M. J., & Reardon, K. K. (1987). Nonverbal signals. In C. Berger & S. Chaffee (Eds.), *Handbook of communication science* (pp. 385–418). Beverly Hills, CA: Sage.

Knapp, M., Wiemann, J., & Daly, J. (1978). Nonverbal communication: Issues and appraisal. *Human Communication Research*, 4, 271–280.

Knitzer, J. & Lefkowitz, J. (2006). *Helping the most vulnerable infants, toddlers, and their families*. Pathways to Early School Success, Issue Brief No. 1. New York: National Center for Children in Poverty.

Knitzer, J., Steinberg, Z., & Fleisch, F. (1990). *At the schoolhouse door: An examination of the programs and policies for children with behavioral and emotional problems*. New York: Bank Street College of Education.

Knoell, C. M. (2012). *The role of the student–teacher relationship in the lives of fifth graders: A mixed methods analysis*. ProQuest, UMI Dissertation Publishing.

Kohn, A. (1993). *Punishment by rewards: The trouble with gold stars, incentive plans, A's, praise, and other bribes*. Boston, MA: Houghton Mifflin.

Kohn, A. (1996). *Beyond discipline: From compliance to community*. Alexandria, VA: Association for Supervision and Curriculum Development.

Kohn, A. (1998). *What to look for in a classroom*. San Francisco, CA: Jossey-Bass.

Kolb, D. A. (1976). *Learning style inventory technical manual*. Boston, MA: McBer & Co.

Kolb, D. A. (1985). *Learning style inventory*. Boston, MA: McBer & Co.

Kozma, R. & Croninger, R. (1992). Technology and the fate of at-risk students. *Education and Urban Society*, 24, 440–453.

Krathwohl, D. (2002). A revision of Bloom's taxonomy: An overview. *Theory into Practice*, 41, 212–218.

Kulik, J. (1994). Meta-analytic studies of findings on computer-based instruction. In E. L. Baker & H. F. O'Neil Jr. (Eds.), *Technology assessment in education and training* (pp. 9–34). Hillsdale NJ: Lawrence Erlbaum Associates.

Kumashiro, D. (2000). Toward a theory of anti-oppressive education. *Review of Educational Research*, 70, 25–54.

Kuykendall, C. (1992). *From rage to hope: Strategies for reclaiming black & hispanic students*. Bloomington, IN: National Educational Service.

Ladd, G. W. (1990). Having friends, keeping friends, making friends, and being liked by peers in the classroom: Predictors of children's early school adjustment? *Child Development*, 61, 1081–1100.

Ladson-Billings, G. (1994). *The dreamkeepers: Successful teachers of African- American children*. San Francisco, CA: Jossey-Bass.

Ladson-Billings, G. (2001). *Crossing over to Canaan: The journey of new teachers in diverse classrooms*. San Francisco, CA: Jossey-Bass.

Ladson-Billings, G. (2006). From the achievement gap to the education debt: understanding achievement in U.S. schools. *Educational Researcher*, 35, 3–12.

LaFrance, M. & Mayo, C. (1979). A review of nonverbal behaviors of women and men. *Western Journal of Speech Communication*, 43, 96–107.

Lam, S.-F., Yim, P.-S., & Ng, Y. I. (2008). Is effort praise motivational? The role of beliefs in the effort-ability relationship. *Contemporary Educational Psychology*, 33, 694–710.

Lang, R. (1986). The hidden dress code dilemma. *Clearing House*, 59, 277–279.

Langer, S. (1942). *Philosophy in a new key*. Cambridge, MA: Harvard University Press.

Larrivee, B. (2005). *Authentic classroom management: Creating a learning community and building reflective practice*. Boston, MA: Pearson Education.

Lee, O. E. & Bertera, E. (2007). Teaching diversity by using instructional technology: Application of self-efficacy and cultural competence. *Multicultural Education & Technology Journal*, 1, 112–125.

Lenroot, R. K., Gogtay, N., Greenstein, D. K., Wells, E. M., Wallace, G. L., Clasen, L. S., Blumenthal, J. D., Lerch, J., Zijdenbos, A. P., Evans, A. C., Thompson, P. M., & Giedd, J. N. (2007). Sexual dimorphism of brain developmental trajectories during childhood and adolescence. *NeuroImage*, 36, 1065–1073.

Levin, J. & Nolan, J. F. (2007). *Principles of classroom management: A professional decision-making mode* (5th ed.). Boston, MA: Allyn & Bacon.

Linn, M. C. & Peterson, A. C. (1985). Emergence and characterization of sex differences in spatial ability: A meta-analysis. *Child Development*, 56, 1479–1498.

Loewen, J. (1995). *Lies my teacher told me: Everything your American history textbook got wrong*. New York: Touchstone.

Long, N. J., Morse, W. C., & Newman, R. G. (1965). *Conflict in the classroom: The education of emotionally disturbed children*. Belmont, CA: Wadsworth.

Lukavsky, J., Butler, S., & Harden, A. (1995). Perceptions of an instructor: Dress and students' characteristics. *Perceptual and Motor Skills*, 81, 231–241.

Lustig, M. W. & Koester, J. (1999). *Intercultural competence* (3rd ed.). Menlo Park, CA: Longman.

Lustig, M. & Koester, J. (Eds.) (2000). *Among us: Essays on identity, belonging, and intercultural competence*. New York: Longman.

Maag, J. W. (1999). *Behavior management: From theoretical implications to practical applications*. San Diego, CA: Singular.

Maag, J. W. (2001). Rewarded by punishment: Reflections on the disuse of positive reinforcement in schools. *Exceptional Children*, 67, (2), 173–186.

Maag, J. W. (2003). *Behavior management: From theoretical implications to practical applications* (2nd ed.). San Diego, CA: Singular.

Maag, J. W. & Katsiyannis, A. (1999). Teacher preparation in E/BD: A national survey. *Behavioral Disorders*, 24, 189–196.

McAllister, G. & Irvine, J. J. (2000). Cultural competency and multicultural teacher education. *Review of Educational Research*, 70, 3–24.

McCroskey, J. C. & Andersen, J. (1976). The relationship between communication apprehension and academic achievement among college students. *Communication Research*, 3, 73–81.

McCroskey, J. C. & McCroskey, L. L. (2002). Willingness to communicate and communication apprehension in the classroom. In J. L. Chesbro & J. McCroskey (Eds.), *Communication for teachers* (pp. 19–34). Boston, MA: Allyn & Bacon.

McCroskey, J. C. & Richmond, V. (1978). Community size as a predictor of development of communication apprehension: Replication and extension. *Communication Monographs*, 27, 212–219.

McCroskey, J. C., Booth-Butterfield, S., & Payne, S. (1989). The impact of apprehension on college student retention and success. *Communication Quarterly*, 37, 100–107.

McKeachie, W. (1986). *Teaching tips: A guidebook for the beginning college teacher* (8th ed.). Lexington, MA: D. C. Heath and Company.

McMillan, D. W. & Chavis, D. M. (1986). Sense of community: A definition and theory. *Journal of Community Psychology*, 14, 6–23.

McPherson, K. (1997). Service learning: Making a difference in the community. *Schools in the Middle*, January/February, 9–15.

McTighe, J. & Wiggins, G. (2004). *Understanding by design: Professional development workbook*. Alexandria, VA: ASCD.

Madden, N. A. & Slavin, R. E. (1983). Mainstreaming students with mild handicaps: Academic and social outcomes. *Review of Educational Research*, 53, 519–569.

Maehr, M. L. & Meyer, H. A. (1997). Understanding motivation and schooling: Where we've been, where we are and where we need to go. *Educational Psychology Review*, 9, 371–409.

Malian, I. M. & Love, L. (1998). Leaving high school: An ongoing transition study. *Teaching Exceptional Children*, 30(3), 4–10.

Malmgren, K., Abbott, R. D., & Hawkins, J. D. (1999). LD and delinquency: Rethinking the "link." *Journal of Learning Disabilities*, 32(3), 201–211.

Manca, P. & Ranieri, M. (2013). Is it a tool suitable for learning? A critical review of the literature on Facebook as a technology-enhanced learning environment. *Journal of Computer Assisted Learning*, (29), 487–504.

Manning, M. L. & Baruth, L. G. (2000). *Multicultural education of children and adolescents* (3rd ed.). Boston, MA: Allyn & Bacon.

Marshall, J. & Caldwell, S. (2007). *Caring School Community implementation study four-year evaluation report*. Rapid City, SD: Marshall Consulting.

Martin, C. L. (1989). Children's use of gender-related information in making social judgments. *Developmental Psychology*, 25, 80–88.

Martin, P. & Midgley, E. (2006). Immigration: Shaping and reshaping America. *Population Bulletin*, 61, 1–28.

Martinez, Y. G. & Velazquez, J. A. (2000). Involving migrant families in education. *ERIC Digest.* ED448010 2000-12-00.

Masi, R. & Cooper, J. L. (2006). *Children's mental health: Facts for policymakers.* New York: National Center for Children in Poverty, Mailman School of Public Health, Columbia University.

Maslow, A. (1968). *Toward a psychology of being.* New York: D. Van Nostrand.

Mathinos, D. A. (1991). Conversational engagement of children with learning disabilities. *Journal of Learning Disabilities,* 24, 439–446.

Mathur, S., Kavale, K., Quinn, M., Forness, S., & Rutherford, R. (1998). Social skills intervention with students with emotional and behavioral problems: A quantitative synthesis of single subject research. *Behavioral Disorders,* 23, 193–202.

Mattox, R. & Harder, J. (2007). Attention deficit hyperactivity disorder (ADHD) and diverse populations. *Child and Adolescent Social Work Journal,* 24(2), 195–207.

Mead, G. H. (1934). *Mind, self, and society.* Chicago, IL: University Press.

Mehrabian, A. (1969a). Significance of posture and position in the communication of attitude and status relationships. *Psychological Bulletin,* 71, 359–372.

Mehrabian, A. (1969b). Some referents and measures of nonverbal behavior. *Behavioral Research Methods and Instruments,* 1, 213–217.

Mehrabian, A. (1970a). The development and validation of measures of affiliative tendency and sensitivity to rejection. *Educational and Psychological Measurement,* 30, 417–428.

Mehrabian, A. (1970b). A semantic space for nonverbal behavior. *Journal of Consulting and Clinical Psychology,* 35, 248–257.

Mehrabian, A. (1971). *Silent messages.* Belmont, CA: Wadsworth.

Mehrabian, A. (1981). *Silent messages* (2nd ed.). Belmont, CA: Wadsworth.

Meichenbaum, D. (1977). *Cognitive-behavior modification: An integrative approach.* New York: Plenum.

Meichenbaum, D. (1980). Cognitive-behavior modification: A promise yet unfulfilled. *Exceptional Education Quarterly,* 1 (1), 83–88.

Menchaca, V. D. & Ruiz-Escalante, J. A. (1995). Instructional strategies for migrant students. *ERIC Digest.* Charleston, WV: ERIC Clearinghouse on Rural Education and Small Schools (ERIC Document Reproduction Service No. ED 388 491).

Meyer, J. C. (2000). Humor as a double-edged sword: Four functions of humor in communication. *Communication Theory,* 10, 310–331.

Miller, J. W. (2000). Exploring the source of self-regulated learning: The influence of internal and external comparisons. *Journal of Instructional Psychology,* 27, 47–52.

Miller, M. (1987). Argumentation and cognition. In M. Hickman (Ed.), *Social and functional approaches in language and thought* (pp. 225–249). San Diego, CA: Academic Press.

Miltenberger, R. G. (2007). *Behavior modification: Principles and procedures* (4th ed.). Belmont, CA: Wadsworth.

Minow, M. L. (2001). *Limited English proficient students and special education.* Wakefield, MA: National Center on Accessing the General Curriculum. Accessed October 3, 2013 at http://aim.cast.org/learn/historyarchive/backgroundpapers/lep_sp_ed

Mishra, P. & Koehler, M. J. (2008). *Introducing technological pedagogical content knowledge.* Paper presented at the annual meeting of the American Educational Research Association, New York (March 24–28).

Molloy, J. T. (1975). *Dress for success.* New York: Warner Books.

Mongeau, P. A. & Blalock, J. (1994). Student evaluations of instructor immediacy and sexually harassing behaviors: An experimental investigation. *Journal of Applied Communication Research*, 22, 256–272.

Montalvo, G. P., Mansfield, E. A., & Miller, R. B. (2007). Liking or disliking the teacher: Student motivation, engagement and achievement. *Evaluation and Research in Education*, 20(3), 144–158.

Montgomery, M. D. & Paul, J. L. (1982). Ecological theory and practice. In J. L. Paul & B. C. Epanchin (Eds.), *Emotional disturbance in children: Theories and methods for teachers* (pp. 214–241). Columbus, OH: Merrill.

Moore, A., Masterson, J. T., Christophel, D., & Shea, K. (1996). College teacher immediacy and student ratings of instruction. *Communication Quarterly*, 44, 29–40.

Moore, J. (2006). *Unaccompanied and homeless youth: Review of literature (1995–2005)*. Washington, DC: National Center for Homeless Education.

Moos, R. H. & Moos, B. S. (1978). Classroom social climate and student absences and grades. *Journal of Educational Psychology*, 70, 263–269.

Morris, R. I. & Butt, R. (2003). Parents' perspectives on homelessness and its effects on the educational development of their children. *Journal of School Nursing*, 19(1), 43–50.

Morse, A. (2005). *A look at immigrant youth: Prospects and promising practices*. Paper presented at the National Conference of State Legislatures: Children's Policy Initiative. Accessed August 19, 2013 at www.ncsl.org/documents/immig/CPIimmigrantyouth.pdf.

Morton, T. (1998). *Cooperative learning and social studies: Towards excellence to equity*. San Clemente, CA: Kagan Cooperative Learning.

Mosteller, F. & Moynihan, D. P. (1972). *On equality of educational opportunity*. New York: Vintage Books, 1972.

Mostert, M. P. (1998). *Interprofessional collaboration in schools*. Boston, MA: Allyn & Bacon.

Moughamian, A. C., Rivera, M. O., & Francis, D. J. (2009). *Instructional models and strategies for teaching English language learners*. Portsmouth, NH: RMC Research Corporation, Center on Instruction.

MTA Cooperative Group. (2004). National Institute of Mental Health multimodal treatment study of ADHD follow-up: 24-month outcomes of treatment strategies for attention-deficit/hyperactivity disorder. (Electronic version). *Pediatrics*, 113, 754–761.

Murphy, P. & Gipps, C. V. (1996). *Equity in the classroom: Towards an effective pedagogy for girls and boys*. Washington, DC: Falmer Press.

Murrell, P. C. (2002). *African-centered pedagogy: Developing schools for African-American children*. Albany, NY: State University Press.

Muscott, H. S. (2000). A review and analysis of service-learning programs involving students with emotional/behavioral disorders. *Education and Treatment of Children*, 23, 346–368.

Muscott, H. S. (2001). An introduction to service-learning for students with emotional and behavioral disorders: Answers to frequently asked questions. *Beyond Behavior*, 10(3), 8–15.

Myrick, R. D. & Erney, T. (1984). *Caring and sharing: Becoming a peer facilitator*. Minneapolis, MN: Educational Media Corporation.

Myrick, R. D. & Erney, T. (1985). *Youth helping youth: a handbook for training peer facilitators*. Minneapolis, MN: Educational Media Corporation.

Nadler, L. & Nadler, M. (1990). Perceptions of sex differences in classroom communication. *Women's Studies in Communication*, 13, 46–65.

National Alliance to End Homelessness. (2013). A research report on homelessness: The state of homelessness in America, April. Accessed September 17, 2013 at http://documents.lahsa.org/Communication/pressrelease/2013/NAEH_State_of_Homeleness_in_America_2013.pdf.

National Assessment of Education Progress (2009). The Nation's Report Card: Mathematics 2009. Accessed August 21, 2013 at http://nces.ed.gov/nationsreportcard/pdf/main2009/2010451.pdf.

National Center for Education Statistics (2006). *The condition of education*. Washington, DC: U.S. Department of Education.

National Center for Education Statistics (2012). *Digest of Education Statistics, 2011* (NCES 2012-001). Washington, DC: Government Printing Office.

National Center for Education Statistics (2013). Children and youth with disabilities. Accessed October 10, 2013 at http://nces.ed.gov/programs/coe/indicator_cgg.asp.

National Center on Family Homelessness (2009). Working to end family homelessness: Annual report. Accessed September 2, 2013 at www.familyhomelessness.org/media/88.pdf.

National Center on Family Homelessness. (2011). State report card on child homelessness: America's youngest outcasts 2010. Accessed September 11, 2013 at www.scribd.com/doc/75506633/Report-Americas-Youngest-Outcasts.

National Clearinghouse for English Language Acquisition (2007). The growing numbers of English learner students 1997/98–2007/08, Accessed August 19, 2013 at www.ncela.gwu.edu/files/uploads/9/growingLEP_0708.pdf.

National Coalition for the Homeless (2007). Education of homeless children and youth. Fact Sheet 10. Accessed October 2, 2013 at www.nationalhomeless.org/publications/facts/education.html.

National Commission on Excellence in Education (1983). *A nation at risk: the imperative for educational reform*. Washington, DC: Author.

National Commission on Teaching and America's Future (2004). *Fifty years after Brown v. Board of Education: A two-tiered education system*. Washington, DC: Author.

National Dissemination Center for Children with Disabilities (2010a). Emotional disturbance: NICHCY Disability Fact Sheet No. 5. Accessed August 5, 2013 at http://nichcy.org/disability/specific/emotionaldisturbance.

National Dissemination Center for Children with Disabilities (2010b). Deafness and hearing loss. Accessed August 10, 2013 at http://nichcy.org/disability/specific/hearingloss.

National Dissemination Center for Children with Disabilities (2013). Attention-deficit/hyperactivity disorder (AD/HD) Fact Sheet 19. Accessed July 8, 2013 at http://nichcy.org/disability/specific/adhd.

National Professional Development Center on ASD (2010). Evidence-based practices for children and youth with ASD. Accessed September 12, 2013 at http://autismpdc.fpg.unc.edu/content/briefs.

National Registry of Evidence-based Programs and Practices (n.d.). *Caring school community*. U.S. Department of Health and Human Services. Accessed on October 30, 2013 at www.nrepp.samhsa.gov/ViewIntervention.aspx?id=152.

National Resource Center on ADHD (2009, September). Diagnosis and treatment of ADHD. Accessed August 11, 2013 at www.help4adhd.org/en/treatment/treatmentoverview.

Neitzel, J. & Wolery, M. (2009). *Overview of prompting.* Chapel Hill, NC: National Professional Development Center on Autism Spectrum Disorders, Frank Porter Graham Child Development Institute, University of North Carolina.

Nelson, J., Lott, L., & Glenn, H. S. (1993). *Positive discipline in the classroom.* Rocklin, CA: Prima.

Neuliep, J. W. (1991). An examination of the content of high school teachers' humor in the classroom and the development of an inductively derived taxonomy of classroom humor. *Communication Education*, 40, 343–355.

Newhouse, R. C. (1984). Teacher appearance in cooperative initiation processes. *Journal of Instructional Psychology*, 11, 158–164.

Nieto, S. (2002). *Language, culture, and teaching: Critical perspectives for a new century.* Mahwah, NJ: Lawrence Erlbaum Associates.

No Child Left Behind (2002). No Child Left Behind (NCLB) Act of 2001. Public Law 107–110 (January 8).

Noddings, N. (1995). Teaching themes of care. *Phi Delta Kappan*, May, 675–679.

Noguera, P. (1995). Preventing and producing violence: A critical analysis of responses to school violence. *Harvard Educational Review*, 65, 189–212.

Norton, R. & Nussbaum, J. (1980). Dramatic behaviors of the effective teacher. In D. Nimmo (Ed.), *Communication yearbook 5* (pp. 565–582). New Brunswick, NJ: Transaction Books.

Nussbaum, J. & Scott, M. (1979). The relationship among communicator style, perceived self-disclosure, and classroom learning. In D. Nimmo (Ed.), *Communication Yearbook 3* (pp. 533–552). New Brunswick, NJ: Transaction.

Nussbaum, J., Comadena, M. E., & Holladay, S. J. (1985). *Verbal communication within the college classroom.* Paper presented at the annual meeting of the International Communication Association, May, Chicago, IL.

Oakes, J. (1995). Two cities tracking and within-school segregation. *Teachers College Record*, 96(4), 681–691.

Ogbu, J. U. (1999). Beyond language: ebonics, proper English, and identity in a black-American speech community. *American Educational Research Journal*, 36, 147–186.

Oliver, R., Omari, A., & Herrington, J. (1998). Investigating implementation strategies for www-based learning environments. *International Journal of Instructional Media*, 25, 121.

O'Loughlin, M. (1995). Daring the imagination: Unlocking voices of dissent and possibility in teaching. *Theory into Practice*, 34, 107–116.

Onafowora, L. L. (2004). Teacher efficacy issues in the practice of novice teachers. *Educational Research Quarterly*, 28, 34–43.

O'Neil, D. K., Wagner, R., & Gomez, L. M. (1996). Online mentors: Experimenting in science class. *Educational Leadership*, 54, 39–42.

Opt, S. K. & Loffredo, D. (2000). Rethinking communication apprehension: A Meyers-Briggs perspective. *The Journal of Psychology*, 134, 556–568.

Orbe, M. P. & Harris, T. M. (2001). *Interracial communication: Theory into practice.* Belmont, CA: Wadsworth.

Orlich, D. C., Harder, R. J., Callahan, R. C., & Gibson, H. W. (2001). *Teaching strategies: A guide to better instruction* (6th ed.). Boston, MA: Houghton Mifflin.

Osterman, K. F. (2000). Students' need for belonging in the school community. *Review of Educational Research*, *70*(3), 323–367.

Paley, V. G. (1989). *White teacher.* Cambridge, MA: Harvard University Press.

Park, H. S. (2008). The impact of technology use on Hispanic students' mathematics achievement within family and school contexts: Subgroup analysis between English- and non-English speaking students. *Journal of Educational Computing Research*, 38, 453–468.

Parks, J. B. & Roberton, M. A. (1998). Contemporary arguments against nonsexist language: Blaubergs (1980) revisited. *Sex Roles*, 39, 445–461.

Patrick, B., Hisley, J., & Kempler, T. (2000). "What's everybody so excited about?" The effects of teacher enthusiasm on student intrensic motivation and vitality. *The Journal of Experimental Education*, 68, 217–236.

Pavri, S. & Monda-Amaya, L. (2000). Loneliness and students with learning disabilities in inclusive classrooms: Self-perceptions, coping strategies, and preferred interventions. *Learning Disabilities Research & Practice*, 15(1), 22–33.

Perry, N. E., VandeKamp, K. O., Mercer, L. K., & Nordby, C. J. (2002). Investigating teacher-student interactions that foster self-regulated learning. *Educational Psychologist*, 37, 5–15.

Philbin, M., Meier, E., Huffman, S., & Boverie, P. (1995). A survey of gender learning styles. *Sex Roles: A Journal of Research*, 32, 485–495.

Piaget, J. (1955). *Thought and language of the child*. Cleveland, OH: The World Publishing Company.

Piaget, J. (1965). *The moral judgment of the child*. New York: Basic Books.

Pianta, R. C. & Steinberg, M. (1992). Teacher-child relationships and the process of adjusting to school. In R. C. Pianta (Ed.), *Beyond the parent: The role of other adults in children's lives* (pp. 61–80). San Francisco, CA: Jossey-Bass.

Pipher, M. (1994). *Reviving Ophelia: Saving the selves of adolescent girls*. New York: Putnam.

Placier, M. L. (1993). The semantics of policy making: the case of "at risk." *Educational Evaluation and Policy Analysis*, 15(2), 380.

Pollack, J. P. & Freda, P. D. (1997). Humor, learning, and socialization in middle level classrooms. *The Clearing House*, 70, 176–179.

Pollack, W. (1998). *Real boys: rescuing our sons from the myths of boyhood*. New York: Henry Holt & Company.

Pomerantz, S. & Raby, R. (2011). 'Oh, she's so smart,: Girls complex engagements with post-feminist narratives of academic success. *Gender and Education*, 23, 544–564.

Portelli, J. P., Shields, C. M., Vibert, A. B. (2007). *Toward an equitable education: Poverty, diversity, and students at risk*. Academica.edu.

Portes, A. & Rumbaut, R. G. (2001). *Legacies: The story of the immigrant second generation* (pp. 255, 279). Berkeley, CA: University of California Press.

Postman, N. (1995). *The end of education*. New York: Vintage Books.

Powell, R. & Aston, W. (July, 1994). *Teacher classroom immediacy and time on task: An exploratory study*. Paper presented at the annual meeting of the International Communication Association, Sydney, Australia.

Powell, R. G. & Avila, D. R. (1986). Ethnicity, communication competency and classroom success: A question of assessment. *Western Journal of Speech Communication*, 50, 269–278.

Powell, R. G. & Harville, B. (1990). The effects of teacher immediacy and clarity on instructional outcomes: An intercultural assessment. *Communication Education*, 39, 369–379.

Pumariega, A. J., Rothe, E., & Pumariega, J. B. (2005). Mental health of immigrants and refugees. *Community Mental Health Journal*, 41(5), 581–597.

Raffaele Mendez, L. M. & Knoff, H. M. (2003). Who gets suspended from school and why: A demographic analysis of schools and discipline infractions in a large school district. *Education and Treatment of Children*, 26, 30–51.

Ravitch, D. (2009). Time to kill "no child left behind." *Education Digest*, 75(1), 4–6.

Rawlins W. K. (1992). *Friendship matters: Communication, dialectics, and life course*. New York: Aldine de Gruyter.

Rawlins, W. K. (2000). Teaching as a mode of friendship. *Communication Theory*, 10, 5–26.

Ray, N. (2006). *Lesbian, gay, bisexual and transgender youth: An epidemic of homelessness*. New York: National Gay and Lesbian Task Force Policy Institute and the National Coalition for the Homeless.

Reagan, T. (2002). *Language, education, and ideology: Mapping the linguistic landscape of U.S. schools*. Westport, CT: Prager.

Redl, F. & Wineman, D. (1952). *Controls from within: Techniques for the treatment of the aggressive child*. New York: Free Press.

Renzulli, J. & Reis, S. (2013). The school-wide enrichment model: Developing creative and productive giftedness. In R. M. Gargiulo & D. Metcalf (Eds.), *Teaching in today's inclusive classrooms: A universal design for learning approach* (2nd ed., p. 143). Belmont, CA: Wadsworth, Cengage Learning.

Revenaugh, M. (2000). At home use of computers casts a new light on the ways schools educate students and their parents. *Educational Leadership*, 58, 25–28.

Rex, L. A. (2003). Loss of the creature: The obscuring of inclusivity in classroom discourse. *Communication Education*, 52, 30–46.

Reyes, P., Scribner, J. D. & Scribner, A. P. (Eds.) (1999). *Lessons from high-performing hispanic schools*. New York: Teachers College Press.

Rezmierski, V. & Kotre, J. (1974). A limited review of theory of the psychodynamic model. In W. C. Rhodes & M. L. Tracy (Eds.), *A study of child variance, Vol. I*. Ann Arbor, MI: University of Michigan.

Rhodes, W. C. (1967). The disturbing child: A problem of ecological management. *Exceptional Children*, 33, 449–455.

Rhodes, W. C. (1970). A community participation analysis of emotional disturbance. *Exceptional Children*, 36, 306–314.

Richmond, V. P. (1990). Communication in the classroom: Power and motivation. *Communication Education*, 39, 181–195.

Richmond, V. P. (2002). Teacher nonverbal immediacy: Use and outcomes. In J. L. Chesebro & J. C. McCroskey (Eds.), *Communication for teachers* (pp. 65–82). Boston, MA: Allyn & Bacon.

Richmond, V. & Dyba, P. (1982). The roots of sexual stereotyping: The teacher as model. *Communication Education*, 31, 265–274.

Richmond, V., McCroskey, J., & Payne, S. K. (1987). *Nonverbal behavior in interpersonal relations*. Englewood Cliffs, NJ: Prentice Hall.

Rimm-Kaufman, S. (2011). Improving students' relationships with teachers to provide essential supports for learning. American Psychological Association. Accessed May 25, 2013 at www.apa.org/educationk12/relationships.aspx.

RMC Research Corporation (2007). Fact sheets: Why districts, schools, and classrooms should practice service-learning. In National Service-Learning Clearinghouse (2013). Accessed November 3, 2013 at www.servicelearning.org/fact-sheets.

Roach, D. D. (1997). Effects of graduate teaching assistant attire on student learning, misbehaviors, and ratings of instruction. *Communication Quarterly*, 45, 125–141.

Robertson, K. & Breiseth, L. (2008). How to support refugee students in the ELL classroom. Colorin Colorado. Accessed September 23, 2013 at www.colorincolorado.org/article/23379/.

Rockwell, S. (2001). Service-learning: Barriers, benefits, and models of excellence. *Beyond Behavior*, 10(3), 16–21.

Rodriguez, J., Plax, T., & Kearney, P. (1996). Clarifying the relationship between teacher nonverbal immediacy and student cognitive learning: Affective learning as the central causal mediator. *Communication Education*, 45, 293–305.

Roeser, R. W., Midgley, C., & Urdan, T. (1996). Perceptions of the school psychological environment and early adolescents' psychological and behavioral functioning in school: The mediating role of goals and belonging. *Journal of Educational Psychology*, 88, 408–422.

Rong, X. L. & Preissle, J. (2009). *Educating immigrant students in the twenty-first century: What educators need to know*. California, CA: Corwin Press.

Roorda, D. L., Koomen, H. M. Y., Spilt, J. L., & Oort, F. J. (2011). The influence of affective teacher–student relationships on students' school engagement and achievement: A meta-analytic approach. *Review of Educational Research*, 81(4), 493–529.

Roschelle, J. M., Pea, R. D., Hoadley, C. M., Gordon, D. N., & Means, B. M. (2000). Changing how and what children learn in school with computer-based technologies. *Children and Computer Technology*, 10, 76–101.

Rose, D. H. & Meyer, A. (2002). *Teaching every student in the Digital Age: Universal design for learning*. Alexandria, VA: Association for Supervision and Curriculum Development (ASCD).

Rosenfeld, L. B. & Richman, J, R. (1999). Supportive communication and school outcomes, part II: Academically "at-risk" low income high school students. *Communication Education*, 48, 294–306.

Rosenfeld, L. B., Grant, H., & McCroskey, J. C. (1995). Communication apprehension and self-perceived communication competence of academically gifted students. *Communication Education*, 44, 79–86.

Ross, J. L., Drysdale, M. T. B., Schulz, R. A. (2001). Cognitive learning styles and academic performance in two postsecondary computer application courses. *Journal of Research on Technology in Education*, 33, 400–411.

Rowe, K. J. (2001). Educational performance indicators. In M. Forster, G. N. Masters & K. J. Rowe (Eds.), *Measuring learning outcomes: Options and challenges in evaluation and performance monitoring* (Revised ed., pp. 2–20). Strategic Choices for Educational Reform; Module IV – Evaluation and Performance Monitoring. Washington, DC: The World Bank Institute.

Rowen, K. (1999). Explanatory skills. In A. Vangelisti, J. Daly, & G. Friedrich (Eds.), *Teaching communication* (2nd ed., pp. 319–331). NJ: Lawrence Erlbaum.

Rubin, J. Z. Provensano, F. & Luria, Z. (1974). The eye of the beholder: Parent's views on sex of newborns. *American Journal of Orthopsychiatry*, 44, 312–319.

Ryan, A. (2001). The peer group as a context for the development of young adolescent motivation and achievement. *Child Development*, 72, 1135–1160.

Ryan, A. M. & Patrick, H. (2001). The classroom social environment and changes in adolescents' motivation and engagement during middle school. *American Educational Research Journal*, 38(2), 437–460.

Ryan, R. M., Stiller, J. D., & Lynch, J. H. (1994). Representations of relationships to teachers, parents, and friends as predictors of academic motivation and self-esteem. *Journal of Early Adolescence*, 14(2), 226–249.

Sadker, M. & Sadker, D. (1994). *Failing at fairness: How America's schools cheat girls*. New York: Charles Scribner's Sons.

Sagor, R. (1996). Building resiliency in students. *Educational Leadership*, September, 38–43.

Samovar, L., Porter, R., & Stefani, L. A. (2000). *Communication between cultures* (3rd ed.). Belmont, CA: Wadsworth.

Sanders, J. & Wiseman, W. R. (1990). The effects of verbal and nonverbal teacher immediacy on perceived cognitive, affective, and behavioral learning in the multicultural classroom. *Communication Education*, 39, 341–353.

Santamaria, L. J. (2009). Culturally responsive differentiated instruction: Narrowing gaps between best pedagogical practices benefiting all learners. *Teachers College Record*, 111, 214–247.

Sato, M. & Lensmire, T. J. (2009). Poverty and Payne: Supporting teachers to work with children of poverty. *Phi Delta Kappan*, 90(5), 365–370.

Savage, T. V. & Savage, M. K. (2010). *Successful classroom management and discipline: teaching self-control and responsibility* (3rd ed.). Los Angeles, CA: Sage.

Scheuermann, B. K. & Hall, J. A. (2007). *Positive behavioral supports for the classroom*. Upper Saddle River, NJ: Pearson Education.

Schierloh, J. M. (1991). Teaching standard English usage: A dialect based approach. *Adult Learning*, 2, 20–22.

Schneider, D. J. (1974). Effects of dress on self-presentation. *Psychological Reports*, 35, 167–170.

Schonert-Reichl, K. A. (1993). Empathy and social relationships in adolescents with behavior disorders. *Behavioral Disorders*, 18(3), 189–204.

Schulte, A. C., Osborne, S. S., & McKinney, J. D. (1990). Academic outcomes for students with learning disabilities in consultation and resource programs. *Exceptional Children*, 57, 162–172.

Schutz, W. (1966). *The interpersonal underworld*. Palo Alto, CA: Science and Behavior Books.

Scruggs, T. E. & Mastropieri, M. A. (1996). *Advances in learning and behavioral disabilities*. Greenwich, CT: JAI Press.

Scruggs, T. E., Mastropieri, M. A., Berkeley, S., & Graetz, J. E. (2010). Do special education interventions improve learning of secondary content? A meta-analysis, *Remedial & Special Education*, 31*(6)*, 437–449.

Seidel, J. F. & Vaughn, S. (1991). Social alienation and the learning disabled school dropout. *Learning Disabilities Research & Practice*, 6, 152–157.

Seifert, T. L. (2004). Understanding student motivation. *Educational Research*, 46, 137–149.

Selfe, C. L. (1999). *Technology and literacy in the twenty-first century: The importance of paying attention*. Carbondale, IL: Southern Illinois University Press.

Shade, B. J. (1989). The influence of perceptual development on cognitive styles: Cross ethnic comparisons. *Early Child Development and Care*, 51, 137–155.

Shannon, C. & Weaver, W. (1949). *The mathematical theory of communication*. Urbana, IL: University of Illinois.

Sharan, S. (1994). *Handbook of cooperative learning methods*. Westport, CT: Greenwood Press.

Sharan, S., Kussell, P., Hertz-Lazarowitz, R., Bejarano, Y., Raviv, S., & Sharan, Y. (1984). *Cooperative learning in the classroom: Research in desegregated schools*. Hillsdale, NJ: Erlbaum.

Share Our Strengths. (2012). *Hunger in the classroom: Share Our Strengths Teacher Report*. Washington, DC: Author.

Shinn, M. R. & Powell-Smith (1997). The effects of reintegration into general education reading instruction for students with mild disabilities. *Exceptional Children*, 64, 59–79.

Silver, H. F., Strong, R. W., & Perini, M. J. (2000). *So each may learn: Integrating learning styles and multiple intelligences*. Alexandria, VA: Association for Supervision and Curriculum Development.

Sim, L., Whiteside, S. P., Dittner, C. A., & Mellon, M. (2006). Effectiveness of a social skills training program with school age children: Transition to the clinical setting. *Journal of Children and Family Studies*, 15, 409–418.

Simmons, B. J. (1996). Teachers should dress for success. *The Clearing House*, 69, 297–299.

Simonsen, B., Sugai, G., & Negron, M. (2008). Schoolwide positive behavior supports primary systems and practices. *Teaching Exceptional Children*, 6, 32–40.

Sine, C. (1995). *Teacher immediacy and time on task*. Unpublished master's thesis. California State University Fresno, Fresno, CA.

Sitler, H. C. (1997). The spaced lecture. *College Teaching*, 45, 108–111.

Skiba, R. J. & Peterson, R. L. (2000). School discipline at a crossroads: From zero tolerance to early response. *Exceptional Children*, 66(3), 335–347.

Skiba, R. J., Horner, R. H., Chung, C. G., Rausch, M. K., May, S. L. & Tobin, T. (2011). Race is not neutral: A national investigation of African American and Latino disproportionality in school discipline. *School Psychology Review*, 40, 85–107.

Skiba, R. J., Michael, R. S., Nardo, A. C., & Peterson, R. (2002). The color of discipline: Sources of racial and gender disproportionality in school punishment. *The Urban Review*, 34, 317–342.

Skinner, B. F. (1971). *Beyond freedom and dignity*. New York: Alfred A. Knopf.

Skinner, E. A. & Belmont, M. J. (1993). Motivation in the classroom: Reciprocal effects of teacher behavior and student engagement across the school year. *Journal of Educational Psychology*, 85, 571–581.

Slavin, R. E. (1995). *Cooperative learning: Theory, research, and practice* (2nd ed.). Boston, MA: Allyn & Bacon.

Smith, D. D. (2001). *Introduction to special education: Teaching in an age of opportunity* (4th ed.). Boston, MA: Allyn & Bacon.

Smith, H. (1984). Nonverbal behavior aspects in teaching. In A. Wolfgang (Ed.), *Nonverbal behavior: Perspectives, applications, intercultural insights* (pp. 171–202). New York: C. J. Hofgrefe.

Smith, P. K., Mahdavi, J., Carvalho, M., Fisher, S., Russell, S., & Tippett, N. (2008). Cyberbullying: Its nature and impact in secondary school pupils. *Journal of Child Psychology and Psychiatry*, 49, 376–385.

Smith, T. E. C., Polloway, E. A., Patton, J. R., & Dowdy, C. A. (2001). *Teaching students with special needs in inclusive settings* (3rd ed.). Boston, MA: Allyn & Bacon.

Smith-Davis, J. (2004). The new immigrant students need more than ESL. *The Education Digest*, 69(8), 21–26.

Snyder, T. D. & Dillow, S. A. (2012). *Digest of education statistics*. Washington, DC: U.S. Department of Education.

Solomon, D., Battistich, V., Watson, M., Schaps, E., & Lewis, C. (2000). A six district study of educational change: Direct and mediated effects of the Child Development Project. *Social Psychology of Education*, 41(1), 3–51.

Solomon, D., Watson, M., Battistich, V., Schaps, E., & Delucchi, K. (1996). Creating classrooms that students experience as communities. *American Journal of Community Psychology*, 24(6), 719–748.

Sorensen, G. (1989). The relationships among teachers: Self-disclosive statements, students' perceptions, and affective learning. *Communication Education*, 38, 259–276.

Sprague, J. (1992). Expanding the research agenda for instructional communication: Raising some unasked questions. *Communication Education*, 41, 1–25.

Stahl, S. A. & Clark, C. H. (1987). The effects of participation expectations in classroom discussion on the learning of science vocabulary. *American Educational Research Journal*, 24, 541–351.

Stern, M. & Karrakar, K. H. (1989). Sex stereotyping in infants: A review of gender labeling studies. *Sex Roles*, 20, 501–522.

Stevens, R. J. & Slavin R. E. (1995). The cooperative elementary school: Effects on students' achievement, attitudes and social relations. *American Educational Research Journal*, 32, 321–351.

Stewart, J. (1986). Speech and human being: A complement to semiotics. *Quarterly Journal of Speech*, 72, 55–73.

Stone, W. L. & LaGreca, A. M. (1983). Comprehension of nonverbal communication: A reexamination of the social competencies of learning-disabled children. *Journal of Abnormal Child Psychology*, 12, 505–518.

Strangeman, N., Hitchcock, C., Hall T., Meo, G., Gersten, R., & Dimino, J. A. (2006). Response-to-instruction and universal design for learning: How might they intersect in the general education classroom. Accessed September 25, 2009 at www.ldonline.org/article/13002.

Strekalova, E. & Hoot, J. L. (2008). What is special about special needs of refugee children: Guidelines for teachers. *Multicultural Education*, 16(1), 21–24.

Stronge, J. H., Tucker, P. D., & Hindman, J. L. (2004). *Handbook for qualities of effective teachers*. Alexandria, VA: Association for Supervision and Curriculum Development

Suarez-Orozco, C. & Suarez-Orozco, M. (2001). *Children of immigration*. Cambridge, MA: Harvard University Press.

Sugai, G. & Horner, R. H. (2002). The evolution of discipline practices: School-wide positive behavior supports. *Child and Family Behavior Therapy*, 24, 23–50.

Sutherland, K. S. & Wehby, J. H. (2001). Exploring the relationship between increased opportunities to respond to academic requests and the academic and behavioral outcomes of students with EBD. *Remedial and Special Education*, 22, 113–121.

Swain, C. & Pearson, T. (2001). Bridging the digital divide: A building block for teachers. *Learning & Leading with Technology*, 28, 10.

Sylwester, R. (1995). *A celebration of neurons: An educator's guide to the human brain*. Alexandria, VA: ASCD.

Tanno, D. (1997). Names narratives, and the evolution of ethnic identity. In A. Gonzalez, M. Houston, & V. Chen (Eds.), *Our voices* (2nd ed.). Los Angeles, CA: Roxbury.

Taylor, H. U. (1989). *Standard English, Black English, and bidialectalism.* New York: Peter Lang.

Teven, J. J. & Hanson, T. L. (2004). The impact of teacher immediacy and perceived caring on teacher competence and trustworthiness. *Communication Quarterly*, 52, 39–53.

Tharp, R. & Gallimore, R. (1988). *Rousing minds to life.* New York: Cambridge University Press.

Thomas, W. P. & Collier, V. P. (2002). A national study of school effectiveness for language minority students' long term academic achievement. Accessed September 23, 2013 at www.crede.uscs.edu/research/llaa/1.1final.html.

Thompson, S. M. (1996). Peer mediation: A peaceful solution. *The School Counselor*, 44, 151–154.

Tienken, C. H., Goldberg, S., & DiRocco, D. (2009). Questioning questions. *Kappa Delta Pi*, 39–43.

Tomlinson, C. A. (1999). *The differentiated classroom: Responding to the needs of all learners.* Alexandria, VA: Association for Supervision and Curriculum Development.

Tomlinson, C. A. (2001). *How to differentiate instruction in mixed-ability classrooms* (2nd ed.). Alexandria, VA: Association for Supervision and Curriculum Development.

Tomlinson, C. A. (2003). *Fulfilling the promise of the differentiated classroom: Strategies and tools for responsive teaching.* Alexandria, VA: Association for Supervision and Curriculum Development.

Tomlinson, C. A. & Kalbfleisch, M. L. (1998). Teach me, teach my brain: A call for differentiated classrooms. *Educational Leadership*, 56, 52–55.

Tomlinson, C. A. & McTighe, J. (2006). *Integrating differentiated instruction and understanding by design.* Alexandria, VA: Association for Supervision and Curriculum Development.

Toro, P. A., Weissberg, R. P., Guare, J., & Liebenstein, N. L. (1990). A comparison of children with and without learning disabilities on social problem-solving skill, school behavior, and family background. *Journal of Learning Disabilities*, 23, 115–120.

Townsend, B. L. (2000). The disproportionate discipline of African American learners: Reducing school suspensions and expulsions. *Exceptional Children*, 66(3), 381–391.

Truebridge, S. (2010). *Tell me a story: Influencing educators' beliefs about student resilience in an effort to enhance student success.* Unpublished doctoral dissertation, Mills College, Oakland CA.

Tschannen-Moran, M. & Hoy, W. (2001). Teacher efficacy: Capturing an elusive construct. *Teaching and Teacher Education*, 17, 783–805.

Turnbull, R., Turnbull, A., Shank, M., Smith, S., & Leal, D. (2002). *Exceptional lives: Special Education in today's schools* (3rd ed.). Columbus, OH: Merrill/Prentice Hall.

Tyler, J. S. & Mira, M. P. (1999). *Traumatic brain injury in children and adolescents: A sourcebook for teachers and other school personnel.* Austin, TX: Pro-Ed.

U.S. Census Bureau (2011). American community survey. Accessed August 28, 2013 at http://factfinder2.census.gov/faces/nav/jsf/pages/searchresults.xhtml?refresh=t.

U.S. Citizenship and Immigration Services (2013). Accessed September 9, 2013 at www.uscis.gov/graphics/services/refugees/Definition.htm.

U.S. Conference of Mayors (2004). A status report on hunger and homelessness in America's cities. Accessed September 10, 2013 at www.usmayors.org.

U.S. Department of Education (1996). *Getting America's students ready for the twenty-first century: Meeting the technology literacy challenge.* Washington, DC: U.S. Department of Education.

U.S. Department of Education (1998). *Twentieth annual report to Congress on the implementation of the Individuals with Disabilities Education Act.* Washington, DC: U.S. Government Printing Office.

U.S. Department of Education (2000). *Twenty-second annual report to Congress on the implementation of the Individuals with Disabilities Education Act.* Washington, DC: Author.

U.S. Department of Education (2002). Executive summary: The No Child Left Behind Act of 2001. Washington, DC: Author.

U.S. Department of Education (2008). A Nation Accountable: Twenty-five Years After A Nation at Risk, Washington, DC: Author.

U.S. Department of Education (2011). Individuals with Disabilities Education Improvement Act (IDEA) data: Data Accountability Center. Accessed May 3, 2013, www.ideadata.org.

U.S. Department of State (2008). Bureau of population, refugees, and migration releases other. Accessed October 3, 2013 at http://2001-2009.state.gov/g/prm/rls/c13076.htm.

Vang, C. T. (2005). Hmong-American students still face multiple challenges in public schools. *Multicultural Education*, 13(1), 27–35.

Vasquez, J. A. (1991). Cognitive style and academic achievement. In J. Lynch, C. Modgil, & S. Modgil (Eds.), *Cultural diversity and the schools: Consensus and controversy*. London: Falconer Press.

Vaughn, S. & Hogan, A. (1994). The social competence of students with learning disabilities over time: A within-individual examination. *Journal of Learning Disabilities*, 27, 292–303.

Vygotsky, L. (1962/1981). *Thought and language* (A. Hanfmann & G. Vakar, Trans.). Cambridge, MA: MIT Press.

Vygotsky, L. (1978). *Mind in society*. Cambridge, MA: Harvard University Press.

Wade, R. C. (1994). Community service learning: Commitment through active citizenship. *Social Studies and the Young Learner*, 6(1), 1–4.

Waldron, N. L. & McLeskey, J. (1998). The effects of an inclusive school program on students with mild and severe learning disabilities. *Exceptional Children*, 64, 395–405.

Walker, D. W. & Leister, C. (1994). Recognition of facial affect cues by adolescents with emotional and behavioral disorders. *Behavioral Disorders*, 19(4), 269–276.

Walker, H. M., McConnell, S., Holmes, D., Todis, B., Walker, J., & Golden, N. (1983). *The Walker social skills curriculum: The ACCEPTS program*. Austin, TX: Pro-Ed.

Walker, H. M., Todis, B., Holmes, D., & Horton, G. (1988). *The Walker social skills curriculum: The ACCESS program*. Austin, TX: Pro-Ed.

Walker, J. E. & Shea, T. M. (1999). *Behavior management: A practical approach for educators* (7th ed.). Upper Saddle River, NJ: Merrill.

Wanzer, M. B. (1998). An exploratory investigation of student and teacher perceptions of student-generated affinity-seeking behaviors. *Communication Education*, 47, 373–382.

Warner-Burke, N. (2014). Revamping the classroom research project. *Educational Leadership*, 71, 40–45.

Watkins, C. (2005). *Classrooms as learning communities: What's in it for schools?* Taylor Francis. Accessed September 20, 2013 at http://myilibrary.com/.

Watson, M. & Battistich, V. (2006). Building and sustaining caring communities. In C. M. Evertson & C. S. Weinstein (Eds.), *Handbook of classroom management: Research, practice, and contemporary issues* (pp. 253–279). Mahwah, NJ: Lawrence Erlbaum.

Weber, K. & Custer, R. (2005). Gender-based preferences toward technology education, content activities, and instructional methods. *Journal of Technology Education*, 16, 55–71.

Wehby, J. H., Symons, F. J., Canale, J. A., & Go, F. J. (1998). Teaching practices in classrooms for students with emotional and behavioral disorders: Discrepancies between recommendations and observations. *Behavioral Disorders*, 24, 51–56.

Wehmeyer, M. L. & Schwartz, M. (1997). Self-determination and positive adult outcomes: A follow up study of youth with mental retardation or learning disabilities. *Exceptional Children*, 63, 245–255.

Wehmeyer, M. L., Argan, M., & Hughes, C. A. (1998). *Teaching self-determination to students with disabilities: Basic skills for successful transition*. Baltimore, MD: Brookes.

Weiner, B. (1984). Principles for a theory of student motivation and their application with an attributional framework. In R. E. Ames & C. Ames (Eds.), *Research on motivation in education: Student motivation Vol. I* (pp. 15–38). New York: Academic Press.

Weiner, B. (1985). An attributional theory of achievement motivation and emotion. *Psychological Review*, 92, 548–573.

Weiner, J. & Harris, P. J. (1997). Evaluation of an individualized, context-based social skills training program for children with learning disabilities. *Learning Disabilities Research & Practice*, 12, 40–53.

Wells, S. E. (1990). *At-risk youth: Identification, programs, and recommendations*. Englewood, CO: Teacher Idea Press.

Wenger, E. (1998). *Communities of practice: Learning, meaning, and identity*. Cambridge, UK: Cambridge University Press.

Wentzel, K. R. (2002). Are effective teachers like good parents? Teaching styles and student adjustment in early adolescence. *Child Development*, 73, 287–301.

Wentzel, K. B. & Asher, S. R. (1995). The academic lives of neglected, rejected, popular, and controversial children. *Child Development*, 66, 754–763.

Werner, E. E. & Smith, R. S. (1982). *Vulnerable to invincible: A longitudinal study of resilient children and youth*. New York: McGraw-Hill.

Westby, C. & Atencio, D. J. (2002). Computers, culture and learning. *Topics in Language Disorders*, 22, 70–98.

Wielkiewicz, R. M. (1995). *Behavior management in the schools: Principles and procedures* (2nd ed.). Boston, MA: Allyn & Bacon.

Wiggins, G. (2012). 7 keys to effective feedback. *Educational Leadership*, 70, 10–16.

Wiliam, D. (2012). Feedback: Part of a system. *Educational Leadership*, 70, 31–34.

Williams, P. A., Alley, R. D., & Hensen, K. T. (1999). Managing secondary classrooms. *Principles and strategies for effective management & instruction*. Boston, MA: Allyn & Bacon.

Wlodkowski, R. J. & Ginsberg, M. B. (1995). *Diversity and motivation: Culturally responsive teaching*. San Francisco, CA: Jossey Bass.

Wolpe, J. (1961). The systematic desensitization treatment of neuroses. *Journal of Nervous and Mental Disease*, 132, 189–203.

Wolvin, A. D. & Coakley, C. G. (1993). A listening typology. In A. D. Wolvin & C. G. Coakley (Eds.), *Perspectives on listening* (pp. 15–22). Norwood, NJ: Ablex Publishing Corporation.

Wood, J. T. (2001). *Gendered lives: Communication, gender and culture* (4th ed.). Belmont, CA: Wadsworth.

Yeung, A. S., Marsh, H. W., & Suliman, R. (2000). Can two tongues live in harmony: Analysis of the national education longitudinal data on the maintenance of home language. *American Educational Research Journal*, 37, 1001–1026.

Yeung, W. J., Linver, M. R., & Brooks-Gunn, J. (2002). How money matters for children's development: Parental investment and family processes. *Child Development*, 73(6), 1861–1879.

Yoder, D., Retish, E., & Wade, R. (1996). Service-learning: Meeting student and community needs. *Teaching Exceptional Children*, 28(4), 14–18.

Yoder, M. B. (2001). The digital divide. *Learning and Leading with Technology*, 28, 10.

Zehler, A. M., Fleischman, H. L., Hopstock, P. J., Stephenson, T. G., Pendzick, M. L., & Sapru, S. (2003). *Descriptive study of services to LEP students and LEP students with disabilities* (Contract No. ED-00-CO-0089). Report prepared for U.S. Department of Education, Office of English Language Acquisition (OELA), Language enhancement, and Academic Achievement of Limited English Proficient Students.

Zhang, D. & Katsiyannis, A. (2002). Minority representation in special education: A persistent challenge. *Remedial and Special Education*, 23(3), 180–187.

Zhao, Y., Englert, C. S., Chen, J., Jones, S. C., & Ferdig, R. E. (2000). The development of a web-based literacy learning environment: A dialogue between innovation and established practices. *Journal of Research on Computing in Education*, 32, 435–454.

Zionts, P. & Fox, R. W. (1998). Facilitating group classroom meetings: Practical guidelines. *Beyond Behavior*, 9(2), 8–13.

Zirpoli, T. J. & Melloy, K. J. (2001). *Behavior management: Applications for teachers*. Upper Saddle River, NJ: Merrill.

Zirpoli, T. J. & Melloy, K. J. (2007). *Behavior management: Applications for teachers* (5th ed.). Upper Saddle River, NJ: Merrill.

INDEX